Lecture Notes in Computer Science

Edited by G. Goos and J. Hartmanis

T0216165

149

Cryptography

Proceedings of the Workshop on Cryptography
Burg Feuerstein, Germany, March 29 – April 2, 1982

Edited by Thomas Beth

Springer-Verlag
Berlin Heidelberg New York 1983

Editor
Thomas Beth
Friedrich-Alexander Universität Erlangen-Nürnberg
Institut für Mathematische Maschinen und Datenverarbeitung (Informatik 1)
Martensstr. 3, 8520 Erlangen, FRG

Gesellschaft für Informatik e.V.
– Fachausschuß 8 –

Institut für Mathematische
Maschinen und Datenverarbeitung

ARBEITSTAGUNG ÜBER KRYPTOGRAPHIE – BURG FEUERSTEIN – 29. 3. – 2. 4. 82

Diese erste europäische Arbeitstagung über Kryptographie wurde von folgenden Institutionen gemeinsam getragen:

Lehrstuhl I (Prof. Dr. K. Leeb) des Instituts für Mathematische Maschinen und Datenverarbeitung (Informatik) der Universität Erlangen-Nürnberg

Gesellschaft für Informatik e.V. (Fachausschuß 8)

Deutsche Forschungs-Gemeinschaft

CR Subject Classifications (1982): D 3

ISBN 3-540-11993-0 Springer-Verlag Berlin Heidelberg New York
ISBN 0-387-11993-0 Springer-Verlag New York Heidelberg Berlin

Library of Congress Cataloging in Publication Data. Main entry under title: Cryptography: proceedings, Burg Feuerstein, 1982. (Lecture notes in computer science ; 149)
1. Cryptography–Congresses. I. Beth, Thomas, 1949-. II. Series. Z102.5.C78 1983 001.54'36 83-430
ISBN 0-387-11993-0

Printing and binding: Beltz Offsetdruck, Hemsbach/Bergstr.
2145/3140-543210

Wir werden in der Folge Gelegenheit nehmen, die mancherlei Arten dieses Versteckens näher zu betrachten. Symbolik, Allegorie, Rätsel, Attrape, Chiffrieren wurden in Übung gesetzt. Apprehension gegen Kunstverwandte, Marktschreierei, Dünkel, Witz und Geist hatten alle gleiches Interesse, sich auf diese Weise zu üben und geltend zu machen, so daß der Gebrauch dieser Verheimlichungskünste sehr lebhaft bis in das siebzehnte Jahrhundert hinübergeht und sich zum Teil noch in den Kanzleien der Diplomatiker erhält.

Goethe: Farbenlehre-Historischer Teil,aus:"Lust am Geheimnis"

ace

book contains the proceedings of a workshop on cryptography that took plac March 29th to April 2nd, 1982, at Burg Feuerstein in the lovely surrounding e Fränkische Schweiz near Erlangen.

Burg Feuerstein is an extensive estate run by the diocese of Bamberg. It serve purposes, mainly of social character.

Our workshop on cryptography, however, proved to be in the best traditions o grounds, since the `Burg´ is not a genuine castle: it was built in the earl ´s as a camouflaged center for communications engineering emphasizing crypto hic research. The unintended coincidence gives a good opportunity to note th ges that cryptographic research has undergone since then. One of the mos rkable was the fact that there were 76 participants from 14 nations.

This volume contains 26 articles altogether. The introduction is an expositor y for non-specialists and places in context the other 25 papers submitted. Thes grouped into 10 sections within which they are arranged with regard to content editor has refrained judiciously from judging the significance or consistency of al results. Together with its rather extensive (doubly linked) bibliography the book be used as a self-contained text. At the back of the book are a list o cipants as well as a list of the talks for which no paper was submitted.

The organizer is indebted to the Deutsche Forschungs - Gemeinschaft and to the llschaft für Informatik for supporting the conference.

The advice given by H.J.Beker (Racal-Comsec,Salisbury), by H.-R. Schuchmann ens-Forschungslaboratorien,München), and by N.J.A. Sloane (Bell Laboratories ay Hill) were of substantial help.

inally it is a pleasure to thank R.Dierstein (DFVLR Oberpfaffenhofen) for his ex- nced aid in organizing the workshop.

T.B.

Contents

Section 1

Introduction

Having all of a sudden left the shady corner of semi-military art, modern cryptography has become a central topic of research in all areas of communication science.

Definitions

(cf. Bauer pp. 31 - 48) Cryptographic measures are applied to protect valuable data during transmission

against unwanted interception

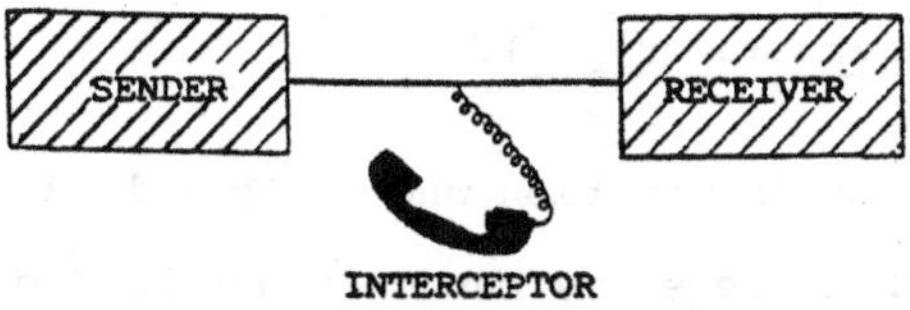

Fig. 1: passive violation

and (possibly undectable) forgery .

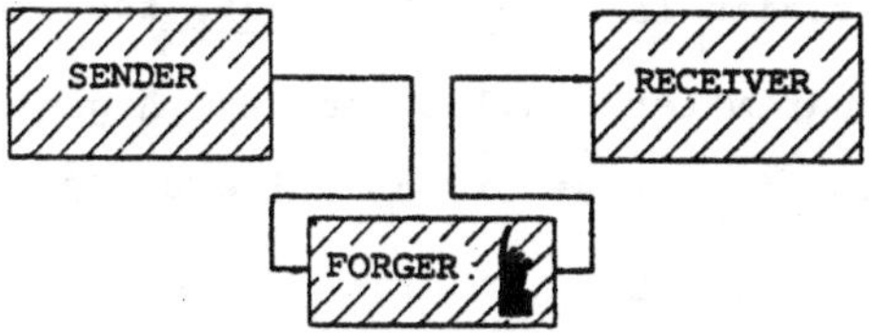

Fig. 2: active violation

In accordance with the subsequent paper of Bauer (pp. 31 - 48), the technique applied to meet these requirements is called encryption. In this process the transmitter enciphers (or encrypts) a plaintext message into a ciphertext .

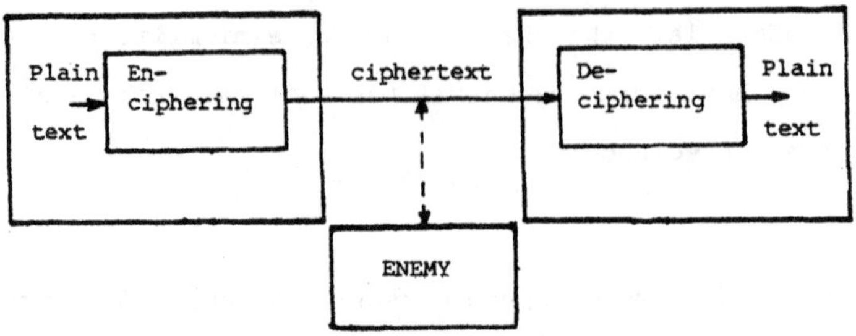

Fig. 3: The Wire-tap-channel

This transformation is called a cipher(function) which the autorized receiver deciphers (decrypts).

An enemy is a person or institution who wants illegal access to the messages. Assuming that the enemy can only get hold of the ciphertexts, he has to perform a cryptanalysis in order to reconstitute the plaintexts.

To add to the difficulties for a cryptanalyst, the cipher functions are chosen to a varying parameter, called the key. A generator cryptosystem consists of a class of injective cipher functions

$$E_S : M \to C \quad ,$$

mapping plaintext messages($\in M$) into ciphertexts($\in C$) .

The parameter s runs through the set K of keys.

These formulations are best demonstrated by the basic, classical examples.

Historical Ciphers

A rather extensive portion of today's cryptographic research is still concerned with the study of classic crypto-systems. One of the most simple systems, the socalled CAESAR,

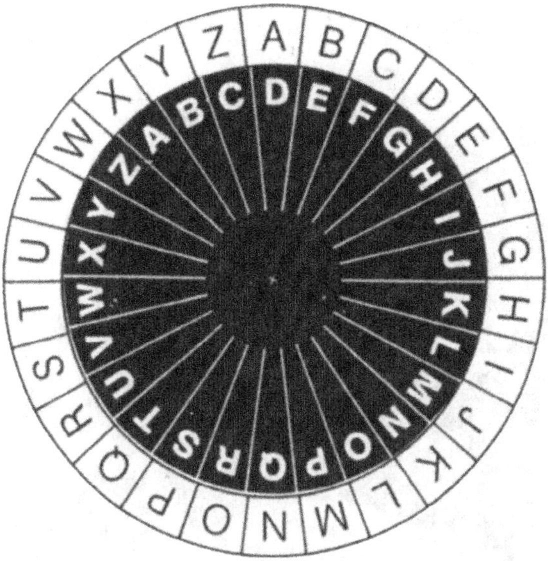

Fig. 4: A Cipher Wheel (taken from Franke 1982)

is probably known to everybody who has ever thought about encrypting messages, cf. Kahn 1968. The article "Cryptology - Methods and Maxims" by Bauer, pp. 31 - 48, gives a rather detailed introduction to the principles of designing cryptographic devices. Bauer also places special emphasis on the weakness of most known systems, some of which were cryptanalysed more than a century ago, cf. Kasiski, 1822, Kerckhoffs, 1822.

In spite of these very old publications crypto-machines were still built without their constructors' realizing that they were practically worthless.

An example is the beautiful looking machine invented by Alexander von Kryha

Fig. 5: A Kryha machine (Phote credit: K. Wirl)
This model was shown at Burg Feuerstein by
K.O. Widman, Crypto AG

The article by Konheim pp. 49 - 64, gives a short summary of the history of this machine and its inventor, followed by a complete cryptanalysis of its function.

This paper is an addition to the introductory chapters on cryptanalysis which for instance can be found in the recent textbooks by Beker and Piper (1982) - e.g. for analyzing the Hagelin M-209 -

or that by Konheim (1981), where a complete analysis of the (in-) famous German cipher machine ENIGMA is demonstrated.

The reader, who is interested in the historical and political implications of the ENIGMA's security being so wrongly overestimated, will find good references in Bauer's article, pp. 31 - 48, including the book by Kahn 1964.

Schuchmann's contribution is yet presenting further aspects that have arisen from his occupation with the ENIGMA-machine.

Fig. 6: An ENIGMA (Photo credit: K. Wirl)
This model was shown at Burg Feuerstein by
H.-P. Schuchmann, Siemens AG

The weakness of all these "classical" systems is mainly owing to the principal mistake of using the same key more than once.

Towards Modern Cryptography

By a small modification most of the classical though simple systems can be made secure. The idea goes back to the AT&T-engineer G.S. Vernam, who already in 1917 (published as late as 1926) proposed to use simply Vigenère-ciphers with a random key. Vigenère-ciphers are basically CAESAR-like ciphers; for an exact definition see Bauer, pp.

The socalled Vernam-cipher had been developed for the use in telegraph systems where the plaintext, which is a binary sequence in this case, is superimposed by a binary key sequence via mod 2 addition.

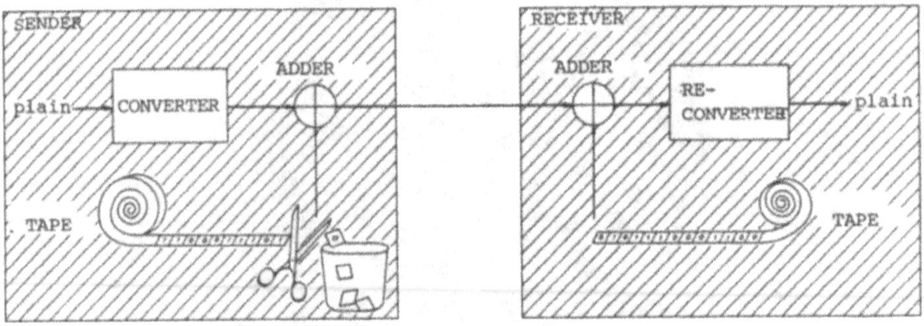

Fig. 7: Vernam cipher with one-time-pad

This key sequence could be realized as a sequence on a paper tape being used by both transmitter and receiver, who synchronously apply each portion of this tape only once (one-time-pad).

Thus emphasis has to be placed upon the question how to generate the key-sequences in order to make the Vernam-system secure, see again Bauer, pp. 31 - 48. It was C.E. Shannon (Shannon 1942), who gave sufficient conditions for absolute cryptographic security of cipher systems. So the proposed Vernam-system would be secure if the key-sequence was generated by a random process such as coin-tossing, giving a binomial distribution of maximal entropy.

Although this procedure endows the users with a system of utmost security - there are reports that such system are used on extremely sensitive lines, cf. Kahn 1963 - it is obvious that the secure distribution of huge sets of key tape generates other problems, cf. Ryska/Herda 1979, Beth 1982.

A possible way to get around this problem will be discussed in the paragraph on Sequential Ciphers.

Modern Cryptosystems

The few examples given so far show that modern cryptographic systems have to be designed with a substantial portion of interdisciplinary work.

Pursuing the directions shown by Vernam 1926, Hill 1926 and Albert 1941, modern cryptography cannot be thought of without mathematics - ranging over all areas from analysis, combinatorics, probability to geometry and algebra.

This should be clear from almost all the articles in this volume. On the other hand, main tools and intrinsic kowledge from many other areas, e.g. physics, electrical engineering, computer science, systems engineering and linguistics are required. This is probably best demonstrated by the fascinating article "Encrypting by Random

Rotations" , pp. 71 - 128, contributed by Sloane. This paper, which originally has arisen from the problem of secure speech transmission, is really giving a wide-ranging survey of methods in modern cryptography.

Secure Speech Transmission

Major attention has always been paid to the problem of persons speaking to each other via telephone or radio without being overheard. With the Vernam-system at disposal a secure speech transmission could just as easily be designed as follows:

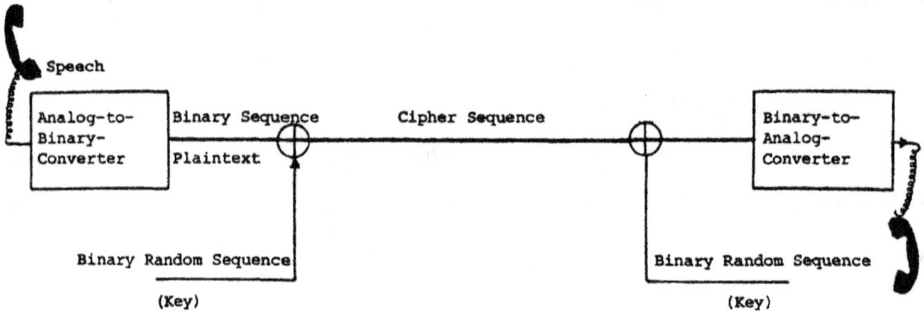

Fig. 8: Secure Digital Speech Transmission

But every simple solution has its drawbacks: Let alone the quoted disadvantages associated with the design of secure Vernam ciphers, there is a more serious problem which is essentially due to a law of physics. For the design of a secure voice transmission via a telephone line one has to be aware of the fact, that standard (wire-) telephone lines are only capable of transmitting in a frequency range of 300-3400 Hz.

Assuming the mentioned Analog-to-Binary-Converter works as a standard

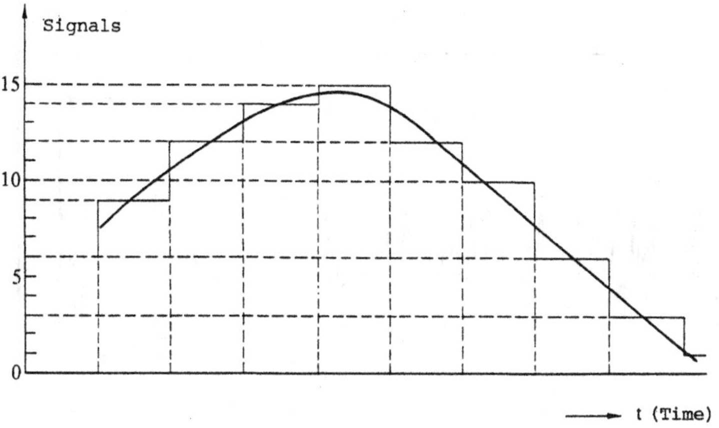

Fig. 9: PCM-Modulation (taken from Franke 1982).

Puls-Code-Modulator, it has to operate at a sampling frequency of at least 2×3.400 Hz (Nyquist rate). This is due to a law of communications engineering, the socalled sampling theorem (for this see Sloane's article, pp. 71 - 128), which is very similar to the renowned Heisenberg uncertainty principle in quantum physics, cf. Dym/McKean 1972.

Furthermore assuming a sampling precision of 8 bit the Analog-to-Binary-Converter in consideration would produce more than 50k Bit per sec.

Obviously it would be impossible to transmit at such a rate via a standard telephone line.

Several remedies are possible

(i) Wyner's scrambling scheme (cf. Wyner 1980)

(ii) Analog Voice scrambling systems using Time-Division-Scrambling and Frequency-Domain-Scrambling: (cf. the recent book Beth/Heß/Wirl 1983).

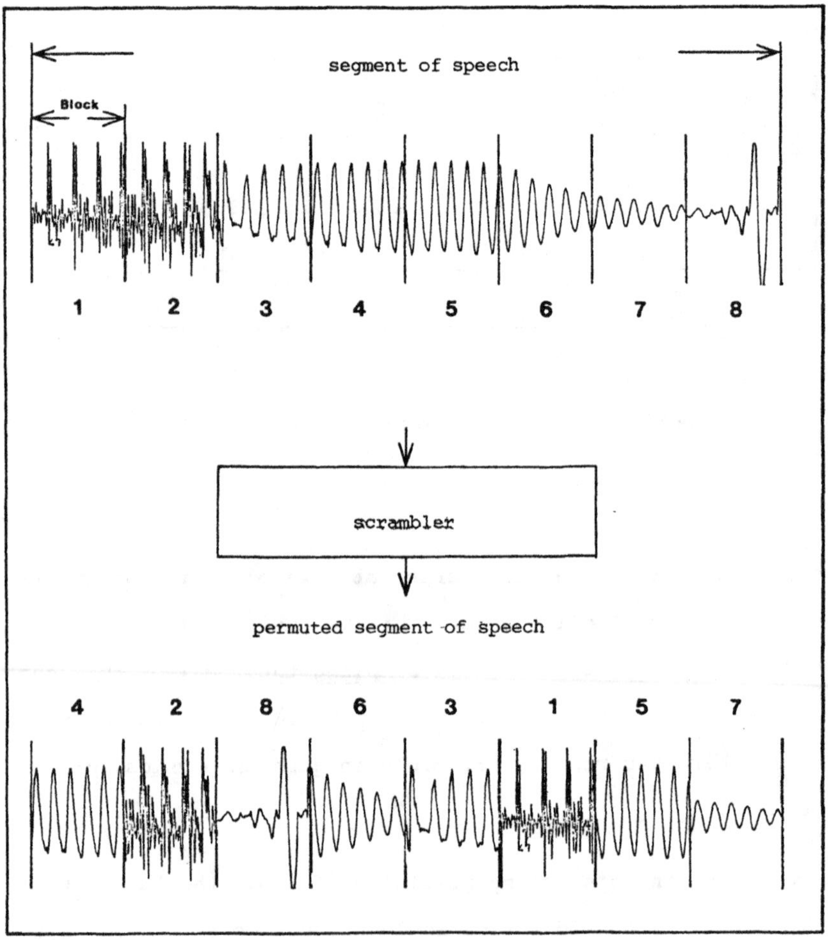

Fig. 10: The effect of time-division scrambling
(taken from Beth/Heß/Wirl 1982)

N.J.A. Sloane's article, pp. 71 - 128, includes a very concise description of the Wyner scheme. Then, in a marvelous excursion through probability, analysis, representation theory and combinatorics, Sloane shows how Wyner's system can be endowed with the suitable probabilistic properties in order to make it cryptographically secure in the strict sense mentioned before. Until today the Wyner system, though extremely appealing, has one major drawback: No feasible implementation is known. So for all practical purposes voice scrambling systems still have to be built as a mixture of Time- and Frequency-Domain-Scramblers.

As these two procedures correspond to the wellknown classes of Transposition-respectively Substitution-ciphers (cf. Bauer, pp. 31 - 48) the quoted security measures have to be applied again. Beker's survey paper "Analogue Speech Security Systems" (pp. 131 - 146) gives an excellent introduction to the present day techniques which finally lead to very refined combinatorical investigations concerning the availability of large key spaces as required for high security. The paper by Heß and Wirl, pp. 147 - 156, "A Voice Scrambling System for Testing and Demonstration" describes a Time-Domain-Scrambler

Fig. 11: The EVOCS-system, cf. pp. 147 - 156, (Photo credit: K. Wirl)

which has been developed at the Department of Computer Sciences at the University of Erlangen. A report on the state of the art (at the beginning of 1982) is contained in the book Beth/Heß/Wirl 1983 which also deals with a description of some experiments to determine subjective understandability of scrambled speech.

The contribution by Timmann, pp. 157 - 163, throws some new light upon this important topic. Other analogue scrambling schemes than those described in the paper by Heß and Wirl, pp. 147 - 156, are the ones which manipulate the spectra. Pichler's contribution, pp. 173 - 178, proposes an interesting way of designing an analogue scrambler via the Fast Fourier Transform (Aho/Hopcroft/Ullman 1974). This technique provides the links with the very new and powerful technique of spread spectra and frequency hopping. These systems, which are mainly developed for large bandwidths (see below), are the topic of the paper by Györfi and Kerekes, pp. 165 - 179.

Digital Cipher Systems

Since the investigations of the preceding section apply merely to low frequency transmission systems, for most computers, data banking systems, VHF- and UHF-communication nets the question of bandwidth is neglectable and, besides, most of the digitized data are already available in a form which supports their processing by means of discrete mathematics and algebra. Digital cipher systems roughly fall into two classes:

- Sequential Ciphers,
- Block Ciphers.

The reader may be warned that these classes are not necessarily disjoint.

Sequential Ciphers

Sequential Ciphers have already been considered in the context of Vernam systems. In applying these systems it is crucial to provide both at the transmitter's and receiver's end binary random sequences longer than the expected sequence of messages.

To give a mathematical model: a Sequential Cipher is a cryptosystem of arbitrary injective enciphering functions, in which the sets of plaintexts (M), of keys(K) and ciphertexts(C) coincide with the set $\{0,1\}^{\mathbb{N}}$ of all countable 0-1-sequences.

For the most restricted class of stream ciphers the set of enciphering functions

$$E_{\underline{s}} : M \to C \qquad \underline{s} \in K$$

consists of the simple additions

$$\underline{m} \mapsto E_{\underline{s}}(\underline{m}) = \underline{m} \oplus \underline{s} \bmod 2$$

(cf. Picture No.).

More complicated sequential ciphers will be discussed in the context of the contribution by Davies/Parkin, pp.

Since coin-tossing - aside from all other aspects - is not quite what one would call a real-time random process for the use in modern computer systems, one has to refer back to "approximate random" (cf. Sloane's article, pp. 71 - 128) by Pseudo Random Generators. Under the assumption that such systems are available, an electronic stream cipher system basically has the following form:

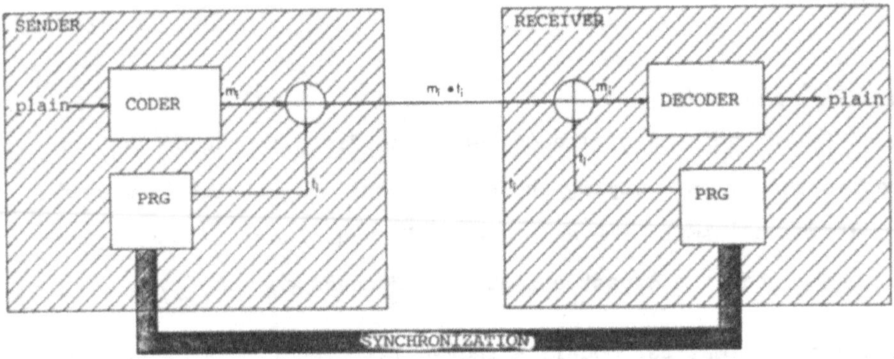

Fig. 12: A sequential cipher system

Piper's article "Stream Ciphers" (pp. 181 - 188) shows why the PRG's, which up to the 1960's were realized via Linear Feedback Shift-Registers (cf. Golomb 1967, Selmer 1966, Lüneburg 1979),

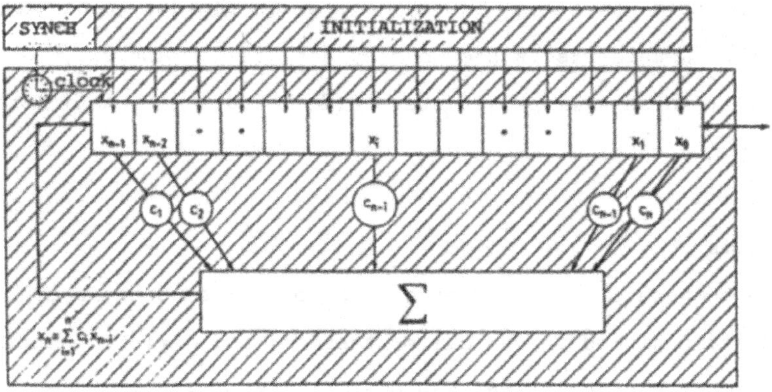

Fig. 13: A linear feed-back-shift-register

are totally insecure. Their replacement by socalled Non-Linear-Feedback Shift Registers

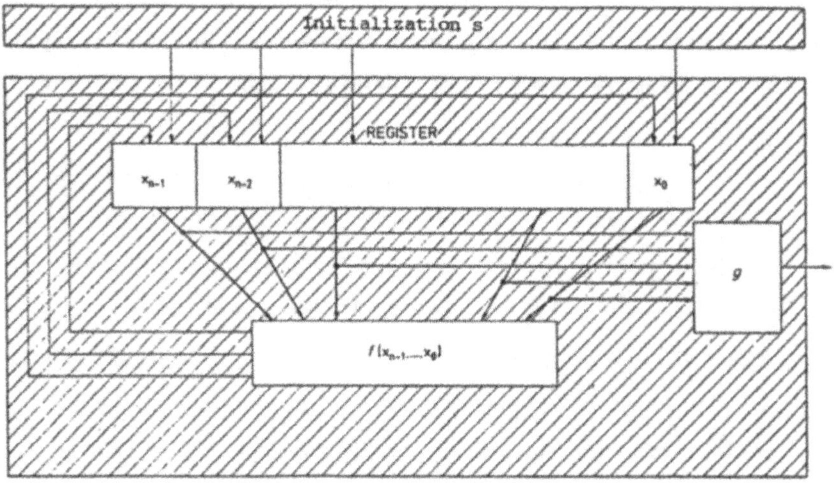

Fig. 14: A non-linear feed-back-shift-register

is being discussed by Jennings' contribution, pp. 189 - 206 , where she describes one of the most powerful practical Pseudo Random Generators. The behaviour of it can be described wholly in terms of Polynomial Algebra over Finite Fields, Discrete Fourier Transforms and Auto-Correlation Functions.

Another tool from Polynomial Theory needed for the design of good Pseudo Random Generators is provided by Herlestam's article, pp. 107 - 216, which will prove interesting to pure mathematicians also.

Block Ciphers

While cryptogenerators for the large class of stream ciphers can be described and designed in the quite beautiful and efficient setup of Algebra over Finite Fields, the development of equally good block ciphers seems to be a much harder problem.

A block cipher consists, of an arbitrary set of injective mappings

$$E_s : M \rightarrow C$$

where in most cases the sets M and C consist of the space $\{0,1\}^n$ of binary vectors of length n for some integer n , while the key space K can be parametrized in many different ways.

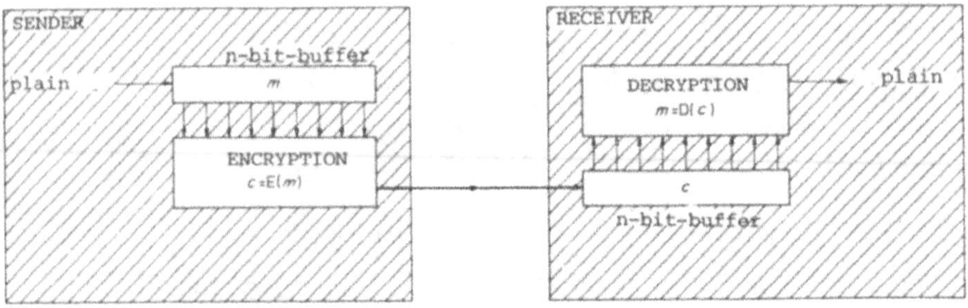

Fig. 15: A Block Cipher System

The figure in principle shows how to operate block ciphers.
It seems to be a challenge for most cryptographers to design secure block ciphers.

For further reading the references Beker/Piper 1982, Ryska/Herda 1980, Konheim 1981, or Feistel 1973 are suggested.

The best-known, but not yet fully understood block cipher appears to be the Data Encryption Standard (DES) as published by the U.S. National Bureau of Standards, Federal Register, August 1st, 1975. Here the messages as well as the ciphertexts are binary words of length 64. The key space consists of binary vectors of 56 bit, extended by (additional) 8 control bits.

The following flow chart

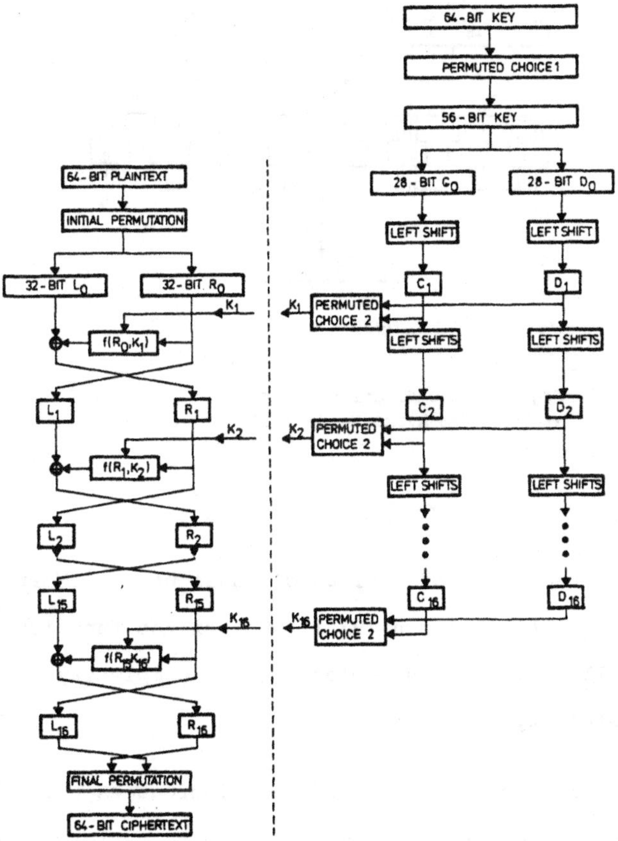

Fig. 16: The principle of DES
(taken from Ryska/Herda 1980)

shows the operational logic of DES which meanwhile is available as a chip produced by several manufacturers.

The procedures in this flow chart are made public (cf. Federal Reg. 1975, Konheim 1981).

The crucial part of the algorithm seems to lie in the construction of socalled S-Boxes, which dominantly determine the functions f(R,K) .

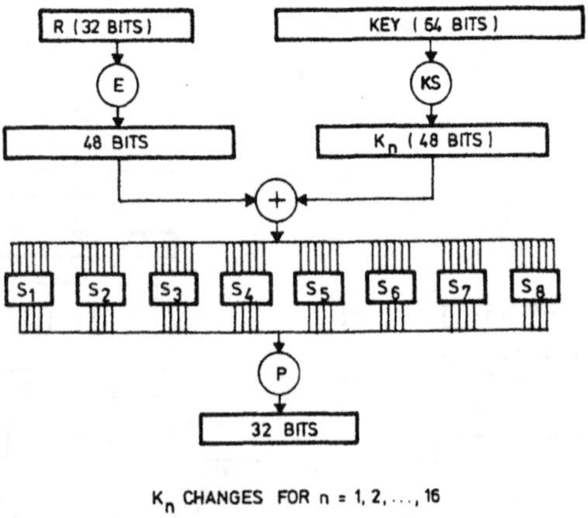

Fig. 17: the function f(R,K)
(taken from Ryska/Herda 1980)

It has been the topic of serious discussions (cf. Morris/Sloane/ Wyner 1977, Diffie/Hellman 1976), whether the function of these S-Boxes will guarantee sufficient crypto-complexity to withstand even forceful attacks.

In her contribution Schaumüller-Bichl introduces a complexity measure through which an attempt is made to perform a security analysis of DES.

Gordon's article on large S-Boxes, pp. 256 - 261, aims at a more constructive approach to increase the security of DES-like block ciphers by proposing larger classes of enciphering algorithms. There is a natural implementation of block ciphers for producing sequential ciphers (which are not stream ciphers in the narrow sense). This principle is best demonstrated by the functional diagram

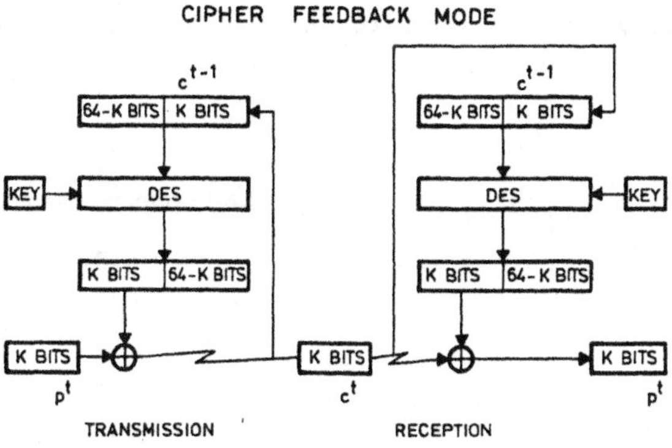

Fig. 18: The cipher feed-back-mode of DES
(taken from Ryska/Herda 1980)

of the DES in the socalled Cipher Feedback Mode.

The paper by Davies and Parkin, pp. 263 - 279 , examines the behaviour of the encryption procedure in terms of combinatorical aspects towards the possible periodicities. This is a very promising approach, which, being merely automata theoretic, may well prove to extend the linear algebraic considerations as introduced by Piper, pp. 181 - 188, or Jennings, pp. 189 - 206.

Cryptography in Communication Nets

As DES has been chosen as a standard encryption procedure for huge information systems (cf. Oberman's paper, pp. 219 - 227) between government authorities, insurance companies and hospitals (cf. Horbach's contribution, pp. 228 - 232), banks and point of sales terminals in department stores, etc., it was essential to design a key distribution system of a kind that let the users communicate with each other in a secure way.

For this purpose the model of a key library has been developed, very much in analogy to that well-known "key library" known as "telephone books".

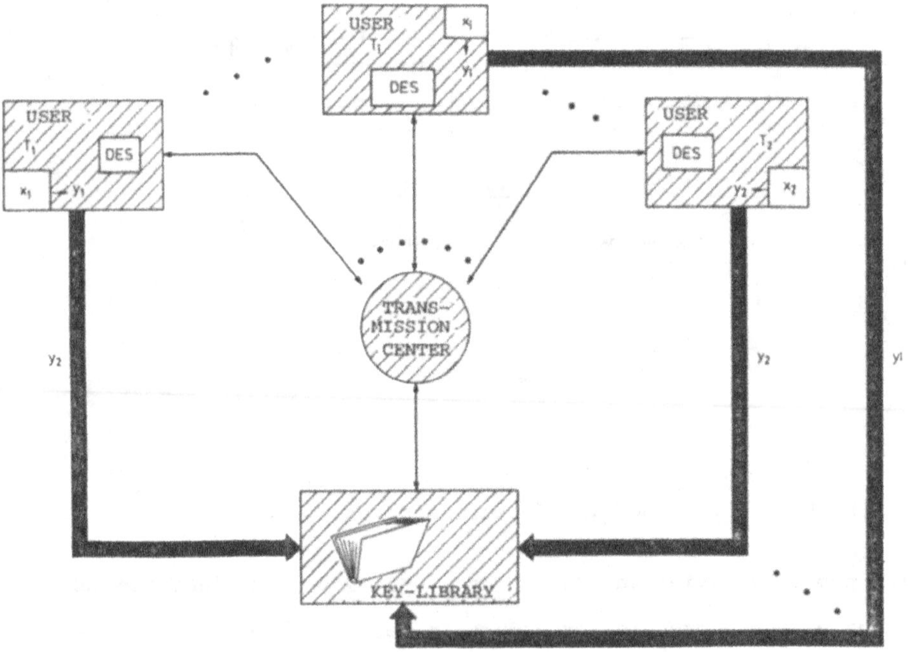

Fig. 19: A communication system based on DES

The concept of a key distribution system helped to develop the concept of a socalled One-Way-Function. Loosely speaking, an injective function $f : X \to Y$ is called a "one-way-function", if

(i) for any $x \in X$ it is "easy" to compute y " $f(x)$.

(ii) for given $y \in Y$ it is "practically" infeasible to find the $x \in X$ solving the equation $y = f(x)$.

For some more explanations of these see the articles by Davio, Goethals and Quisquater, pp. 283 - 288, and Schöbi and Massey, pp. 289 - 306. A one-way-function, which in the context of key distribution probably has become known best, is the one given by Pohlig/Hellman 1978. For this let $Y = GF(p)$ be the finite field of prime order p with a primitive element w, cf. Dornhoff/Hohn 1978, Lüneburg 1979. Then the function

$$f : [1 : p-2] \to GF(p)$$

given by

$$x \mapsto f(x) = w^x$$

is a one-way-function cf. Pohlig/Hellman 1978, Ryska/Herda 1980, Beth 1982.

For an implementation in a key distribution system, e.g. for DES, it can be used as follows:

Each user T_i chooses a number x_i (kept secret) and sends the value $y_i = w^{x_i}$ to the key library. Suppose T_1 and T_2 want to communicate under DES.

T_1 looks up T_2's key and uses $k_{1,2} = y_2^{x_1}$ as a key.

T_2 looks up y_1 and uses $k_{2,1} = y^{x_2}$. But as

$$k_{2,1} = y_1^{x_2} = x^{x_1 x_2} = w^{x_2 x_1} = y_2^{x_1} = k_{1,2} ,$$

both happen to use the same key as is required.

This concept had been developed to provide secure pairwise communication lines on the base of a common cryptosystem like DES. For most communication systems a different model is of equally important use. Consider a communication system, in which any user T_1 wants to be able to send a message to some arbitrary other user T_2 exclusively, even without identifying himself or having any feedback. This model applies to satellites addressing certain authorized ground stations, measuring instruments reporting to certain authorized controllers, etc.

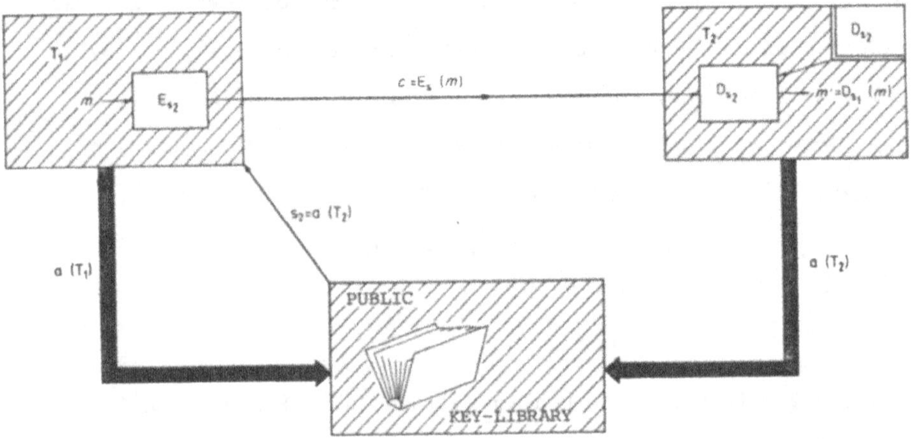

Fig. 20: A public key crypto system

It is realized by a cryptosystem with a public key library, based on the idea of "trap-door-functions". These, loosely speaking, are one-way-functions whose inversion becomes easy if some hidden (trap-door-)information is known, cf. Diffie/Hellman 1976, Hellman 1977.

The public-key-system now operates as follows:

The receiver T_2 has made his trap-door-function E_{s_2} public via the key library, where any sender T_1 can look up E_{s_2} and then encipher his message m by E_{s_2}. Any other possible receiver - except T_2 - will be locked out, as $c = E_{s_2}(m)$ is scrambled under the one-way-function E_{s_2}. But T_2 knows the hidden trick to invert E_{s_2} by D_{s_2}. So T_2 (and only T_2) is able to read m .

It is one of the amazing properties of this system, cf. Diffie/ Hellman 1976, Hellman 1977, that it can be used for the contrary purpose - i.e. the identification of the sender T_2 - as well.

To do this the sender only has to encipher all his messages by "his" inverse function D_{s_1} (which is only known to him). Any receiver T_2 , who wants to convince himself that it is indeed T_1 who is transmitting, looks up E_{s_1} in the library and deciphers with its help. He obtains the plaintext if T_1 is the sender.

In the light of this concept the contribution by Davio, Goethals and Quisquater, pp. 283 - 288, describes an interesting setup for new authentication procedures.

The paper by Schöbi and Massey, pp. 289 - 306, deals with a fast authentication algorithm based on the concrete trap-door-function, known as the Trap-door-knapsack.

Trap-Door-Functions

Two examples of trap-door-functions have become well-known:

- the RSA-Scheme,
- the Merkle-Hellman-Scheme.

The Merkle-Hellman-Scheme (cf. Merkle/Hellman 1978) is based on a special knapsack problem (cf. Aho/Hopcroft/Ullman 1974), which is nicely described in the contributions by Schöbi and Massey, pp. 289 - 306, or Eier and Lagger, pp. 316 - 322.

But - since very shortly after the publication of the MH-Scheme - there have been misgivings with respect to the security of cryptosystems linked to NP-hard problems (cf. Aho/Hopcroft/Ullman 1974, Garey/Johnson 1979). Especially the MH-Scheme, which depends on a very special subclass of the general Knapsack-Problem, shows a surprising weakness.

Already in 1977 it was shown by Even, Lempel and Yacobi (cf. Lempel 1978) that a slight modification, which seemingly increased the security, makes the MH-Scheme almost trivial to "break".

One proposal to launch an attack against the MH-Scheme is made in the paper by Eier and Lagger, pp. 316 - 322, giving at the same time a good starting point for the contribution by Ingemarsson (pp. 309 - 315). Ingemarsson describes a procedure transforming the original knapsack into a system of modified knapsack problems in elementary geometry of numbers and linear programming.

Along the same lines is a paper by Shamir (Shamir 1982) in which he describes a method*) solving almost all the knapsack-equations of fixed length n in polynomial computing time. Shamir's method uses a result of Lenstra's (Lenstra 1981), which proves that the integer linear programming problem (Garey/Johnson 1977) with a fixed number of variables is polynomially solvable.

---

*) This result was already announced during a Workshop on Cryptography, Burg Feuerstein. The editor would have been happy to be able to include this paper in this volume.

So there remains to consider the other famous Public-Key-Crypto-System, the renowned RSA-System (Rivest/Shamir/Adleman 1978).

The RSA-System uses as a set of plaintext M the set $M = [0:m]$. The set K of keys consists of the pairs (N,d) of positive integers with $N > m$ and g.c.d. $(d,\varphi(N)) = 1$.

Each user selects a pair of distinct prime numbers p,q with $N = p \cdot q > m$ and a number d with

- $(p,q) < d < \varphi(n) = (p-1)(q-1)$
- g.c.d. $(d,\varphi(N)) = 1$.

His private trap-door-information is the factorization $n = p \cdot q$.

As a public key the user publishes the pair of numbers (N,e), where e is a multiplicative inverse of d mod $\varphi(n)$, i.e.

$$e \cdot d \equiv 1 \mod \varphi(n) .$$

The encryption function - for speaking to r - is to be

$$E_r : [0 : m] \to \mathbb{Z}_n$$

as given by

$$x \to E_r(x) = x^e \mod n .$$

The receiver, who knows the trap-door-information $n = p \cdot q$, can easily compute

$$x = D_r(E_r(x)) = (E_r(x))^d = x^{de} \equiv x \mod n$$

(cf. Knuth 1967).

But breaking this system would rest upon the ability to apply the Chinese remainder theorem (Dornhoff/Hohn 1978) in order to determine d from e . This probably cannot be done without the prime factorization of n .

The contribution by Sattler and Schnorr gives an excellent introduction to the present state of the art of factoring large numbers while analysing the security of the RSA system.

Additional rules for security precautions can be excerpted from Schnorr's paper, pp. 325 - 329, in which an attempt is made to break the RSA-Scheme.

Finally the contribution by Ecker, pp. 353 - 369, describes the background needed to generalize RSA-like schemes to different algebraic systems.

A closely related question is treated in Mignotte's paper, pp. 371 - 375, on the problem

"How to share a secret?"

Section 2

Classical Cryptography

C R Y P T O L O G Y - M E T H O D S A N D M A X I M S

Friedrich L. Bauer
Technical University Munich

Summary.

This paper gives a survey of classical cryptographic methods and of the maxims to their proper use in order to resist illegitimate decryption, as a basis for an understanding of modern commercial, computer-based cryptographic systems and for a critical analysis of those.

Key words: Cryptology, cryptography, cipher systems, encryption, cryptanalysis, computational complexity.

Computing Reviews Classification: D.3

INTRODUCTION

A few years ago, cryptology, the study of the principles of secret writing and of methods of breaking ciphers and codes, rather was a wall-flower: Flowering, since it was over the centuries a profitable pursuit for the professionals, among which are included mathematicians like VIETE or WALLIS. And remaining hidden is in its nature: with the rise of omnipotent governments, professional cryptologists are forced into anonymity and have at least to accept censorship of their publications. Correspondingly, thé open literature never reflected the state of the art completely - one can safely assume that this has continued to be so. In this respect, different nations show varying degrees of retention: while the United States of America - who wonders - rather generously released information about the situation in World War II, the Soviet Union kept silent. But even Great Britain was unduly secretive, in particular on the subject of the 'Colossi', electronic machines used for breaking the German Geheimschreiber.Only about the state of cryptology in Germany an open report was issued after the breakdown of the Nazi regime [Rohrbach 1948].

World War II definitely brought mathematicians to the cryptological front, for example HANS ROHRBACH in Germany and ALAN TURING in England. In the USA, the great algebraist A. A. ALBERT mobilized mathematicians for the work in cryptology. In Germany, several people (who later on became university professors of mathematics) could be listed. Again, little is known about the mathematicians the British recruited (but some are still among us) and nothing, of course, about Soviet mathematicians.

Among the great professionals of the last 50 years, names like FRIEDMAN, KULLBACK, SINKOV, ROWLETT in the USA, EYRAUD, GIVIERGE in France, SACCO in Italy, GYLDEN in Sweden, HÜTTENHAIN, KUNZE, SCHAUFFLER, PASCHKE in Germany, FIGL in Austria, LANGER in Poland, DE GREY, DENNISON and KNOX in Great Britain are all related to World War II. Today, names of professional cryptographers are kept secret. In general, this is well understandable: they cannot risk exposure to the activities of intelligence agencies. Even the smallest detail would be revealing: It is important to keep the enemy in the dark concerning one's own views about the selection of methods and particularly about one's own capability in breaking ciphers and codes. Thus, until 1944 the Germans remained convinced that their ENIGMA machines could not be compromised. However, once a solution is found - the British accomplished this, with Polish help, in 1940 for the ENIGMA enciphering - then it is of paramount importance to hide this fact from the enemy and not to arouse his suspicions by unwise reactions. In World War II, this has meant that material and even human lives had to be sacrificed in order to prevent greater losses.

Side by side with governmental cryptology, there are the amateurs, particularly since the epoch of liberalization following the French Revolution. This reaches from retired professionals like ETIENNE BAZERIES (1846-1924) who investigated historical French events, to the entertainment CHARLES WHEATSTONE (1802-1875) and CHARLES BABBAGE (1792-1871) found in decrypting messages published by loving couples in London newspapers - love messages being anyhow one of the oldest incentives for secret writing. It has literary and journalistic aspects: EDGAR ALLAN POE, besides writing the famous short story 'The Gold Bug', had cryptological articles in the Philadelphia newspaper 'Alexanders Weekly Messenger' and in other journals which have found wide interest. In our times, the Los Angeles Times daily publishes a 'Cryptoquip' and VLADIMIR NABOKOV, in *Lolita*, used eccentric enigmas. There are amateurs in cryptology with records reaching from occultism to espionage, from smuggling to terrorism. Such a fascinating picture of cryptography, mixed with sensational reports on World War II events, was first presented in compact form to a wide public in the 1967 book 'The Code Breakers' by DAVID KAHN, a journalistic masterpiece of popularization [Kahn 1967]. In the seventies, after Great Britain had released certain informations that supplemented the war stories, BRIAN JOHNSON wrote 'The Secret War' [Johnson 1978], PATRICK BEESLEY 'Very special intelligence' [Beesley 1977].

After the invention of the telegraph, commercial interest in cryptology was restricted to the production of code books and, roughly since the turn of the century, to the construction of mechanical and electromechanical enciphering and deciphering machines. In continuation of the successful start in World War II, electronic computers then found ample use for breaking cryptograms. As soon as programmable pocket calculators were available, enciphering and deciphering at low cost, but at a considerable degree of security, was in principle available to everybody. But only in the mid-seventies, a wide-spread commercial interest in encrypting private message channels became manifest. Here, the possibilities of microminiature circuitry on a single chip are effectively combined with the needs that originate in computer-supported message systems ('electronic mail'). Further incentives came from laws that required data protection, not to forget scandal news about tapped wires and wide-spread industrial espionage.

Thus suddenly private commercial applications of cryptology are in the forefront of interest.

'Cryptology for everybody', however, is a postulate that is contradictory in itself. In particular, occupation of a great number of scientists with this discipline leads, in the large nations, to problems of national security. A ban on private research in cryptology - comparable with the ban on private research in atomic bombs - can only be prevented, if scientists adhere to some form of voluntary self-control.

Freedom of Science has its price.

CRYPTOGRAPHIC METHODS

In the following survey on known cryptographic methods, we omit some details and restrict attention to the genuine cryptological aspect of protecting an established communication channel against (passive) eavesdropping and (active) forging. We are not concerned with *noisy channels* and assume that appropriate countermeasures are taken by using *error-detecting* and *error-correcting codes*. Likewise we do not deal with *steganographic* methods, which even try to conceal the existence of messages by technical means (invisible inks, microdots, spread spectra methods etc.) or by linguistic tricks (open codes, jargons).

Thus, it remains *cryptography* in the proper sense: the *plain message* ('plain text') is transformed into a *crypto message* which is 'unintelligible to outsiders' in the twofold sense that they can neither read nor forge it; the transformation is called *encryption* and is to be carried out by the sender. The recipient performs a transformation into the original message: the mapping, which is the inverse of encryption, is called *decryption*.

In agreement with technological conditions, we make the usual (although specializing) assumption that both the plain and the crypto message are represented as *strings* of *finite length* ('words') over finite sets $\mathbb{V}$, $\mathbb{W}$ of marks ('symbols', 'letters', 'digits') called *alphabets* or *vocabularies*.

Of course, the choice of the *plain alphabet* or *plain vocabulary* $\mathbb{V}$ depends on the underlying natural or artificial language. In the Renaissance, 20 letters were sufficient. Classical cryptographic systems mostly use the 26 letters of the 'Latin' alphabet $\mathbb{Z}_{26}$. In commercial systems using typewriters, figures and punctuation marks are needed, too; even upper and lower case is often to be distinguished. This usually results in 88 symbols, 96 symbols are available in the ISO (ASCII) 7-bit code $\mathbb{Z}_{96}$. The plain text can also be expressed in a binary alphabet $\mathbb{Z}_2 = \{0, 1\}$ For our purposes these last two cases can be considered to be normal.

The choice of the crypto alphabet or crypto vocabulary $\mathbb{W}$ is rather free. It may depend on the circumstances of the communication channel. In classical situations, $\mathbb{W}$ sometimes has been different from $\mathbb{V}$, e.g. has been the set $\mathbb{Z}_{10}$ of ten decimal digits or the set $\mathbb{Z}_6$ of six well-distinguishable Morse groups .- , -.. , ..- , --. , ...- , -... . Very often, and in particular in modern methods, $\mathbb{W}$ will coincide with $\mathbb{V}$, and we may often find $\mathbb{Z}_2$ or $\mathbb{Z}_{96}$ for $\mathbb{W}$.

Let $\mathbb{V}^*$, $\mathbb{W}^*$ denote the set of all words over $\mathbb{V}$, $\mathbb{W}$ resp., $\mathbb{V}^{(n)}$, $\mathbb{W}^{(m)}$ the set of all words of maximal length n , m resp., $\mathbb{V}^n$, $\mathbb{W}^m$ the set of all words of exact length n , m resp.

We then define an *encryption* σ to be an *injective partial mapping* from V^* into W^* :

$$\sigma : V^* \longrightarrow W^*$$

or more generally, a *left-unique correspondence* between V^* and W^* :

$$\sigma : V^* \dashrightarrow W^*$$

Left-uniqueness means that for all $x , y \in V^* , z \in W^*$

$$x \overset{\sigma}{\mapsto} z \wedge y \overset{\sigma}{\mapsto} z \succ x = y .$$

The inverse of the mapping or the correspondence σ is then uniquely determined, even in the latter case it is a partial mapping σ^{-1} , called *decryption*

$$\sigma^{-1} : W^* \dashrightarrow V^*$$

which maps σV^* , the image of V^* under σ , onto V^* , if σ is a total mapping.

σ , followed by σ^{-1} , is the identity (on the domain of σ) .

Words from W^* , which correspond to the same word from V^* , are called *homophones*. In particular, words from W^* which correspond to the empty word $\varepsilon \in V^*$, are called *nulls*.

If the encryption is not a mapping, it defines a non-deterministic transformation rule. The choice of homophones and nulls should not be subject to any recognizable law. If the encryption is a mapping, there are no proper homophones and the only null is usually the trivial empty word from W ; σ^{-1} , followed by σ is the identity, too (on the range of σ) .

It is not necessary that the domain of σ is the whole V^* and that the range is the whole W^* . For example, σ could be a mapping of 32 ready-made messages on political events onto 32 5-bit words. Practically, σ will often be a correspondence $V^{(n)} \dashrightarrow W^{(m)}$ for some rather large and usually unknown n .

For perpetual traffic, no maximum length can be accepted. Thus, some rather small n is chosen and the stream of messages is decomposed into segments of maximal length n , which are encrypted, transmitted and decrypted consecutively. In this way, $\sigma : V^{(n)} \dashrightarrow W^{(m)}$ induces a correspondence

$$\sigma^* : V^* \dashrightarrow W^*$$

σ^* is not necessarily left-unique even if σ is. A sufficient requirement is the *Fano condition*: No word from the range of σ may be beginning (or may be the end) of another word from the range.

Very often, all words from the range of σ have equal length,

$$\sigma : \quad \mathbb{V}^{(n)} \dashrightarrow \mathbb{W}^{m}$$

Then, the Fano condition holds trivially. Originating from the tariff construction of international telegraphy, classically the use of groups of five crypto symbols or of a multiple thereof is customary. For $\mathbb{W} = \mathbb{Z}_2$, powers of 2 may be used for m , in particular $m = 32$ or $m = 64$.
Often, all words from the domain of σ have a equal length, too.

$$\sigma : \quad \mathbb{V}^{n} \dashrightarrow \mathbb{W}^{m}$$

The use of encrypted words of unequal length ('straddling') as well as the use of homophones and nulls, makes the cryptanalytic attack much more difficult, as it has been known since MATTEO ARGENTI's work (1590). It is, however, inconvenient for the cypher clerk.

For a correspondence $\mathbb{V}^{(n)} \dashrightarrow \mathbb{W}^{(m)}$ or a mapping $\mathbb{V}^{(n)} \longrightarrow \mathbb{W}^{(m)}$, a finite listing of all pairs of words is possible. If the plaintext groups are all of equal and rather small length, say $n = 1$, $n = 2$, it is customary to speak of a *cipher* (which may be noted down in a *cipher table*) and to call encryption *enciphering*, decryption *deciphering*. If the plaintext groups rather follow linguistic structures like syllables, words, sentences (and thus normally are of different length), it is customary to speak of a *code* (which may be contained in a *code book*) and to call encryption *encoding*, decryption *decoding*. The border line in the use of these two terms is vague.

More refined ciphers and codes can also be obtained by (deterministic or nondeterministic) algorithms: these algorithms can be parametrized by a *key*. In order to make cryptanalytic attacks more difficult, one thus obtains a family $S = \{\sigma^{(k)}\}$ of ciphers or codes - in the simplest case a family of cipher tables or code books. For every new message, or at least every day, if not every hour, the key is changed according to previous agreement. This agreement is to be done under special precautions in order to prevent the enemy from obtaining the key.

The size of the family of *all* (left-unique) correspondences $\mathbb{V}^{(n)} \dashrightarrow \mathbb{W}^{(m)}$ or (injective) mappings $\mathbb{V}^{(n)} \longrightarrow \mathbb{W}^{(m)}$ may be, depending on the cardinalities N of $\mathbb{V}$ and M of $\mathbb{W}$, quite enormous; if $N = M$ and $n = m$, there are $(N^N)!$ bijections $\mathbb{V}^n \longleftrightarrow \mathbb{W}^n$ and $((N^{n+1} - 1)/(N-1))!$ bijections $\mathbb{V}^{(n)} \longleftrightarrow \mathbb{W}^{(n)}$.
In practical cryptography, smaller families are used. It is a common mistake, to use unnecessarily small families.

All commonly used ciphers and codes fall into the family of *general substitutions* - transpositions included, as we shall see - defined to be

$$\sigma : \quad \mathbb{V}^{(n)} \dashrightarrow \mathbb{W}^{(m)}$$

where (with $\nu \leq n$, $\mu \leq m$)

$$(x_1 \dots x_\nu) \overset{\sigma}{\longmapsto}$$

$$(\Upsilon_1(x_1 \dots x_{k_1})\ \Upsilon_2(x_{k_1+1} \dots x_{k_2})\ \dots\ \Upsilon_r(x_{k_{r-1}+1} \dots x_\nu))$$

and where the Υ_i themselves are ciphers or codes

$$\Upsilon_i : \mathbb{V}^{(k_i - k_{i-1})} \dashrightarrow \mathbb{W}^{(m_i)} \quad \text{with } k_0 = 0\ ,\ k_r = \nu\ ,\ \sum_{i=1}^{r} m_i = \mu\ .$$

A substitution is called *monographic*, if $k_i = i$ (and thus $r = \nu$) ; then Υ_i is $\mathbb{V}^{(1)} \dashrightarrow \mathbb{W}^{(m_i)}$. Otherwise, it is called *polygraphic*. In this case, it is customary to take $k_i - k_{i-1} = k$ constant, then Υ_i is $\mathbb{V}^{(k)} \dashrightarrow \mathbb{W}^{(m_i)}$; one speaks of a *k-gram cipher* or a *k-gram code*. With the use of a computer, a tetragram cipher over $\mathbb{Z}_{96}$ or a 32-gram code over $\mathbb{Z}_2$ (i.e. a mapping of 32-bit words) is realistic.

A substitution is called *monoalphabetic*, if $r = 1$ (and thus $k_1 = \nu$) ; then $\sigma = \Upsilon_1$. Otherwise, it is called *polyalphabetic* with the *period* r . Each Υ_i is from a family $S_i = \{\Upsilon_i^{(k_i)}\}$ of ciphers or codes, the families may be pairwise distinct. It is a common mistake, to use - for reasons of convenience - the same family throughout.

The key for σ is a r-tuple of keys belonging to the individual $\Upsilon_1 \dots \Upsilon_r$; there are $s_1 \cdot s_2 \cdot \ldots s_r$ different keys, if s_i is the size of the family S_i .

A special case of (monoalphabetic or polyalphabetic) substitution is *linear substitution*: every Υ_i is a unimodular linear mapping L_i of a $(k_i - k_{i-1})$-dimensional (usually a k-dimensional)vector space over the quotient ring modulo N in itself; here N is again the cardinality of the alphabet $\mathbb{V}$ which in its linear order is mapped onto $0, 1, 2, \dots N-1$ (Lester S. Hill, 1891-1961, [Hill 1929]). What the mathematician likes most about linearity: the availability of the superposition principle, cryptologically is the snag: the matrix L_i can too easily be reconstructed (see [Konheim 1981], p. 116ff.).
Quite a special case of linear substitution works with k-dimensional permutation matrices P_i , the effect being a permutation of the symbols positions. This is usually called *transposition* of degree k . It has all the weaknesses of linearity. k , however, is usually taken rather large.

Restricting our attention to monographic methods, we have to study correspondences $\Upsilon_i : \mathbb{V}^{(1)} \dashrightarrow \mathbb{W}^{(m)}$. For simplicity, we assume mappings $\Upsilon_i : \mathbb{V}^1 \longrightarrow \mathbb{V}^1$. The size of the full family over $\mathbb{Z}_{26}$ is $26! = 4.03 \cdot 10^{26}$. The individual bijection ('mixed alphabet', «alphabet desordonné», "Tauschalphabet") is usually written in substitution notation[1]

$$\Upsilon = \begin{pmatrix} a & b & c & d & e & f & g & h & i & j & k & l & m & n & o & p & q & r & s & t & u & v & w & x & y & z \\ N & F & O & B & V & G & H & J & T & K & M & S & P & D & U & Q & W & A & C & Z & R & I & X & Y & E & L \end{pmatrix}$$

Shorter is the cycle notation

$$\Upsilon = (\, e\ v\ i\ t\ z\ l\ s\ c\ o\ u\ r\ a\ n\ d\ b\ f\ g\ h\ j\ k\ m\ p\ q\ w\ x\ y \,)$$

which shows that in our case the order or the substitution is the maximal one, namely 26 ('cyclic substitution'). In general, there are several cycles and sometimes even invariat symbols: the substitution

$$\Upsilon = \begin{pmatrix} a & b & c & d & e & f & g & h & i & j & k & l & m & n & o & p & q & r & s & t & u & v & w & x & y & z \\ S & E & C & U & R & I & T & Y & A & B & D & F & G & H & J & K & L & M & N & O & P & Q & V & W & X & Z \end{pmatrix}$$

reads in cycle notation

$$\Upsilon = (\, a\ s\ n\ h\ y\ x\ v\ q\ l\ f\ i \,)(\, b\ e\ r\ n\ g\ t\ o\ j \,)(\, d\ u\ p\ k \,)(\, c \,)(\, z \,)$$

Since the times of G. B. Porta (1535-1615), a restriction to involutory mappings can be found. This makes encryption and decryption identical. An involutory substitution has cycles of order 2 or 1 only:

$$\Upsilon = (az)(by)(cx)(dw)(ev)(fu)(gt)(hs)(ir)(jq)(kp)(lo)(mn)$$

This reduces the size of the family over $\mathbb{Z}_{26}$ to $26!\,/\,(2^{13}.13!\,) = 7.91\cdot 10^{12}$.

Surprisingly often the actual family is quite drastically small. In many polyalphabetic systems, it consists of just 26 substitutions which are obtained as powers of a single cyclic substitution σ_i of order 26 ,

$$\gamma_i^{(k_i)} = (\sigma_i)^{k_i} .$$

Here, the key elements k_i can be denoted by the 26 letters themselves.

In 1795, Thomas Jeefferson (1743-1826) used a polyalphabetic substitution of period 36 , based on powers of 36 different cyclic substitutions. The same system (with period 20) was proposed by Etienne Bazeries (1846-1924). In both cases, a cylindrical device was used to support encryption und decryption mechanically, and in order to simplify the use, the *same* power $k_i = k$ was used for every substitution. The same weakness showed the machine M-94 of the US Army (period 25), also a cylindrical device and the machine M-138-A of the US State Department (period 30), using slides. Security of these systems rested solely with the free choice of the order these different substitutions σ_i were to be used. In the M-138-A, there was even a choice of 30 out of 100 available alphabets - still, the system was vulnerable.

---

[1] Following general use, plain text is set in lower case, crypto text is set in SMALL CAPS, keys are set in LARGE CAPS.

Another weakness is shown by polyalphabetic systems which use different powers of the *same* cyclic substitution σ

$$\gamma_i^{(k_i)} = \sigma^{k_i}$$

Using the above cycle

σ = (e v i t z l s c o u r a n d b f g h j k m p q w x y)

and period 4 , we obtain with the key word A B E L (where $A \cong \sigma^1$, $B \cong \sigma^2$, $E \cong \sigma^5$, $L \cong \sigma^{12}$)

plain text	c r y p t o l o g y
key	A B E L A B E L A E
crypto text	O N Z C Z R R M H V

A particular simple case uses a cyclic substitution σ_0 with the cycle in common alphabetic order

σ_0 = (a b c d e f g h i j k l m n o p q r s t u v w x y z)

With period 4 again and with the key word A B E L , we obtain

plain text	c r y p t o l o g y
key	A B E L A B E L A B
crypto text	D T D E U Q Q A H A

Polyalphabetic enciphering of this kind is called a VIGENERE (Blaise de Vigenere, 1523-1596). In the monoalphabetic case, one speaks of a CAESAR (according to Suetonius, Caesar in letters to Cicero replaced every plaintext letter by the one standing three places further down the alphabet).
VIGENERE and in particular CAESAR can be viewed as addition modulo N , if in text and key the i-th letter of the cycle is represented by the number i . Thus, they are monographic special cases of *inhomogenous linear* substitutions.

Especially for N = 2 , i.e. for a binary plain and cryptic vocabulary, VIGENERE reduces to addition modulo 2, which is called a VERNAM cipher (Gilbert S. Vernam, 1890-1960).

Instead of working with powers of a single substitution σ_0 , VIGENERE already used an arbitrary substitution ρ , followed by a power of σ_0

$$\gamma_i^{(k_i)} = \sigma_0^{k_i}\,\rho$$

('parallel mixed alphabets').

This line is followed by the rotor machines, an example being the ENIGMA, used by the German Army before and during World War II. It used j specially chosen fixed substitutions $\rho^{(1)}$, $\rho^{(2)}$ ... $\rho^{(j)}$ which were sandwiched between similarity transformations with powers of σ_0 (the use of similarity transformations being motivated by an electro-mechanical realization) :

$$\gamma_i^{(k_i^{(1)}, k_i^{(2)}, \ldots k_i^{(j)})} = \sigma_0^{(k_i^{(j)})} \rho^{(j)} \sigma_0^{(k_i^{(j-1)} - k_i^{(j)})} \ldots \rho^{(2)} \sigma_0^{(k_i^{(1)} - k_i^{(2)})} \rho^{(1)} \sigma_0^{(-k_i^{(1)})}$$

Here, the single key is the j-tuple $(k_i^{(1)}, k_i^{(2)}, \ldots k_i^{(j)})$ of letters. There is also a choice in the use of the $\rho^{(k)}$ - in the 1943 Navy ENIGMA, 4 were to be chosen out of 10 .

The rotor machines showed about the most involved polyalphabetic encryption that was practically manageable before the advent of electronic computers. These allowed to increase the size of the key family dramatically; in particular polyalphabetic polygraphic substitution could be used effectively.

SOME REMARKS ON CRYPTANALYSIS

There is neither room nor reason to discuss cryptanalysis here at length. However, a few remarks of general nature are appropriate in order to judge the use of cryptological methods. Monoalphabetic substitution offers no security, not even in the polygraphic case. This was already well known to ALBERTI (1466) and VIETE (1589). After FRIEDRICH W. KASISKI, a Prussian Army officer (1805-1881) had shown [Kasiski 1863] how to determine the period of a general polyalphabetic substitution and then reducing the analysis to the monoalphabetic case, it took only a few decades until better cryptologists knew that polyalphabetic substitution with periodic key offers no security either, unless the key is of about the length of the message. In addition, AUGUSTE KERKHOFFS (1835-1903) had shown [Kerkhoffs 1883] how to break general polyalphabetic substitutions with nonperiodic keys, if the same key is used several times. He also gave the <<symêtrie de position>> method to facilitate solution when parallel mixed alphabets are used, in particular against a VIGENERE. And the Marquis G. H. L. DE VIARIS (1847-1901), a French army officer, could show [de Viaris 1893] how to facilitate breaking a JEFFERSON-BAZERIES polyalphabetic substitution. These methods were still refined by WILLIAM FREDERICK FRIEDMAN (1891-1969), the leading cryptologist of our century, and his school (SINKOV, KULLBACK), introducing sensitive test functions. In 1915, PARKER HITT (1877-1950) gave an open warning [Hitt 1916] of the dangers of repeating or repeated keys.

Thus, the way led naturally to *running keys* for *one-time use* ('one-time pads'). Amateurs were inclined to use widely available books of the world literature, which offered no security: A meaningful text contains too many repetitions. Much better was the method of professional spies to use statistical yearbooks. But finally, it was only consequent to use a running key of totally stochastic nature. This came up around 1920 in Germany, in France, in the USA; priority probably goes to JOSEPH C. MAUBORGNE, US Army Signal Corps, who introduced stochastic one-time keys in 1918 on the basis of a VERNAM encryption (which had been invented in 1917 for teletype machines by GILBERT S. VERNAM). The probabilistic aspect of the one-time key was studied, among others, by FRIEDMAN who coined the word 'holocryptic', and by Claude E. SHANNON who defined 'perfect secrecy' in looking at message and key as stochastic sources; in fact SHANNONS Information Theory was motivated by his work.

Soon, however, the disadvantages of practical nature the one-time key showed came to the open: the distribution of key material was difficult and dangerous, and the production of good random keys was problematic. Thus, everywhere pseudo random keys, which could be produced mechanically, came into use, - but then, the holocryptic property is, at least theoretically, lost. How some practical pseudo random generators can be attacked, is treated in the article by T. BETH and F. C. PIPER.

To make things worse, known rotor machines did not even use pseudo random key, but just keys of somewhat irregular patterns, with a rather huge period.

> 'Success in dealing with unknown ciphers is measured by these four things in the order named: perseverance, careful methods of analysis, intuition, luck.'
>
> Parker Hitt, 1916

MAXIMS

Over the centuries, cryptology has gathered a wealth of experience; even the open literature shows this. From this experience originate maxims for the cryptographic work, in particular in defense of illegitimate decryption, which cannot be neglected, even - or rather just - in todays era of computers. In addition to the trivial 'keep the enemy in the dark', there is

Rule Nr. 1: Don't underestimate the enemy.

Until 1944 the Germans did not suspect the Allies to be continously reading the 3-rotor ENIGMA encryption - only the German Navy in 1942 switched in the U-boat war to the more complicated 4-rotor ENIGMA. The British Navy realized only in 1942, that the German Navy xB-Dienst was reading their traffic. American cryptologists were unsuspicious, too, and could not imagine that Hans Rohrbach had broken their M-133-A enciphering - which, however, was of importance only for a short while, since the USA was in the process of introducing new cipher machines. It included M-134-C, also called SIGABA, a rotor machine FRIEDMAN had devised. The Signal Security Agency, US Army, in vain had tried to break this encryption. Did that mean that the Germans would not be up to it? Did the Americans know all about the British success in breaking the ENIGMA - was the information they received from this source called ULTRA also covered with 'a bodyguard of lies' (WINSTON S. CHURCHILL)? Typically, F. D. ROOSEVELT, the intellectual among the allied statesmen, distrusted cryptographers' asseverations. He certainly knew about the deep-rooted human bias towards ignoring the unwanted.

In this respect, inventors of encryption methods are particularly endangered. 'Nearly every inventor of a cipher system has been convinced of the unsolvability of his brainchild' (KAHN). BAZERIES offers an extreme example: Commissioned by his French government and army, he had ruined numerous inventions by breaking test examples. He then conceived the cylinder which he now thought of as being absolutely unbreakable: <<Je suis indéchiffrable>>, see [Bazeries 1901]. DE VIARIS, one of the victims of BAZERIES, took revenge on BAZERIES.
This brings us to

Rule Nr. 2: Only the cryptanalyst can judge the security of an encryption method.

This finding, dating back to PORTA and ANTOINE ROSSIGNOL (1599-1682), was formulated by KERKHOFFS in 1883. He critized the way of demonstrating the analytical security of a method by counting how many years it would take to run through all possible cases. Indeed, such counts can only give an upper limit, they are concerned with the time the most inefficient of all cryptanalytic methods, *exhaustive search*, needs, and can be utterly misleading.

KERKHOFFS was one of the first to discuss cryptography from a practical point of view: <<il faut bien distinguer entre un système d'écriture chiffrée imaginé pour un échange momentané de lettres entre quelques personnes isolées, et une méthode de cryptographie destinée a régler pour un temps illimité la correspondance des differents chefs d'armée entre eux>>. We will come back to the questions of encryption discipline. His particular merit was to distinguish between the class of methods (<<le système>>) and the key in the proper sense. He postulated

Rule Nr. 3: In judging the security of a cryptographic method one has to assume that the enemy knows the class of methods (the system).

For practical reasons, in certain situations some methods are to be preferred to others. Inertia of the established apparatus creates certain prejudices ('cipher philosophy') which can not be hidden from the enemy. And the simplest cryptanalytical tests differentiate, for example, reliably between monoalphabetic substitution, transposition and polyalphabetic substitution.

In a war, encrypting devices can fall into the hands of the enemy, they can also be stolen. This included machines like the ENIGMA; following KERKHOFFS' advice, the ENIGMA should have been extended at the beginning of World War II to a 5-rotor machine, and the rotors should have been permuted three times a day much earlier than 1942; in particular the whole set of rotors should have been exchanged every few months. Of course, this would not have been easy since estimates say that roughly 200 000 ENIGMAs have been built and used.

But the Americans were vulnerable, too, in this respect: Their cipher machine M-209, built by HAGELIN and used in military units from divisions down to battalions, was also used by the Italian Navy. No wonder that the Germans from 1942 to 1944 in North Africa and Italy were often well informed about the plans of the American troops.

The desire of the cryptologist, to make it not too easy for the enemy, frequently leads him to devise complications of known methods. A classical scheme is the composition of methods. Sometimes this does not help: Double substitution is a substitution again (the period, however, may be longer), double transposition is again a transposition. There is more hope with 'mixing' methods: Polyalphabetic substitution of a code from a code book ('enciphered code'), transposition of a monoalphabetic substitution. Specific cryptanalytical methods, however, are often insensitive against such complications. In 1924, MARCEL GIVIERGE, French general of World War I, has stated the

Rule Nr. 4: Superficial complications can be illusory: they then induce a delusive feeling of security.

In the worst case, an illusory complication can even facilitate illegitimate decryption. If a letter is never substituted by itself, then the position of a suffiently long 'probable word' can be detected quite reliably. This situation arises, if somebody thinks it would be better to exclude the identical substitution from a VIGENERE. It also happens with all pairwise involutory substitutions. In the ENIGMA, by a reflection in the last disk the number of rotors that were actually used was numerically doubled, and the system was known. This led to pairwise involutory substitutions and to a simple possibility to start a break.

Last not least, human weakness is to be mentioned. An encryption is not better than the cipher clerk. Illegitimate decryption thrives on the cryptographer's sins: 'A cryptographer's error is the cryptanalyst's only hope'. And this hope is justified. There is the stress under which a cipher clerk works in military and diplomatic traffic. Once an enciphering mistake happens, the decipherer may obtain a lot of garbled clear text - methods which give a thorough mix, polygraphic ones in particular, have a tendency to achieve this. Under pressure of time, it may then be inevitable to repeat the same message without thorough reformulation. GIVIERGE wrote <<Chiffrez bien, ou ne chiffrez pas>> and ROHRBACH formulated the

Rule Nr. 5: In judging the security of a cryptographic method, enciphering mistakes and other offences to encryption discipline are to be taken into account.

The simplest and therefore most frequent ones are:

Repeated transmission of the same plain text with different keys,

repetition of the enciphered message in clear text,

frequent use of stereotype words and phrases (there is ample supply in the language of the military and diplomacy and elsewhere),

the use of key words which are too short or can easily be guessed,

the use of a common word for a sudden event ('probable word'),

when using code books, not to use homophones and nulls and to spell rarely used words, and finally

the use of double letters and combinations like ch and qu , of punctuation marks and of spaces.

The ideal plain text is orthographically wrong, linguistically poor, stilistically ghastly. Which Commanding Officer will phrase an order in this way, which diplomat will send such a report to his head? And what should be done with commercial letters?

In addition, ambassadors and generals, like presidents, rarely take the time to supervise their cipher clerks. As a rule, they lack understanding for the necessity anyhow, since they are mostly cryptographically ignorant. Thus, all efficient intelligence services know that supervision of their own units is of the same importance as knowledge about the units of the enemy.

MODERN COMMERCIAL CRYPTOGRAPHY

Looking at the existing proposals for encryption of commercial message channels, first of all one finds that the general method is made openly known. Rule Nr. 3 is followed to the extreme: security rests with the key only. This, however, has other than sheer cryptological reasons, it comes from practical needs.

In contrast to the classical communication between just two partners who beforehand have agreed on a mutual key, a 'public key' system [Diffie, Hellman 1976] allows a participant to send an encrypted message to any partner who has publicized his 'own' key. 'key' is to be understood as a generator for a running key. Here, even the encrypting algorithm is made openly known. Nevertheless, breaking the encryption is not trivial since 'trapdoor mappings' σ_i are used, encrypting algorithms the inverses σ_i^{-1} of which are only obtainable with a great amount of work, are 'hard to compute' without additional information and are supposed to be only in the possession of the key owner.

In such a public key system, both privacy and authenticity are to be protected. If partner A wants to send a message to partner B , he therefore first encrypts it with σ_A^{-1} (which is known only to him) and then with σ_B (which is public), the recipient B first decrypts it with σ_B^{-1} (which distinguishes him as legitimate recipient) and then with σ_A (which qualifies A as sender).
For more details, in particular on the generation of pairs $(\sigma_i , \sigma_i^{-1})$, confer the article by T. BETH.
While the class of trapdoor mappings found the enthusiastic theoretical interest of specialists in complexity theory, the practical schemes proposed so far for public key systems have certainly given joy to professional cryptanalysts. Apart from the lack of homophones, nulls and straddling, all classical avenues of attack are wide open, in particular under heavy traffic the same running key will be used repeatedly. The whole situation is liable to awake delusive confidence of the user. Reference to SHANNON's recommendation to mix thoroughly transposition ('diffusion') and substitutions ('confusion'), if accompanied by the analogy to the HOPF 'pastry dough' principle, may unduly impress the mathematician. Papers which give the mere combinatorial complexity of the proposed methods support the calming impression. Yet, it is characteristic of the present state of complexity theory that it produces only upper limits, it only deals with the worst case. To obtain lower limits for, say, the effort to factorize a number into primes seems to be out of present reach.
Replacement of the 'cipher clerk', who attends the traffic, by a machine makes things worse: it eliminates some enciphering errors, but also the alert mind which alone helps to avoid grave mistakes.
While it can be expected that the proposed public cryptosystems will resist attacks by amateurs, even if they have medium-size machines at their disposal, it can also be expected that they are vulnerable to attacks by top experts. The National Security Agency of the United States of America is likely to be able to supervise any traffic that has come under suspicion. By definition, it should be able to do so anyhow: one cannot expect that the President of the United States will allow a foreign intelligence service to operate freely under the cover of a commercial communication system. The times are over, when HENRY L. STIMSON, then Secretary of State under President HOOVER, dismissed on ethical grounds the Black Chamber of the State Department, with the explanation "Gentlemen do not read each other's mail" (1929!). Not even President CARTER showed similar scruple - or does this perhaps mean, that the Americans did not succeed in breaking Russian secrets?
Not only in the Great Powers, but also in smaller nations, in the long run it will become necessary for private and commercial cryptography to come to terms with the requirements of the governmental authorities. Great Britain, a classical country of Democracy, here gives an example. If a nation does not protect its own security, it endangers also the security of its friends. On the other hand, demands of the commercial side cannot be suppressed in free countries.

Therefore, scientific work in cryptosystems for private and commercial channels has to be carried on. Its aim should be - under realistic assumptions on the lack of discipline among laymen users - to establish lower limits for the complexity of breaking such systems on the basis of precisely specified machine characteristics. This will be hard work, but rewarding one: it will give the user a guaranteed measure of security and will end the present obfuscation.

HINTS TO THE LITERATURE

Good introductions for the amateur to classical cryptography and elementary cryptanalysis are [Gaines 1956] and [Smith]. Mathematically oriented readers will probably find [Sinkov 1966] more appealing; it is written by a professional cryptologist of high ranking - although it certainly does not reflect the full knowledge of its author. Still unsurpassed, but quite voluminous, is the *Manuale de Crittografia* [Sacco 1947]; most readers prefer the French translation [Sacco 1951]. On some special topics, it may be worthwhile to consult also [Eyraud 1953], [Figl 1926], [Givierge 1925], [Lange, Soudart 1925], [Hitt 1916], [Delastelle 1902], [Valerio 1893]. A good source on classical cryptographic machines is [Türkel 1927]. Some now classical works are [Kasiski 1863] and [Kerkhoffs 1883], an excellent source for the early history is [Meister 1906] and [Meister 1902].

A comprehensive historical presentation of cryptology with all its implications has appeared with [Kahn 1967]. It is supplemented for topics on World War II by [Johnson 1978] and [Beesly 1977]. New material from the other side is found in [Rohwer, Jäckel 1979].

A rather mathematically oriented introduction to modern cryptography is [Konheim 1981], [Beker, Piper 1982]; there are several other books pending, [Denning 1982] has just appeared.

A surprisingly complete bibliography has been compiled by [Shulman 1976]. But also [Kahn 1967] meticulously lists a great number of sources.

There are excellent articles on CRYPTOLOGY in Encyclopedia Brittannica by W. F. FRIEDMAN, in Encyclopedia Americana by D. KAHN, on CRYPTOGRAPHY in World Book Encyclopedia by L. D. CALLIMAHOS, in Chamber's Encyclopedia by W. W. JAMES.

Mechanical Cryptographic Devices I

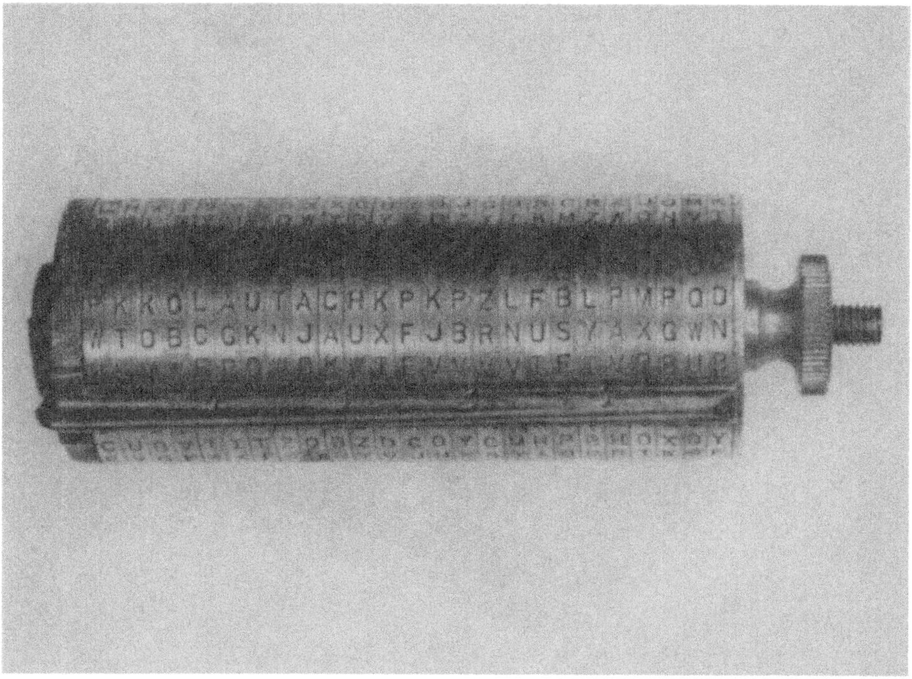

Thomas Jefferson's wheel cipher , cf. Kahn 1964 .

Mechanical Cryptographic Devices 2

Hagelin's machine BC - 543 , cf. Franke 1982.

CRYPTANALYSIS OF A KRYHA MACHINE

Alan G. Konheim

Mathematical Sciences Department
IBM Thomas J. Watson Research Center
P. O. Box 218, Yorktown Heights, New York 10598/USA

1. Introduction

In the early part of this century, a mechanical "ciphering machine" was invented by a German engineer, Alexander von Kryha of Berlin. The *Kryha-Ciphering-Machine* received both the State Prize from the Prussian Ministry of the Interior at the 1926 Police Fair (Berlin) and a Diploma in 1928 from Dr. Konrad Adenauer at the International Press Exhibition (Cologne). Georg Hamel, who was to become famous for his work in set theory, published an analysis in 1927 of the size of the *key space*, which was quoted extensively by "Internationale Kryha-Maschinen-Gelleschaft" (Hamburg) to infer the unbreakability of the Kryha machines.

The standard Kryha machine contains two basic components; the first, a *cipher disk* (FIGURE 2) consists of two rings. On the outer (fixed) ring the letters A, B, ..., Z of the (plaintext) alphabet are written, while on the inner (moveable) ring a substitution $\pi(A)$, $\pi(B)$, ..., $\pi(Z)$ of the letters of the (ciphertext) alphabet is recorded twice. The *cipher wheel* (shown in FIGURE 1) is the second component; it has a number of *pins* $\mathbf{k} = (k_0, k_1, ..., k_{S-1})$ located at *stop points* and controls the (counterclockwise) rotation of the inner ring.

The letters of the ciphertext alphabet are on tabs inserted into 52 slots on the inner ring, so that the permutation π is one component of the key. It appears that many cipher wheels were available and thus the number of stop points S as well as the pin values $\mathbf{k}$ form a second component of the key. Assuming, as we may, that $0 \le k_i < 26$, there are

- $26! \approx 4.03 \times 10^{26}$ possible cipher disks

•• 26^S possible cipher wheels

For the machine we have examined, $S = 17$, providing a total of 4.57×10^{50} possible key values.

The purpose of this note is to give an example of the cryptanalysis of a Kryha machine.

2. Mathematical Description And Analysis

The *Kryha machine* produces a polyalphabetic substitution. The key has three components:

- the number of *pins* $\boldsymbol{k} = (k_0, k_1, \ldots, k_{16})$ at each *stop point* on a *cipher wheel*

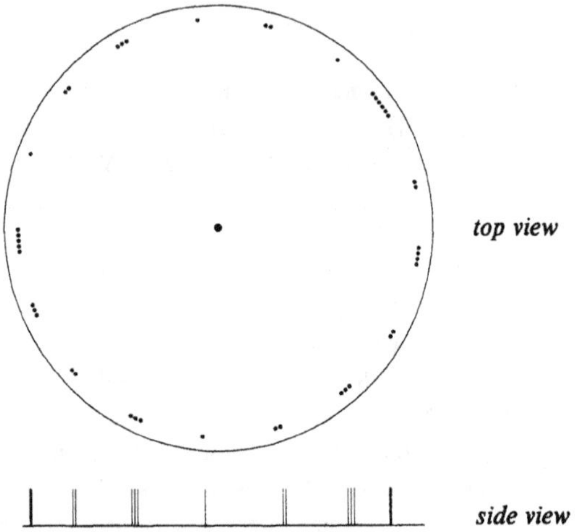

FIGURE 1 : A Cipher Wheel

•• a *cipher disk* specifying a monalphabetic substitution

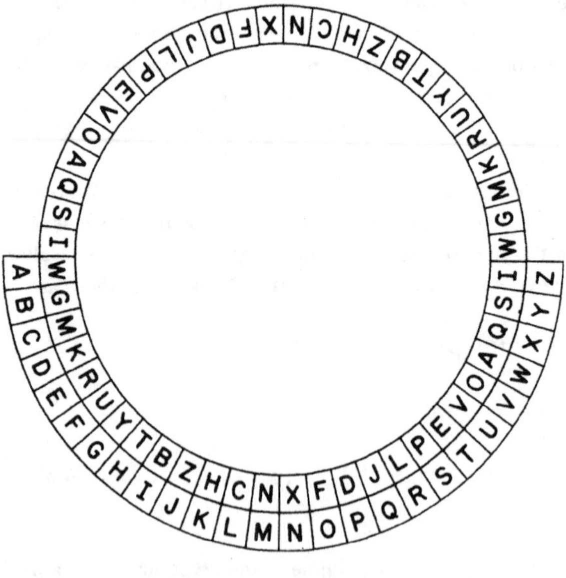

FIGURE 2 : A Cipher Disk

••• an *initial displacement* d, $0 \leq d < 17$ of the pin wheel.

The inner (moveable) ring of the cipher disk in FIGURE 2 rotates counterclockwise relative to the outer (fixed) ring. The rotation is controlled by the pin wheel as follows; for the encipherment of the ith-letter of plaintext ($0 \leq i < \infty$), the inner ring rotates $k_i + 3$ positions (counterclockwise) from its current position. For example, if $d = 0$, $k_0 = 5$, $k_1 = 3$, $k_2 = 2$ and $k_3 = 3$, plaintext HELP... is enciphered into ciphertext IJPJ....

Let[1] $\mathcal{Z}_{26} = \{0, 1, ..., 25\}$ denote the plaintext and ciphertext alphabets with the coding (A $\Leftrightarrow$ 0, B $\Leftrightarrow$ 1, ..., Z $\Leftrightarrow$ 25) and

$$K_i = k_0 + k_1 + ... + k_i \qquad 0 \leq i < \infty$$

$$K = k_0 + k_1 + ... + k_{16}.$$

The *Kryha transformation* (with key $\boldsymbol{k}$, π, d) applied to plaintext

$$\boldsymbol{x} = (x_0, x_1, ..., x_{n-1})$$

produces the ciphertext

$$\boldsymbol{y} = (y_0, y_1, ..., y_{n-1})$$

(1) $y_i = \pi(x_i - (K_{i+d} - K_{d-1}) - 3(i+1)) \qquad 0 \leq i < n$

We may clearly assume $d = 0$ and replace equation (1) by

(2) $y_i = \pi(x_i - K_i - 3(i+1))$

When we introduce the *shifted keys* $\{L_i\}$ defined by

$$l_i = k_i + 3 \quad 0 \leq i < 17$$

$$L_i = l_0 + l_1 + ... + l_i \qquad 0 \leq i < \infty$$

$$L = L_{16}$$

equation (2) further simplies to

(3) $y_i = \pi(x_i - L_i) \qquad 0 \leq i < \infty$

---

[1] Unless otherwise noted, all arithmetic operations are modulo 26.

We shall assume that the sequence $L_0, L_1, \ldots, L_{16}$ is not constant. It follows that the period of the polyalphabetic substitution (equation (3)) can be one of three values:

- $26 \times 17 = 442$ if $\gcd\{L,26\} = 1$
- $2 \times 17 = 34$ if $\gcd\{L,26\} = 13$
- $13 \times 17 = 221$ if $\gcd\{L,26\} = 2$

For the particular Kryha machine we have examined, the number of pins is shown in FIGURE 3. For this machine L = 16 and the period is 221.

i	k_i	K_i	L_i
0	5	5	8
1	3	8	14
2	2	10	19
3	3	13	25
4	1	14	3
5	2	16	8
6	3	19	14
7	2	21	19
8	4	25	0
9	2	1	5
10	6	7	14
11	1	8	18
12	2	10	23
13	1	11	1
14	3	14	7
15	2	16	12
16	1	17	16

FIGURE 3 : k_i, K_i, L_i $\quad i = 0(1)16$

FIGURE 4 specifies the substitution π while FIGURE 5 displays the ciphertext.

A	B	C	D	E	F	G	H	I	J	K	L	M	N	O	P	Q	R	S	T	U	V	W	X	Y	Z
↓	↓	↓	↓	↓	↓	↓	↓	↓	↓	↓	↓	↓	↓	↓	↓	↓	↓	↓	↓	↓	↓	↓	↓	↓	↓
W	G	M	K	R	U	Y	T	B	Z	H	C	N	X	F	D	J	L	P	E	V	O	A	Q	S	I

FIGURE 4 : The Substitution π

```
CECZDHYCFWGNVRTUA MZEDCQAMRUDWGAKCQ GQUSIFIZBMXMDOGOY WTSZRJBDOLZESLLSO
VVFBPHTKYMFXDGNRN MIIPITFWNRRIZCRGN LMKNXXIDHAARQEGAH PLIYXSQYARQRQSSVX
BVLUIULXQGISVXIKU YNUIZQUQVIJFEEQNH YGKIXTNIKOOQYIBFB UUGPLRJOSIYBACPGV
QYFZOWOGKRLPHTKNE YLAPCOYZEXBJAYGWI EHNDHRHZKNVTVXJXS KCDNKNEKSLXMFEDGB
XSKSZSBRCKKFOJDCF EEYXAHWSYMFIOUDBC BYXPMHQSDGFZGHVYO MSYMUBTVNKXHMCECA
GNXAVGPCCVBBBIRFM UJQJGSKMHCGSHGXFR QMUUZOWWVWMABUAWT LNOUIGGLRHWTIKWBV
XARTAYYWYYCPWXNNZ BXBLYJJHUDEYTPLLE IJCGFKHACOIOCNIKL MFOINMZOYTHRMKAMC
RREFOSOPBPWRJOGVJ AZPZXAKUZIPUGVGZW WPFZKWWYITNAGLWSN ZBVKXRDVDQXFKJIWO
DSYLEKXANBMTKWVVT FNLNKDPJADRPFHPHD VTKVKBEZLNIPTGFSW LJEWNQUQQCESWKEUF
NWAGUHAVYMARMXKDI UAUCKXTSFKPTLENNU NEUUJDYFVRZMNEWJA YKLNCPDEROIWUXUWH
HZAISFAMOKSYIOKLG JYXZCIIDITHEPGDNO WYUXPWMDLPBGPKIAL VXFADSSXTXNCORDJG
NFQYOGOZZECVPQHJV FCEQPABYPFBJFZBAZ HYPQYPKICOPXKRKHR XAQJXTPSJUGKHDDTG
BDGGNQUQRCWBMFSSC PABNHPCCSHJPNKTNV CVLSJMOZFVITJZGGR JRGPLGSGVSMDOALQR
VUGPQKDCPKPOKHNPG DAHEMYFESLBPFZOMQ WEBOBDMGCEYDWCGXQ PJMZVWPPLXGWXCGHT
XWFCELCAPZOAISTKZ VPPPMVXZEQOVJZOIG DSYLEKBVGHSUATFZA XAQCBFJFARNFSSDQY
XOXUJMTXEUMQEYXVQ BWNOQLYCBFSXCDTWT IHLDNOYPKOOEKNVSQ HPWZTLZXZUYEFVKCS
AUJSLBRIHMMWLKFAV VEAPGOVZEKWOVKCTM OHLXODFIXZXPFVTML UHFFUIVOCLYLQVOEN
DFIHXAUWNNAUFTNAU CFNGCEMIJJWXLDWYD SMSTQBSHLWFSIDHJV MBGSEXSMGOMKROVKA
SIKHDODLJUQRTSZOZ SGVTVSISYFESAXOKF BWWXWRWNJSYNBETPC PICCAYMUKHIRNXWHI
YYWAVNVLZOZPGUJSL YDCKLBDDBRESGOJQU YKKGFOWSAIQETLNFC XRZPCUCOGXHOGAUMX
EHGNEEFVSLIAFESCB SSKXDZBPRVVXCTHRF ZROMFITIYTPDOIHYJ SJPIBEPLXRFPUHHNG
BBMGSWCBNYARQEGDI FAGTRFPRTLOUZBQYD APSVKQACOUMQUFSVT RZXXMNNYXCWBGDQNH
UNONQJJBREQBJKKXM UPYDOLILTUHTCNXMP NJMKXHZUKDJDIDANI PUDDHBYCPFVAJOWFK
HFHPCJCOGUDWWDOAN UHXFURWJZKQOQYJRC AZCAUDQDZEKFWCCUY FEXAIWCSKWFLIJCPP
VMSTZKKNMGQIUFLFG BBMGUNBMFAGVIAUXP KNNITBAPAIYFTYIEY TTGHQZOXDQIJEPKZE
JJSGWXNVRZUSPUJBZ VHLZUFQVHENALZYMB UAJGFYUEBDRWZUNQB GJFLENFQKCBMUEAQT
JGFUHRYIEAJMJMQUM OHUFZJBKHUZOYJTYC JCYIEUSDTBXYNQRXP XMCPKWMUAPLJAVGOA
BEIPWHLKMNEKOYCRU KPOEIBRQMADVPNOKX FCGZPMSEKKUHCWZHU HLMBYFTTVYNFBVUQH
TVMHKQPGHKGHPRKMG DMULAQSNVOCZACQRF UBJKQEILBZJJFYELY CODTFWNSYVWMASXHH
JOGOSBKCTCOMCQOSC PUDDHTJSBZDHLCBFG HZQRFYCBFBRVYXYXS KCDNKNEKSCFORNVNR
SZUUNAPPNKCJHPGZE VLTDSBRZEMRZBLMYS GMLIRRGBMSFBVDIIG TSPXQBWMAVSTMOPFW
QQYQTBAPAIELZQMYF YAAZFSULJWAKXEBRB RVGJXDAEFZMZBDBGW IJTMNOBADSNEKNVSQ
HPWZTXZLZZVTLENVK CYPLSMMJSIDXHKCBP HRFDLKDBROIJJPQVG MTYCSOHAKNWOLRTZB
GPUBHJCYBYIVJWRAS MQIIVCVMNXE
```

FIGURE 5 : *CIPHER* = $T_{k,\pi,0}$(*PLAIN*)

The number of coincidences between $\boldsymbol{y} = (y_0, y_1, \ldots, y_{2271})$ and the *shifted ciphertext* $\boldsymbol{y}^{(s)} = (y_s, y_{s+1}, \ldots, y_{2271}, y_0, \ldots, y_{s-1}) = \sigma^s \boldsymbol{y}$ is

$$\kappa_s = \sum_{0 \le i < 2272} \chi\{y_i = y_{(i+s)\ (\text{modulo } 2272)}\}$$

κ_s shown in FIGURE 6 has local maxima at s = 221 and 442 which is consistent with

$$L = 0 \text{ (modulo 2)} \qquad L \neq 0 \text{ (modulo 13)}$$

For $0 \le i < n$, we write $i = 17r_i + c_i$, $0 \le c_i < 17$, $r_i = 0, 1, \ldots$ and set

$$\Lambda_{r,c} = \{i : 0 \le i < 2272,\ r_i = r, c_i = c\} \qquad 0 \le r, 0 \le c < 17$$

$$\boldsymbol{x}_{\Lambda_{r,c}} = \{x_i : i \in \Lambda_{r,c}\} \qquad \boldsymbol{y}_{\Lambda_{r,c}} = \{y_i : i \in \Lambda_{r,c}\}$$

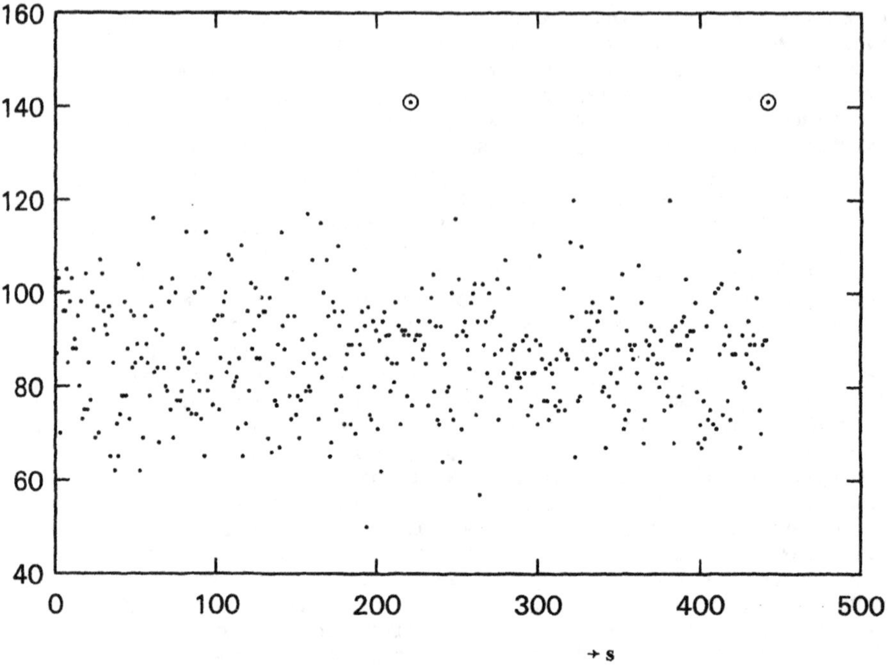

FIGURE 6 : κ_s **s = 1(1)442**

Encipherment is the composition of the substitution π and Caesar substitution C_{-rL-L_c}

$$\pi C_{-rL-L_c} : \mathbf{x}_{\Lambda_{r,c}} \mapsto \mathbf{y}_{\Lambda_{r,c}}$$

The letters in $\mathbf{y}_{\Lambda_{r,c_1}}$ and $\mathbf{y}_{\Lambda_{r+s,c_2}}$ are enciphered by the same monalphabetic substitution if and only if

(4) $sL = L_{c_1} - L_{c_2}$

If equation (4) holds, both of the subsets of ciphertext $\mathbf{y}_{\Lambda_{r,c_1}}$ and $\mathbf{y}_{\Lambda_{r+s,c_2}}$ arise from the same monalphabetic substitution (depending upon r) for *every* r, $0 \le r < 13$. We will test if L_{c_1} and L_{c_2} are related as in equation (4) using a variant of the *chi test*; define

$$\rho_{i,j}(s) = \frac{\sum_{0 \le r < 13} \sum_{0 \le t < 26} N_t(\mathbf{y}_{\Lambda_{r,i}}) N_t(\mathbf{y}_{\Lambda_{r+s,j}})}{13 \, |\Lambda_{r,i}| \, |\Lambda_{r+s,j}| \, s_2}$$

$$\rho_{i,j} = \rho_{i,j}(\tau_{i,j}) = \max_{0 \le s < 13} \rho_{i,j}(s)$$

where $N_t(\mathbf{y}_{\Lambda_{r,i}})$ is the number of times the "letter" t occurs in $\mathbf{y}_{\Lambda_{r,i}}$, {p(t)} are the "probabilities" of the occurrence of letters in English, and

$$s_2 = \sum_{0 \le t < 26} p^2(t) \approx 0.06875$$

$\rho_{i,j}(s)$ is a (normalized) average of the cross-correlations between the vectors

$$(N_0(\Lambda_{r,i})/|\Lambda_{r,i}|, (N_1(\Lambda_{r,i})/|\Lambda_{r,i}|, \ldots, (N_{25}(\Lambda_{r,i})/|\Lambda_{r,i}|)$$

and

$$(N_0(\Lambda_{r+s,j})/|\Lambda_{r+s,j}|, (N_1(\Lambda_{r+s,j})/|\Lambda_{r+s,j}|, \ldots, (N_{25}(\Lambda_{r+s,j})/|\Lambda_{r+s,j}|)$$

$\rho_{i,j}$ is the maximum (over s) of $\rho_{i,j}(s)$ and $\tau_{i,j}$ is the (smallest) value of s at which the maximum is attained. We tabulate the values $\rho_{i,j}$ and $\tau_{i,j}$ ($i,j = 0(1)16$, $i \neq j$) in FIGURE 7 and in FIGURE 8, the values of $L_i - L_j$ ($i,j = 0,(1)16$, $i \neq j$) and the solution $s = s_{i,j}$ (if it exists) of $sL = L_i - L_j$. Since the entries in FIGURE 7 have been normalized (relative to s_2), we expect $\rho_{i,j}$ to be "large" when there exists a solution to $sL = L_i - L_j$ and "small" otherwise.

i↓/j→	0	1	2	3	4	5	6	7	8	9	10	11	12	13	14	15	16
0		0.89	0.70	0.68	0.72	0.89	0.94	0.91	0.91	0.83	1.08	1.10	0.76	0.85	0.75	0.78	0.83
		11	6	8	12	0	11	0	4	9	11	1	0	11	1	6	6
1	0.84		0.73	0.75	0.81	1.08	0.92	0.80	1.30	0.95	0.99	1.02	0.75	0.69	0.74	1.12	1.11
	2		12	0	0	2	0	2	9	8	0	3	4	8	6	5	8
2	0.72	0.75		1.04	0.98	0.88	0.70	0.91	0.88	0.96	0.89	0.68	0.88	0.85	1.12	0.75	0.82
	12	10		11	1	3	11	0	7	9	0	5	3	6	4	6	5
3	0.81	0.75	0.98		0.89	0.77	0.77	1.19	0.78	0.92	0.74	0.77	0.95	0.90	0.88	0.72	0.74
	5	0	2		3	5	3	2	0	11	3	6	5	8	6	0	7
4	0.67	0.81	0.96	0.93		0.83	0.82	1.04	0.75	1.10	0.68	0.70	0.97	1.00	1.03	0.73	0.66
	1	0	12	10		12	0	12	6	8	0	0	2	5	3	10	0
5	0.89	1.06	0.84	0.77	0.79		0.79	0.77	0.94	0.78	1.05	0.99	0.74	0.75	0.99	1.11	0.71
	0	11	10	8	1		11	0	4	6	11	1	4	3	1	3	6
6	0.98	0.92	0.69	0.78	0.82	0.94		0.78	0.79	0.88	0.89	0.91	0.75	0.73	0.83	0.81	0.93
	2	0	0	10	0	2		12	9	8	0	3	2	5	3	5	8
7	0.91	0.78	0.91	1.15	1.09	0.77	0.78		0.83	1.10	0.88	0.91	0.86	1.07	0.99	0.81	0.75
	0	11	0	11	1	0	6		7	9	11	4	3	6	4	6	1
8	0.87	1.24	0.80	0.78	0.76	0.94	0.77	0.83		0.84	0.98	0.99	0.91	0.77	0.93	1.02	1.08
	9	4	6	0	4	9	4	3		2	4	7	9	12	10	9	12
9	0.83	0.94	0.91	0.92	1.08	0.81	0.90	1.07	0.94		0.71	0.84	0.93	0.95	1.12	0.91	0.79
	4	5	4	2	5	7	5	4	11		10	8	7	10	8	10	0
10	1.10	0.99	0.89	0.75	0.68	0.97	0.89	0.89	0.94	0.70		0.96	0.71	0.67	0.77	0.95	0.80
	2	0	0	10	0	2	0	2	9	11		3	10	0	8	5	5
11	1.13	1.07	0.71	0.69	0.70	0.94	0.93	0.89	1.05	0.81	1.03		0.81	0.79	0.78	0.99	0.92
	12	10	10	7	5	12	10	9	6	5	10		2	2	12	2	5
12	0.76	0.75	0.87	0.96	0.93	0.74	0.78	0.86	0.88	0.86	0.77	0.82		0.82	1.07	0.76	0.78
	0	8	10	8	11	3	12	10	4	6	3	11		3	1	8	6
13	0.75	0.69	0.87	0.86	0.96	0.74	0.72	1.03	0.77	0.92	0.67	0.83	0.84		1.01	0.77	0.73
	2	9	7	5	8	10	8	7	1	3	0	11	10		11	5	3
14	0.74	0.70	1.08	0.82	1.05	1.04	0.81	0.89	0.88	1.08	0.76	0.84	1.04	0.98		0.70	0.81
	12	10	9	11	10	12	10	9	3	5	6	1	12	2		2	2
15	0.75	1.09	0.76	0.72	0.77	1.11	0.80	0.82	1.04	0.87	0.97	0.96	0.73	0.78	0.79		1.04
	0	8	2	0	3	10	8	7	4	3	8	11	5	8	11		3
16	0.81	1.09	0.78	0.73	0.71	0.74	0.89	0.76	1.10	0.79	0.74	0.84	0.77	0.73	0.82	0.99	
	7	5	7	6	5	7	5	7	1	0	5	8	7	10	8	10	

FIGURE 7 : $\rho_{i,j}$, $\tau_{i,j}$ $\quad i,j = 0(1)16$

i↓/j→	0	1	2	3	4	5	6	7	8	9	10	11	12	13	14	15	16
0		20	15	9	5	0	20	15	8	3	20	16	11	7	1	22	18
		11				0	11		7		11	1				3	6
1	6		21	15	11	6	0	21	14	9	0	22	17	13	7	2	24
	2					2	0		9		0	3				5	8
2	11	5		20	16	11	5	0	19	14	5	1	22	18	12	7	3
				11	1			0		9			3	6	4		
3	17	11	6		22	17	11	6	25	20	11	7	2	24	18	13	9
			2		3			2		11			5	8	6		
4	21	15	10	4		21	15	10	3	24	15	11	6	2	22	17	13
			12	10				12		8			2	5	3		
5	0	20	15	9	5		20	15	8	3	20	16	11	7	1	22	18
	0	11					11		7		11	1				3	6
6	6	0	21	15	11	6		21	14	9	0	22	17	13	7	2	24
	2	0				2			9		0	3				5	8
7	11	5	0	20	16	11	5		19	14	5	1	22	18	12	7	3
			0	11	1					9			3	6	4		
8	18	12	7	1	23	18	12	7		21	12	8	3	25	19	14	10
	6	4				6	4				4	7				9	12
9	23	17	12	6	2	23	17	12	5		17	13	8	4	24	19	15
			4	2	5			4					7	10	8		
10	6	0	21	15	11	6	0	21	14	9		22	17	13	7	2	24
	2	0				2	0		9			3				5	8
11	10	4	25	19	15	10	4	25	18	13	4		21	17	11	6	2
	12	10				12	10		6		10					2	5
12	15	9	4	24	20	15	9	4	23	18	9	5		22	16	11	7
			10	8	11			10		6				3	1		
13	19	13	8	2	24	19	13	8	1	22	13	9	4		20	15	11
			7	5	8			7		3			10		11		
14	25	19	14	8	4	25	19	14	7	2	19	15	10	6		21	17
			9	7	10			9		5			12	2			
15	4	24	19	13	9	4	24	19	12	7	24	20	15	11	5		22
	10	8				10	8		4		8	11					3
16	8	2	23	17	13	8	2	23	16	11	2	24	19	15	9	4	
	7	5				7	5		1		5	8				10	

FIGURE 8 : $L_i - L_j$, $s_{i,j}$ $\quad i,j = 0(1)16 \ i \neq j$

In FIGURES 9-10, we list the pairs (i,j) which have the smallest and largest values of $\rho_{i,j}$.

i	j	$\rho_{i,j}$	i	j	$\rho_{i,j}$
4	16	0.66	6	2	0.69
10	13	0.67	1	13	0.69
13	10	0.67	4	11	0.70
4	0	0.67	2	6	0.70
0	3	0.68	14	1	0.70
2	11	0.68	0	2	0.70
10	4	0.68	10	9	0.70
4	10	0.68	11	4	0.70
11	3	0.69	14	15	0.70
13	1	0.69	10	12	0.71

FIGURE 9 : 20 Smallest Values Of $\rho_{i,j}$

i	j	$\rho_{i,j}$	$\tau_{i,j}$	i	j	$\rho_{i,j}$	$\tau_{i,j}$
1	8	1.30	$L_1 - L_8 = 9L$	8	1	1.24	$L_8 - L_1 = 4L$
3	7	1.19	$L_3 - L_7 = 2L$	7	3	1.15	$L_7 - L_3 = 11L$
11	0	1.13	$L_{11} - L_0 = 12L$	1	15	1.12	$L_1 - L_{15} = 5L$
9	14	1.12	$L_9 - L_{14} = 8L$	2	14	1.12	$L_2 - L_{14} = 4L$
15	5	1.11	$L_{15} - L_5 = 10L$	5	15	1.11	$L_5 - L_{15} = 3L$
1	16	1.11	$L_1 - L_{16} = 8L$	10	0	1.10	$L_{10} - L_0 = 2L$
0	11	1.10	$L_0 - L_{11} = 1L$	16	8	1.10	$L_{16} - L_8 = 1L$
4	9	1.10	$L_4 - L_9 = 8L$	7	9	1.10	$L_7 - L_9 = 9L$
16	1	1.09	$L_{16} - L_1 = 5L$	7	4	1.09	$L_7 - L_4 = 1L$
15	1	1.09	$L_{15} - L_1 = 8L$	1	5	1.08	$L_1 - L_5 = 2L$
0	10	1.08	$L_0 - L_{10} = 11L$	8	16	1.08	$L_8 - L_{16} = 12L$
14	9	1.08	$L_{14} - L_9 = 5L$	14	2	1.08	$L_{14} - L_2 = 9L$
9	4	1.08	$L_9 - L_4 = 5L$	12	14	1.07	$L_{12} - L_{14} = 1L$
9	7	1.07	$L_9 - L_7 = 4L$	11	1	1.07	$L_{11} - L_1 = 10L$
7	13	1.07	$L_7 - L_{13} = 6L$	5	1	1.06	$L_5 - L_1 = 11L$

FIGURE 10 : 30 Largest Values Of $\rho_{i,j}$

Next, we partition the indices $\mathcal{Z}_{17}$ into two sets *EV* and *OD* with

$$EV = \{i : L_i = 0 \text{ (modulo 2)}\} \qquad OD = \{i : L_i = 1 \text{ (modulo 2)}\}$$

using the following heuristic;

- $\rho_{i,j}$ "small" $\Rightarrow$ $i \in EV, j \in OD$ *or* $i \in OD, j \in EV$
- •• $\rho_{i,j}$ "large" $\Rightarrow$ $\{i,j\} \subseteq EV$ *or* $\{i,j\} \subseteq OD$

$L_{16} = L = 0$ (modulo 2) $\Rightarrow 16 \in EV$. From FIGURES 8-10 we are able to reach the following conclusions:

Conclusion	Reason	Conclusion	Reason
1. $4 \in OD$	$\rho_{4,16}$ is "small"	*2.* $0 \in EV$	$\rho_{0,4}$ is "small" and $4 \in OD$
3. $3 \in OD$	$\rho_{0,3}$ is "small" and $0 \in EV$	*4.* $7 \in OD$	$\rho_{3,7}$ is "big" and $3 \in OD$
5. $11 \in EV$	$\rho_{11,0}$ is "big" and $0 \in EV$	*6.* $2 \in OD$	$\rho_{2,11}$ is "small" and $11 \in EV$
7. $10 \in EV$	$\rho_{10,4}$ is "small" and $4 \in OD$	*8.* $13 \in OD$	$\rho_{10,13}$ is "small" and $10 \in EV$
9. $1 \in EV$	$\rho_{13,1}$ is "small" and $13 \in OD$	*10.* $8 \in EV$	$\rho_{1,8}$ is "big" and $1 \in EV$
11. $15 \in EV$	$\rho_{1,15}$ is "big" and $1 \in EV$	*12.* $14 \in OD$	$\rho_{2,14}$ is "big" and $2 \in OD$
13. $9 \in OD$	$\rho_{9,14}$ is "big" and $14 \in OD$	*14.* $6 \in EV$	$\rho_{6,2}$ is "small" and $2 \in OD$
15. $5 \in EV$	$\rho_{15,5}$ is "big" and $15 \in EV$	*16.* $12 \in OD$	$\rho_{10,12}$ is "small" and $10 \in EV$

This yields the partition

$$EV = \{0, 1, 5, 6, 8, 10, 11, 15, 16\} \qquad OD = \{2, 3, 4, 7, 9, 12, 13, 14\}$$

Each L_i can be expressed as $L_i = \alpha_i L_2 + \beta_i L$ ($\alpha_i = 0$ if $i \in EV$). We use FIGURES 8,10 to infer the values of $\{\alpha_i\}$ and $\{\beta_i\}$ listing the results in FIGURE 11.

Line	i	j	$\rho_{i,j}$	$L_i - L_j = s_{i,j}L$	Conclusion	
1	1	8	1.30	$L_1 - L_8 = 9L$		
2	3	7	1.19	$L_3 - L_7 = 2L$		
3	11	0	1.13	$L_{11} - L_0 = 12L$		
4	1	15	1.12	$L_1 - L_{15} = 5L$		
5	9	14	1.12	$L_9 - L_{14} = 8L$		
6(a)	2	14	1.12	$L_2 - L_{14} = 4L$	$L_{14} = L_2 + 9L$	
6(b)					$L_9 = L_2 + 4L$	*5,6(a)*
7(a)	1	16	1.11	$L_1 - L_{16} = 8L$	$L_1 = 9L$	
7(b)					$L_8 = 0$	*1,7(a)*
7(c)					$L_{15} = 4L$	*4,7(a)*
8	5	15	1.11	$L_5 - L_{15} = 3L$	$L_5 = 7L$	*7(c)*
9	4	9	1.10	$L_4 - L_9 = 8L$	$L_4 = L_2 + 12L$	*6(b)*
10(a)	7	9	1.10	$L_7 - L_9 = 9L$	$L_7 = L_2$	*6(b)*
10(b)					$L_3 = L_2 + 2L$	*2,10(a)*
11	10	0	1.10	$L_{10} - L_0 = 2L$		
12	7	13	1.07	$L_7 - L_{13} = 6L$	$L_{13} = L_2 + 7L$	*10(a)*
13(a)	11	1	1.07	$L_{11} - L_1 = 10L$	$L_{11} = 6L$	*7(a)*
13(b)					$L_0 = 7L$	*2,13(a)*
13(c)					$L_{10} = 9L$	*11,13(a)*
14	12	14	1.07	$L_{12} - L_{14} = L$	$L_{12} = L_2 + 10L$	*6(a)*
15	6	0	0.98	$L_6 - L_0 = 2L$	$L_6 = 9L$	*13(b)*

FIGURE 11 : $L_i = \alpha_i L_2 + \beta_i L$

While FIGURE 11 expresses L_i as a linear combination of L and L_2, the value of L and L_2 is not yet determined. For this purpose, define

$$\alpha(M,M_2) = (a_0(M,M_2), a_1(M,M_2), ..., a_{16}(M,M_2))$$

$$A_i(M,M_2) = \sum_{0\le j\le i} a_j(M,M_2) \qquad 0 \le i < 221$$

where $\{a_i(M,M_2) : 0 \le i < 17\}$ are given in FIGURE 12.

If M = 0 (modulo 2), m ≠ 0 (modulo 13) and M_2 = 1 (modulo 2), there exists a solution s = $s_{i,j}(M,M_2)$ to

$$sM = A_i(M,M_2) - A_j(M,M_2)$$

whenever $\{i,j\} \subseteq EV$ or $\{i,j\} \subseteq OD$.

In FIGURE 12 we summarize the results in FIGURE 11, expressing each $\{A_i(M,M_2)\}$ in terms of M and M_2.

i	$A_i(M,M_2)$	i	$A_i(M,M_2)$	i	$A_i(M,M_2)$
0	7M	1	9M	2	M_2
3	$2M+M_2$	4	$12M+M_2$	5	7M
6	9M	7	M_2	8	0
9	$4M+M_2$	10	9M	11.	6M
12	$10M+M_2$	13	$7M+M_2$	14	$9M+M_2$
15	4M	16	M		

FIGURE 12

To recover the actual key values (L and L_2) we make use of the following

Lemma: Suppose (M, M_2) satisfy:

(i) M = 0 (modulo 2)

(ii) M ≠ 0 (modulo 13)

(iii) M_2 = 1 (modulo 2)

Then, the 13 by 17 array $\mathcal{A}(M,M_2) = (A_{17i+j}(M,M_2))$ $(0 \le i < 13, 0 \le j < 17)$ of key values

$$\mathcal{A}(M,M_2) = \begin{vmatrix} A_0(M,M_2) & A_1(M,M_2) & \cdots & A_{16}(M,M_2) \\ A_{17}(M,M_2) & A_{18}(M,M_2) & \cdots & A_{33}(M,M_2) \\ & & \cdots & \\ & & \cdots & \\ & & \cdots & \\ A_{204}(M,M_2) & A_{205}(M,M_2) & \cdots & A_{220}(M,M_2) \end{vmatrix}$$

is related to the array $\mathcal{A}(L,L_2)$ by a permutation

$$\lambda : \mathcal{Z}_{26} \mapsto \mathcal{Z}_{26}$$

$$A_i(M,M_2) = \lambda(A_i(L,L_2)) = \lambda(L_i) \qquad 0 \le i < 221.$$

In particular, if $A_i(M,M_2) - A_j(M,M_2) = s_{i,j}M$, then $A_i(L,L_2) - A_j(L,L_2) = s_{i,j}L$

Proof: For $0 \le r < 13, 0 \le i < 17$ we have

$$A_{17r+i}(L,L_2) = (\alpha_i+r-1)L + \beta_i L_2 \qquad A_{17r+i}(M,M_2) = (\alpha_i+r-1)M + \beta_i M_2$$

with $\{\beta_i,\beta_j\} \subseteq \{0,1\}$. If $A_{17r+i}(M,M_2) = A_{17s+j}(M,M_2)$, then $(\alpha_i-\beta_j+r-s)M = (\alpha_j-\beta_i)M_2$ which implies $A_{17r+i}(L,L_2) = A_{17s+j}(L,L_2)$. ■

For each pair (M, M_2) satisfying

- • $M = 0$ (modulo 2)
- •• $M \neq 0$ (modulo 13)
- ••• $M_2 = 1$ (modulo 2)

define the partition $\{\Gamma_i(M,M_2) : 0 \le i < 26\}$ of $\mathcal{Z}_{221}$ by

$$\Gamma_i(M,M_2) = \{n : 0 \le n < 2272, A_n(M,M_2) = i\} \qquad 0 \le i < 26$$

and

$$\mathcal{x}_{\Gamma_i(M,M_2)} = \{x_n : n \in \Gamma_i(M,M_2)\} \qquad \mathcal{y}_{\Gamma_i(M,M_2)} = \{y_n : n \in \Gamma_i(M,M_2)\}$$

On $\Gamma_i(M,M_2)$ the Kryha transformation is the monalphabetic substitution $\pi C_{-\lambda^{-1}(i)}$ since

$$\Gamma_{-i}(M,M_2) = \Gamma_{-\lambda(i)}(L,L_2)$$

Define

$N_{i,j}(M,M_2)$: number of times the "letter" j appears in $\mathscr{Y}_{\Gamma_i(M,M_2)}$

In FIGURES 13-14 we list the array $\mathscr{N}(M,M_2) = (N_{i,j}(M,M_2))$ for (M, M_2) equal to (2,1) and (16,19) = (L, L_2).

	A	B	C	D	E	F	G	H	I	J	K	L	M	N	O	P	Q	R	S	T	U	V	W	X	Y	Z
$\Gamma_{-0}(2,1)$	3	7	4	2	9	10	1	0	1	0	2	4	4	5	1	7	0	9	2	4	3	2	7	4	0	0
$\Gamma_{-1}(2,1)$	6	1	16	5	3	5	3	3	2	0	1	1	2	2	5	2	0	0	7	4	0	0	6	1	0	8
$\Gamma_{-2}(2,1)$	1	4	2	4	0	13	8	6	2	2	7	2	6	1	4	6	5	3	9	0	0	0	0	5	2	0
$\Gamma_{-3}(2,1)$	2	4	1	1	6	0	1	10	7	0	5	6	3	1	14	1	2	2	5	0	4	2	0	0	2	4
$\Gamma_{-4}(2,1)$	4	15	8	0	0	1	4	1	2	0	0	1	5	4	0	0	5	0	20	5	3	2	1	6	1	4
$\Gamma_{-5}(2,1)$	0	2	0	10	3	3	9	0	2	2	5	0	0	2	2	9	0	2	0	0	9	8	0	6	4	6
$\Gamma_{-6}(2,1)$	7	8	2	3	3	0	0	0	1	5	1	7	0	12	4	6	14	8	2	2	0	0	0	1	4	2
$\Gamma_{-7}(2,1)$	2	0	8	12	4	4	0	0	8	0	6	0	6	0	0	8	3	7	4	0	7	0	2	1	0	1
$\Gamma_{-8}(2,1)$	5	1	0	0	6	6	5	1	7	3	3	3	4	1	5	10	0	0	0	11	6	4	4	0	6	0
$\Gamma_{-9}(2,1)$	2	5	0	1	0	10	0	0	9	0	10	0	2	6	7	0	2	1	5	3	0	0	1	8	3	7
$\Gamma_{-10}(2,1)$	2	0	5	6	2	0	1	2	0	4	0	4	15	7	0	2	0	1	4	0	9	1	8	7	7	4
$\Gamma_{-11}(2,1)$	3	3	1	0	8	0	0	4	2	1	1	3	0	4	1	6	6	0	7	4	9	4	1	7	0	7
$\Gamma_{-12}(2,1)$	7	6	3	1	2	1	11	5	3	9	1	0	3	15	8	1	3	1	0	0	0	3	4	3	2	0
$\Gamma_{-13}(2,1)$	5	8	3	4	7	0	4	0	0	0	7	3	8	0	1	5	1	1	0	5	0	5	3	2	8	1
$\Gamma_{-14}(2,1)$	13	1	5	0	0	0	0	5	4	3	3	0	0	1	9	10	0	4	1	5	4	7	4	0	8	6
$\Gamma_{-15}(2,1)$	0	0	2	0	2	3	3	1	7	4	11	5	3	9	1	10	2	2	0	3	0	2	0	7	5	0
$\Gamma_{-16}(2,1)$	1	2	0	9	6	3	0	6	0	9	2	3	10	0	9	1	2	7	2	0	2	1	0	3	12	3
$\Gamma_{-17}(2,1)$	8	0	3	1	0	2	5	0	0	4	3	8	7	4	2	0	4	1	4	2	0	2	5	9	0	7
$\Gamma_{-18}(2,1)$	0	3	0	5	6	6	8	1	7	11	5	1	0	3	0	1	3	6	1	1	9	5	6	2	5	0
$\Gamma_{-19}(2,1)$	3	2	5	0	5	0	7	4	4	0	0	1	0	10	3	0	12	2	2	3	7	2	5	2	3	0
$\Gamma_{-20}(2,1)$	12	3	8	7	0	7	0	11	1	1	5	1	1	0	0	1	0	4	5	3	0	2	7	6	1	9
$\Gamma_{-21}(2,1)$	7	3	5	0	0	3	0	3	1	9	8	7	0	0	6	2	0	0	0	10	5	10	0	0	2	1
$\Gamma_{-22}(2,1)$	0	6	5	0	6	7	0	9	9	0	0	1	2	0	2	2	6	1	4	1	0	10	5	4	8	5
$\Gamma_{-23}(2,1)$	0	0	0	5	2	2	9	0	5	5	0	12	1	0	5	0	0	6	6	0	4	3	6	4	6	1
$\Gamma_{-24}(2,1)$	1	9	1	0	2	2	3	5	0	2	12	2	5	1	0	4	2	6	7	6	4	11	0	0	1	7
$\Gamma_{-25}(2,1)$	0	1	8	7	0	9	11	7	3	5	2	2	2	6	0	2	6	1	0	0	6	0	2	0	0	2

FIGURE 13 : $\mathscr{N}(2,1)$

	A	B	C	D	E	F	G	H	I	J	K	L	M	N	O	P	Q	R	S	T	U	V	W	X	Y	Z
$\Gamma_{-0}(16,19)$	3	7	4	2	9	10	1	0	1	0	2	4	4	5	1	7	0	9	2	4	3	2	7	4	0	0
$\Gamma_{-1}(16,19)$	0	0	2	0	2	3	3	1	7	4	11	5	3	9	1	10	2	2	0	3	0	2	0	7	5	0
$\Gamma_{-2}(16,19)$	2	0	5	6	2	0	1	2	0	4	0	4	15	7	0	2	0	1	4	0	9	1	8	7	7	4
$\Gamma_{-3}(16,19)$	0	1	8	7	0	9	11	7	3	5	2	2	2	6	0	2	6	1	0	0	6	0	2	0	0	2
$\Gamma_{-4}(16,19)$	12	3	8	7	0	7	0	11	1	1	5	1	1	0	0	1	0	4	5	3	0	2	7	6	1	9
$\Gamma_{-5}(16,19)$	2	5	0	1	0	10	0	0	9	0	10	0	2	6	7	0	2	1	5	3	0	0	1	8	3	7
$\Gamma_{-6}(16,19)$	4	15	8	0	0	1	4	1	2	0	0	1	5	4	0	0	5	0	20	5	3	2	1	6	1	4
$\Gamma_{-7}(16,19)$	3	2	5	0	5	0	7	4	4	0	0	1	0	10	3	0	12	2	2	3	7	2	5	2	3	0
$\Gamma_{-8}(16,19)$	13	1	5	0	0	0	0	5	4	3	3	0	0	1	9	10	0	4	1	5	4	7	4	0	8	6
$\Gamma_{-9}(16,19)$	2	4	1	1	6	0	1	10	7	0	5	6	3	1	14	1	2	2	5	0	4	2	0	0	2	4
$\Gamma_{-10}(16,19)$	1	9	1	0	2	2	3	5	0	2	12	2	5	1	0	4	2	6	7	6	4	11	0	0	1	7
$\Gamma_{-11}(16,19)$	5	8	3	4	7	0	4	0	0	0	7	3	8	0	1	5	1	1	0	5	0	5	3	2	8	1
$\Gamma_{-12}(16,19)$	5	1	0	0	6	6	5	1	7	3	3	3	4	1	5	10	0	0	0	11	6	4	4	0	6	0
$\Gamma_{-13}(16,19)$	0	0	0	5	2	2	9	0	5	5	0	12	1	0	5	0	0	6	6	0	4	3	6	4	6	1
$\Gamma_{-14}(16,19)$	0	3	0	5	6	6	8	1	7	11	5	1	0	3	0	1	3	6	1	1	9	5	6	2	5	0
$\Gamma_{-15}(16,19)$	2	0	8	12	4	4	0	0	8	0	6	0	6	0	0	8	3	7	4	0	7	0	2	1	0	1
$\Gamma_{-16}(16,19)$	1	4	2	4	0	13	8	6	2	2	7	2	6	1	4	6	5	3	9	0	0	0	0	5	2	0
$\Gamma_{-17}(16,19)$	8	0	3	1	0	2	5	0	0	4	3	8	7	4	2	0	4	1	4	2	0	2	5	9	0	7
$\Gamma_{-18}(16,19)$	7	6	3	1	2	1	11	5	3	9	1	0	3	15	8	1	3	1	0	0	0	3	4	3	2	0
$\Gamma_{-19}(16,19)$	6	1	16	5	3	5	3	3	2	0	1	1	2	2	5	2	0	0	7	4	0	0	6	1	0	8
$\Gamma_{-20}(16,19)$	0	6	5	0	6	7	0	9	9	0	0	1	2	0	2	2	6	1	4	1	0	10	5	4	8	5
$\Gamma_{-21}(16,19)$	3	3	1	0	8	0	0	4	2	1	1	3	0	4	1	6	6	0	7	4	9	4	1	7	0	7
$\Gamma_{-22}(16,19)$	7	8	2	3	3	0	0	0	1	5	1	7	0	12	4	6	14	8	2	2	0	0	0	1	4	2
$\Gamma_{-23}(16,19)$	7	3	5	0	0	3	0	3	1	9	8	7	0	0	6	2	0	0	0	10	5	10	0	0	2	1
$\Gamma_{-24}(16,19)$	1	2	0	9	6	3	0	6	0	9	2	3	10	0	9	1	2	7	2	0	2	1	0	3	12	3
$\Gamma_{-25}(16,19)$	0	2	0	10	3	3	9	0	2	2	5	0	0	2	2	9	0	2	0	0	9	8	0	6	4	6

FIGURE 14 : $\mathscr{N}(16,19)$

If $\pi^{-1}(0) = j$, then $N_{0,0}(16,19)$ is the number of times the "letter" j appears in the plaintext $\mathscr{x}_{\Gamma_0(16,19)}$. It also follows that $N_{i,0}(16,19)$ is the number of times the "letter" j+i appears in the plaintext $\mathscr{x}_{\Gamma_i(16,10)}$ for every i, $0 \le i < 25$. That is, the cyclic rotation to the left by j places of the vector $(N_{0,0}(16,19), N_{1,0}(16,19), \ldots, N_{25,0}(16,19))$

$$\sigma^{-j}(N_{0,0}(16,19), N_{1,0}(16,19) \ldots, N_{25,0}(16,19)) = (N_{-j,0}(16,19), N_{1-j,0}(16,19), \ldots, N_{25-j,0}(16,19))$$

will be the vector listing the number of appearances of each of the "letters" 0, 1, ..., 25 in the plaintext in positions $\{n : y_n = 0\}$.

On the other hand, if $(M, M_2) \neq (16,19) = (L, L_2)$ and $\pi^{-1}(0) = j$, then $N_{t,0}(M,M_2)$ is the number of times the "letter" $j + \lambda^{-1}(t)$ appears in the plaintext $x_{\Gamma_t(M,M_2)}$ where λ is the permutation referred to in the Lemma. Thus no cyclic rotation

$$\sigma^{-s}(N_{0,0}(M,M_2), N_{1,0}(M,M_2) \ldots, N_{25,0}(M,M_2))$$

will yield a count of the number of appearances of the "letters" 0, 1, ..., 25 in the plaintext in positions $\{n : y_n = 0\}$.

For each admissible pair (M, M_2), we determine the vector of shifts

$$\mathbf{s} = (s_0, s_1, \ldots, s_{25})$$

by maximizing the covariance

$$\sum_{0 \le i < 26} N_{i-s_j,j}(M,M_2)p(i) = \max_{0 \le s < 26} \sum_{0 \le i < 26} N_{i-s,j}(M,M_2)p(i)$$

Having determined the vector of shifts $\mathbf{s}$, the addition of the shifted vectors

$$(N_{0-s_j,j}(M,M_2), N_{1-s_j,j}(M,M_2), \ldots, N_{25-s_j,j}(M,M_2))$$

will give the number of appearances of the "letters" 0, 1, ..., 25 in the entire plaintext if $(M, M_2) = (L, L_2)$. Define

$$\mu(M,M_2) = \frac{\sum_{0 \le i < 26} p(i) \sum_{0 \le j < 26} N_{i-s_j,j}(M,M_2)}{\sum_{0 \le j < 26} N_{i-s_j,j}(M,M_2)}$$

In FIGURE 15 we list the 20 largest values of $\mu(M,M_2)$ with $M = 2(2)24$, $M_2 = 1(2)25$.

M	M_2	$\mu(M,M_2)$	M	M_2	$\mu(M,M_2)$
16	19	0.06732	16	21	0.05847
16	17	0.05827	16	15	0.05748
16	23	0.05712	16	7	0.05663
16	5	0.05658	16	13	0.05655
16	25	0.05618	4	11	0.05585
10	9	0.05545	4	5	0.05544
16	3	0.05539	12	5	0.05522
14	17	0.05508	16	9	0.05503
14	25	0.05502	14	5	0.05492
22	1	0.05486	14	13	0.05485

FIGURE 15 : 20 Largest Values Of $\mu(M,M_2)$

We expect $\mu(M,M_2)$ to be a maximum when $(M, M_2) = (L,L_2)$. From FIGURE 15, we deduce that $L = 16$ and $L_2 = 19$.

All that remains is to recover π. We use the same idea; if the vector $s = (s_0, s_1, ..., s_{25})$ satisfies

$$\sum_{0\leq i<26} N_{i-s_j,j}(16,19)p_i = \max_{0\leq s<26} \sum_{0\leq i<26} N_{i-s,j}(16,19)p_i$$

then the permutation π then should satisfy $\pi(s_j) = j$, $(0 \leq j < 26)$. We have carried out this program and list the results in FIGURE 16. A segment of the plaintext is given in FIGURE 17.

j	s_j	$\pi(s_j) = j$	j	s_j	$\pi(s_j) = j$
0	22	π(W) = A	13	12	π(M) = N
1	8	π(I) = B	14	21	π(V) = O
2	11	π(L) = C	15	18	π(S) = P
3	15	π(P) = D	16	23	π(X) = Q
4	19	π(T) = E	17	4	π(E) = R
5	14	π(O) = F	18	24	π(Y) = S
6	1	π(B) = G	19	7	π(H) = T
7	10	π(K) = H	20	5	π(F) = U
8	25	π(Z) = I	21	20	π(U) = V
9	16	π(Q) = J	22	0	π(A) = W
10	3	π(D) = K	23	13	π(N) = X
11	17	π(R) = L	24	6	π(G) = Y
12	2	π(C) = M	25	9	π(J) = Z

FIGURE 16 : Recovery Of Cipher Disk Substitution π

```
The issue of performance evaluation and prediction has concerned users throughout
the history of computer evolution. In fact, as in any other technological develop-
ment, the issue is most acute when the technology is young; the persistent pursuit
of products with improved cost-performance characteristics then constantly leads to
designs with untried uncertain ...
```

FIGURE 17 : *PLAIN*

Hishahi Kobayashi, "Modelling And Analysis: An Introduction To Performance Evaluation Methodology

I would like to thank Dr. Kjell-Ove Widman of Crypto AG for the historical material.

ENIGMA Variations

H.-R. Schuchmann
Siemens AG, München

Following Webster's Dictionary, the term 'enigma' signifies something "intentionally obscure - as a riddle or a complex metaphor - that depends for full comprehension on the alertness and ingenuity of the hearer or reader". This in mind, in 1896 the British composer Edgar Elgar named his 14 Variations for Large Orchestra, op. 36, 'Enigma Variations'. He wanted to keep secret the underlying theme - and indeed, up to now nobody was able to find out the hidden melody. About 30 years later, the German engineer Arthur Scherbius invented an electro-mechanical ciphermachine which he also called ENIGMA. In this case, however, the programmatic name did not prove as successful in actual practice. Though in a very different sense, the machine became as famous as the aforementioned piece of music.

Meanwhile, much has been written about the ENIGMA, its history in the twenties and its intensive military application during the Second World War /Kahn, 1967/. Thus the following are just marginal notes on a fascinating subject, originally prepared for a demonstration of an ENIGMA machine owned by the Siemens Museum in Munich. They summarize the main technical and historical facts about the ciphermachine, and conclude with a short remark on the role of cryptotechniques in today's commercial data processing.

The ENIGMA is based on the concept of rotors, a simple and robust - but nevertheless quite effective - way for implementing a non-static substitution scheme.

A rotor is a round disk made of electrically insulating material, which in case of the ENIGMA is about 10 cm in diameter and 2,5 cm thick. On each side it carries 26 contacts - corresponding in an adjustable way to the letters of the alphabet -, which are pairwise connected internally in an irregular manner. Several rotors are mounted on a common axis, forming together with a stator on the right of the ensemble and a reflector - i.e. a short circuit stator - on the left the kernel of the ciphermachine. The trick is that after the encipherment of every single letter the position of one or more rotors on the axis is changed, thus leading to a permanently changing substitution function.

The rotor as a cryptomechanism was invented and patented shortly after World War I independently by four persons: The American Edward Hugh Hebern, the Dutch Hugo Alexander Koch, the Swedish Arvid Gerhard Damm, and the already mentioned German Arthur Scherbius. During that early period of public telegraphy, there was a subtle disposition for cryptography, stimulating many inventors of cryptodevices. It turned out, however, that - with only very few exceptions - it was extremely difficult to market such products successfully for commercial applications.

Arthur Scherbius was one of the unsuccessful manufacturers. Having broad technical interests in such different fields as ceramics, motor control, heating, and electrical switches - where he held more than 30 patents -, he also invented in 1923 his ENIGMA ciphermachine and got it patented. For production he founded the Chiffriermaschinen AG in Berlin. Two models of the machine where designed: a huge and heavy printing version, sold for 8,000 Reichsmark, and a much simpler and smaller version with lamps displaying the specific corresponding letter, which was sold for 1,000 Reichsmark. Despite the fact - or probably just because of it - that the company had problems in delivering the ordered machines, the Chiffriermaschinen AG was dissolved in 1933. Only a few month later it was reestablished as Chiffriermaschinen Gesellschaft Heimsoeth und Rinke, again in Berlin. In 1935 the new formed company officially took over from Arthur Scherbius a package of about 20 German patents concerning the ENIGMA. Nothing more is known about the inventor of the machine himself. The specific date of the company´s decline and reorganisation, however, could be an indication for political reasons of his disappearence.

Since the mid-thirties several military versions of the ENIGMA were built. All of them were based on the non-printing model which was equipped with an additional switch board for a static interchange of the alphabet characters by manual cabeling. The cipher key of these ENIGMA machines consisted of the following parameters, which were set independently:

- The selected set of rotors; there existed about ten differently wired wheels.
- The labeling (01 to 26) of the rotor contacts; this parameter also fixed the carry-over-position of the rotor.
- The sequence of the different rotors on the common axis.
- The initial position of each of the rotors.
- The special plugging of the switch-board.

The operational instructions for key selection and key transmission have been changed several times during pre-war and war times. The first significant alteration took place in 1938 and 1939; it had a major impact on early attempts to break the ENIGMA cipher.

From the very beginning of its military or quasi-military applications, the seemingly complex key of the ENIGMA proved to be less secure than was expected. Besides operational flaws in the field, the main weakness of the machine concept results from the fact that in the case of typical short and stereotypic military messages normally only one rotor - the rightmost one - is moved, while all the others remain in their position.

Heavy and systematic attacks on ENIGMA enciphered messages were successfully executed mainly at two places: during pre-war times in Warschau (Poland), and later, in the early forties, at Bletchley Park near London (UK). The geographical places of these attempts, the underlying methods, and the people involved form part of a long, but only historically interesting story, which cannot be spread out here /Rejewski, 1981; Kahn, 1982/. There exists, however, a remarkable bridge from the codebreaking techniques of those days to the origins of modern electronic data processing.

At their intelligence center at Bletchley Park, the British began from the very beginning of World War II to develop electro-mechanical and later electronic tools as an aid for breaking German coded messages. The most successful one of these tools, a machine called COLOSSUS, in retrospect appears as the earliest implementation of an electronic digital computer /Randell, 1980/. It enabled the British intelligence service to get an ENIGMA enciphered message deciphered into plaintext within about an hour.

The first version of COLOSSUS was put into operation in December 1943. This is six months earlier than MARK I at Harvard University, and two years earlier than ENIAC at Moore School; usually these two are referred to as the oldest computers. Most of the documentation on COLOSSUS is still classified, so that no full technical details are accessible. But even the few known characteristics read quite impressively. The COLOSSUS was a fully electronical, plug-board programmable computer containing about 1.500 tubes. A redesigned version, named MARK II COLOSSUS, was equipped with 2.500 tubes and became operational in June 1944. Both machines contained built-in operations for counting, binary arithmetic, and boolean connections. Data was input at a rate of 5.000 char/s by a paper tape reader - a figur given by Randell that appears, however, too high for the technology of that time. One of the later celebrated pioneers of data processing, Alan M. Turing, had been working at Bletchley Park during that period, but "did not have any direct involvement in, or influence on, the design or use of COLOSSUS".

Today, the ENIGMA ciphermachine itself is of historical value only. Technology has changed dramatically, so that it is possible to implement the functions of its several kilogramme of electro-mechanical hardware on a single chip now. What has remained is the hesitation or reluctance for applying cryptographic techniques in commercial information techniques, i.e. in modern data recording and data transmission. A major European manufacturer of crypto-devices recently stated that only less than 1 % of the sales in this area is done on the commercial field. It appears that the "information society" does not care much for data accidents, probably occurring quite frequently in our large computer centers and on public transmission lines with their high data traffic. Thus, manufacturers of modern integrated chips for the Data Encryption Standard (DES), e.g. Intel, Motorola, or Western Digital, are in a similar position as the manufacturers of crypto--devices in the twenties: They have available a meaningful technical product for which they cannot get acceptance on the market /Iversen, 1981/.

Section 3

Mathematical Foundations

Encrypting by Random Rotations

N. J. A. Sloane

Mathematics and Statistics Research Center
Bell Laboratories
Murray Hill, New Jersey 07974, USA

Abstract

This paper gives some well-known, little known, and new results on the problem of generating random elements in groups, with particular emphasis on applications to cryptography. The groups of greatest interest are the group of all orthogonal $n \times n$ matrices and the group of all permutations of a set. The chief application is to A. D. Wyner's analog scrambling scheme for voice signals.

1. Introduction

This work was originally motivated by three questions: How long does it take to shuffle a deck of cards? How secure is the Data Encryption Standard? How does one generate random rotations?

The first question involves a certain set of *permutations* of a set of 52 elements (namely the permutations that are produced by the shuffling process), and asks how many permutations from this set must be multiplied together before a truly random permutation is obtained (cf. [Diaconis and Shahshahani,

1981], [Diaconis, Graham and Kantor, 1982]).

The controversial Data Encryption Standard, or DES, encrypts blocks of 64 bits of plain-text into blocks of 64 bits of cipher-text using a 56-bit key (see [Diffie and Hellman, 1976 and 1977], [Morris, Sloane and Wyner, 1977], [Davis, 1978], [Morris, 1978], [Bernhard, 1982]). If the 56-bit key is fixed, the DES carries out a certain permutation of the 2^{64} possible 64-bit words. (In other words it is a simple substitution cipher on an alphabet of size 2^{64}.) A natural question to ask is what are the properties of these DES permutations? In particular, do they look like random permutations? Well, what does a random permutation look like? Of course the same questions can be asked about any block cipher.

The third question arose in connection with the voice encryption scheme proposed by [Wyner, 1979 and 1979a]. This will be described in Section II, but in the end requires that one be able to produce large numbers of random real *orthogonal matrices*.

A common feature of the three questions is that they all involve random elements from a group: in the first two cases the group is the *symmetric group* S_n, i.e. the group of all $n!$ permutations of an n-element set (with n equal to either 52 or 2^{64}), while in the third case it is the *orthogonal group* $O(n)$, the group of all $n \times n$ real orthogonal matrices (i.e. matrices A satisfying

$AA^{tr} = I$, where tr denotes transpose). Another important group is the *special orthogonal group* $SO(n)$, consisting of all matrices in $O(n)$ having determinant +1 (these are the proper rotations in $O(n)$).

This discussion has thus led to the following questions. Let G be a group.

(Q1). How does one generate elements of G "at random"?

(Q2). How can one test if certain given elements of G really are random?

(The DES permutations, for example.) One test is to multiply them together in all possible ways and see if they produce the whole group. More generally, one can ask:

(Q3) Does a given subset H generate the whole group G?

(Q4) If so, how long does it take? (This is the card shuffling problem.)

This paper will examine some of the known results (and in Section 4.5 present some new ones) on these questions, concentrating on the special cases when G is the group S_n (of all permutations) or $O(n)$ (of all orthogonal matrices). There are a considerable number of results, but they are widely scattered through the literature, and their possible applications to cryptography have received little attention. As will appear, many open problems remain.

A related topic, which will be mentioned only briefly, comes from the classic paper on cryptography by [Shannon, 1949]. In this paper Shannon introduced what he called product ciphers (an ancestor of the DES) by analogy with the well-known algorithm for mixing dough. Take two non-commuting operations (rolling the dough and folding it) and apply them again and again (see Figure 1). It had been proved many years earlier by [Hopf, 1937] that this process eventually will mix the dough thoroughly. This is an answer to question (Q3) for yet another group. However transformations of this type belong to *ergodic theory*, which as usually defined is outside the scope of the present article (see for example [Halmos, 1956] or [Walters, 1981]).

The following works deal with probability distributions on groups and so are also closely related to the subject of this paper: [Diaconis, 1982], [Furstenberg, 1980], [Grenander, 1963], [Guivarc'h et al., 1977], [Heyer, 1977 and 1982]. Then of course in the background is the enormous literature on harmonic analysis on groups — see for example [Boothby and Weiss, 1972], [Hewitt and Ross, 1963-1970], [Moore, 1973], and [Warner, 1972].

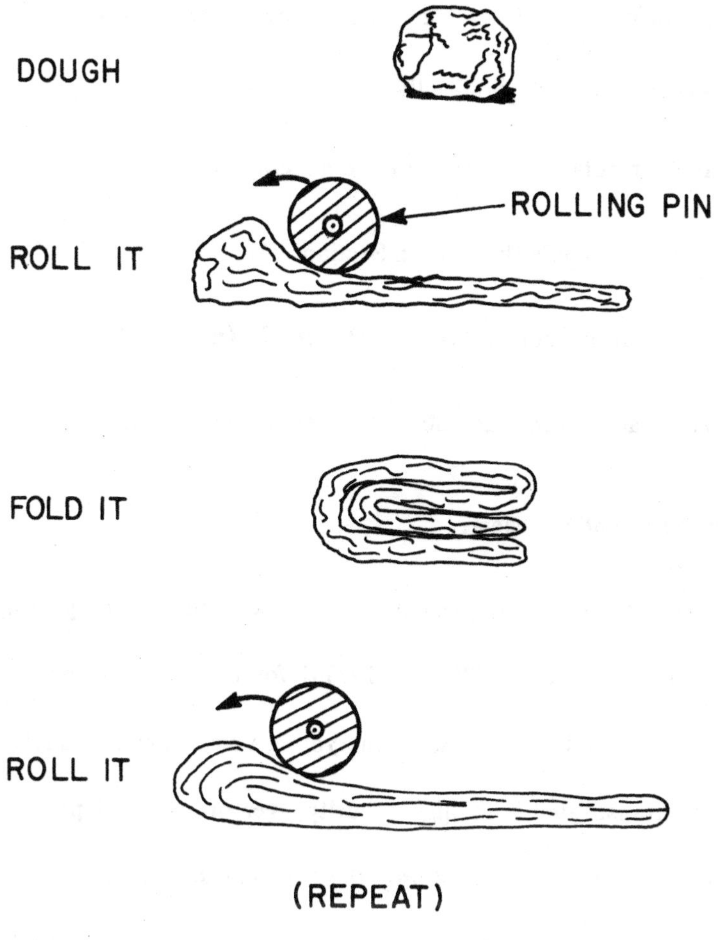

Figure 1. The classical algorithm for mixing dough uses two non-commuting operations (rolling and folding).

To end this Introduction I shall give a preview of two results, using the format of the currently popular light-bulb jokes*:

Q: How many permutations does it take to generate S_n?

A: 2, usually (see Dixon's theorem in Section 3.4).

Q: How many rotations does it take to generate $SO(n)$?

A: 2, almost certainly (see Auerbach's theorem in Section 4.5).

2. Wyner's Voice Encryption Scheme

Only a brief sketch of the simplest of Wyner's schemes will be given. The reader is referred to [Wyner, 1979 and 1979a] for the complete description. The problem to be considered is that of encrypting voice signals in such a way that they can be transmitted with high security over ordinary telephone lines. There are two standard ways of doing this, analog scrambling and digital scrambling ([MacKinnon, 1980] gives an excellent survey; see also [Jayant, 1982] and the article by Beker in the present volume). Both methods have their drawbacks. The analog schemes typically involve permutations in the time and/or frequency domains, produce high quality speech at the receiving

* For example, here is the classic New York City version. Q: How many Upper East Siders does it take to screw in a light-bulb? A: Two, one to mix the martinis, the other to call the superintendent.

end, but have low security. On the other hand the digital schemes offer very high security but low fidelity, and in fact usually degrade the speech so much that although it can be understood, the speaker cannot be recognized. The reason is the low bandwidth of the channel, which necessitates a very low bit rate.

Wyner's scheme appears to combine the best features of both methods: high fidelity *and* high security. Before describing it we state some properties of sequences of real numbers. An infinite sequence $a = \{a(k)\}_{-\infty}^{\infty}$ has the *discrete Fourier transform*

$$A(\omega) = \sum_{k=-\infty}^{\infty} a(k) e^{-2\pi i k \omega} \quad (-\infty < \omega < \infty) .$$

Note that $A(\omega)$ is periodic with period 1. The sequence a is said to have *finite support* if $a(k) = 0$ except for $k_1 \leq k \leq k_2$, and is *bandlimited* (with bandwidth $W < ½$) if

$$A(\omega) = 0 \quad \text{for} \quad W < |\omega| \leq ½ .$$

A central fact in this theory is that a sequence cannot both have finite support and be bandlimited. However we say that a is *approximately bandlimited* (with bandwidth $W < ½$) if it has finite energy and most of its energy lies in the band $-W \leq \omega \leq W$, so that

$$\int_{W}^{1/2} A(\omega) d\omega \approx 0 .$$

The encryption scheme makes use of the fact that there is a known basis for the space of approximately bandlimited sequences. More precisely (see [Slepian, 1978], [Wyner, 1979, Theorem 3.1]), the vector space of sequences $(a(1),...,a(N))$ which are approximately bandlimited has dimension $d \approx 2WN$ (thus $d < N$), and has a basis $\phi_1, \ldots, \phi_d$ consisting of certain sequences called *discrete prolate spheroidal* sequences.

The scrambling method operates as follows. Let $x(t)$ be the voice waveform to be transmitted (or a portion thereof), having bandwidth W_0 cycles per second (in other words the ordinary Fourier transform $X(\omega)$ of $x(t)$ is zero for $|\omega| > W_0$). The waveform is sampled every T seconds, where T is less than the Nyquist rate $1/2W_0$. We take a finite segment of this sequence, say

$$a = (a(1), a(2), ..., a(N)) ,$$

where N is large enough so that this contains most of the energy in $x(t)$. Then a is approximately bandlimited, with bandwidth $W = TW_0 < ½$. We express a in terms of the discrete prolate spheroidal sequences ϕ_j, obtaining

$$a = \sum_{j=1}^{d} \alpha_j \phi_j ,$$

where the coefficients are calculated using

$$\alpha_j = \sum_{k=1}^{N} a(k)\phi_j(k) , \quad j = 1,...,d .$$

The scrambling is performed by multiplying the coefficient vector $(\alpha_1, \alpha_2, \ldots, \alpha_d)$ by a secret $d \times d$ orthogonal matrix Q, producing

$$(\beta_1, \ldots, \beta_d) = (\alpha_1, \ldots, \alpha_d)Q .$$

A new matrix Q will be used for each sequence a. The scrambled *sequence* is

$$b = \sum_{j=1}^{d} \beta_j \phi_j ,$$

from which we form the scrambled *waveform*

$$y(t) = \sum_{k=1}^{N} b(k)g(t-kT) ,$$

where $g(t)$ is any waveform whose Fourier transform $G(\omega)$ satisfies

$$G(\omega) = \begin{array}{ll} T & \text{for } |\omega| \le W_0 \\ \text{bounded} & \text{for } W_0 < |\omega| \le 1/2T \\ 0 & \text{for } |\omega| > 1/2T \end{array}$$

The scrambled waveform $y(t)$ can be shown to have the same bandwidth and approximately the same energy as $x(t)$ (since Q is orthogonal), and therefore can be sent over an ordinary telephone line to the receiver.

At the receiving end the waveform $y(t)$ is sampled every T seconds, producing a sequence of samples $(\hat{b}(1), \ldots, \hat{b}(N))$. The receiver reverses the scrambling procedure (using the inverse matrix Q^{tr}), and finds

$(\hat{a}(1),...,\hat{a}(N))$. This is used to construct a waveform

$$\hat{x}(t) = \sum_{k=1}^{N} \hat{a}(k)g(t-kT)$$

which Wyner shows is very close to the original waveform $x(t)$. He also shows that if N and d are large enough and the matrices Q are chosen independently and uniformly from the orthogonal group, then this method offers essentially perfect security. So provided we can generate random (and secret) orthogonal matrices at a sufficiently high rate, the problem is solved. We shall return to this question in Sections 4.4 and 4.5.

3. Random Permutations

We begin our discussion of random elements of groups with the symmetric group S_n, since it is somewhat simpler than the orthogonal group and has certainly been more extensively studied. We shall describe some of the answers to questions $Q1-Q4$ for this group. A typical permutation in S_n will be written $\sigma = \{\sigma_1, \ldots, \sigma_n\}$, meaning $1 \rightarrow \sigma_1,...,n \rightarrow \sigma_n$.

3.1 (Q1) Generating random permutations

The problem can be stated very simply. We wish to find a procedure which will generate permutations from S_n, in such a way that every permutation is equally likely to be chosen each time. (More formally, the output should be a sequence of independent, identically distributed random variables $X_0, X_1, X_2,...,$

with Prob$\{X_i = \sigma\} = 1/n!$ for all $\sigma \in S_n$ and $i = 0,1,2,\ldots$.)

Although many methods have been proposed for solving this problem [Plackett, 1968], there is one very simple and fast algorithm which stands out above all the others. It is the following ([Durstenfeld, 1964], [Page 1967], [Nijenhuis and Wilf, 1978, p. 62], [Knuth, 1981, p. 139]).

> Start with $\sigma_1 = 1,\ \sigma_2 = 2, \ldots, \sigma_n = n$.
>
> For $i = n, n-1, \ldots, 2$ do the following.
>
> > Generate a random number U, uniformly distributed between 0 and 1, set $k = [iU]+1$, and exchange the values of σ_i and σ_k.

Then $\{\sigma_1, \sigma_2, \ldots, \sigma_n\}$ is the desired permutation. $[x]$ denotes the largest integer $\leq x$. Provided we have a method for producing uniformly distributed random numbers U in the range $[0,1)$, a problem that is discussed in Section 4.1, this algorithm does indeed produce random permutations. (For generalizations see [Diaconis and Shahshahani, 1982]. A recent paper by [Ayoub, 1981] describes a method for using a secret key to generate permutations that can be used to encrypt binary data.)

The algorithm uses $n-1$ uniform random numbers U, which at first glance appears to be the smallest possible number. However, if we are willing to sacrifice some randomness, faster methods can be found.

3.2 Quasi-Random Permutations

For example we may choose a fixed set of say M permutations in advance, and store them. When a permutation is called for, we pick a number i at random between 1 and M, and supply the i-th permutation. The Erlangen Voice Scrambler [Hess and Wirl, 1982] for example makes use of $M = 256$ carefully chosen permutations from S_8. (See also [McGonegal et al. 1981]).

This may be called a *quasi-random* method, and has two advantages over the random method described above. (i) Speed: if M is not too large, a single uniformly distributed random number U is sufficient to specify a number between 1 and M (use $[UM] + 1$). (ii) Greater control: many permutations do a poor job of scrambling (the identity permutation, single transpositions, etc.), and with this algorithm they can be avoided. In the random method there is always a chance that a poor permutation will be produced.

A similar situation occurs when random numbers are used in numerical analysis — there are often good reasons for preferring quasi-random numbers (or quasi-Monte Carlo methods as they are also called) over more genuinely random numbers. See the excellent discussion in [Niederreiter, 1978].

3.3 (Q2) Tests for random permutations

Someone is supplying us with a sequence of permutations, which he claims are being produced independently and at random from S_n. How can we test if this is true? This problem has not been studied as intensively as the corresponding question for random *numbers*, and there does not seem to be any discussion of tests comparable to that given by [Knuth, 1981] for random number generators. However, a number of individual tests have been studied (some in connection with permutations used for conscription — see [Fienberg, 1971], [Rosenblatt and Filliben, 1971]), and others can be constructed from the known properties of random permutations. Here we list just a few.

Number of cycles.

Theorem 1 [Goncharov, 1944].

Let c_n be the number of cycles in a random permutation from S_n. Then the mean and variance of c_n are both approximately equal to log n. (See also [Feller, 1957, p. 242], [Riordan, 1958, p. 72].)

Length of cycles.

Let l_r (resp. m_r) be the length of the rth longest (resp. shortest) cycle. [Shepp and Lloyd, 1966] have found the average values of l_r and m_r, as well as their higher moments and the limiting distribution of l_r. In particular the length l_1 of the longest cycle satisfies $l_1/n \to 0.624...$ as $n \to \infty$, a result discovered empirically by [Golomb, 1964].

Length of monotonic subsequence

Theorem 2 ([Hammersley, 1972], [Logan and Shepp, 1977], [Veršik and Kerov, 1977].)

Let $\{\sigma_1, \ldots, \sigma_n\}$ *be a random element of* S_n, *and let* α_n *be the length of the longest monotonic subsequence of* $\sigma_1, \ldots, \sigma_n$. *Then the average value of* α_n *satisfies*

$$\alpha_n/\sqrt{n} \to 2 \quad as \quad n \to \infty .$$

Open Problem: Find the variance of α_n. [Baer and Brock, 1968] give extensive tables.

Distance between permutations

There are many ways to define a metric on S_n (see for example [Kendall, 1970]). Four common examples are

$$d_1(\sigma,\tau) = \sum_{i=1}^{n} |\sigma_i - \tau_i| ,$$

$$d_2(\sigma,\tau) = \left\{ \sum_{i=1}^{n} (\sigma_i - \tau_i)^2 \right\}^{1/2} ,$$

$d_3(\sigma,\tau)$ = minimum number of transpositions needed

to bring $\{\sigma_1, \ldots, \sigma_n\}$ into the order $\{\tau_1, \ldots, \tau_n\}$,

$d_4(\sigma,\tau)$ = minimum number of pairwise adjacent transpositions

needed to bring $\{\sigma_1^{-1}, \ldots, \sigma_n^{-1}\}$ into the order $\{\tau_1^{-1}, \ldots, \tau_n^{-1}\}$.

Here σ^{-1} and τ^{-1} are the permutations inverse to σ and τ. Consider $d_k(\sigma,\tau)$ when σ and τ are chosen independently and uniformly from S_n. Then, for large n, $d_k(\sigma,\tau)$ approaches a normal distribution with known mean and variance (see [Diaconis and Graham, 1977] for the cases $k = 1$ and 3, [Kendall, 1970] for $k = 2$ and 4).

Tests for multivariate time series

We may regard our sequence of permutations $\sigma^{(i)} = \{\sigma_1^{(i)}, \ldots, \sigma_n^{(i)}\}$, $i = 0,1,2,\ldots$, as a sequence of points in real n-dimensional space $\mathbf{R}^n$. Then any of the standard tests for multivariate time series may be applied. For example we may look at the correlation between $\sigma^{(i)}$ and $\sigma^{(i+k)}$ for $k = 1,2,3,\ldots$ (see [Hannan, 1960], [Brillinger, 1975], [Chatfield, 1975] or [Bloomfield, 1976]).

3.4 (Q3) Generating S_n from a subset

The basic fact is that it is very easy to generate S_n: just about any two permutations will do.

Theorem 3 [Dixon, 1969]

If two permutations are chosen independently and uniformly from S_n, then with probability very close to 3/4 they generate S_n, and with probability close to 1/4 they *generate the alternating subgroup A_n.*

A permutation is equally likely to be even or odd, and the even ones form the alternating subgroup A_n. There is a probability of 1/4 that a pair of permutations are both in A_n, in which case the theorem says they are very likely to generate A_n. In the remaining 3/4 of the cases they are likely to generate S_n. [Bovey and Williamson, 1978] and Bovey [1980] have sharpened Dixon's estimates.

Another test for the randomness of a set of permutations is to see if they generate A_n or S_n. But in view of Theorem 3 this is a very weak test: we would be surprised if a set of permutations did not generate either A_n or S_n. It is not surprising therefore that [Coppersmith and Grossman, 1975] were able to show that, for a certain simple class of product ciphers, the associated permutations do indeed generate A_n. However it appears that so far no one has applied the tests mentioned in Section 3.3 to the permutations associated with product ciphers. Of course this will not be easy in view of the large values of n involved (2^{64} for the DES).

3.5 (Q4) How long does it take to generate S_n?

The answer to Q4 for a random pair of permutations appears to be open. This may be stated more precisely as follows.

Open Problem: Let σ and τ be chosen independently and uniformly from S_n, and consider a product $\rho = \pi_1 \pi_2 \cdots \pi_k$, where each π_i is equally likely to be σ or τ. Then how large must k be before ρ is close to random, for example in the sense explained below?

On the other hand one elegant result of this type is known. Place n cards labeled $1,2,...,n$ in a row. Apply random transpositions, by choosing numbers i and j independently and uniformly from the set $\{1,2,...,n\}$, and interchanging the cards in positions i and j. (If $i = j$ this does nothing.) How many transpositions are needed before the resulting permutation of the cards is close to random?

Theorem 4 [Diaconis and Shahshahani, 1981.]

$$\tfrac{1}{2}\, n \log_e n \quad \textit{transpositions are needed}\ .$$

The precise result that Diaconis and Shahshahani proved is as follows (this will also give one possible definition of what it means for a permutation to be close to random). The process of choosing the random transposition is represented by the probability distribution

$$\begin{aligned} P\{\text{identity}\} &= 1/n, \\ P\{\sigma\} &= 2/n^2 \quad \text{if } \sigma \text{ is a transposition}, \\ P\{\sigma\} &= 0 \quad \text{otherwise}. \end{aligned}$$

The result of applying k transpositions is the k-fold convolution $P^{(k)}$ of this distribution. Then Diaconis and Shahshahani prove that, if $k > \tfrac{1}{2} n \log_e n$,

$P^{(k)}$ is close to the uniform distribution $Q(\sigma) = 1/n!$ for all $\sigma \in S_n$. In fact they show that, for $n \geq 10$,

$$\sum_{\sigma \in S_n} |P^{(k)}(\sigma) - Q(\sigma)| < ce^{-2(k-\frac{1}{2} n \log n)/n}$$

where c is a constant, which clearly implies Theorem 4.

Of course the distribution $P^{(k)}$ is never exactly uniform, and [Robbins and Bolker, 1981] have investigated how biased the distribution can be in some cases.

Leo Flatto has recently proved a kind of converse to Theorem 4.

Theorem 5 (Flatto, private communication)
Starting with a random ordering of n cards, let a_n be the number of random transpositions needed to return the cards to their original order of $1,2,...,n$. *Then the average value of a_n is $n!$.*

The difference between Theorems 4 and 5 is easily explained. Starting at the conference center in Burg Feuerstein where this meeting was held, it does not take long before one is lost in the surrounding forest. On the other hand, starting at a random place in the forest, it takes a very long time before one returns to the conference center.

For some other very interesting results on card shuffling see [Even and

Goldreich, 1981], [Diaconis, Graham and Kantor, 1982], and [Kantor, 1982].

4. Random Numbers, Random Points on a Sphere, and Random Rotations

In this section we consider questions (Q1)-(Q4) for the orthogonal group $O(n)$ and the rotation subgroup $SO(n)$. We shall approach the construction of orthogonal matrices gradually, by considering in turn

uniformly distributed random numbers,

normally distributed random numbers,

random points on an n-dimensional sphere, and

random orthogonal matrices.

4.1 Uniformly distributed random numbers

The problem of generating numbers that are (as nearly as possible) independent and uniformly distributed between 0 and 1 has been very extensively studied. (This amounts to solving question (Q1) for the torus group **R/Z**.) Chapter 3 of [Knuth, 1981] surveys many of the standard methods of generating such numbers and the tests that can be applied to see how close they come to being truly "random". Some standard random number generators are tabulated in [Abramowitz and Stegun, 1972, §26.8]. Other tests are described in [MacLaren and Marsaglia, 1965], [Jansson, 1966], [Lewis, 1975], [Niederreiter, 1978] (which has an extensive bibliography), and [Bright and Enison, 1979]. See also [Chambers, 1967],

[Mihram, 1972], [Li and Yorke, 1978], and [Kennedy and Gentle, 1980].

It is surprising, however, that most of these accounts concentrate on statistical tests for randomness, and pay little attention to the cryptographic aspects. For cryptographic applications one wants a random number generator which not only passes all the standard statistical tests, but is also hard to "break". For example, if the sequence is produced by a multiplicative congruential generator (see [Knuth, 1981, p. 9]) then it should be difficult to recover the seed, or if it is produced by a linear or nonlinear feedback shift register ([Feistel, 1973], [Feistel, Notz and Smith, 1975], [Sloane, 1981]) then it should be difficult to discover the initial contents of the register and the feedback rule. The fact that a particular random number generator may be easily broken in this way should be of as much concern to the statistician as to the cryptographer. In other words the set of tests should be enlarged to include tests for cryptographic strength.

One obvious test, for example, that is not mentioned in any of the above references, is to find the length of the shortest *linear* feedback shift register that can produce the sequence. There is a well-known algorithm of Berlekamp which does this efficiently, at least for sequences over a finite field. This is an essential step in decoding certain error-correcting codes — see [Berlekamp, 1968, Algorithm 7.4], [Massey, 1969], [MacWilliams and Sloane, 1981, Chapters 9 and 12].

Open Problem: Generalize the Berlekamp algorithm so as to apply to sequences of integers modulo m, when m is not a prime.

In any case it is known that the two commonest random number generators, namely multiplicative congruential generators and Tausworthe linear shift register generators [Knuth, 1981, p. 30] are cryptographically very weak. See the attacks described in [Geffe, 1967], [Meyer and Tuchman, 1972], [Reeds, 1977, 1979 and 1979a], [Knuth, 1980 and 1981, Problem 3.6.7].

Composite Random Number Generators

There are several ways of combining the outputs from two random number generators to produce a more random sequence. One way is simply to add the two output sequences (where the addition is modulo m, if the two generators produce numbers between 0 and $m-1$). Other methods are described by [MacLaren and Marsaglia, 1965] and [Knuth, 1981, pp. 31-33]. Such composite random number generators are used in some mathematical subroutine libraries [Marsaglia, Ananthanarayanan and Paul, 1973], [Fox, 1976]. Intuitively they appear to be more random than the original generators, and [Brown and Solomon, 1979] have partially confirmed this statistically. However there does not seem to have been any study made of the cryptographic strength of composite random number generators.

Open Problem: How hard is it for example to break the [Marsaglia et al., 1973] Super-Duper uniform random number generator?

On the other hand any good conventional cipher can be used (in many ways) as a random number generator. Suppose the cipher is described by the equation $y = F(k, x)$, where k, x and y are respectively the key, plain-text and cipher-text. Choose "seeds" k_0 and x_0. Then for example we expect that

$$y_0 = F(k_0, x_0) \ , \quad y_i = F(y_{i-1}, x_0) \ , \quad i = 1,2,...$$

will be a random sequence which is hard to break (although we may be uncertain about its statistical properties).

Finally, then, it is clear that by combining the output from a composite random number generator (good statistics, possibly weak cryptographically) with a random number generator based on a conventional cipher (strong cryptographically, uncertain statistics), we can obtain a fast uniform random number generator which is satisfactory from both points of view. Figure 2 shows one possible configuration, using either the Lucifer ([Smith, 1971], [Girsdansky, 1971]) or DES ciphers. The Lucifer cipher is similar in design to the DES, except for being considerably stronger because both the key and the data blocks are 128 bits long. The configuration shown in Figure 2 seems unnecessarily complicated, however, and it is hoped that this discussion will stimulate readers to find more efficient schemes.

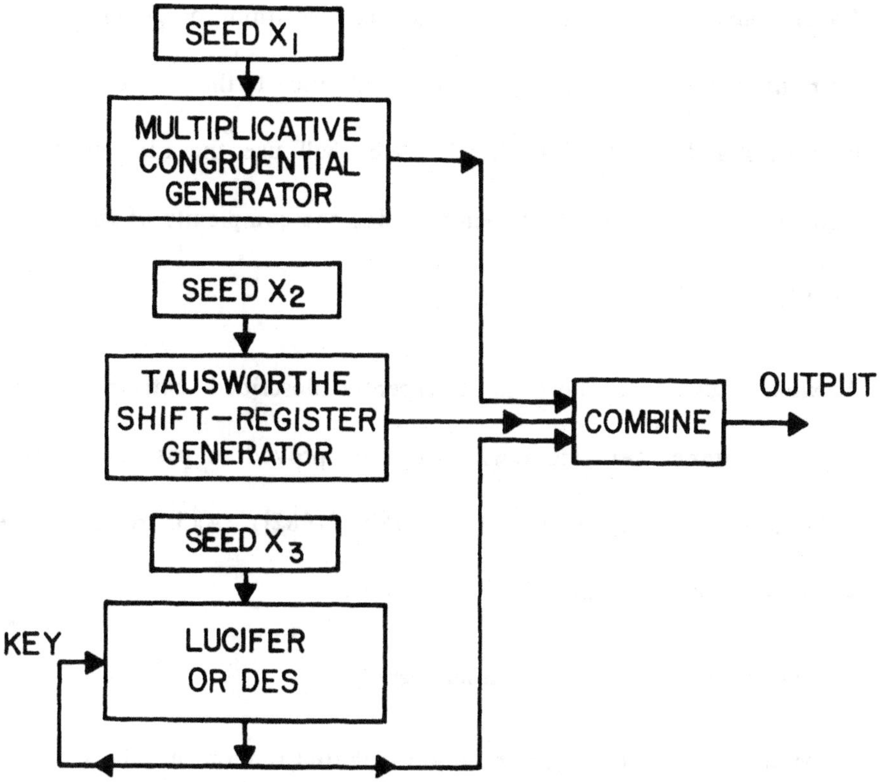

Figure 2. Prototype uniform random number generator that has good statistical properties and is hard to break. The outputs from two standard random number generators are combined with the output from a conventional cipher (such as the Lucifer or DES ciphers). Here x_1, x_2, x_3 are seeds, and a fourth seed is used as the initial value of the key for the cipher.

Conclusion. It is possible to find a fast algorithm for generating uniformly distributed random numbers between 0 and 1 that have good statistical properties and are hard to break. We shall use the running time of this algorithm as a standard by which to judge the complexity of the algorithms in the following sections.

Remark. Several authors have recently described extremely complicated random number generators which can be proved to pass any statistical test ([Blum et al., 1982], [Shamir, 1981], [Yao, 1982]). As is to be expected these generators are quite slow.

4.2 Normally distributed random numbers

Methods of generating normally distributed random numbers have received almost as much attention as methods for uniform random numbers. Some selected references are [Box and Muller, 1958], [Marsaglia and Bray, 1964], [Abramowitz and Stegun, 1972, §26.8], [Ahrens and Dieter, 1972, 1973], [Dieter and Ahrens, 1973], [Brent, 1974], [Atkinson and Pearce, 1976], [Marsaglia, Ananthanarayanan and Paul, 1976], [Sakasegawa, 1978], [Schmeiser, 1980], [Knuth, 1981, §3.4.1].

Here we shall just mention three methods, each of which has certain desirable features. They all produce (approximations to) standard normal random numbers, with mean 0 and variance 1. $U_1, U_2, \ldots$ will denote independent uniform random numbers between 0 and 1 (see the previous section).

Approximate Normal Distribution.

Compute $U_1+U_2+...+U_{12}-6$.

This is one of the oldest methods (see for example [Abramowitz and Stegun, 1972, p. 952], [Ahrens and Dieter, 1972]), and, recalling the central limit theorem, we see that it produces numbers which are roughly normally distributed. It has the advantage of being very simple and of producing numbers at a fixed rate. On the other hand it takes about $12u$ seconds per number, where u is the time to generate a single uniform random number. The other two methods are much faster than this, and also produce numbers whose distribution is almost exactly normal.

The Box-Muller Method [Box and Muller, 1958].

Compute U_1 and U_2; set $V_1 = 2U_1-1$, $V_2 = 2U_2-1$.

Reject this pair unless $r = V_1^2+V_2^2 \leq 1$.

Compute $s = \sqrt{\dfrac{-2 \log_e r}{r}}$.

Then sV_1 and sV_2 are independent and normally distributed.

This is slightly more complicated to program than the previous method, but only takes about $5u$ seconds per number [Ahrens and Dieter, 1972].

The Method of Mixtures.

There have been a series of methods of this type, culminating in an algorithm described in [Marsaglia, Ananthanarayanan and Paul, 1976]. The idea is to write the normal density function

$$\phi(x) = \frac{1}{\sqrt{2\pi}} e^{-x^2/2}$$

as a sum

$$\phi(x) = 0.960...f_1(x)+0.023f_2(x)+0.011...f_3(x)+0.006...f_4(x) \ ,$$

where f_1 is a simple step function approximation to ϕ which is used 96% of the time. Then f_2 is a density function which accounts for most of the difference between ϕ and $0.960...f_1$, and f_3 and f_4 take care of what is left. The result is an extremely fast algorithm, with an average running time of about $1.5u$ seconds. The program is naturally more complicated than the other two methods (although less so than one would expect: the algorithm is extremely ingenious).

Neither of the last two methods produces numbers whose distribution is precisely normal, of course, because of the inevitable inaccuracies in the logarithm and square-root functions, and round-off errors. Nevertheless the deviation from the true normal distribution can be made very small.

4.3 Random points on an n-dimensional sphere

In this section we consider the problem of generating points which are uniformly distributed over the surface of the n-dimensional unit sphere

$$\Omega_n = \{(x_1, \ldots, x_n) \in \mathbf{R}^n : x_1^2 + \ldots + x_n^2 = 1\} .$$

(To be precise, the points should have uniform Lebesgue measure on Ω_n.) This is already a sufficiently complicated problem that it may be worthwhile to consider as an alternative the use of *quasi-random* points. As in Section 3.2 we take this to mean a fixed, finite set of say M points on Ω_n which are determined in advance. Then when a point on Ω_n is called for, a randomly chosen one of the M is supplied. The set of M points should be picked carefully so as to be regularly spaced over Ω_n. Quite a lot can be said about the construction of such sets of points, but for reasons of space this topic will be postponed to a later paper.

In the rest of this section we shall therefore consider methods which produce points on Ω_n with uniform Lebesgue measure. The following references deal with this problem: [Von Neumann, 1951], [Brown, 1956], [Cook, 1957 and 1959], [Hicks and Wheeling, 1959], [Muller, 1959], [Sibuya, 1964], [Knop, 1970], [Schrack, 1972], [Marsaglia, 1972], [Tashiro, 1977], [Knuth, 1981, p. 130], and especially [Deak, 1979]. We shall describe the four most important methods, beginning with algorithms for three and four dimensions, which are somewhat special. As before, $U_1, U_2, \ldots$ denote independent uniform random numbers between 0 and 1 (see Section 4.1).

Random points on the three-dimensional sphere Ω_3.

Compute U_1, U_2; set $V_1 = 2U_1 - 1$, $V_2 = 2U_2 - 1$.

Reject this pair unless $r = V_1^2 + V_2^2 \leq 1$.

Then $(2V_1(1-r)^{1/2},\ 2V_2(1-r)^{1/2},\ 1-2r)$ is uniformly distributed on Ω_3.

(See [Knop, 1970), [Schrack, 1972], [Marsaglia, 1972].)

Random points on the four-dimensional sphere Ω_4.

Compute U_1, U_2; set $V_1 = 2U_1 - 1$, $V_2 = 2U_2 - 1$.

Reject this pair unless $r_1 = V_1^2 + V_2^2 \leq 1$.

Compute U_3, U_4; set $V_3 = 2U_3 - 1$, $V_4 = 2U_4 - 1$.

Reject this pair unless $r_2 = V_3^2 + V_4^2 \leq 1$.

Then $(V_1, V_2, V_3\{(1-r_1)/r_2\}^{1/2},\ V_4\{(1-r_1)/r_2\}^{1/2})$ is uniformly distributed on Ω_4.

(See [Marsaglia, 1972].)

The uniform projection method.

Compute $U_1, \ldots, U_n$; set $V_i = 2U_i - 1$ $(1 \leq i \leq n)$.

Reject unless $r = \sqrt{V_1^2 + \ldots + V_n^2} \leq 1$.

Then $\frac{1}{r}(V_1,...,V_n)$ is uniformly distributed on Ω_n.

This method is excellent for small dimensions, but for large n the rejection rate is too high.

The normal projection method

Compute independent, normally distributed random numbers $X_1,...,X_n$ with mean 0 and variance 1 (see Section 4.2).

Find $r = \sqrt{X_1^2+...+X_n^2}$.

Then $\frac{1}{r}(X_1,...,X_n)$ is uniformly distributed over Ω_n.

Since this algorithm never rejects any of the X_i's (compare the second step of the previous algorithm) it is the fastest for large n (for $n \geq 5$ say). See [Brown, 1956], [Muller, 1959], [Deák, 1979].

4.4 Random orthogonal matrices

Finally we arrive at the problem of constructing random orthogonal matrices. "Random" here means that the matrices should be produced with Haar measure, which is the unique translation-invariant measure on $O(n)$ (see for example [Halmos, 1950, Chapter XI]). Since the fastest known methods for doing this have running time proportional to n^2 or n^3, this is a time-consuming task, and therefore as an alternative we discuss quasi-random methods in Section 4.5.

Algorithms for generating random orthogonal matrices have been proposed by [Lloyd, 1977 and 1978], [Heiberger, 1978] and [Stewart, 1980]. Stewart's algorithm seems to be the most efficient, although as far as the author knows no one has compared the actual running times of the different algorithms, for example when $n = 50$.

The simplest algorithm is based on the observation that if Q is a random element of $O(n)$ then the first column of Q represents a random point on Ω_n (which is why we discussed this problem in the previous section), the second column is a random point on the $(n-1)$-dimensional sphere perpendicular to the first point, and so on. This leads to the following algorithm. We shall write vectors as column vectors $x = (x_1, \ldots, x_n)^{tr}$, and the length of x is denoted by $\|x\| = (x^{tr}x)^{1/2} = x \cdot x$.

Gram-Schmidt method (see for example [Lloyd, 1977]).

Compute n^2 independent, normally distributed random numbers X_{ij} with mean 0 and variance 1 (see Section 4.2). Let $p_1,\ldots,p_n$ be the columns of the matrix $X = (X_{ij})$.

Compute $q_1 = p_1/\|p_1\|$ and, for $i = 2,\ldots,n$,

$$q_i = \frac{p_i - \sum_{j=1}^{i-1} (p_i \cdot q_j) q_j}{\| p_i - \sum_{j=1}^{i-1} (p_i \cdot q_j) q_j \|}$$

Then $Q = (q_1, ..., q_n)$ is a random orthogonal matrix.

The number of steps required by this algorithm is proportional to n^3, so it is only useful for small values of n.

Stewart's algorithm also takes on the order of n^3 steps to produce a random orthogonal matrix Q, but if what we are really interested in is not Q itself but the product Qv of Q with a given vector v, this can be computed in time proportional to n^2. The algorithm is based on the fact ([Schwerdtfeger, 1950, p. 193], [Cartan, 1966, p. 10]) that an orthogonal matrix can be written as the product of (at most) n reflection matrices, where a reflection (or Householder) matrix has the form

$$R = I - \frac{2 a\, a^{tr}}{a^{tr} a}, \tag{1}$$

where a is a column vector. Then the mapping $x \to Rx$ is a reflection in the hyperplane perpendicular to a. For any vector $x \in \mathbf{R}^n$ there is a unique reflection R_x such that

$$R_x x = \pm \| x \| e_1 ,$$

where $e_1 = (1,0,...,0)^{tr}$. Furthermore R_x can be found in time proportional to n.

Product of reflections method [Stewart, 1980].

Compute ½ $n(n+1)$ independent, normally distributed random numbers X_{ij} $(1 \le j \le i \le n)$ with mean 0 and variance 1 (see Section 4.2). Then $p_j = (X_{j,j}, X_{j+1,j},...,X_{n,j})^{tr}$ for $1 \le j \le n-1$ is a column vector with $n-j+1$ components.

Find the reflection R_{p_j} such that

$$R_{p_j} = \epsilon_j \|p_j\| e_1 ,$$

where $\epsilon_j = \pm 1$, and let $R_j = diag(I_{j-1}, R_{p_j})$.

Set $D = diag(\epsilon_1, \ldots, \epsilon_{n-1}, sgn(X_{n,n}))$.

Then the matrix $Q = DR_1R_2...R_{n-1}$ is a random orthogonal matrix.

Multiplying a vector by a reflection matrix takes time proportional to n. Therefore with this algorithm we can multiply a given vector by a random orthogonal matrix in time proportional to n^2. This includes the time needed to generate ½ $n(n+1)$ normally distributed random numbers, which by Section 4.2 is about $0.75n^2u$ seconds. If we wish to use random matrices from $SO(n)$ rather than $O(n)$, the only modification needed to the algorithm is that the last diagonal entry of D should be chosen to be $+1$ or -1 so as to make $\det Q = 1$ (remember that the determinant of any reflection matrix is -1). When used for scrambling speech in Wyner's scheme (see Section 2) this method is relatively slow but extremely secure.

4.5 Quasi-random orthogonal matrices

In contrast, in this section we describe a quasi-random procedure which does the scrambling much faster, in time proportional to $n \log_2 n$, but for which the level of security is at present unknown.

The method (expanding on a suggestion of [Wyner, 1979, p. 269]) is to use only a certain predetermined set of orthogonal matrices for the scrambling. Let H be a fixed $n \times n$ *Hadamard* matrix, scaled so as to be orthogonal. In other words H is an orthogonal matrix in which all entries are either $1/\sqrt{n}$ or $-1/\sqrt{n}$. A 4×4 example is

$$H_4 = \frac{1}{2}\begin{bmatrix} 1 & 1 & 1 & 1 \\ 1 & -1 & 1 & -1 \\ 1 & 1 & -1 & -1 \\ 1 & -1 & -1 & 1 \end{bmatrix}.$$

Hadamard matrices are believed to exist whenever n is 1,2 or a multiple of 4, and numerous constructions are known. See for example [Hall, 1967], [Wallis, Street and Wallis, 1972], [Turyn, 1974], [Harwit and Sloane, 1979], [Geramita and Seberry, 1979]. Then as our set S of matrices we shall use the matrices of the form

$$D_1\, P\, H\, Q\, D_2$$

where P and Q are arbitrary $n \times n$ permutation matrices, and D_1 and D_2 are arbitrary diagonal matrices of the form $\mathrm{diag}(\pm 1, \pm 1, \ldots, \pm 1)$. In words, S consists of all the matrices that can be obtained from one fixed Hadamard matrix by permuting its rows and columns and changing the signs of any rows and columns.

When a random orthogonal matrix is called for we choose a random element from S. To do this we choose $2n$ uniformly distributed random numbers between 0 and 1 and use them to construct P and Q (see the algorithm for generating permutations in Section 3.1), and a further n uniform random numbers to choose the signs in D_1 and D_2.

In the following paragraphs we discuss some of the properties of this scheme.

Complexity.

When this set of matrices is used for scrambling we need to form the product $D_1\, P\, H\, Q\, D_2\, v$, where v is a vector in $\mathbf{R}^n$. Provided n has only a few distinct prime factors (e.g. if $n = 2^a$ or $3 \cdot 2^a$ etc.) this can be done in time proportional to $n \log_2 n$ by using the Fast Hadamard Transform (see [Good, 1958], [Pratt, 1969], [Brigham, 1974], [Fino and Algazi, 1976], [Harwit and Sloane, 1979], [Diaconis, 1980], [Rose, 1980]).

Time- and frequency-domain scrambling.

As pointed out by Franz R. Pichler (private communication) this method can be regarded as a discrete analog of the joint time- and frequency-domain scrambling technique used in conventional voice encryption. Hadamard matrices are often used as transformations from the spatial or time domains to the frequency (or "sequency") domain (see [Pratt, Kane and Andrews, 1969], [Harwit and Sloane, 1979]). In our application, when the set S is used in Wyner's encryption scheme, the initial domain is the space of sequences $(\alpha_1, \ldots, \alpha_d)$ (see Section 2). The matrices Q, D_2 scramble v in this domain, and then P, D_1 perform further scrambling in the transformed domain.

Security.

Open Problem: How secure is this scheme?

The argument of the previous paragraph suggests that the security may be high if the matrices P, Q, D_1 and D_2 are changed frequently. The remaining paragraphs of this section contain some partial results on this subject.

The number of different matrices.

A *monomial* matrix has exactly one $+1$ or -1 in each row and column, the other entries being zero. Then we can describe S more concisely by

$$S = \{M_1 H M_2 : M_1, M_2 \text{ monomials}\} .$$

The *automorphism group* Aut(H) of a Hadamard matrix H consists of all monomials M_1 such that there is a monomial M_2 with $M_1 H M_2 = H$. From this it follows easily that S contains

$$|S| = \frac{2^{2n}(n!)^2}{|\mathrm{Aut}(H)|} \tag{3}$$

elements (the vertical bars indicate the cardinality of a set). Two Hadamard matrices H_1, H_2 are called *equivalent* if there exist monomials M_1, M_2 with $M_1 H_1 M_2 = H_2$. Obviously equivalent Hadamard matrices produce the same set S. The numbers of inequivalent Hadamard matrices of small dimensions are as follows (see [Ito, Leon and Longyear, 1981]):

n	:	1	2	4	8	12	16	20	24	28
number	:	1	1	1	1	1	5	3	59	?

Examples

The unique 4×4 Hadamard matrix (shown in Eq. (2) above) has $|\mathrm{Aut}(H_4)| = 192$, and S contains 768 elements. For $n = 8$, $|\mathrm{Aut}(H_8)| = 2^{10} \cdot 3 \cdot 7$, and $|S| = 4954521600$.

If H is an $n \times n$ Hadamard matrix of Paley type, where $n-1 = p \geq 19$ is a prime of the form $4a-1$, then $|\mathrm{Aut}(H)| = p(p^2-1)$ [Kantor, 1969] and so from (3)

$$|S| = \frac{2^{2n}(n!)^2}{(n-1)(n^2-2n-2)} .$$

When $n = 48$, $|S| = 1.1765...\cdot 10^{146}$. So S certainly contains large numbers of matrices. Of course this by itself is no guarantee of security. For further information about the automorphism groups of Hadamard matrices see [Hall, 1975], [Ito et al., 1981].

The covering radius of S.

How well does the set S cover the orthogonal group? Let us define the distance between the two $n \times n$ matrices $A = (a_{ij})$, $B = (b_{ij})$ by

$$\mathrm{dist}(A,B) = \left\{ \sum_{i=1}^{n} \sum_{j=1}^{n} (a_{ij}-b_{ij})^2 \right\}^{1/2} . \tag{4}$$

The *covering radius* of any subset $S \subseteq O(n)$ is then

$$\max_{A \in O(n)} \min_{B \in S} \mathrm{dist}(A,B) .$$

The smaller the covering radius, the better S covers $O(n)$. The matrices in $O(n)$ at maximum distance from S are called the *deep holes* in S (using the terminology of [Conway, Parker and Sloane, 1982]).

Theorem 6.

The covering radius of S is $\sqrt{2n(1-1/\sqrt{n})}$, and the deep holes in S are the *monomial matrices.*

Proof. Let $A \in O(n)$ be a deep hole in S, and suppose $\rho_1,\ldots,\rho_n$ are the rows of A. Suppose $H \in S$ has rows $\sigma_1,\ldots,\sigma_n$. The σ_i belong to the set $n^{-1/2}(\pm 1,\ldots,\pm 1)$, forming a cube inscribed in Ω_n. The points of Ω_n furthest from this cube are the $2n$ vertices $(\pm 1,0,\ldots,0)$ of a generalized octahedron dual to the cube. The distance from a vertex of the cube to the nearest vertex of the generalized octahedron is $(2-2/\sqrt{n})^{1/2}$. Then

$$\mathrm{dist}^2(A,H) = \sum_{i=1}^{n} \|\rho_i - \sigma_i\|^2 \le n\left(2 - \frac{2}{\sqrt{n}}\right),$$

with equality if and only if every row of A contains a single nonzero entry ± 1.

The subgroup generated by S.

In this paragraph we answer question (Q3) for the set S. If G is a subgroup of $O(n)$, $\bar{G}$ will denote the topological closure of G (using the metric of Eq. (4)). G is called irreducible if there is no nontrivial subspace V of $\mathbf{R}^n$ with $V^G \subseteq V$. We shall make use of the following result.

Theorem 7. [Eaton and Pearlman, 1977].

Let G be a closed subgroup of $O(n)$ which is generated by reflections (see Eq. (1)), and is infinite and irreducible. Then $G = O(n)$.

From this we can prove several analogs of Dixon's theorem for permutations (see Theorem 3 above).

Theorem 8.

Let H be a fixed $n \times n$ Hadamard matrix, with $n \geq 8$. Let G be the subgroup of $O(n)$ generated by H and all monomial matrices. Then $\bar{G} = O(n)$.

Proof. Let L be the monomial subgroup of $O(n)$. Clearly Aut(H) $\neq L$, so there is a monomial M_1 (say) such that $H\ M_1\ H^{-1} \notin L$. Now L is generated by reflections (it is actually the Weyl group of type B_n [Bourbaki, 1968]). Let J be the largest subgroup of G generated by reflections, so that $L \subseteq J \subseteq G$. Then J is a normal subgroup of G, so $HM_1H^{-1} \in J \setminus L$. Thus J is a reflection group which properly contains L. From the classification of reflection groups ([Bourbaki, 1968], [Humphreys, 1972], [(Coxeter, 1973]), using $n > 4$, it follows that J is infinite. It is easily seen that J is irreducible and therefore $\bar{J} = O(n)$ by Theorem 7. Since $\bar{G} \supseteq \bar{J}$ the theorem follows.

Corollary 9.

For $n \geq 8$, let G be the subgroup of $O(n)$ generated by the elements of the set S. Then $\bar{G} = O(n)$.

Proof. For all n, G contains H, H^{-1} and therefore all monomials, and so is the same as the group G described in Theorem 8.

When $n = 2$ or 4 the conclusions of Theorem 8 and Corollary 9 do not hold. In fact in these two cases G simply consists of the union of S and the monomial matrices. When $n = 2$, this is a dihedral group of order 16; and when $n = 4$, G is the Weyl group of type F_4, of order 1152 [Bourbaki, 1968, p. 273].

The argument used to prove Theorem 8 also establishes the following result.

Theorem 10.

Let A be any element of $O(n)$ which is not in the normalizer of the monomial subgroup. Let G be the subgroup generated by A and all monomial matrices. Then $\bar{G} = O(n)$.

Other analogs of Dixon's theorem

Finally we mention a more direct analog of Dixon's theorem.

Theorem 11. [Auerbach, 1933-34].

Let G be any compact, simply connected Lie group. Let A and B be chosen independently and at random (with Haar measure) from G. Then, with probability one, the topological closure of the subgroup generated by A and B is equal to G.

Corollary 12.

Let A and B be randomly chosen matrices in $SO(n)$. With probability one, the *topological closure of the subgroup they generate is equal to* $SO(n)$.

Acknowledgements.

While writing this paper I have benefitted from conversations with many colleagues. I should particularly like to thank C. L. Mallows and L. A. Shepp for helpful suggestions, and W. M. Kantor for simplifying the proof of Theorems 8 and 10.

References

Abramowitz, M. and Stegun, I. A. (1972), *Handbook of Mathematical Functions,* National Bureau of Standards Applied Math. Series **55**, U.S. Dept. Commerce, Washington, D.C.

Ahrens, J. H. and Dieter, U. (1972), *Computer methods for sampling from the exponential and normal distributions,* Commun. ACM, **15**, 873-882.

Ahrens, J. H. and Dieter, U. (1973), *Extensions of Forsythe's method for random sampling from the normal distribution,* Math. Comp., **27**, 927-937.

Atkinson, A. C. and Pearce, M. C. (1976), *The computer generation of beta, gamma and normal random variables,* J. Royal Statist. Soc., **A139**, 431-461.

Auerbach, H. (1933-34), *Sur les groupes linéaires bornés,* Studia Math., **4**, 113-127 and 158-166; **5**, 43-49.

Ayoub, F. (1981), *Encryption with keyed random permutations,* Electronics Letters, **17**, 583-585.

Baer, R. M. and Brock, P. (1968), *Natural sorting over permutation spaces,* Math. Comp., **22**, 385-410.

Berlekamp, E. R. (1968), *Algebraic Coding Theory,* McGraw-Hill, New York.

Bernhard, R. (1982), *Breaching system security,* IEEE Spectrum, **19** (No. 6), 24-31.

Bloomfield, P. (1976), *Fourier Analysis of Time Series: An Introduction,* Wiley, New York.

Blum, L., Blum, M. and Shub, M. (1982), *A simple secure pseudo-random number generator,* presented at "Crypto 82", Univ. of Calif., Santa Barbara, August 1982.

Boothby, W. M. and Weiss, G. L., editors (1972), *Symmetric Spaces,* Dekker, New York.

Bourbaki, N. (1968), *Groupes et algèbras de Lie, Chap. 4-6,* Hermann, Paris.

Bovey, J. D. (1980), *The probability that some power of a permutation has small degree,* Bull. London Math. Soc., **12**, 47-51.

Bovey, J. D. and Williamson, A. (1978), *The probability of generating the symmetric group,* Bull. London Math. Soc., **10**, 91-96.

Box, G. E. P. and Muller, M. E. (1958), *A note on the generation of normal deviates,* Annals Math. Stat., **29**, 610-611.

Brent, R. P. (1974), *A Gaussian pseudo-random number generator,* Commun. ACM, **17**, 704-706.

Brigham, E. O. (1974), *The Fast Fourier Transform,* Prentice-Hall, Englewood Cliffs, N.J.

Bright, H. S. and Enison, R. L. (1979), *Quasi-random number sequences from a long-period TLP generator with remarks on application to cryptography,* Computing Surveys, **11**, 357-370.

Brillinger, D. R. (1975), *Time Series: Data Analysis and Theory,* Holt, Rinehart and Winston, New York.

Brown, G. W. (1956), *Monte Carlo methods,* in *Modern Mathematics for the Engineer,* edited E. F. Beckenbach, McGraw-Hill, New York, pp. 279-303.

Brown, M. and Solomon, H. (1979), *On combining pseudorandom number generators,* Ann. Statistics, **7**, 691-695.

Cartan, E. (1966), *The Theory of Spinors,* Hermann, Paris. Reprinted by Dover Publications, New York, 1981.

Chambers, R. P. (1967), *Random-number generation,* IEEE Spectrum, **4** (No. 2), 48-56.

Chatfield, C. (1975), *The Analysis of Time Series: Theory and Practice,* Chapman and Hall, London.

Conway, J. H., Parker, R. A. and Sloane, N. J. A. (1982), *The covering radius of the Leech lattice,* Proc. Royal Soc. London, A **380**, 261-290.

Cook, J. M. (1957), *Rational formulae for the production of a spherically symmetric probability distribution,* Math. Tables Other Aids Comp., **11**, 81-82.

Cook, J. M. (1959), *Remarks on a recent paper*, Commun. ACM, **2** (No. 10), 26.

Coppersmith, D. and Grossman, E. (1975), *Generators for certain alternating groups with applications to cryptography*, SIAM J. Applied Math., **29**, 624-627.

Coxeter, H. S. M. (1973), *Regular Polytopes,* Dover, New York, third edition.

Davis, R. M. (1978), *The Data Encryption Standard in perspective,* IEEE Communications Society Magazine, **16** (November), 5-9.

Deák, I. (1979), *Comparison of methods for genercting uniformly distributed random points in and on a hypersphere,* Problems of Control and Information Theory, **8**, 105-113.

Diaconis, P. (1980), *Average running time of the fast Fourier transform*, J. Algorithms, **1**, 187-208.

Diaconis, P. (1982), *Group Theory in Statistics,* lecture notes, Harvard University.

Diaconis, P. and Graham, R. L. (1977), *Spearman's footrule as a measure of disarray,* J. Royal Stat. Soc., B **39**, 262-268.

Diaconis, P., Graham, R. L., and Kantor, W. M. (1982), *The mathematics of perfect shuffles,* Advances in Applied Math., in press.

Diaconis, P. and Shahshahani, M. (1981), *Generating a random permutation with random transpositions,* Z. Wahrscheinlichkeitstheorie, **57**, 159-179.

Diaconis, P. and Shahshahani, M. (1982), *Factoring probabilities on compact groups*, preprint.

Dieter, U. and Ahrens, J. H. (1973), *A combinatorial method for the generation of normally distributed random variables,* Computing, **11**, 137-146.

Diffie, W. and Hellman, M. E. (1976), *A critique of the proposed Data Encryption Standard*, Commun. ACM, **19**, 164-165.

Diffie, W. and Hellman, M. E. (1977), *Exhaustive analysis of the NBS Data Encryption Standard,* Computer, **10**, 74-84.

Dixon, J. D. (1969), *The probability of generating the symmetric group,* Math. Zeit., **110**, 199-205.

Durstenfeld, R. (1964), *Random permutation,* Commun. ACM, **7**, 420.

Eaton, M. L. and Perlman, M. (1977), *Generating $O(n)$ with reflections*, Pacific J. Math., **73**, 73-80.

Even, S. and Goldreich, O. (1981), *The minimum-length generator sequence problem is NP-hard,* J. Algorithms, **2**, 311-313.

Feistel, H. (1973), *Cryptography and computer privacy*, Scientific American, **228** (May), 15-23.

Feistel, H., Notz, W. A. and Smith, J. L. (1975), *Some cryptographic techniques for machine-to-machine data communications*, Proc. IEEE, **63**, 1545-1554.

Feller, W. (1957), *An Introduction to Probability Theory and Its Applications*, Volume I, Wiley, New York, second edition.

Fienberg, S. E. (1971), *Randomization and social affairs: the 1970 draft lottery*, Science, **167** (22 January), 255-261.

Fino, B. J. and Algazi, V. R. (1976), *Unified matrix treatment of the fast Walsh-Hadamard transform*, IEEE Trans. Computers, **C-25**, 1142-1146.

Fox, P. A., editor (1976), *The PORT Mathematical Subroutine Library*, Bell Laboratories, Murray Hill, New Jersey.

Furstenberg, H. (1980), *Random walks on Lie groups*, in *Harmonic Analysis and Representations of Semisimple Lie Groups*, edited by J. A. Wolf et al., Reidel Publ., Dordrecht, Holland, pp. 467-489.

Geffe, P. R. (1967), *An open letter to communication engineers*, Proc. IEEE, **55**, 2173.

Geramita, A. V. and Seberry, J. (1979), *Orthogonal Designs*, Dekker, New York.

Girsdansky, M. B. (1971), *Data privacy—cryptology and the computer at IBM*

Research, IBM Research Reports, **7** (No. 4), 12 pages. Reprinted in Computers and Automation, **21** (April, 1971), 12-19.

Golomb, S. W. (1964), *Random permutations,* Bull. Amer. Math. Soc., **70**, 747.

Goncharov, V. (1944), *Du domaine d'analyse combinatoire* (Russian, French summary), Bull. de l'Académie URSS, Sér. Math. **8**, 3-48. English translation in Amer. Math. Soc. Translations, (2) **19** (1962), 1-46.

Good, I. J. (1958), *The interaction algorithm and practical Fourier analysis,* J. Roy. Stat. Soc. **B 20**, 361-372 and **B 22**, 372-375.

Grenander, U. (1963), *Probability on Algebraic Structures,* Wiley, New York.

Guivarc'h, Y., Keane, M. and Roynette, B. (1977), *Marches aleatoires sur les groupes de Lie,* Lecture Notes in Math. **624**, Springer-Verlag, New York.

Hall, M., Jr. (1967), *Combinatorial Theory*, Blaisdell, Waltham, Mass.

Hall, M., Jr. (1975), *Semi-automorphisms of Hadamard matrices*, Math. Proc. Camb. Phil. Soc., **77**, 459-473.

Halmos, P. R. (1950), *Measure Theory*, Van Nostrand, Princeton, N.J.

Halmos, P. R. (1956), *Lectures on Ergodic Theory,* Chelsea, New York.

Hammersley, J. H. (1972), *A few seedlings of research*, in *Proc. Sixth Berkeley Symp. Math. Stat. and Prob.*, Vol. 1, pp. 345-394.

Hannan, E. J. (1960), *Time Series Analysis*, Methuen, London.

Harwit, M. and Sloane, N. J. A. (1979), *Hadamard Transform Optics*, Academic Press, New York.

Heiberger, R. M. (1978), *Generation of random orthogonal matrices*, Applied Statistics, **27**, 199-206.

Hess, P. and Wirl, K. (1983), *A voice scrambling system for testing and demonstration*, in this volume.

Hewitt, E. and Ross, K. A. (1963-1970), *Abstract Harmonic Analysis*, 2 vols., Springer-Verlag, New York.

Heyer, H. (1977), *Probablity Measures on Locally Compact Groups*, Springer-Verlag, New York.

Heyer, H., editor (1982), *Probability Measures on Groups*, Lecture Notes in Math. **928**, Springer-Verlag, New York.

Hicks, J. S. and Wheeling, R. F. (1959), *An efficient method for generating uniformly distributed points on the surface of an n-dimensional sphere*,

Commun. ACM, **2** (No.4), 17-19.

Hopf, E. (1937), *Ergodentheorie*, J. Springer, Berlin. Reprinted by Chelsea, New York, 1948.

Humphreys, J. E. (1972), *Introduction to Lie Algebras and Representation Theory*, Springer-Verlag, New York, second printing.

Ito, N., Leon, J. S. and Longyear, J. Q. (1981), *Classification of 3-(24,12,5) designs and 24-dimensional Hadamard matrics*, J. Combinatorial Theory, **A31**, 66-93.

Jansson, B. (1966), *Random Number Generators*, Stockholm.

Jayant, N. S. (1982), *Analog scramblers for speech privacy*, preprint.

Kantor, W. M. (1969), *Automorphism groups of Hadamard matrices*, J. Combinatorial Theory, **6**, 279-281.

Kantor, W. M. (1982), *Polynomial-time perfect shuffling*, preprint.

Kendall, M. (1970), *Rank Correlation Methods*, Griffin, London, fourth edition.

Kennedy, W. J., Jr. and Gentle, J. E. (1980), *Statistical Computing*, Dekker, New York.

Knop, R. E. (1970), *Random vectors uniform in solid angle*, Commun. ACM, **13**, 326.

Knuth, D. E. (1980), *Deciphering a linear congruential encryption*, Report STAN-CS-80-800, Computer Science Dept., Stanford Univ., Stanford, Calif.

Knuth, D. E. (1981), *The Art of Computer Programming, Volume 2: Seminumerical Algorithms*, Addison-Wesley, Reading Mass., second edition.

Lewis, T. G. (1975), *Distribution Sampling for Computer Simulation,* Lexington Books, Lexington, Mass.

Li, T. Y. and Yorke, J. A. (1978), *Ergodic maps on [0,1] and nonlinear pseudo-random number generators*, Nonlinear Analysis, Theory, Methods and Applications, **2**, 473-481.

Lloyd, S. P. (1977), *Random rotation secrecy systems*, unpublished memorandum, Bell Laboratories, Murray Hill, N.J.

Lloyd, S. P. (1978), *Choosing a rotation at random*, unpublished memorandum, Bell Laboratories, Murray Hill, N.J.

Logan, B. F. and Shepp, L. A. (1977), *A variational problem for random Young tableaux*, Advances in Math., **26**, 206-222.

McGonegal, C. A., Berkley, D. A. and Jayant, N. S. (1981), *Private communications,* Bell Syst. Tech. J. **60**, 1563-1572.

MacKinnon, N. R. F. (1980), *The development of speech encipherment*, Radio and Electronic Engineer, **50**, No. 4, 147-155.

MacLaren, M. D. and Marsaglia (1965), *Uniform random number generators*, J. Assoc. Comput. Mach., **12**, 83-89.

MacWilliams, F. J. and Sloane, N. J. A. (1981), *The Theory of Error-Correcting Codes*, North-Holland, Amsterdam.

Marsaglia, G. (1972), *Choosing a point from the surface of a sphere*, Annals. Math. Stat., **43**, 645-646.

Marsaglia, G., Ananthanarayanan, K., and Paul, N. (1973), *Random number generator package — "Super-Duper"*, School of Computer Science, McGill University, Montreal, Quebec.

Marsaglia, G., Ananthanarayanan, K., and Paul, N. J. (1976), *Improvements on fast methods for generating normal random variables*, Information Processing Letters, **5** (No. 2), 27-30.

Marsaglia, G. and Bray, T. A. (1964), *A convenient method for generating normal variables*, SIAM Review, **6**, 260-264.

Massey, J. L. (1969), *Shift-register synthesis and BCH decoding*, IEEE Trans. Inform. Theory, **IT-15**, 122-127.

Meyer, C. H. and Tuchman, W. L. (1972), *Pseudorandom codes can be cracked*, Electronic Design, **20** (Nov. 9), 74-76.

Mihram, G. A. (1972), *Simulation: Statistical Foundations and Methodology*, Academic Press, New York.

Moore, C. C., editor (1973), *Harmonic Analysis on Homogeneous Spaces*, Proc. Sympos. Pure Math. **26**, Amer. Math. Soc., Providence, Rhode Island.

Morris, R. (1978), *The Data Encryption Standard — retrospective and prospects*, IEEE Communications Society Magazine, **16** (November), 11-14.

Morris, R., Sloane, N. J. A. and Wyner, A. D. (1977), *Assessment of the National Bureau of Standards proposed Federal Data Encryption Standard*, Cryptologia, **1**, 281-306.

Muller, M. E. (1959), *A note on a method for generating points uniformly on n-dimensional spheres*, Commun. ACM, **2** (No. 4), 19-20.

Von Neumann, J. (1951), *Various techniques used in connection with random digits*, in *Monte Carlo Methods*, National Bureau of Standards Applied Math. Series **12**, U. S. Dept. Commerce, Washington, D.C. pp. 36-38.

Niederreiter, H. (1978), *Quasi-Monte Carlo methods and pseudo-random numbers,* Bull. Amer. Math. Soc., **84**, 957-1041.

Nijenhuis, A. and Wilf, H. S. (1978), *Combinatorial Algorithms,* Academic Press, New York, second edition.

Page, E. S. (1967), *A note on generating random permutations,* Applied Statist., **16**, 273-274.

Plackett, R. L. (1968), *Random permutations,* J. Royal Stat. Soc., **30**, 517-534.

Pratt, W. K. (1969), *An algorithm for a fast Hadamard matrix transform of order twelve,* IEEE Trans. Computers, **C-18**, 1131-1132.

Pratt, W. K., Kane, J. and Andrews, H. C. (1969), *Hadamard transform image coding,* Proc. IEEE, **57**, 58-68.

Reeds, J. (1977), *"Cracking" a random number generator*, Cryptologia, **1** (No. 1), 20-26.

Reeds, J. (1979), *Cracking a multiplicative congruential encryption algorithm,* in *Information Linkage Between Applied Mathematics and Industry* (Proc. First Annual Workshop, Naval Postgraduate School, Monterey, Calif., 1978), Academic Press, New York, pp. 467-472.

Reeds, J. (1979a), *Solution of challenge cipher,* Cryptologia, **3**, 83-95.

Riordan, J. (1958), *An Introduction to Combinatorial Analysis,* Wiley, New York.

Robbins, D. P. and Bolker, E. D. (1981), *The bias of three pseudo-random shuffles,* Aequationes Math., **22**, 268-292.

Rose, D. J. (1980), *Matrix identities of the fast Fourier transform*, Linear Alg. Applic., **29**, 423-443.

Rosenblatt, J. R. and Filliben, J. J. (1971), *Randomization and the draft lottery,* Science, **167** (22 January), 306-308.

Sakasegawa, H. (1978), *On generation of normal pseudo-random numbers,* Ann. Inst. Statist. Math., **A30,** 271-279.

Schmeiser, B. W. (1980), *Random variate generation: a survey*, in *Simulation with Discrete Models: A State-of-the-Art Survey*, edited by T. I. Oren, C. M. Shub and P. F. Roth, IEEE Press, New York.

Schrack, G. F. (1972), *Remark on Algorithm 381*, Commun. ACM, **15**, 468.

Schwerdtfeger, H. (1950), *Introduction to Linear Algebra and the Theory of Matrices*, Noordhoff, Groningen.

Shamir, A. (1981), *The generation of cryptographically strong pseudo-random sequences,* presented at "Crypto 81", Univ. of Calif., Santa Barbara, August 1981.

Shannon, C. E. (1949), *Communication theory of secrecy systems*, Bell Syst. Tech. J., **28**, 656-715.

Shepp, L. A. and Lloyd, S. P. (1966), *Ordered cycle lengths in a random permutation*, Trans. Amer. Math. Soc., **121**, 340-357.

Sibuya, M. (1964), *A method for generating uniformly distributed points on n-dimensional spheres*, Ann. Inst. Stat. Math., **14**, 81-85.

Slepian, D. (1978), *Prolate spheroidal wave functions, Fourier analysis, and uncertainty, Part V: the discrete case*, Bell Syst. Tech. J., **57**, 1371-1430.

Sloane, N. J. A. (1981), *Error-correcting codes and cryptography*, in *The Mathematical Gardner*, edited by D. A. Klarner, Prindle, Weber and Schmidt, Boston, pp. 346-382. Reprinted in *Cryptologia*, **6** (1982), 128-153 and 258-278.

Smith, J. L. (1971), *The design of Lucifer, a cryptographic device for data communications,* Report RC-3326, IBM Thomas Watson Research Center, Yorktown Heights, N.Y.

Stewart, G. W. (1980), *The efficient generation of random orthogonal matrices with an application to condition estimators*, SIAM J. Numer. Anal., **17**, 403-409.

Tashiro, Y. (1977), *On methods for generating uniform random points on the surface of a sphere,* Ann. Inst. Stat. Math., **A29**, 295-300.

Turyn, R. J. (1974), *Hadamard matrices, Baumert-Hall units, four-symbol sequences, pulse compression, and surface wave encodings*, J. Combinatorial Theory, **16A**, 313-333.

Veršik, A. M. and Kerov, S. V. (1977), *Asymptotics of the Plancherel measure of the symmetric group and the limiting form of Young tableaux* (Russian), Dokl. Akad. Nauk SSSR, **233**, No. 6. English translation in Soviet Math. Doklady, **18** (1977), 527-531.

Wallis, W. D., Street, A. P. and Wallis, J. S. (1972), *Combinatorics: Room Squares, Sum-Free Sets, Hadamard Matrices*, Lecture Notes in Math., **292**, Springer-Verlag, New York.

Walter, P. (1981), *An Introduction to Ergodic Theory*, Springer-Verlag, Berlin and New York.

Warner, G. (1972), *Harmonic Analysis on Semi-Simple Lie Groups,* 2 vols., Springer-Verlag, New York.

Wyner, A. D. (1979), *An analog scrambling scheme which does not expand bandwidth, Part I: discrete time*, IEEE Trans. Inform. Theory, **IT-25**, 261-274.

Wyner, A. D. (1979a), *An analog scrambling scheme which does not expand bandwidth, Part II: continuous times*, IEEE Trans. Inform. Theory, **IT-25,** 415-425.

Yao, A. C. (1982), private communication.

Section 4

Analogue Scrambling Schemes

ANALOGUE SPEECH SECURITY SYSTEMS

Dr. H.J. Beker,
Chief Mathematician,
Racal-Comsec Limited,
Milford Industrial Estate,
Tollgate Road,
Salisbury,
Wiltshire SP1 2JG.

1. Introduction

Speech is probably the most fundamental form of communication available to us and our society has become highly dependent on our modern, fast and accurate means of transmitting spoken messages. Usually the main aim of communicants is merely to transmit a message as quickly, accurately and cheaply as possible. There are, however, a number of situations where the information is confidential and where an interceptor might be able to benefit immensely from the knowledge gained by monitoring the information circuit. In such situations the communicants must take steps to conceal and protect the content of their spoken message. Of course, the amount of protection will vary. On occasions it is sufficient to prevent a casual 'listener' from understanding the message but there are other times when it is crucial that even a determined interceptor must not be able to deduce it.

One basic problem facing the designer of speech security equipment is that there already exist a great variety of communications circuits for the transmission of speech signals. Many of the techniques at his disposal might necessitate the restriction, of the communicator, to only a few of these types of channel. Furthermore, the designer must remain aware, at all times, that almost all speech security systems reduce, at least to some extent, the audio quality of a voice transmission. Clearly, security will not be enhanced if the link has been so badly degraded that we have to repeat the same message a number of times. There is, therefore, a need to take into consideration the type of transmission link that might be used and, for any particular security equipment, to choose an encryption system that will give the least degradation of audio quality. There is no point in having a very high security level if it is no longer possible to communicate!

There are, essentially, two techniques for encrypting speech: digital and analogue. Figure 1 illustrates the basic block diagram for a digital system.

The serial data stream that results, after the voice input has been converted to a digital signal, commonly takes one of the following values: (i) 64 kbit/s, (ii) 32 kbit/s, (iii) 16kbit/s, (iv) 9.6 kbit/s, (v) 4.8 kbit/s or (vi) 2.4 kbit/s. Utilising bit rates of 9.6 kbit/s or more normally implies an increase in the signal bandwidth after encipherment. Thus for many communication channels they cannot be used. Achievement of the lower bit rates is normally associated with a reduction in voice recognition and because of the complex algorithms required to achieve these low bit rates such devices are, at present, large and expensive. Thus, applications which involve narrowband channels and tactical levels of security (i.e relatively short cover times) require an alternative approach.

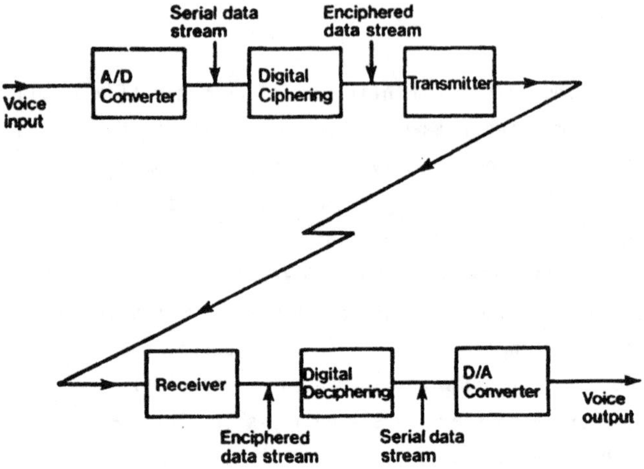

Figure 1
Digital cipher system

The object of this paper is to trace the development of analogue scrambling systems and to discuss both the advantages and disadvantages of the various techniques available. For a fuller discussion of both analogue and digital techniques see [Beker and Piper, 1982] .

2. Speech Inversion

One of the earliest forms of frequency scrambler was a device known as a speech inverter. Suppose we have a speech signal which is band-limited to the 300-3000Hz range as in Figure 2.

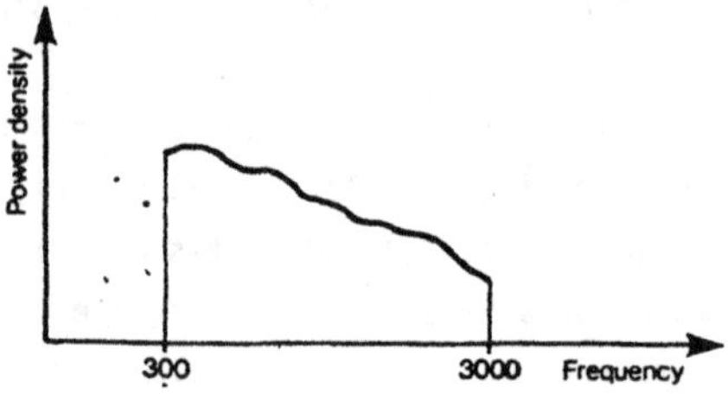

Figure 2
A speech signal band-limited to 300-3000 Hz

The basic idea of an inverter is to interchange the high and low frequencies. This can be achieved relatively easily and the result is illustrated in Figure 3.

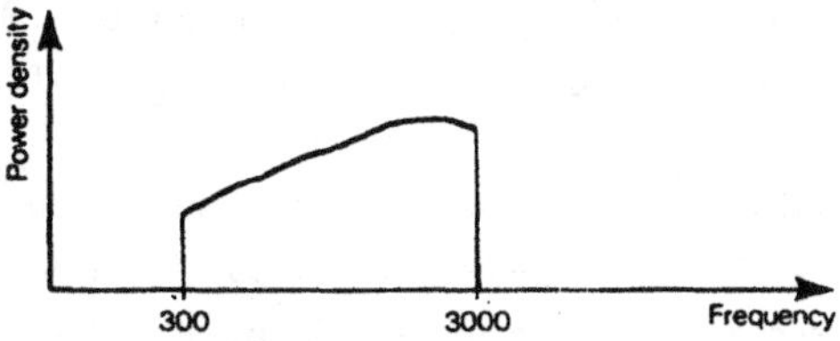

Figure 3
Power density spectrum of inverted speech signal

So far we have not introduced a key. Thus the system is simply a code which, as such, is not secure against any interceptor with a similar piece of equipment to reinvert the signal. Some improvement on this basic inversion code is obtained by using a device known as a band-shift inverter. Once this device is introduced we at least have a genuine cipher system in the sense that the concept of varying keys is introduced. One theoretical way of considering band-shift inversion is the following.

When we discussed inversion we began with a signal which was bandwidth-limited to 300-3000Hz. If our system were designed such that the inverted signal occupied a different band, say 1000-3700Hz, then we would get the signal whose spectrum is shown in Figure 4 (a). This signal is no longer in the same band as our original one, but we can arrange for it to be in this band by taking that part of the signal above 3000Hz and putting it at the low frequency end. (Note that although the signal of Figure 4 (a) has a different frequency range it has, of necessity, the same bandwidth as our original signal). This is the principle of band-shift inverting and is illustrated in Figure 4 (b).

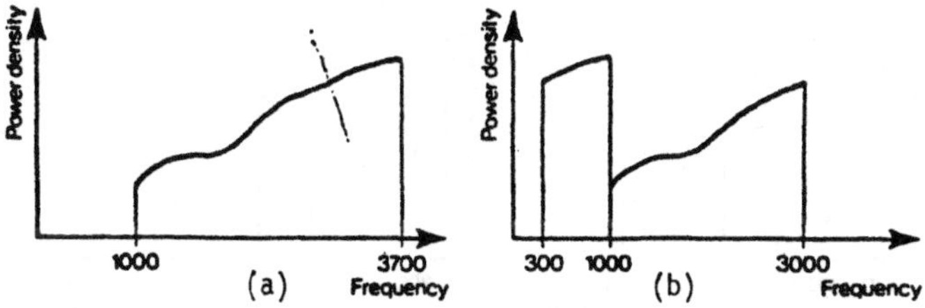

Figure 4
The principle of band-shift inversion

A typical inverter has between 4 and 16 different carrier frequencies which result in the same numbers of different 'shifts'. There are two ways in which a key may operate. The simple way is to select the shift directly. Alternatively it may be used to initialize a pseudo-random number generator, which will then select a different shift every so often. A typical time interval between shifts might be 10 or 20mS. This latter arrangement is often referred to as a cyclical band-shift inversion .

Systems relying on band-shift inverters have two obvious failings. Firstly since, at any given time, there are only a limited number of possibilities for the shift, the original signal can be recovered reasonably easily by using 'trial and error' methods with relatively simple equipment. Secondly, and perhaps more importantly, the residual intelligibility in the output signal is unacceptably high. The residual intelligibility of an output signal is that proportion of the original signal which can be understood directly when listening to the enciphered message. In this case, this is especially high after the message has been reinverted.

3. Bandscramblers

In this section we consider a third speech scrambler in the frequency domain: the bandscrambler or bandsplitter. In this case the spectrum is divided into a number of equal sub-bands and the signal is then scrambled by rearranging their order. In some of the more sophisticated systems certain of the sub-bands may also be inverted. Figure 5 illustrates a simple example with five sub-bands. The sub-bands 1, 2 and 5 have been inverted as well as displaced. For this particular example there are 5! possible re-orderings and 2^5 ways of deciding which, if any, sub-bands to invert. Thus there are $5! \times 2^5 = 3840$ possible ways of rearranging the sub-bands. Unfortunately the residual intelligibility is unacceptably high for most of these arrangements, and it is generally agreed that, if one is forced to rely on reordering alone and not use inversion, less than 10% of the possibilities provide reasonable security. Some of the reasons for the

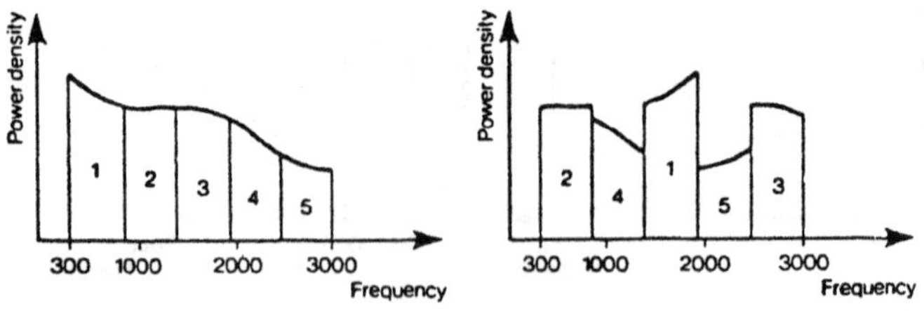

Figure 5
Band scrambling technique

high residual intelligibility are easy to understand. For instance, experiments have shown that reorderings which leave some of the sub-bands in their original positions tend to have high residual intelligibility. Since these reorderings leave part of the signal unaltered this is not completely surprising.

There is another disadvantage to this type of system. It is usual for more than 40% of the energy to lie in the first two sub-bands. So, in our example, no matter which reordering is used, as soon as the cryptanalyst finds the new positions of the first two sub-bands and translates them back, he will have recovered sufficient of the content of the signal to have a good chance of 'understanding the message'. We can improve matters slightly by having a number of different rearrangements and using a pseudo-random number generator sequence to select a new one every few hundred milliseconds. For many practical systems, the 'better' reorderings, i.e those with small residual intelligibility, are stored in a ROM (read only memory) within the equipment. For our example the system may work as follows. In a five sub-band system the number of stored reorderings is typically about 32 and consequently, since there are still 2^5 ways of inverting some or all of the sub-bands, there are 1024 rearrangements available. Each rearrangement needs 10 bits of the sequence to define it; five to determine the re-ordering and five to decide on the inversions. The sequence generator itself may have a period of many millions of bits so that the cycle of rearrangements used does not repeat itself for days. Clearly, then, the size of the key may be chosen so that it is large enough to deter an interceptor from trying all possibilities. Nevertheless, no matter what is done, the residual intelligibility of a large proportion of the arrangements is so high that this sytem cannot be considered fully secure.

In general, scramblers which affect only the frequency domain are regarded more as privacy devices than as fully secure systems. Their use tends to be limited to situations where the aim is to prevent a casual listener from understanding a conversation or possibly even a determined interceptor who does not have any reasonably sophisticated equipment. Unfortunately, the majority of the more secure systems either increase the bandwidth necessary for the signal or introduce a time delay in transmission. Both of these changes introduce their own problems and so, when the strictest security is not essential, the systems just discussed are often preferable.

We must now pay attention to the number of sub-bands in a bandscrambler. In our example we had five sub-bands and, clearly, if this number were significantly increased there would be a considerable increase in the number of reorderings available and we might expect that this would increase the security. However, the introduction of too many sub-bands would introduce too many practical difficulties. It must be remembered that the input signal has to be reconstructed at the receiver's end of the transmission link. The filters and other components used introduce noise into the signal and are not truly linear in their operation. Any modification of the signal results in the introduction of imperfections and degrades the final quality of the signal. Band-scramblers are particularly susceptible to these types of imperfection. Thus introducing a larger number of sub-bands would, for most practical transmission links, render the system either unusable or so expensive as to be uneconomical.

4. Time Element Scramblers

We will now look at scramblers which affect the time element of a signal. These time element scramblers (t.e.s) usually employ the following basic principle. The analogue signal is first divided into (equal) time periods called frames. Each frame is then sub-divided into small equal time periods called segments. Once this has been done the input is scrambled by permuting the segments within each frame. The process is illustrated diagramatically in Figure 6 where we have divided the frame into eight segments.

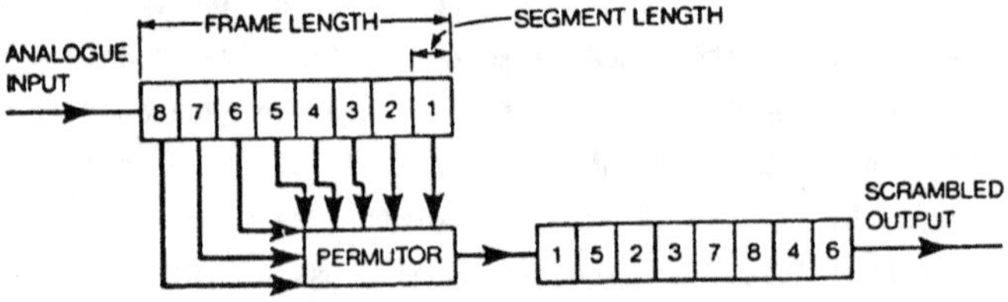

Figure 6
Time Element Scrambler

When setting up a t.e.s system it is necessary to decide upon values for the lengths of the frames and segments. Clearly the message within a segment is not distorted in this type of scrambling. Furthermore the segment length decides how much information is contained within that segment. This makes it desirable to keep the segments as short as possible and, obviously, they must be short enough that whole words cannot be contained within a segment. On the other hand, the segment length has a significant bearing on the audio quality of the transmitted message, and the quality decreases as the segment lengths get smaller. Thus, because of difficulties in implementation, there is a delicate balance to be made when choosing a segment length.

In order to choose a frame length we need to see how this choice affects the delay between the analogue signal being fed into the equipment and the signal being reconstructed as 'clear speech'. To understand this time delay we will look back at our example in Figure 6. Let us suppose that, in this example, the segment length is T seconds. Thus it takes 8T seconds for our eight speech segments to enter the scrambler. Although it is not so in our example, we may wish to permute the segments so that segment 8 is transmitted first. Consequently we will not start to transmit until all 8 segments are in the device and consequently, delays have already occurred. (For instance segment 1 must be delayed by at least 8T seconds). Once the transmission is begun it takes another 8T seconds to complete it. This, of course, causes further delays. If we wish to allow all permutations then, as in the case of our example, the last segment to reach the receiver may be the first that he must output. This means that the receiver cannot begin to decipher until he has received all 8 segments. So, even if we assume negligible time for the actual transmission, there is a time delay of 16T seconds for each speech segment. In general for a system with m segments per frame the time delay is 2mT. This, of course, is provided no restriction is placed upon the permutations to be used. Figure 7 shows which segment is being processed during each of the first 24 T-second periods of transmission, for our example.

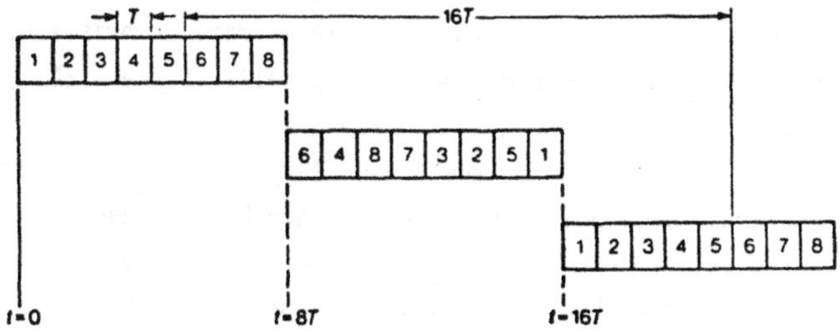

Figure 7
A timing diagram for the t.e.s. process

The effect of this delay is similar to that experienced on international telephone calls which are transmitted via satellite. From the user's point of view they are undesirable and present a case for making the frame as short as possible. Unfortunately from the security point of view we need long frames. One reason for this is that a speech 'sound' can last for quite a long time. To illustrate how disastrous short frames can be, let us suppose that we have a frame which is so short that it consists of a single tone. No matter how we scramble it the result will still be a single continuous tone (but almost certainly degraded in quality as a result of our tampering). Although this example is extreme, it nevertheless shows that if we make our frames too short we may not be able to achieve sufficient dispersement of the segments. This may result in significant parts of words being unaltered and allow a listener to guess part, or all, of the message. Furthermore it is clear that increasing the numbers of segments in a frame increases the number of permutations.

There is no obvious mathematical way for choosing optimal values for the lengths of the segments or frames. In practice it is necessary to test any given choice experimentally. One good, and very demanding, test for a t.e.s system is to read out, in an arbitrary order, some numbers between one and ten, and for some listeners to write down the numbers which they believe they 'hear'. Our reason for claiming that this test is demanding is that the listener is only trying to distinguish between ten possible sounds. This is considerably easier than trying to understand what is being said when he has no idea of the context. Experiments show that, unless the frame length is sufficiently large, most t.e.s systems perform badly against this test. One interesting point about this particular test is that most of the listeners' mistakes arise from confusing 5 and 9. This is because they are the only two of the numbers with the same vowel sound and vowel sounds are far longer than consonant sounds. Thus the listener tends to identify the vowel sounds and then guess the final word from them.

As a general rule the frame length should be as long as the user will accept. Within most of these types of equipment currently available a frame comprises between 8 and 16 segments, and each segment has a duration of, typically, between 20 and 60mS.

Once the lengths of the segments and frames are chosen the final 'ingredient' for a t.e.s is the permutation. Clearly some permutations are better than others and we must now try to decide precisely which ones are 'good'. We must also decide how to use the permutations. As in the case of band-shift inverters or bandscramblers there are a number of ways in which we can use our basic t.e.s system. We can, for instance, have a key which selects one fixed permutation and then use this given permutation for every frame. Another alternative is to let our key select several permutations and then repeatedly use them in some fixed order. However, as before, a better system is to employ some form of sequence generator to select a 'different' permutation for each frame. (Here, when we say 'different' we merely mean that the permutations are not chosen in any fixed order. Two distinct frames may well use the same permutation if the output of the sequence generator, which makes the selection, is the same). With eight segments in a frame the total number of permutations is $8! = 40320$. So, if each segment has a duration of 40mS, after about 3.6 hours of continuous usage we must be using permutations for at least the second time. However, the pattern of permutations used will not begin to repeat until the sequence repeats; i.e the period of the sequence determines the period of repetition of the sequence of permutations used. Although we have said that there are a maximum of 40320 permutations on eight symbols, we may not wish to use them all. As an illustration, consider the following two permutations. For these and future permutations, the top line represents the original order of the segments and the second line represents the order after scrambling. Thus the permutation representing the example of Figure 6 is :

$$\begin{matrix} 1 & 2 & 3 & 4 & 5 & 6 & 7 & 8 \\ 6 & 4 & 8 & 7 & 3 & 2 & 5 & 1 \end{matrix}$$

Example 1 1 2 3 4 5 6 7 8
1 3 2 4 5 7 6 8

Example 2 1 2 3 4 5 6 7 8
3 6 2 5 8 4 7 1

If we were able to listen to the effects of each of these two permutations we would find that the first has a very high residual intelligibility. In fact, after a few repetitions, we would probably begin to understand the message. The second permutation would have a far lower residual intelligibility and it is doubtful whether our understanding would increase after the first few hearings. If we now look closely at our two examples we can see the reason for this. In Example 1 four segments remain unmoved and each of the others is only moved one place. Thus the permutation does not do much to distort the input signal. However, in the second example most of the segments have been displaced much further.

If, for any permutation α, we let $\alpha(i)$ represent the position to which α moves the ith segment then the displacement of i is merely $|i-\alpha(i)|$. (For instance, in Example 2, $\alpha(2)=3$ and the displacement of 2 is $|2-3| = 1$.) We can then easily compute the average displacement of α by computing

$$\frac{1}{8}\sum_{i=1}^{8} |i-\alpha(i)|.$$

For Example 1 this average is $\frac{1}{2}$ whereas for Example 2 it is $2\frac{1}{2}$. The value of this average displacement is called the <u>shift factor</u> of the permutation and a high shift factor is essential if a permutation is to result in low residual intelligibility. But a high shift factor certainly offers no guarantees about the residual intelligibility. The following is an example, with a shift factor of 4, which could perform very badly in listening tests.

Example 3 1 2 3 4 5 6 7 8
5 7 6 8 3 2 4 1

Experiments have shown that in order to lessen the residual intelligibility, after scrambling, it is far more important to inhibit certain patterns in the permutation. In this context the most important rule is to ensure that the permutation does not leave any pair of consecutive segments, still consecutive after permuting; i.e does not contain any patterns i(i+1). Although a little less important patterns of the types i(i+2) and i?(i+1) should also be inhibited. Some authors also recommend that the following patterns should be avoided: i?(i+2), i?(i+3), i??(i+2) and i??(i+3).

The extra conditions which must be imposed are highly subjective and different people use different criteria. This results in considerable discrepancies in values for the number of 'good' permutations. For instance in [Telsy Systems, 1979] it is claimed that about half of the 40320 permutations on eight segments are useful, whereas [MacKinnon, 1980] puts the number as low as about 3000. If there is any reasonable doubt about a permutation then, since his aim is to guarantee security, the cryptographer should not use it. For this reason we feel it is safer to adopt MacKinnon's figure.

Having agreed upon our conditions for good permutations, we must now decide how our key is going to select them. Basically we have two choices. One alternative is to allow the sequence generator to produce arbitrary permutations and then 'screen' them in some way to see which ones meet our requirements. The other is to select some (or all) of the 'good' permutations, store them in a ROM within the equipment and then let the sequence generator select pseudo-randomly from the ROM. We will consider the relative merits of each alternative.

The main disadvantage of the first alternative is the time factor. If a frame lasts for 320mS, say, then at the end of that time we must have selected the next 'good' permutation. But if we merely let our sequence generate permutations at random then, although statistically the probability is very high, we cannot guarantee that it will produce a 'good' one in time. So we need to incorporate some contingency plan to protect ourselves from this possibility. This could, for example, allow the use of a previous permutation for a second time. Another possibility is to relax the screening conditions as time runs out. But both are undesirable. On the other hand the system has one big advantage. This is that, once we have a reasonable sequence generator and algorithm for generating permutations from that sequence, all the good permutations can be used. In contrast the ROM method only allows the use of those permutations which are stored. If our store is not big enough then this will not be all the good permutations. When there are only eight segments per frame then, if we take the 'strictest' definition of 'good', the number of such permutations is small enough that we can probably store them all. When this happens the ROM method is usually considered preferable. But, as soon as we start using more than eight segments per frame, the limitation on the number of permutations which can actually be used is a definite disadvantage of our second method.

In order to understand another of the advantages of the ROM method we must consider the situation of the cryptanalyst with the same machine but no knowledge of the key we are using. In this case he might be trying to decipher a frame scrambled under a permutation λ with some μ^{-1}. Thus, ideally, we also require that $\mu^{-1}\lambda$ leaves a small residual intelligibility for all acceptable pairs λ, μ. If we are using the 'screening' method to obtain our good permutations, i.e using our sequence generator to generate the permutations directly, then there is nothing we can do to ensure this. All we can do is rely on the fact that the number of permutations is so large that the probability of a 'success' of this type is small. However with only eight segments per frame, the total number of 'good' permutations is, in our view, not large enough for us to trust to 'luck' and the system is liable to be broken by straightforward trial and error. If, on the other hand, we are only using permutations which we have chosen and stored in a ROM then, at the cost of further reducing the number of usable 'good' permutations, we can protect ourselves. To do this we simply avoid putting any pair of permutations λ,μ in our ROM before first testing that $\mu^{-1}\lambda$ is sufficiently bad; i.e so that scrambling by λ and then unscrambling by μ does not give a signal which is too similar to our original one. We build up this store by testing any new entry with all the existing ones until either our ROM contains sufficient permutations for our purposes or the list of 'good' permutations is exhausted. (This process of testing permutations against each other is often referred to as <u>testing mutual security</u>).

In Figure 8 we give a block diagram for a typical time element scrambler. If the sequence generator is used to generate patterns in real time then the n-bit register and ROM must be replaced by a processor (or complex piece of hardware) to determine permutations and 'screen' them for low residual intelligibility.

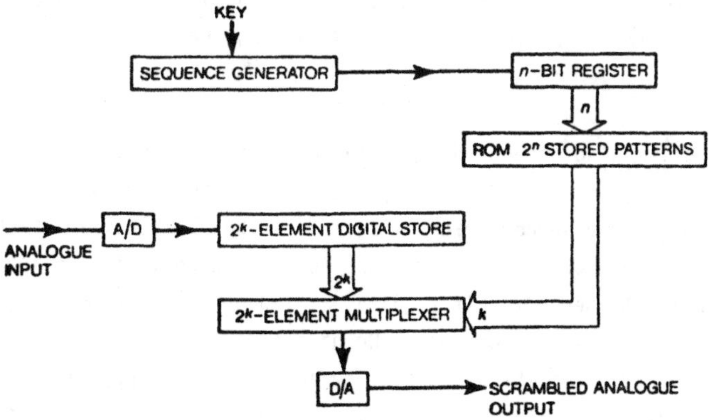

Figure 8
A typical t.e.s. system

The A/D converts the analogue input to a digital form to make the actual storing and processing easier. Once it is converted to a digital form, the signal is fed into a store of 2^k elements, where 2^k is the number of segments in a frame. (So, in our example, where we have been using eight segments per frame, k=3.) Each element of this store contains the number of digital elements appropriate to a particular segment. The segments are then removed from the store by a multiplexer addressed from the ROM containing the permutation. Finally the signal is reconverted to an analogue form for transmission. The signal transmitted still contains many of the characteristics of speech and thus still retains some residual intelligibility. There are a number of techniques for reducing this residual intelligibility still further. We will discuss three.

The first option is simply to reverse the order in which bits are taken from an element of the 2^k element digital store in Figure 8. This more or less reverses the order of a segment of speech. (The sequence generator can be used to decide which segments should be reversed in this way.) Superficially it may appear that reversing in this way will have a significant effect on the residual intelligibility. However a typical segment is 20-60mS and, in comparison, most speech 'sounds' are reasonably long. This means that this type of reversing is often ineffective. In practice use of the numbers test suggests that the success rate of a listener is reduced by about 10% if inversion is used in this way.

The second method of reducing residual intelligibility is to vary the clock rate of the A/D and D/A converters. This method, which is a form of frequency modulation, gives a two-dimensional scrambling system; time and frequency. The clock may either vary in some fixed way or be dependent on the sequence generator. In either case varying the clock rate has the effect of changing the signal in the frequency domain. Use of the numbers test indicates that this method reduces the success rate of a listener by about 15%.

The third alternative also depends on the frequency domain. This time we use a band-scrambler and a t.e.s simultaneously to again, obtain a two-dimensional system. Although such a method reduces the success rate of a listener by about 20% it has a number of disadvantages when compared to the other two. To start with it is considerably more expensive to implement. Secondly, it requires a frequency-stable, noise-free transmission path for good audio performance. (We have already observed that every modification to the signal reduces the audio quality and that frequency distortions are particularly susceptible to noise and non-linearities in the transmission path.)

5. Refinement of the t.e.s

One possible refinement of the basic time element scrambler is to use what is known as a sliding window. The sliding window system is a technique whose aim is to reduce the delay of the time element scrambler and simultaneously increase the number of permutations. The method it employs is to restrict the permutations selected to those in which no segment is delayed for 'too long'. More precisely; for an n-segment frame we restrict ourselves to those permutations in A(n,k) where

$$A(n,k)=\{\alpha\varepsilon\ S_n|\ i^{\alpha}\varepsilon\{\overline{i-1},\ldots.,\ \overline{i-k}\}\}$$

and $\bar{j}$ denotes the residue class of j modulo n with the classes labelled 1, 2,..., n.

To consider an example, let $\alpha\varepsilon A(8,3)$ be given by

$$\begin{matrix} 1 & 2 & 3 & 4 & 5 & 6 & 7 & 8 \\ 6 & 1 & 8 & 3 & 2 & 5 & 4 & 7 \end{matrix}$$

To appreciate how such a permutation is used and what delay is incurred consider the timing diagram of Figure 9 for our example above.

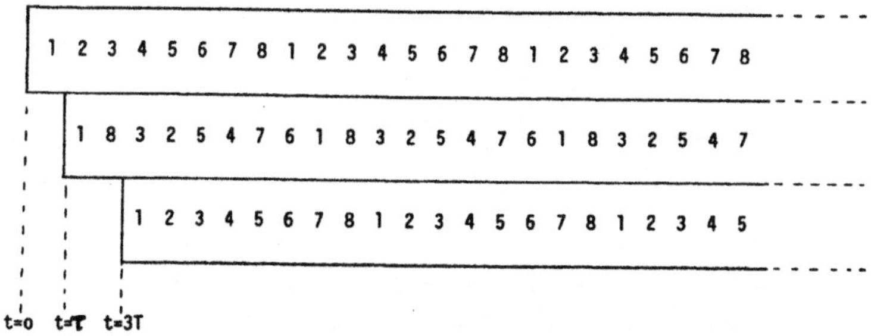

Figure 9
A Timing Diagram for the Sliding Window

In this timing diagram we see that transmission starts at time t=T, i.e as soon as the first segment has been received. Because of the condition imposed on our permutations we know that each segment will be transmitted within k segment time slots. This means that just (k-1) time slots later the receiver can begin unscrambling the speech signal. Thus in total we have a delay of kT seconds.

Certainly the delay time has been reduced but have we really increased the number of permutations? To decide this we must determine |A(n,k)| ; the size of the set A(n,k). A recently developed algorithm (see [Beker and Mitchell, 1982]) has enabled |A(n,k)| to be evaluated for some reasonably large values of n,k. For example (and also to illustrate how quickly A(n,k) grows):

$$|A(8,4)| = 264$$
$$|A(16,8)| = 5.67 \times 10^{8}$$
$$|A(24,8)| = 8.75 \times 10^{12}$$
$$|A(48,8)| = 3.68 \times 10^{25}$$
$$|A(48,12)| = 1.67 \times 10^{33}$$

Of course, as before, not all of the permutations leave a sufficiently low level of residual intelligibility. In order to appreciate some of the problems in deciding whether a permutation is adequate in terms of residual intelligibility, consider the following example of a permutation from A(8,3):

$$\begin{matrix} 1 & 2 & 3 & 4 & 5 & 6 & 7 & 8 \\ 7 & 8 & 2 & 1 & 3 & 4 & 5 & 6 \end{matrix}$$

The effect of this permutation is shown in Figure 10.

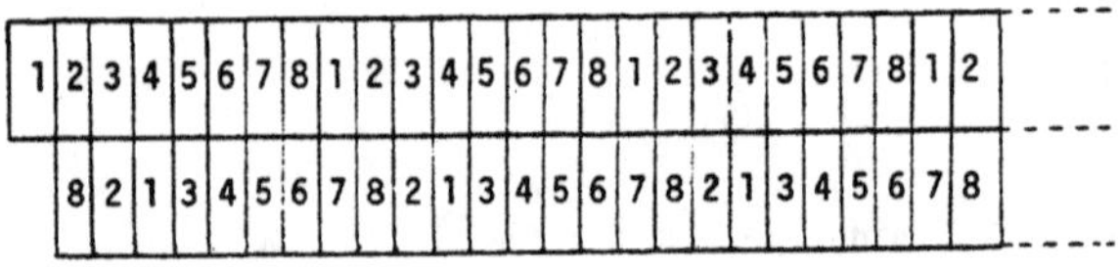

Figure 10
Timing Diagram for our Example

Experimentation has indicated that, as in the case of our earlier t.e.s., the most important property to avoid is that two segments which were originally consecutive should remain so. Thus our choice of permutations should be further restricted to the set B(n,k) where

$$B(n,k) = \{\alpha \varepsilon A(n,k) \mid i^{\alpha} + 1 \neq (i+1)^{\alpha} \text{ for any } i\}$$

For more details of the sliding window system see [Bromfield and Mitchell, 1982].

6. Summary

The analogue speech security systems that we have discussed are characterized by their analogue output which is of the same bandwidth as the original sequence. Furthermore they usually contain the distinctive syllabic rhythms, plus the frequency/power distribution patterns and phonemic sequences, of clear speech (but, of course, in a distorted form). The security depends both on the type of scrambling and on the way in which it is implemented. In particular, the use of a key-dependent sequence generator to pseudo-randomize the scrambling can considerably increase the security level. The particular method chosen for scrambling depends largely on the type and quality of the transmission channel and on the threat considered likely. (This latter consideration affects the likely investment in machinery). Scramblers range from cheap inverters, which are merely privacy devices, right through to sophisticated t.e.s. systems which offer a high level of security and force any would-be cryptanalyst to invest a great deal of time and money before he can have any hope of breaking the system. Nevertheless all scramblers must be considered purely as tactical security systems; i.e we must be prepared to assume that, eventually, any scrambled analogue message may be broken if the cryptanalyst has sufficient determination. Increasing the sophistication merely delays the inevitable. But, in practice, it may be possible to delay it for as long as the situation demands.

Acknowledgement

I would like to thank Racal-Comsec Limited for their support in the preparation of this paper.

7. References

[1] Beker, H.J and Mitchell,C.J. 'Permutations with restricted displacement', to be submitted.

[2] Beker, H.J. and Piper,F.C. 'Cipher Systems : The protection of communications', Northwood Books (1982).

[3] Bromfield, A.J. and Mitchell, C.J. 'Permutation selector for a sliding window time element scrambler', to be submitted.

[4] MacKinnon, N.R.F., 'The development of speech encipherment', Radio and Elect. Eng. Vol 50, No 4, 1980, 147-155.

[5] Telsy Systems, 'Secure Voice : Reality or myth' (1979).

A VOICE SCRAMBLING SYSTEM FOR TESTING AND DEMONSTRATION

Peter Hess
Universität Erlangen
IMMD V
Martensstr. 3
D-8520 Erlangen

Klaus Wirl
Universität Erlangen
IMMD III
Martensstr. 3
D-8520 Erlangen

1. Introduction

The principle of time division multiplexing was known before World War II [Kahn, 76]. But time division multiplexing was not very important, as it was quite complicated to implement this method in analog technique. But since digital memories have become cheaper, more TDM-systems have been introduced. Our system, called Erlangen Voice Scrambling (EVS-) system [Beth,Hess,Wirl, 82] was built for testing and demonstration.

2. The Principle of Time Division Multiplexing

The idea of time division multiplexing is to permute the speech signal in the time domain, as you can see in figure 1. We store one speech segment, say 600 ms, and divide this segment into n, say 8, parts, called blocks. These 8 blocks are now permuted by a permutation π, which is known to the receiver, but only to the receiver. He receives the permuted speech signal and rearranges the blocks by applying the inverse permutation π^{-1}. TDM has two main shortcomings: First, you have to store one whole speech segment in the sender and in the receiver, so the speech is delayed by the length of two speech segments. And second, TDM is not "absolutely" secure, so you speak about a privacy system, not a security system.

In designing a TDM-system it is important to choose the length of a block nearly the length of a phoneme. Because the Germans speak slowly, we decided that one block should last 75 ms. The number of blocks in one speech segment is limited by the delay time - every block needs a delay of 150 ms in the system - but the number of blocks should be large in

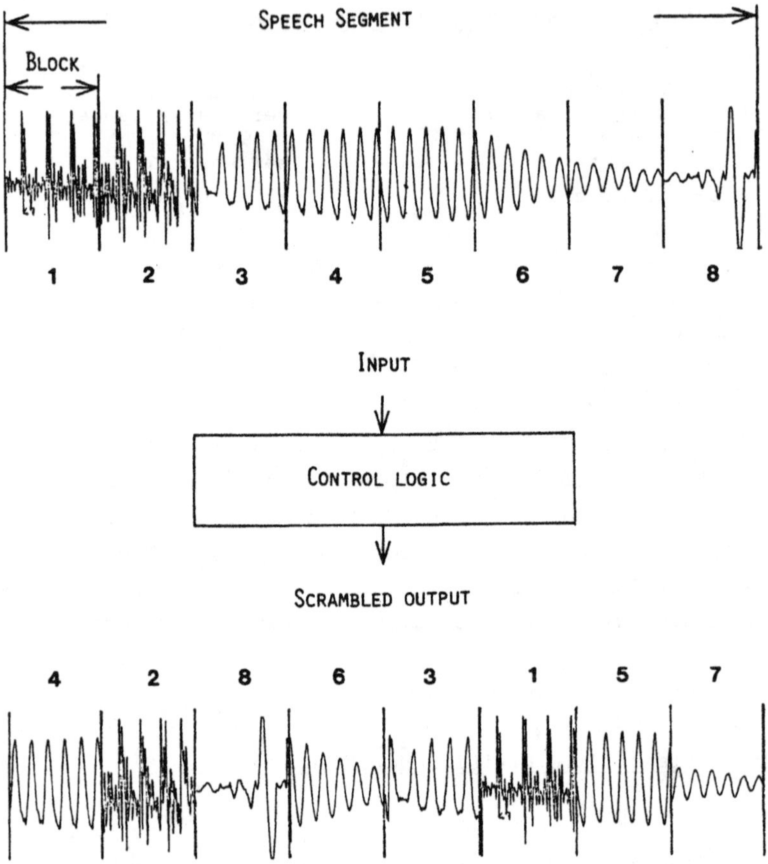

Figure 1 : The Principle of Time Division Multiplexing

order to break the words as widely as possible. Considering these constraints and the complexity of the implementation, we choose 8 blocks for each speech segment.

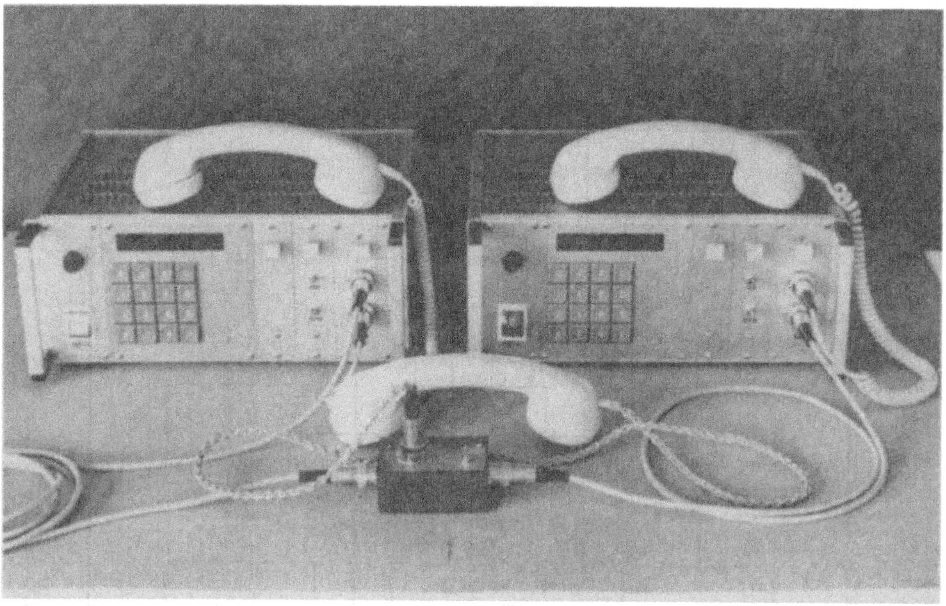

Figure 2 : EVS-System

3. The Erlangen Voice Scrambling System

Figure 2 shows our system which consists of a sender, a receiver and a line you can eavesdrop. For testing only one direction is scrambled. The skeleton of one apparatus is shown in figure 3. The speech signal is deltamodulated and portions of 600 ms are digitally stored in a 24 kbit shift register. By skillful reading, it is scrambled and then digital-analog converted by a deltademodulator.

How do we permute? Remember the definition of an inversion table:

Def.: Let $X = \{1,\dots,n\}$ be a finite set and $\pi = (\pi(1),\dots,\pi(n))$ a permutation of X. The inversion table $inv(\pi)$ is given by $(b_1,\dots,b_n)$ where $b_i = |\{j \mid i<j \wedge \pi(i)>\pi(j)\}|$.

M. Hall has shown that there is a bijective function between the set of permutations and the set of inversion tables. So we can use the inversion table instead of the corresponding permutation to permute the blocks of a speech segment. We will show you a small example, how to do it.

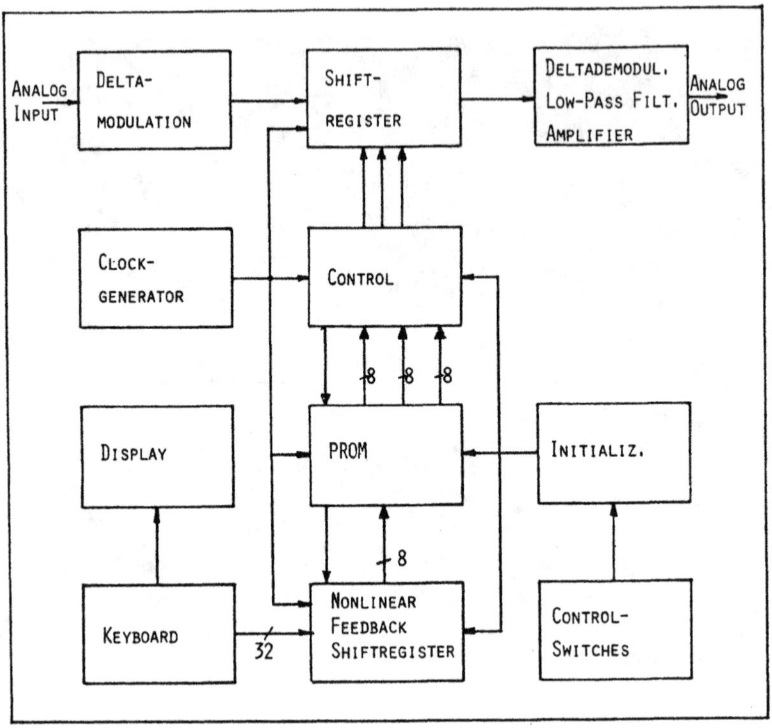

Figure 3 : Block Diagram

Example: Let $\pi = \begin{pmatrix}1,2,3,4,5,6,7,8\\1,7,3,6,5,8,4,2\end{pmatrix}$ and inv(π) = (0,6,1,4,2,1,0,0)

First we store the whole speech segment

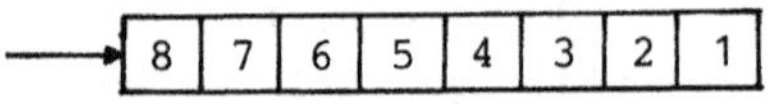

Then we read out the first block according to $b_1 = 0$. At the same time all other blocks are shifted and block 1' of the next speech segment is shifted in.

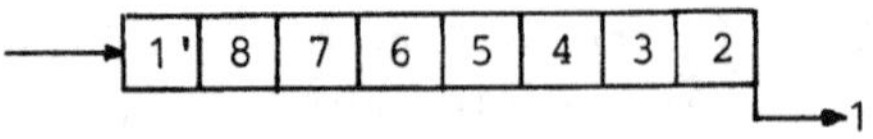

According to $b_2 = 6$ the block that now covers cell 7 is read out. Block 1' is shifted and block 2' is stored.

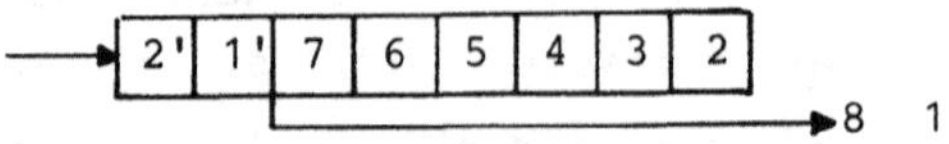

And so on until the whole permutation π is handled and the next speech segment is stored in the shift register

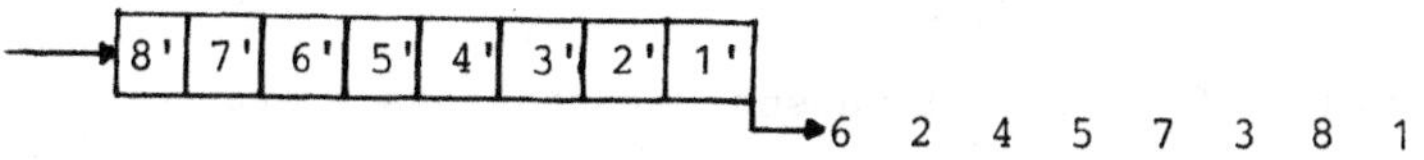

We then only need one 24 kbit shift register in each apparatus instead of two memory blocks we need using RAMs.

Which permutations do we take? We have stored 256 permutations in an EPROM. Here we know that scrambled speech is unrecognizable, and we call such permutations unrecognizable permutations. For every speech segment we take a new permutation that is pseudo-randomly chosen by a nonlinear feedback shift register. The setting of this nonlinear feedback shift register can be done with a keyboard. The key sequence consists of 8 hexadecimal digits, so that we have about 2 billions of keys.
The receiver is nearly identical to the sender. Only the initializing routine is slightly changed and the inverse permutations are stored in the EPROM.

4. Selection of Permutations

To select 256 suitable permutations for our system out of the 40,320 permutations of the symmetric group S_8, we defined a distance function $d(\pi, \varphi)$, where π and φ are permutations. The distance of a permutation π from the identity permutation $d(\pi, id)$ should be high, if π is a unrecognizable permutation; that means that texts scrambled with π are not intelligible.
Definition of $d(\pi, \varphi)$:

$$d : S_n \times S_n \rightarrow \mathbb{N}_0$$

$$d(\pi, \varphi) = \sum_{i=1}^{n} |\pi(i) - \varphi(i)|$$

We require the following properties for the permutations of our EVS-system :

a) $d(\pi, id) \geq 24$

b) $d(\pi, \omega) \geq 18$

This requirement secures that an eavesdropper who tries to understand the speech signal by unscrambling with ω fails, where ω is the permutation which simply reverses the order of the elements, $\omega = (8,7,6,5,4,3,2,1)$.

c) $d(\pi,\varphi) \geq 8$ for all chosen Permutations π and φ. Because $d(\pi,\varphi) = d(\pi^{-1}\varphi, id)$ this property prevents somebody listening, who has the same system but not the correct key.

5. Experimental Results

Next we wish to refer to the tests we made with the scrambler. The object of these two tests was to find out, whether our distance function $d(\pi, id)$ is suitable for finding good permutations for scrambling purposes. As there are only subjective criteria for measuring the intelligibility of a scrambled speech signal, we had a number of listeners who were given the task of recognizing several texts processed by our EVS-system.

In the first test we had 6 texts, which were scrambled by several fixed permutations, one for each text (see table 1). The texts had different topics and lasted about one minute. After each text the persons were asked how much of the text they understood.

TEXT	PERMUTATION	$d(\pi, ID)$	RUNS UP
1	(1,2,3,4,8,6,5,7)	6	3
2	(7,1,3,4,5,2,6,8)	12	3
3	(7,2,6,3,4,5,8,1)	20	4
4	(6,4,8,1,2,7,3,5)	26	4
5	(5,6,7,8,1,2,3,4)	32	2
6	(6,5,8,7,2,1,4,3)	32	6

Table 1 : List of Used Permutations

There were five possible degrees:

literal understanding of the text,
literal understanding of great portions of the text,
understanding the topic of the text,
understanding only single words but not the topic, and
understanding nothing.

Each complete experiment was preceeded by another scrambled text just to let our test persons hear the sound of scrambled speech, since most of them were completely untrained.

To minimize the effect of "learning" on the one hand and "tiredness" on the other hand we reversed the order of the texts in every other experiment. Thus we found the scores listed in table 2 for the six different permutations. The total number of listeners was 45.

ORDER 1 .. 6

TEXT	1	2	3	4	5	6
LITERALLY	-	-	-	-	-	-
LITERALLY (PORTIONS)	1	-	-	-	-	-
THEME	5	1	-	-	3	-
SINGLE WORDS	12	10	2	2	16	1
NOTHING	4	11	20	20	3	21

ORDER 6 .. 1

TEXT	1	2	3	4	5	6
LITERALLY	-	-	-	-	-	-
LITERALLY (PORTIONS)	7	-	-	-	-	-
THEME	1	-	-	-	-	-
SINGLE WORDS	13	19	5	1	22	1
NOTHING	2	4	18	22	1	22

Table 2 : Results of Test 1

You can see that text 1, which is scrambled with permutation 1 has the highes intelligibility score, while the permutations 3, 4 and 6 have low scores.
The intelligibility score of permutation 1 is much better in the experiments with reversed order of the texts. We think that this an effect of "learning". If you listened to such a text for several times you would probably understand it. But this is true only for permutations which are "bad" in respect to our distance function with some modifications. These modifications we got from the following result:
The two permutations 5 and 6 both have the same value of $d(\pi,id)$, but the text scrambled with permutation 5 has a higher intelligibility score than the other. This is due to the fact that permutation 5 has only 2 runs up, while the other has 6 runs up. A run up is an increasing connected subsequence of a permutation.
In our device we use only permutations with more than 3 runs up, so that texts have quite a low intelligibility even if we use only one fixed permutation for scrambling.

In our second test we had "spoken digits" as speech samples. We had seven sets of twenty four-digit-numbers. We refer to such a set also as a text. Each digit in these four-digit-numbers was spoken individually - for instance 3 - 8 - 6 - 4. After each number there was a short pause of about two seconds. These numbers were balanced so that within every set of twenty numbers each of the digits occurred eight times. Each digit also occurred exactly twice in every position within these numbers. To decrease the effect of fatigue, one test person only had to listen to three texts (or sets of numbers) in one experiment. We used a Steiner System S(2,3,7) to fix the order of the sets of numbers. Thus we got seven schemes with three texts, shown in table 3. Each text occurs once in every position of these schemes.
The texts 1 to 6 were scrambled with the same fixed permutations as those listed before. Text 0 was scrambled with randomly chosen permutations changing every 600 milliseconds.
Every test person had to listen to one scheme, that means to three texts. The test persons were told to listen to each number and write the digits they heard on their answer sheets. They were also told, that if some of these numbers were difficult to understand, they should write down their best guess rather than to leave blanks. Table 4 shows the results of this test.
The tendency of our first experiment is unchanged. This means, that texts, scrambled with a permutation with high value of our distance

Scheme	First Text	Second Text	Third Text
0	0	1	3
1	1	2	4
2	2	3	5
3	3	4	6
4	4	5	0
5	5	6	1
6	6	0	2

Table 3 : S(2,3,7)

Text	Identified Digits	Percentage
0	708	29.5 %
1	2 173	90.5 %
2	2 144	89.3 %
3	1 486	61.9 %
4	1 609	67.0 %
5	1 949	81.2 %
6	1 415	59.0 %

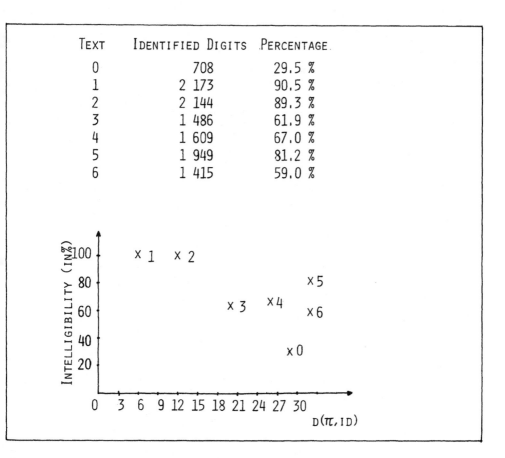

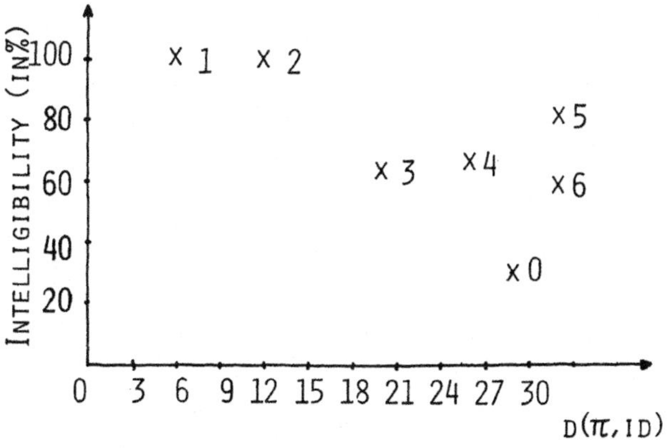

Table 4 : Results of Test 2

function $d(\pi,id)$ have lower intelligibility scores than those where $d(\pi,id)$ has lower values.
Altogether the identification score is higher for spoken digits than for complete sentences. This is caused on the one hand by the small size of the digit vocabulary and on the other hand by the pauses between two numbers. These pauses decrease the typical effect of mixing the blocks of the speech signal into an unintelligible order.
Another interesting result is the score of text 0. This text was scrambled with permutations, changing every 600 milliseconds. This kind of voice scrambling has lower intelligibility than scrambling schemes with fixed permutations. Together with pure security considerations this is the reason to scramble with frequently changing permutations. This also prevents an eavesdropper from "learning".

THE RATING OF UNDERSTANDING

IN

SECURE VOICE COMMUNICATIONS SYSTEMS

by

Klaus-P. Timmann, MSEE

managing director of TST

1) The quality of any voice message communication depends on various electroacoustic and electronic parameters of the communication equipment (frequency response, bandwidth limitation, differential delays, rythmic or arythmic distortions or interruptions, signal/noise ratio with white or frequency selective noise ...) as well as the human parameters of articulation of the speaker and the recognition and comprehension of the received message by the hearer.

2) Although the electroacoustic and electronic qualities of a voice communication system can properly be measured and evaluated, there is no easy way of determining the 'rate of understanding' that actually leads to the comprehension of the message content, which is the reason for communication. This requires first of all its 'understanding' in the means of physically noting the sounds, secondly the ability to understand the words and to make sense of the message and to consume it intellectually.

3) In linguistic research it is well known, that a message is understood even when partly distored or missing, because of the redundancy of speech.

   The elements of message are:

   - 1 The individual sentences.
     Here, one sentence can lead to the next sentence and understanding is made easier through the contextual dead-reckoning (extrapolation) performed by the human brain.
   - 2 The words, forming the sentence.
     The words in their context are easy to identify, missing words are even added by human brain to satisfy the rules of grammer.
   - 3 The syllables, forming the words.
     The redundancy of many words is so high that a missing syllable still leads to understanding of the word in the sentence.
   - 4 The sounds, forming the syllable.

Although there is no clear definition of the syllable, it is generally accepted as the 'basic unit' for the description of the relationships of sounds, which is different in all languages. If we take the syllable out of its textual environment and communicate with disarranged syllables only, the human brain can no longer perform the contextual computations and we have a means to rate the true understandability of the communication. However, the syllable as the basic unit of the word, exhibits 'tones and stresses' which identify the specific syllable in the specific word. For the research of the 'understandability', we will have to neglect the tones and stresses, and take into consideration only the base of a singular syllable.

Syllables are formed of vowels and consonants.

VOWELS are those sounds (a, e, i, o, u), formed by the vocal tract with different lip-configurations only.
Vowels may be of short or long characteristic.
CONSONANTS are b, c, d, f, g, h, j, k, l, m, n, p, q, r, s, t, v, w, x, y, z.
They can be grouped in sounding and not sounding, bilabial (spoken with both lips), labio-dental (spoken with lip and teeth), alveolar, alveolopalatal, palatal, velar, glottal.
The 'r' (in other languages also 'j' and 'ch') can be generated either by the tongue (vibration or not), or the uvula (Arabic, German or Spanish pronounciation) resulting in quite different sounding.

Single syllables are formed by the left consonant C_1, the vowel V, and the right consonant C_r, so that

$$SSYL \rightarrow X \subset C_1 \; , \; Y \times V \; , \; Z \times C_r$$

X and Z can be 0 .. 5, depending on language.
If Z = 1, the syllable is called 'closed syllable',
if Z = 0, the syllable is called 'open'.
The single syllables without 'tones and stresses' are representing the most important parameter for the rating of understanding in communications systems, when defined as the percentage of the correctly understood syllables of all communicated syllables.

e.g.

C_1	V	C_r	
0	1	1	ab, or, un
1	1	0	ba, ru, la
1	1	1	lap, nik, suk
2	1	1	flu, cri, smo

Work-sheets with the indicated mixed disarranged syllables have to be written, with at least 1000 elements for testing.

When designing these work-sheets, care should be taken that

a. the syllables are not meaningfull by themselves and
b. they are pronouncable by a normal speaker,
c. they reflect a good mixture of sounds for the particular language, for which the test is to be performed or for all languages that might be used.

Those syllables are known as Logatomes.

It was tested that the syllable-understanding-rate (SUR) of a perfect communication channel is reduced by 5 %, when the bandwidth was limited to 500-4000 Hz, and by 35 %, when the bandwidth was limited to 500-1700 Hz. (The test was performed for English, French and German). This means that bandwidth reductions from 100 to 500 Hz are much less important, than bandwidth reductions in the higher frequency area.

From the syllable-understanding-rate (SUR), there is a relationship to the word-understanding-rate (WUR), which is highly nonlinear, approximately according to this table, which proves the contextual processing of the human brain.

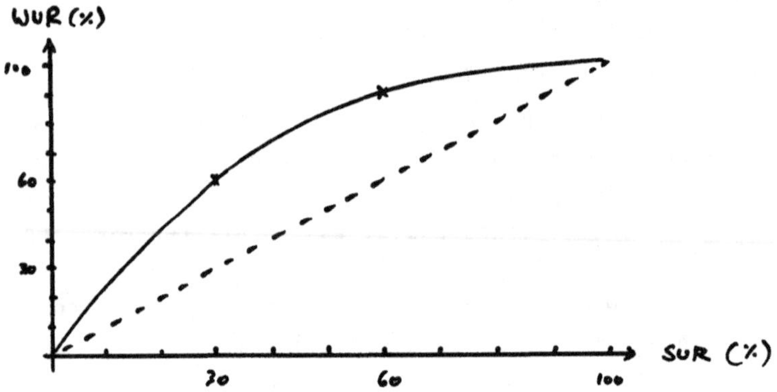

graph showing SUR against WUR

From the WUR the MUR (message-understanding-rate) can be tested and a similar relationship will be found, so that it is obvious that there is a sharp degradation of understanding, when the SUR is less than 35 %, and a perfect comprehension of message text with SUR of better than 65 %. It should be noted that various influences can reduce the SUR, e.g. reduced bandwidth and/or low volume (old telephone systems), in-band white noise (VHF/UHF radio) and in-band splatter and beep-tones (HF radio). It widely depends on the speaker and hearer, how well syllables and thus messages can be understood. There are wide differences in personnel due to training, concentration and mental condition.

4) The rating of understanding in cryptophonic communications differs from normal communications in that the use of cipher equipment (or scramblers) may result in a severe reduction of SUR in addition to those found in 'clear'.

   -1 Most frequently, secure communications reduces the available signal/noise ratio to 20-40 db due to quantizing noise of analogue/digital converters or feedthrough of mixing frequencies.
   At 20 db (most 9 or 16 KHz digital cipher sets), the SUR is heavily reduced and even the word-understanding is degraded.
   at 30 db, the SUR will be slightly reduced,
   at 40 db a reduction was not noticeable.

   -2 Ciphered communication commonly produces distortions of 10 - 20 % by deforming the audio signals, where everything above 10 % surely will reduce the understanding, as it was measured by the SUR test method.

   -3 Distortion through blanking signals and nonconformities in rearranging the time segments of time division equipments.
   This generally is giving a noticeable reduction in SUR.
   Time segments are in the length of 8-52 ms with the equipment on the market, 4 to 32 time elements are used. The audio quality of the equipments as measured by the SUR varies substantially (depending on the exact synchronization between speaker-set and hearer-set and differential delays of the line or radio set).

5) In order to test various equipments for performance and comparison it should be done so that the test can be reproduced by oneself or others with the same results:

-1 Design proper syllable work sheets as explained,
-2 set up the equipment in the lab,
-3 introduce from a tape recorder the attenuation, white noise or splatter and beep tone distortions of the communication channel, as it is expected in real-life and establish SUR.
-4 Make different speaker-hearer tests and note the SUR. Since the tests will vary between every pair of 'speaker-hearer', a true comparison of the equipments is possible only, when comparing the individual results of each speaker-hearer pair.

Only the SUR-method of scientific evaluation with reproduceable system variables gives satisfactory results for the evaluation of secure communication systems.

Field tests are mostly not reproduceable and might lead to the procurement of equipment that is not best for the purpose.

As wrote Lord Kelvin:

> 'I often say, when you can measure what you are speaking about, and express it in numbers, you know something about it, but when you cannot measure it, when you cannot express it in numbers, your knowledge is of a meager and unsatisfactory kind.'

LIST OF USED LITERATURE

Chomsky-Halle 1968 — Noam Chomsky and Morris Halle, _The Sound Pattern of English,_ New York 1968

Delattre 1965 — Pierre Delattre, _Comparing the Phonetic Features of English, French, German and Spanish_, Heidelberg 1965

Hala 1960 — Bohuslav Hâla, "autour de problême de la syllable", _Phonetica_ 5 (1960). 159 - 168

Martens 1965 — Carl und Peter Martens, _Phonetik der deutschen Sprache,_ München 1965

Scholz 1972 — Hans-Joachim Scholz, _Untersuchungen zur Lautstruktur Deutscher Wörter,_ München 1972

ANALYSIS OF MULTIPLE ACCESS CHANNEL USING MULTIPLE LEVEL FSK

László Győrfi István Kerekes
Technical University of Budapest
H-1111 Budapest
Stoczek u. 2.
Hungary

Abstract. For multiple level FSK system of multiple user communication a model is considered containing independent parallel noisy OR channels. The error probability is calculated if a random block code and a majority type decoding rule is applied.

Channel model

Initiated by Viterbi [1], Goodman, Henry and Prabhu [2] investigated the performance of a multiple access channel consisting of multiple frequency bands, and they gave an approximation on the probability of decoding error for a random code and a majority type decoder. Our purpose is to give a channel model for this problem and an exponential bound on the probability of error.

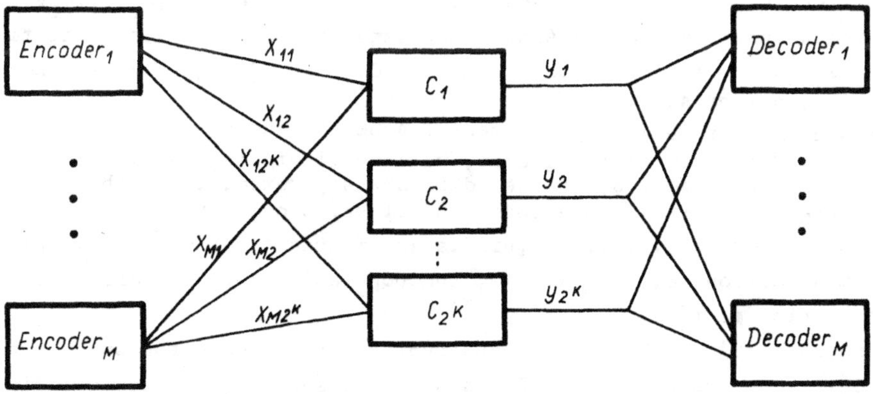

Fig. 1.

Suppose that each of the M users can access the parallel channels C_1, $C_2,\dots C_{2K}$ /Fig. 1./. C_j is assumed to be a noisy OR channel, i.e. C_j is an OR channel followed by a binary memoryless channel with transition probabilities p_F /false alarm, $0\to1$/ and p_D /deletion, $1\to0$/ /$j=1,2,\dots 2^K$ /Fig. 2./. $C_1,C_2,\dots C_{2K}$ are independent.

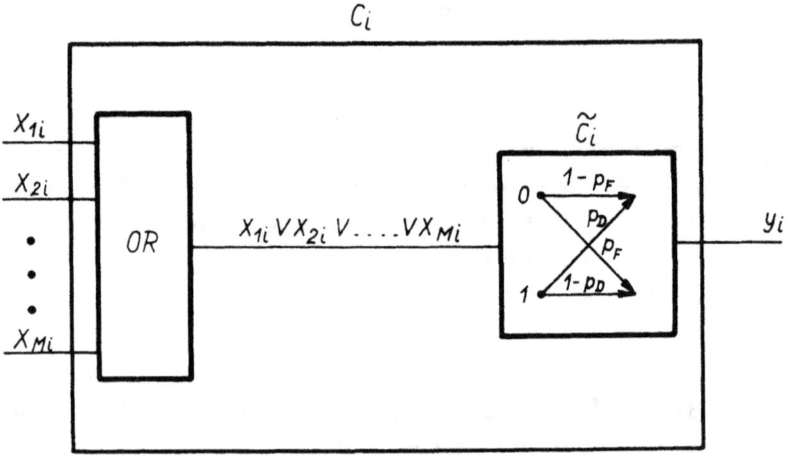

Fig. 2. The channel C_i

The channels $C_1,C_2,\dots C_{2K}$ are the models of the 2^K frequency bands. The transmitters send the bit 1 through one of the channels $C_1,C_2,\dots C_{2K}$, which means that they send a single frequency sinus signal in a bit time. The receivers try to detect the subset of $C_1,C_2,\dots C_{2K}$ through which sinus signals were sent.

This channel is a multiple access channel. Although each of the receivers has the same input sequence, we investigate the case, when the encoders are asynchronous, the decoders are separated, the i-th decoder is synchronized to the i-th encoder and it knows only the codebook of the i-th encoder /i=1,2,...M/. This is an important scheme of multiple user communication if, for example, the population of the users is changing from time to time.

Einarsson [3] and Timor [4] constructed a block code for such channel if $C_1,C_2,\dots C_{2K}$ are noiseless OR channels and supposed a fixed or slightly varying population of users.

Coding-decoding rule

Independent encoder-decoder pairs are assumed and a random coding procedure is applied. The source alphabet is the set $1,2,\ldots 2^K$ for all sources. Each encoder has a memoryless sequence of random variables with uniform distribution on the set $1,2,\ldots 2^K$. The encoder produces a binary matrix of $Lx2^K$ as follows: let E_j be a matrix having 1-s in the j-th row, 0-s otherwise. The source letter j is encoded to a binary matrix D_{ij} the columns of which are the rotations of E_j and the size of the rotations is generated by a segment of length L of the random sequence of the i-th encoder /Fig. 3./. The element a_{nm} of the matrix D_{ij} is transmitted through the channel C_n at the moment m /$n=1,2,\ldots 2^K$, $m=1,2,\ldots L$/.

The i-th decoder has the random sequence of the i-th encoder and it is synchronized to the i-th encoder. For the received block /matrix/ the i-th decoder executes the inverse rotations made by the i-th encoder and decodes the character $\hat{j}$ if the $\hat{j}$-th row has the most 1-s /Fig. 4./. In case of ties arbitrary character is chosen.

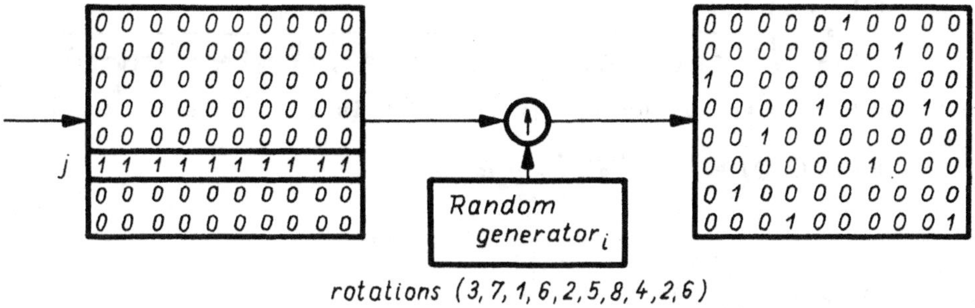

Fig. 3. Encoding

Probability of error

Introduce the notation

$$R_{sum} = \frac{MK}{L2^K}$$

for the sum of the equal code rates of the encoders. Given a source letter j the probability of error does not depend on j because of the properties of the random sequences of the rotations. Let P_e be the probability of the decoding error.

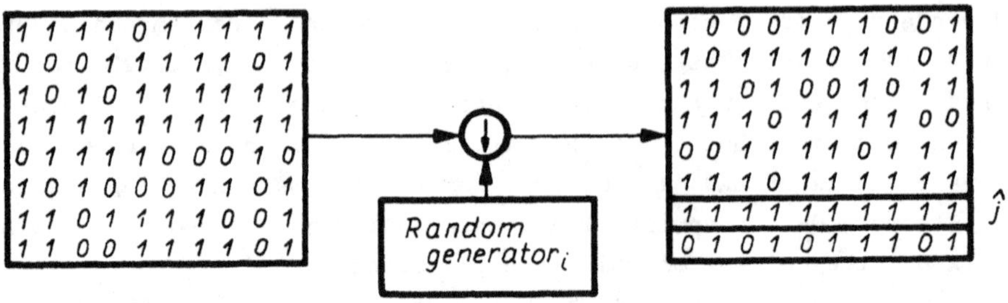

Fig. 4. Decoding

Theorem If $M \le 2^K$ and $p_D + p_F < 1$, then

$$P_e \le 2^{-K\left(\frac{F(M/2^K,\, p_D,\, p_F)}{R_{sum}} - 1\right)}$$

where

$$F(c, p_D, p_F) \triangleq$$

$$\triangleq -2c \cdot \log_2\left(\sqrt{(1-p_D)(1-p_D-(1-p_D-p_F)e^{-c})} + \sqrt{p_D(p_F+(1-p_D-p_F)e^{-c})}\right).$$

In the case of $p_D = p_F = 0$ each C_j $/j=1,2,\ldots 2^K/$ is a noiseless OR channel and

$$F(c,0,0) = -c \log_2(1-e^{-c})$$

implying

$$P_e \le 2^{-K\left(\frac{\ln 2}{R_{sum}} - 1\right)}$$

if $M/2^K \sim \ln 2 = 0.69\ldots$ This particular case was investigated in [5]. Consider some values of $F(c, p_D, p_F)$. If $0.5 \le c \le 1$ then

$F(c,0,10^{-3}) \ge 0.66$	$F(c,10^{-3},0) \ge 0.59$
$F(c,0,10^{-2}) \ge 0.65$	$F(c,10^{-2},0) \ge 0.47$
$F(c,0,10^{-1}) \ge 0.57$	$F(c,10^{-1},0) \ge 0.23$

which shows that the increase of p_F does not affect the probability of error, however, the increase of p_D is crucial.

Proofs

In the proof of the Theorem we apply the following Chernoff-type bound:

Lemma Let $Y_1, Y_2, \ldots Y_n$ be $-1,0,+1$ valued independent random variables such that

$$p_+ \triangleq \mathbb{P}(Y_i = 1)$$
$$p_- \triangleq \mathbb{P}(Y_i = -1)$$
$$p_0 \triangleq \mathbb{P}(Y_i = 0)$$

If $p_+ < p_-$, then $\mathbb{P}(\sum_{i=1}^{n} Y_i \geq 0) \leq [2\sqrt{p_+ p_-} + p_0]^n$

<u>Proof</u> $\frac{p_+}{p_-} < 1$, therefore by the Markov-inequality

$$\mathbb{P}(\sum_{i=1}^{n} Y_i \geq 0) = \mathbb{P}\left(\left(\frac{p_-}{p_+}\right)^{\frac{1}{2}\sum_{i=1}^{n} Y_i} \geq 1\right) \leq$$

$$\leq \mathbb{E}\left[\left(\frac{p_-}{p_+}\right)^{\frac{1}{2}\sum_{i=1}^{n} Y_i}\right] = \prod_{i=1}^{n} \mathbb{E}\left[\left(\frac{p_-}{p_+}\right)^{\frac{1}{2} Y_i}\right] =$$

$$= \left[p_+\sqrt{\frac{p_-}{p_+}} + p_0 + p_-\sqrt{\frac{p_+}{p_-}}\right]^n =$$

$$= \left[2\sqrt{p_+ p_-} + p_0\right]^n$$

<u>Proof of the Theorem</u> We calculate the probability of error for the communication from the 1-st encoder to the 1-st decoder. Without loss of generality assume that the source character 1 was sent. Denote by X_{ij} /$i=1,2,\dots,L$, $j=1,2,\dots 2^K$/ the matrix after the inverse rotations in the decoder, then

$$P_e \leq \mathbb{P}\left(\bigcup_{i=2}^{2^K} \left\{\sum_{j=1}^{L} X_{ij} \geq \sum_{j=1}^{L} X_{1j}\right\}\right)$$

therefore

$$P_e \leq \sum_{i=2}^{2^K} \mathbb{P}\left(\sum_{j=1}^{L} X_{ij} \geq \sum_{j=1}^{L} X_{1j}\right) \leq$$

$$\leq 2^K \mathbb{P}\left(\sum_{j=1}^{L} (X_{2j} - X_{1j}) \geq 0\right) \qquad (1)$$

Apply the Lemma for $Y_j = X_{2j} - X_{1j}$. Clearly

$$\mathbb{P}(X_{2j} = 1) = [1 - (1 - 1/2^K)^{M-1}](1 - p_D) + (1 - 1/2^K)^{M-1} p_F =$$

$$= 1 - p_D - (1 - p_D - p_F)(1 - 1/2^K)^{M-1} \qquad (2)$$

$$\mathbb{P}(X_{1j} = 1) = 1 - p_D \qquad (3)$$

furthermore

$$p_+ = \mathbb{P}(X_{2j}=1)(1-\mathbb{P}(X_{1j}=1)),$$
$$p_- = (1-\mathbb{P}(X_{2j}=1))\,\mathbb{P}(X_{1j}=1),$$
$$p_0 = 1 - p_+ - p_-.$$

The condition $p_+ < p_-$ of Lemma is equivalent to

$$\mathbb{P}(X_{2j}=1) < \mathbb{P}(X_{1j}=1)$$

which is equivalent to the condition $p_D + p_F < 1$. Thus

$$2\sqrt{p_+ p_-} + p_0 =$$
$$= \left(\sqrt{\mathbb{P}(X_{1j}=1)\mathbb{P}(X_{2j}=1)} + \sqrt{\mathbb{P}(X_{1j}=0)\mathbb{P}(X_{2j}=0)}\right)^2. \quad (4)$$

If $M \leq 2^K$, then it is easy to check that

$$\left(1-\frac{1}{2^K}\right)^{M-1} \geq e^{-\frac{M}{2^K}}. \quad (5)$$

For $p_D + p_F < 1$ we have $\mathbb{P}(X_{2j}=1) < \mathbb{P}(X_{1j}=1)$ and in this range (4) is a monoton increasing function of $\mathbb{P}(X_{2j}=1)$, therefore by (3) and (5) for the notation $c = M/2^K$ we get

$$\tilde{F}(c, p_D, p_F) \triangleq 2\sqrt{p_+ p_-} + p_0 \leq$$
$$\leq \left(\sqrt{(1-p_D)(1-p_D-(1-p_D-p_F)e^{-c})} +\right.$$
$$\left. + \sqrt{p_D(p_D+(1-p_D-p_F)e^{-c})}\right)^2$$

Thus

$$P_e \leq 2^K \tilde{F}(M/2^K, p_D, p_F)^L =$$

$$= 2^K \tilde{F}(M/2^K, p_D, p_F)^{\frac{K\frac{M}{2^K}}{R_{sum}}} =$$

$$= 2^{-K\left(\frac{F(M/2^K, p_D, p_F)}{R_{sum}} - 1\right)}$$

<u>Generalization</u>

A possible generalization of model considered is seen on Fig. 5. The output of the channel C_i^* is defined as follows:

$$z_i = \begin{cases} 0 \text{ if } \sum_{j=1}^{M} x_{ij} = 0 \\ 1 \text{ if } \sum_{j=1}^{M} x_{ij} = 1 \\ 2 \quad \text{otherwise.} \end{cases}$$

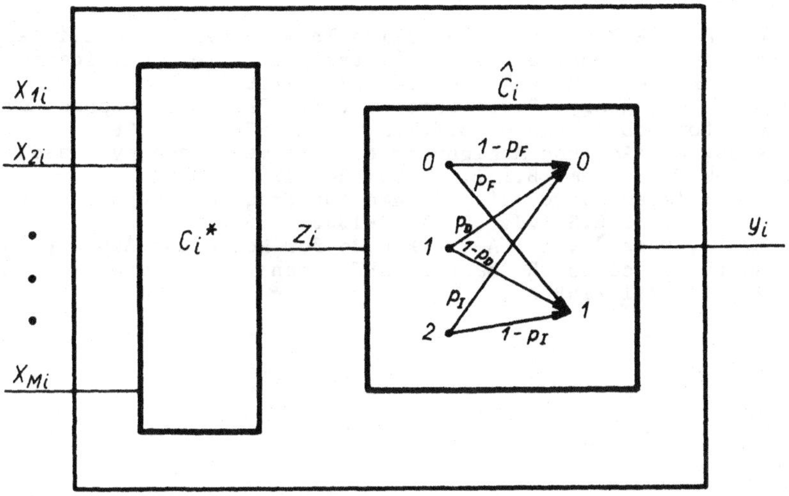

Fig. 5. Generalization

$\hat{C}_i$ denotes a channel with ternary inputs and binary output. p_F /0→1/, p_D /1→0/ and p_I /interference, 2→0/ denote the transition probabilities, respectively. In the case of $p_I = p_D$ the model is reduced to that of Fig. 2. In this model the variables X_{1j} and X_{2j} introduced in the proof of the Theorem are not independent, but the sequence of $Y_j = X_{2j} - X_{1j}$ is independent. After calculating the probabilities p_+, p_-, p_o as a function of p_F, p_D, p_I one can get a similar upper bound for P_e as before with a much more involved function $F(c, p_F, p_D, p_I)$ instead of $F(c, p_D, p_F)$. The condition $p_- > p_+$ of Lemma is met if

$$1 - p_F - p_D p - p_I (1 - p) > 0$$

where

$$p \triangleq \left(1 - \frac{1}{2^K - 1}\right)^{M-1}$$

While the original model is suitable, for example, for mobile digital radiotelephony in the direction base to mobile, this generalization of the model might be applied modeling the direction mobile to base.

References

1 Viterbi, A.J: A Processing Satellite Transponder for Multiple Access by Low-Rate Mobile Users. Digital Satellite Communications Conference, Montreal, October 23-25 /1978/

2 Goodman, D.J., Henry, P.J., Prabhu, V.K.: Frequency-hopped Multilevel FSK for Mobile Radio. B.S.T.J. 59, 1257-1275 /1980/

3 Einarsson, G.: Address Assignment for a Time-Frequency-Coded, Spread-Spectrum System. B.S.T.J. 59, 1241-1255 /1980/

4 Timor, U.: Improved Decoding Scheme for Frequency-Hopped Multilevel FSK System. B.S.T.J. 59, 1839-1855 /1980/

5 Györfi, L., Kerekes, I.: A Block Code for Noiseless Asynchronous Multiple Access OR Channel. IEEE Trans. on Information Theory 27, 788-791 /1981/

ANALOG SCRAMBLING BY THE GENERAL FAST FOURIER TRANSFORM

Franz Pichler[†]
Department of Systems Science
Johannes Kepler University of Linz
A-4040 Linz, Austria

. Introduction

here are many different methods in use to scramble voice signals. Two f them seem to be of special importance: band-splitting and time-divi- ion. In existing devices for scrambling analog signals often only one f these methods is implemented. However, newer equipment, which is ealized by digital circuitry, allow us to use both methods, band split- ing and time division, at the same time.

ur paper presents a methematical basis for that situation. We show how n operation which realizes band-splitting - in a generalized way - and ime division can be designed, and point out that such an operation can e realized by a fast algorithm. The mathematical background is the heory of group-characters for finite abelian groups and the theory of he general fast fourier transfrom (GFFT).

esides voice scrambling the method is well suited for image scrambling f remotely sensed signals ([PI80]). A development project on that topic s under preparation at the Institute of Systems Science at the Univer- ity of Linz.

. The Basic Scrambling Scheme

e assume that the analog signal a is already sampled. Therefore a is discrete time-function $a: N_o \to R: k \to a(k)$. Frequently the signal a as to pass some pre-processing operation T before it is scrambled. T ould be a digital filter, e.g. for data-compression, or the DPSS-trans- orm of Wyner ([WY 79]).

Currently as Visiting Professor at the Department of Systems Science, chool of Advanced Technology, State University of New York at Bingham- on, Binghamton, N.Y. 13901. The work presented in this paper was artially supported by the Oesterreichischen Fonds zur Foerderung der issenschaftlichen Forschung under FWF-Project Nr 4141.

The resulting analog signal x constitutes the "plaintext" for our scrambling operation E_K which is controlled by a key K. The resulting "ciphertext" $y = E_K(x)$ is reprocessed to form the final scrambled output of the system. Figure 1 shows the block-diagram of this basic arrangement.

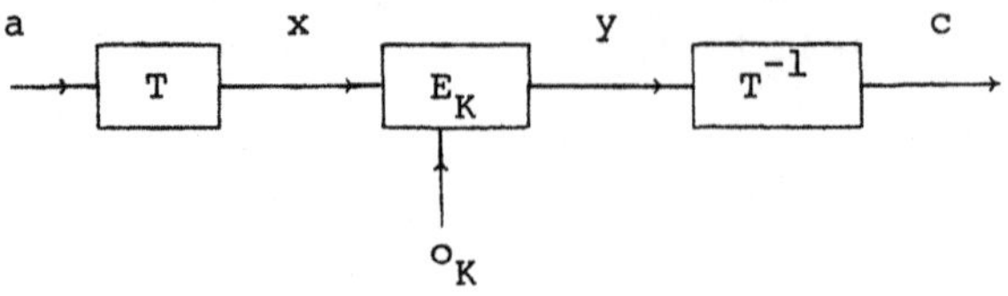

Figure 1: Basic Scrambling Scheme

We assume furthermore that scrambling is done blockwise with block-length N. So the input signal x is divided into blocks $x_i = (x_{io}, x_{i1}, \ldots, x_{iN-1})$; $i = 0,1,2.,,,.$ In every step i the scrambling operation E_K receives the block x_i to compute the block $y_i = (y_{io}, y_{i1}, \ldots, y_{iN-1})$ of the scrambled signal y;

$$y_i = E_K(x_i). \tag{1}$$

In the case of band-splitting E_K is often realized by the conventional discrete fourier-transform F and subsequent coordinate permutation $\hat{\pi}_K$,

$$y_i = \hat{\pi}_K(F(x_i)). \tag{2}$$

$\hat{\pi}_K$ is assumed here to be an operation which permutes the components of the spectrum block $\hat{x}_i = Fx_i = (\hat{x}_{io}, \hat{x}_{i1}, \ldots, \hat{x}_{iN-1})$. Therefore $\hat{\pi}_K$ is in a one-to-one correspondence with a related permutation $\hat{\Pi}_K$ on the set $\{0,1,\ldots,N-1\}$ of indices of x_i.

Time division of x by E_K is realized very simply. It consists of the coordinate permutation of the time-block x_i

$$y_i = \pi_K(x_i). \tag{3}$$

In terms of cryptographic notation time-division of x_i establishes a polyalphabetic substitution-cipher; band-splitting is a product cipher, consisting of a linear cipher as given by the fourier transform F followed by the substitution $\hat{\pi}_K$. In many cases of application K will not tay constant for each block x_i but will change with i: $K = K(i)$.

o finish the basic discussion of the introduced scrambling scheme we ombine band-splitting with time-division and get a scrambling operation $_K = \hat{\pi}_K F \pi_K$ by

$$y_i = E_K(x_i) = \hat{\pi}_K(F(\pi_K(x_i))). \tag{4}$$

quation (4) is the scrambling operation which we would like to generalize y using the generalized discrete fourier-transform Ω replacing F.

. <u>The General Discrete Fourier-Transform</u>

t is well known that the "classical" fourier-transform has been gener-lized in many different ways. A famous example of it is the Laplace-ransform which is produced by extension of the real domain R of the ignals to the complex number field C. Another example is the fourier-ransform as discussed in abstract harmonic analysis. In this theory n arbitrary locally compact abelian group G takes the place of R. It s this generalization of the fourier-transform which we will use. How-ver, for our purposes it will be sufficient to consider finite abelian roups. Let G denote an arbitrary finite abelian group and let f denote function defined on G with values in the set C of complex numbers; $: G \to C$. Then the fourier-transform $\hat{f}$ of f is defined as the function $: \Omega \to C$ which is given by

$$\hat{f}(\omega) = \sum_{g \in G} \overline{\omega(g)}\, f(g), \tag{5}$$

here Ω denotes the character-group of G which consists of the set of haracter-functions $\omega: G \to C$, with their multiplication as group-compo-ition; $\overline{\omega(g)}$ denotes the complex conjugate of $\omega(g)$. The inverse trans-orm which maps $\hat{f}$ to f is given by

$$f(g) = \frac{1}{|G|} \sum_{\omega \in \Omega} \omega(g)\, \hat{f}(\omega). \tag{6}$$

or a more detailed treatment of the fourier-transform for functions efined on abelian groups consult for example the book of Rudin ([RU62]).

ur goal is to represent the transforms as given in (5) and (6) in matrix notation. For that we define an ordering in both groups G and Ω by numbering the elements from 0 to N-1 (we assume that G as N elements); $G = \{g_0, g_1, \ldots, g_{N-1}\}$ and $\Omega = \{\omega_0, \omega_1, \ldots, \omega_{N-1}\}$. Then equations (5) and (6) can be written in the form

$$\underline{\hat{f}} = \underline{\Omega}\ \underline{f} \text{ and} \tag{7}$$

$$\underline{f} = \frac{1}{N}\ \underline{\Omega}^*\ \underline{\hat{f}} \tag{8}$$

where $\underline{f}$ and $\underline{\hat{f}}$ denote the column-vectors of length N which are given by $\underline{f}^T = [f(g_0), f(g_1), \ldots, f(g_{N-1})]$ and $\underline{\hat{f}}^T = [\hat{f}(\omega_0), \hat{f}(\omega_1), \ldots, \hat{f}(\omega_{N-1})]$; the symbol T denotes transposition of matrices. $\underline{\Omega}$ denotes the $N \times N$ matrix $\underline{\Omega} = [\omega_{ij}]$ which is given by $\omega_{ij} = \overline{\omega_{i}(g_j)}$; Ω^* denotes the adjoint matrix of Ω. We call $\underline{\Omega}$ the fourier-matrix of G. From equations (7) and (8) we see that $\frac{1}{N}\ \underline{\Omega}^*\ \underline{\Omega} = I$ (the unity matrix). Therefore $\underline{\Omega}$ is basically unitary.

After this mathematical exposition we return to the scrambling scheme.

4. Generalized Band-Splitting

We identify now the set of indices $\{0,1,2,\ldots,N-1\}$ of a block $x_i = (x_{io}, x_{i1}, \ldots, x_{iN-1})$ of input-text with the arbitrary abelian group G of order N. Then x_i can be considered as a function $x_i: G \to C$. Since now the (generalized) fourier-transform $\hat{x}_i$ of x_i is defined we are able to define a generalized version of band-splitting by permuting the spectrum-text $\hat{x}_i$ with $\hat{\pi}_K$. In matrix notation this reads as

$$\underline{y}_i = \underline{\hat{\pi}}_K\ \underline{\Omega}\ \underline{x}_i \tag{9}$$

where $\underline{\hat{\pi}}_K$ denotes the matrix representation of $\hat{\pi}_K$. Using the matrix representation $\underline{\pi}_K$ for the permutation $\pi_K: G \to G$ we are in the position to combine time-division with generaliced band-splitting to establish the scrambling operation

$$\underline{y}_i = E_K(\underline{x}_i) = \underline{\hat{\pi}}_K\ \underline{\Omega}\ \underline{\pi}_K\ \underline{x}_i. \tag{10}$$

The matrix $\underline{\Omega}\ (\hat{\pi}_K, \pi_K) := \underline{\hat{\pi}}_K\ \underline{\Omega}\ \underline{\pi}_K$ of this operation is derived from _ by row permutation according to $\hat{\pi}_K$ and column permutation according π_K.

5. Fast Realization of $\Omega(\hat{\pi}_K,\pi_K)$

In order that the operation as described in equation (10) is of practical use in analog signal scrambling it is necessary to have efficient algorithms for hardware or software realization available. For the general fourier-transform it is known that there exist algorithms which reduce the number of primitive operations from $O(N^2)$ to $O(N \log N)$ ([Nl 71], [KU 77]). If we assume that the permutation π_K and $\hat{\pi}_K$ do not reduce the effectiveness of the algorithm, then we have found also a fast realization for the matrix-operation $\underline{\Omega}(\hat{\pi}_K,\pi_K) = \underline{\hat{\pi}}_K \, \underline{\Omega} \, \underline{\pi}_K$. However, since in practical application the group G has to be chosen depending on the key K, i.e., $G = G_K$, we have to make sure also that the related scrambling operation $\underline{\hat{\pi}}_K \, \underline{\Omega}_K \, \underline{\pi}_K$ is easy to realize for any choice of the key K. For implementations in software this is the case since the specific group-structure of G_K does not change the effectiveness of the realization algorithm ([FE 82]). For hardware implementation which depends on a fixed wiring scheme, the applicability of our general scrambling scheme remains to be investigated.

6. Conclusion

The concepts which have been presented in this paper show that it is possible to generalize the common scrambling method of band-splitting such that fast algorithms for digital realization are also available. By the generalization an additional parameter for the key K is obtained, which determines the specific group G_K and therefore also the related character-group Ω_K on which the spectral representation of the signals are based. The method also provides a tool for the cryptanalyst since it enables one to represent signals and systems by the different possible spectral-representations. Such an application could be to eliminate time-division permutations π_K which are of convolution type with respect to a certain group G and therefore provide little security.

An extension of the method to nonabelian groups seems to be possible and also desirable, since in that case also fast realization algorithms exist ([KA 77]).

Finally it should be mentioned that the paper received its final form after listening to a lecture of N.J.A. Sloane on "Encyrption by Random Rotations" ([SL 82]). In this lecture a randomly chosen orthogonal matrix M was suggested for the transform of the signals. As parameters determining the user-key, permutations of the rows and columns of M and sign-changes were proposed. By the framework presented in our paper we see that for the special case that a fourier-matrix $\underline{\Omega}$ is chosen for M, the method suggested by the Sloane lecture is, neglecting the sign-change operation, exactly our generalized scrambling method.

References

[FE 82] Fellner, H.: Master Thesis (in German), Institut für Systemwissenschaften, Universität Linz, 1982

[KA 77] Karpovsky, M.G.: Fast Fourier Transforms on Finite Non-Abelian Groups, IEEE Trans. on Computers, Vol. C-26, No. 10, October, 1977, pp. 1028-1030.

[KU 77] Kunz, H.: Approximation optimaler linearer Transformationen durch eine Klasse schneller, verallgemeinerter, Fourier-Transformationen. Dissertation ETH5832, Zurich, Juris Druck & Verlag, Zurich, 1977.

[NI 71] Nicholson, P.: Algebraic Theory of Finite Fourier Transforms. Journal of Comp. and Systems Sc. 5 (1971), pp. 524-547.

[PI 80] Pichler, F.: Fast Linear Methods for Image Filtering, in: Applications of Information and Control Systems (D.G. Lainiotis and N.S. Tzannes, eds.) Reidel Publishing Corp., Denhaag, 1980, pp. 3-11.

[RU 62] Rudin, W.: Fourier Analysis on Groups Interscience, New York, 1962.

[SL 82] N.J.A. Sloane: "Encryption by Random Rotations" Lecture presented at the "Workshop on Cryptography" Burg Feuerstein March 29 - April 2, 1982 organized by Institut für Mathematische Maschinen und Datenverarbeitung, Universität Erlangen (Thomas Beth).

[WY 79] Wyner, A.D.: An Analog Scrambling Scheme which does not Expand Bandwith, IEEE Trans. on Informational Theory, Vol. 25, Part I (May 1979), Part II (July 1979).

Section 5

Stream Ciphers

STREAM CIPHERS

Fred Piper

INTRODUCTION

The object of this talk is to give a general introduction to stream ciphers. It will provide the general background for the other four talks on this topic. We begin by giving a diagramatic definition of a stream cipher :

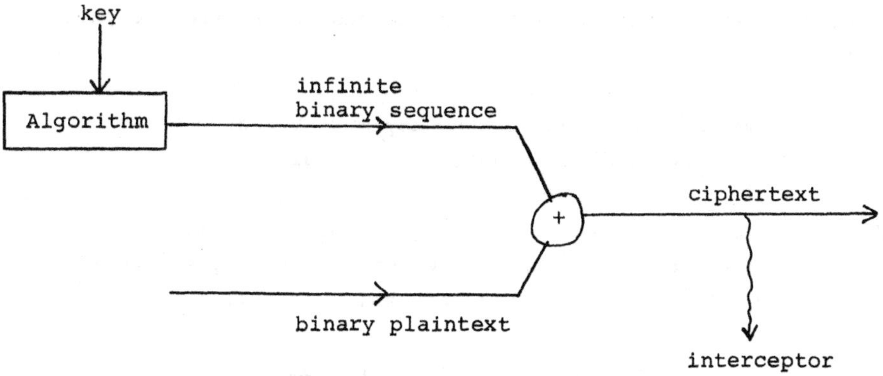

(Of course the interceptor is not part of the system. He is included in the diagram merely to indicate where interceptions are likely to take place.)

Before discussing stream ciphers we must mention one of their most important properties; there is no error propagation. Although it is not always the case, error propagation is often undesirable and, on these occasions, stream ciphers may be preferable to block ciphers. We also note that the algorithm is usually a finite state machine.

In his lecture Professor Bauer stressed the importance of never underestimating the interceptor. This, of course, is vital and in this context it means we must assume :

<u>C1</u> The cryptanalyst has a complete knowledge of the cipher system, (i.e. all security lies in the key).

C2 The cryptanalyst has obtained a considerable amount of the ciphertext.

C3 The cryptanalyst knows the plaintext equivalent of a certain amount of the ciphertext.

Assumptions C1, C2, C3 may sound pessimistic but they are almost certainly realistic, and any cipher system should be secure under these assumptions. (Of course in any given situation the terms 'considerable' and 'certain amount' will need to be quantified. Their precise values will depend on the system in use and the level of security required.) If we accept these assumptions then, in the case of a stream cipher, we require :

A1 The number of choices for the key must be large enough that the cryptanalyst cannot try them all.

A2 The infinite sequences must have a guaranteed minimum length for their periods. (We will then only encipher messages which are shorter than this period.)

A3 The ciphertext must appear to be 'random'.

In general terms, a 'random' sequence is one in which knowledge of a number of consecutive elements does not help anyone trying to predict the next one. Of course any sequence generated by a finite state machine is periodic and, consequently, cannot be truly random. (Clearly knowledge of a complete cycle enables one to determine the entire sequence.) Nevertheless if the period is large enough then we can obtain sequences which are effectively random.

Golomb has suggested the following randomness postualtes for a binary sequence of period p.

R1 A cycle of length p has $\left[\frac{p}{2}\right]$ 0s or 1s.

R2 In a cycle of length p, ½ the runs have length 1, ¼ have length 2, and, in general, for each i for which there are 2^{i+1} runs, $\frac{1}{2^i}$ of the runs have length i. Moreover for each of these lengths there are equally many gaps and blocks.

R3 The out-of-phase autocorreclation is a constant.

If a sequence satisfies R1, R2, R3 then it is said to be G-random. It must not be forgotten that G-randomness is a property which relates to the entire sequence. In practice the cryptographer hopes that the length of the sequence obtained by the cryptanalyst will be small in comparison with the period. Thus it is important that our sequence also has 'good' local randomness properties, and there are many statistical tests for investigating local randomness.

Now that we have stated some requirements for our sequence we must look at ways of achieving them. In most practical systems the finite state machine is a shift register and we will devote the rest of this talk to sequences which can be generated by shift registers.

SHIFT REGISTER SEQUENCES

An n-stage shift register produces a sequence of state vectors $(s_0(t),s_1(t),\ldots,s_{n-1}(t))$, (where $t = 0,1,2,..$), such that $s_i(t+1) = s_{i+1}(t)$ for $i = 0,1,\ldots,n-2$ and $s_{n-1}(t+1) = f(s_0(t),s_1(t),\ldots, s_{n-1}(t))$. If we write s_t for $s_0(t)$ then we get the shift register sequence $s_0s_1s_2\ldots$ which we write as (s_t). The function f is called the feedback function of the register and if $f(s_0,s_1,\ldots,s_{n-1}) = c_0s_0+c_1s_1+\ldots+c_{n-1}s_{n-1}$ then we say that the register is linear. Clearly, for any linear shift register,

(1) (s_t) is completely determined by $c_0,c_1,\ldots,c_{n-1},s_0,s_1,\ldots,s_{n-1}$.

(2) $s_{n+t} = \sum_{i=0}^{n-1} c_{t+i}s_{t+i}$ for $t = 0,1,2,\ldots$

(3) (s_t) has period $\leq 2^n-1$.

In order to study the relation between (s_t) and the parameters listed in (1) we define the characteristic polynomial f(x) by $f(x) = c_0+c_1x+\ldots+c_{n-1}x^{n-1}+x^n$. If, adopting Selmer's notation, we let $\Omega(f)$ be the set of all sequences generated by f(x) then $\Omega(f)$ is an n-dimensional vector space over Z_2.

For any polynomial g(x) in $Z_2[x]$ the exponent of g(x) is e if $g(x)\,|\,x^e+1$ but $g(x)\nmid x^r+1$ for any $r < e$. The important properties of exponents are

(a) $e \leq 2^n-1$ for all polynomials of degree n

(b) if $(s_t) \in \Omega(f)$ and f(x) have exponent e then the period of (s_t) divides e

(c) if f(x) is irreducible with exponent e and $(s_t) \in \Omega(f)$ then the period of (s_t) is e.

(Note: (b) and (c) assume that (s_t) is not the sequence of all zeros.)

From (a) we know that the maximum possible size for the exponent of a polynomial of degree n in $Z_2[x]$ is 2^n-1. If f(x) has degree n and exponent 2^n-1 then f(x) is called primitive and any non-null $(s_t) \in \Omega(f)$ is often called a PN-sequence. The following are true :

T1 If f(x) is primitive then any non-zero choice for $s_0, s_1, \ldots, s_{n-1}$ will result in a sequence of period 2^n-1.

T2 PN-sequences are G-random, (the out-of-phase autocorrelation being $\frac{-1}{2^n-1}$).

T3 There are $\frac{\phi(2^n-1)}{n}$ primitive polynomials of degree n.

From these results it is clear that we can produce sequences satisfying A1, A2, A3. Since these conditions were chosen to ensure that our system satisfied the conditions C1, C2, C3 we might, (but of course will not!), be tempted to assume we have a 'good' system. The 'flaw' in our system is a consequence of the fact that a PN-sequence with period 2^n-1 is completely determined by any set of 2n consecutive terms. Thus if a cryptanalyst knows 2n consecutive bits of plaintext and ciphertext equivalents he will be able to deduce the entire message. To do this he will have to invert a suitable n by n binary matrix whose entries are the 2n known bits of the sequence. So if the 'certain amount' in C3 is more than 2n consecutive bits the cover time for our system will be roughly the time needed for the inversion of an n by n binary matrix. This weakness comes from the use of a linear feedback function and forces us to add a fourth requirement :

A4 The system must appear to be non-linear. (For a shift register this means that the feedback function f must contain at least one product involving two (or more) of the s_i.)

There are two standard ways of introducing non-linearity :

(a) use a non-linear feedback function,

(b) use more than one linear shift register.

I do not intend to say much about (a). There does not appear to be the same type of 'neat' mathematical theory as for linear shift registers. For instance there is no natural analogue to T1. Anyone interested in studying non-linear feedbacks should consult the recent survey article of Ronse (1980).

With (b) it is absolutely crucial to realise that a complex looking system with numerous shift registers is not necessarily secure. In fact it is imperative to combine the registers in such a way that it is possible to analyse the overall system. An important concept in this type of analysis is the linear equivalence of a sequence. The linear equivalence of a binary sequence is the length of the shortest linear shift register which can generate it. If (s_t) has linear equivalence n then knowledge of 2n consecutive bits completely determine (s_t). Thus, no matter how we actually generate (s_t), we must ensure that it has a large linear equivalence. In fact large enough that the cryptanalyst should not be able to invent an n by n matrix with our required cover time. This means that we now require our sequence to have a long period, large linear equivalence and good statistical properties. However it is important to realize that these three properties only offer necessary conditions for a good sequence. They certainly do not guarantee a secure system.

It is also important to realize that no two of these properties guarantee the third and that each of the three of them must be carefully checked. As an illustration of what can go wrong, consider the following two 'bad' examples of ways of combining registers.

Example 1

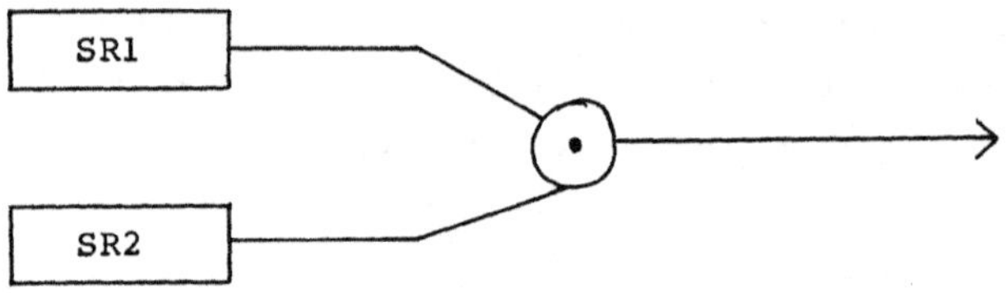

SR1 is a shift register generating a PN-sequence of period 2^n-1
SR2 is a shift register generating a PN-sequence of period 2^m-1
$\odot$ is an AND gate, or modulo 2 multiplier.

If $(2^m-1, 2^n-1) = 1$ it is easy to show that the period of the resulting sequence is $(2^m-1)(2^n-1)$. However the sequence will not have good statistical properties because roughly $\frac{3}{4}$ of its entries will be 0. (This is because $0\times 1 = 1\times 0 = 0\times 0 = 0$ and $1\times 1 = 1$.) Thus, no matter what the linear equivalence this example is unsuitable.

Example 2 A J-K flip-flop

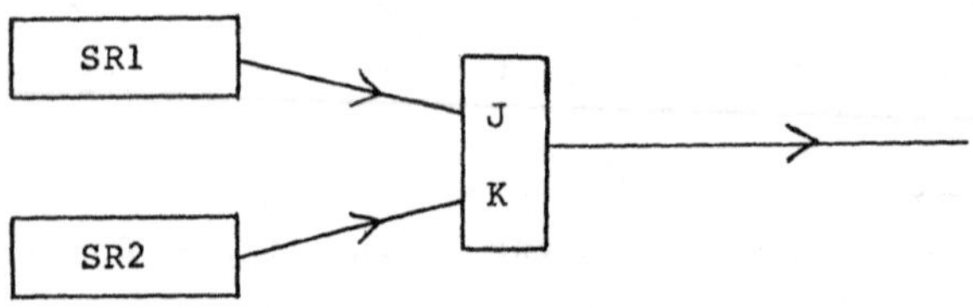

Here SR1 and SR2 are as in Example 1 and the action of the J-K flip-flop is described by :

J	K	q_n
0	0	q_{n-1}
0	1	0
1	0	1
1	1	$\bar{q}_{n-1}$

where $q_0q_1q_2\ldots$ is the output sequence.

Here the problem is not the periodicity or the statistical properties. It arises from the fact that knowledge of two consecutive entries of the output sequence determines an entry in one of the two shift register sequences. Thus knowledge of a certain amount of the output sequence will eventually give enough information to determine each of the two shift register sequences.

In general it is often difficult to actually determine the linear equivalence of a sequence. But it is probably dangerous to use one with an unknown linear equivalence. At present one of the most promising ways of combining two registers is by multiplexing. This is the topic of the next lecture and provides a suitable place for this talk to end. However, to put things into perspective, we must not forget that the sequence generator is only a part of the overall system and that, although crucial, a good sequence in no way guarantees a secure system.

Professor F.C. Piper,
Department of Mathematics,
Westfield College, (University of London),
Kidderpore Avenue,
London, NW3 7ST. U.K.

REFERENCES

The standard references for shift register sequences are Golomb (1967) and Selmer (1966). As mentioned earlier Ronse (1980) is a survey of shift registers with non-linear feedback. An overall discussion of stream ciphers can be found in Beker and Piper (1982).

Beker, H.J. and Piper, F.C.	Cipher Systems : the protection of communications Northwood Books, 1982.
Golomb, S.W.	Shift Register Sequences Holden-Day, 1967.
Ronse, C.	Non-linear shift registers : A survey MBLE Research Report R430, 1980.
Selmer, E.S.	Linear recurrence relations over finite fields Univ. of Bergen, 1966.

MULTIPLEXED SEQUENCES : SOME PROPERTIES OF THE MINIMUM POLYNOMIAL

S.M. Jennings,
Racal Research Ltd.,
Worton Grange Industrial Estate,
Reading, Berks. RG2 0SB,
England.

1. INTRODUCTION

In recent years considerable interest has been shown in the generation of binary sequences which have good randomness properties. Such sequences play an important role in cipher systems. In many situations the enciphering process begins with the conversion of the plaintext into a string of bits by means of a binary "alphabet". The sequence is then added to the plaintext bit by bit, using modulo 2 arithmetic and the resulting ciphertext is then transmitted. Decipherment is accomplished simply by adding the sequence to the ciphertext in a similar manner.

Any sequence generated by a finite-state machine cannot be considered truly random, since if the input is ultimately periodic then the output must be also. An interceptor who knows the plaintext equivalent of k bits of ciphertext also knows k bits of the sequence. If it takes less than k bits of sequence to determine its entirety, then the whole message may be discovered. If the generated sequence has minimum polynomial of degree d, then knowledge of any 2d consecutive bits is sufficient to determine it completely. Thus we have three important requirements for a sequence used in a cipher system :-

1. The period of the sequence must be long (at least as long as any message to be enciphered).

2. The sequence should have a minimum polynomial of large degree.

3. The sequence must appear random.

It must be emphasized that for a good sequence generator within a a cipher system, these requirements are certainly necessary but clearly not sufficient (for example see [Beker & Piper, 1982]).

In this paper we show how a special class of sequences, called multiplexed sequences, satisfy the first two requirements. This provides some evidence that multiplexed sequences may be eligible for use as a building block ([Beker & Piper, 1982]) towards a complete sequence generator. In practice, a sequence used in a cipher system would be far more complex than those we shall consider here.

This work is contained in my Ph.D. thesis entitled "A Special Class of Binary Sequences" submitted to the University of London in 1980. I would like to thank Dr. Henry Beker and Professor Fred Piper for their invaluable advice and encouragement and Racal Electronics Ltd. for their help and support.

2. PRELIMINARIES

An n-stage (binary linear feedback) shift register consists of n binary storage elements $S_0, S_1, \ldots, S_{n-1}$ called stages, connected in series. The contents of the stages change in time with a clock pulse according to the rule :-

Let $S_i(t)$ denote the content of S_i after the t-th time pulse ($t = 0,1,2,\ldots$). Then

$$S_i(t+1) = S_{i+1}(t) \quad \text{for } i = 0,1,\ldots,n-2$$

and $$S_{n-1}(t+1) = \sum_{i=0}^{n-1} c_i S_i(t) \qquad (\text{mod } 2)$$

where the c_i are all specified as 0 or 1.

This is represented by the diagram below where $c_i = 1$ denotes a closed connection and $c_i = 0$ an open one.

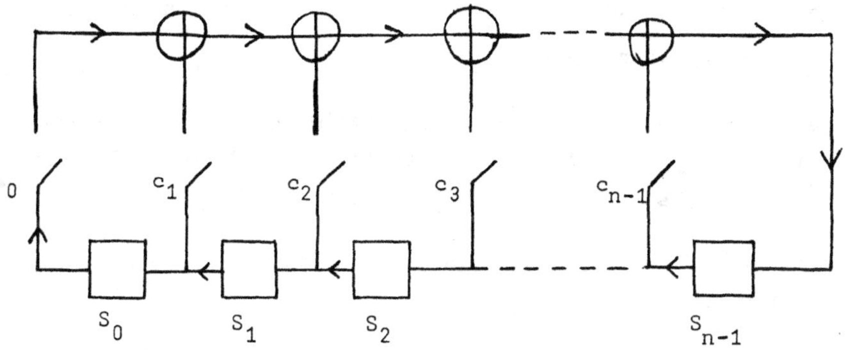

We assume $c_0 = 1$ so that $S_{n-1}(t+1)$ is dependent on $S_0(t)$.
If we put $s_t = S_0(t)$, we get an infinite binary sequence denoted (s_t) satisfying the linear recurrence relation

$$s_{t+n} = \sum_{i=0}^{n-1} c_i s_{t+i} \quad \text{for } t = 0,1,2,\ldots \qquad (1)$$

We often identify a shift register with its characteristic polynomial $f(x) = 1+c_1x+c_2x^2+\ldots+c_{n-1}x^{n-1}+x^n$ (remembering $c_0 = 1$). The set of all infinite binary recurring sequences (s_t) generated by $f(x)$ is called the solution space of f and is denoted $\Omega(f)$. Each of the 2^n possible initial states corresponds to a unique sequence in $\Omega(f)$. It is well-known [Selmer, 1966] that $\Omega(f)$ is a vector space of dimension n over GF(2), where addition and scalar multiplication of sequences are the obvious termwise operations. The infinite sequence of all zeros arising from an initial state of n zeros is the null sequence.

For proof of the following, the reader is referred to [Zierler, 1959].

Result 1 For any non-null periodic binary sequence (s_t), there exists a unique polynomial $g(x)$ with $g(0) \neq 0$, such that for any polynomial $h(x)$ with $h(0) \neq 0$, $(s_t) \in \Omega(h)$ if and only if $g(x)|h(x)$.

The polynomial $g(x)$ of Result 1 is the minimum polynomial of the sequence (s_t).

We let ${}_\tau(s_t)$, or ${}_\tau(s)$ denote the sequence $(s_{t+\tau})$, the translate of (s_t) by τ. It can be shown that if the minimum polynomial $g(x)$ has degree d, then the d sequences $(s_t), {}_1(s_t), \ldots, {}_{d-1}(s_t)$ are linearly independent in $\Omega(g)$ [Selmer, 1966].

For an arbitrary polynomial $f(x)$ over GF(2) with $f(0) \neq 0$, we say $f(x)$ belongs to exponent e if $f(x)|x^e+1$, $f(x)\nmid x^r+1$ for $0<r<e$. Zierler has proved the following :-

Result 2 If $f(x)$ is the minimum polynomial of (s_t), then the period of (s_t) equals the exponent of f.

Consequently if $f(x)$ has degree n and is primitive (irreducible over GF(2 and of exponent 2^n-1), the period of any non-null sequence in $\Omega(f)$ is 2^n-1. That is, the shift register goes through all 2^n-1 non-zero states before repeating. Such sequences are called PN sequences and their properties are described in [Golomb, 1967].

As shown by Zierler, the general solution of a linear recurrence relation (1) can be given explicitly in terms of the roots (assumed distinct) of the characteristic polynomial.

<u>Result 3</u> Let $f(x) = 1+c_1x+\ldots+c_{n-1}x^{n-1}+x^n$ be a polynomial over GF(2). Let $GF(2^r)$ be a splitting field of f(x) over GF(2) and suppose that the roots $\alpha_0,\alpha_1,\ldots,\alpha_{n-1}$ of f(x) in $GF(2^r)$ are distinct. Then for each binary sequence $(s_t) \in \Omega(f)$, there exist uniquely determined elements $\delta_0,\delta_1,\ldots,\delta_{n-1}$ in $GF(2^r)$ such that for t = 0,1,2,...

$$s_t = \sum_{j=0}^{n-1} \delta_j \alpha_j^{\,t} \qquad (2)$$

Conversely, if for any n-tuple $\delta_0,\delta_1,\ldots,\delta_{n-1}$ of elements of $GF(2^r)$, all the terms of the sequence (s_t) of elements of $GF(2^r)$ defined by (2) lie in GF(2), then $(s_t) \in \Omega(f)$.

<u>Remark</u> If f(x) is irreducible over GF(2) with roots α^{2^j} (j = 0,1,...,n-1) in $GF(2^n)$, it may be shown [Selmer, 1966] that the δ_j in equation (2) are of the form $\delta_j = \gamma^{2^j}$ (j = 0,1,...,n-1), for some $\gamma \in GF(2^n)$. The one-to-one correspondence $(s_t) \leftrightarrow \gamma$ is then an isomorphism between $\Omega(f)$ and $GF(2^n)$ considered as a vector space over GF(2).

Let $f_1(x), f_2(x)$ be polynomials of degrees n_1, n_2 respectively, satisfying the conditions of Result 3. Let $(s_t) \in \Omega(f_1)$ and $(v_t) \in \Omega(f_2)$. It is easy to show that the <u>product sequence</u> (w_t) defined by $w_t = s_t \cdot v_t$ (t = 0,1,2,...) is generated by the polynomial of degree n_1n_2 over GF(2) whose roots are all products of one root of $f_1(x)$ and one root of $f_2(x)$. If $f_1(x) = \prod_{i=0}^{n_1-1}(x+\omega_i)$, $f_2(x) = \prod_{j=0}^{n_2-1}(x+\theta_j)$ we define the polynomial $f_1 \S f_2$ by

$$(f_1 \S f_2)(x) = \prod_{i=0}^{n_1-1} \prod_{j=0}^{n_2-1} (x+\omega_i\theta_j).$$

Then $(w_t) \in \Omega(f_1 \S f_2)$, though $(f_1 \S f_2)(x)$ is not necessarily the minimum polynomial of (w_t).

3. MULTIPLEXED SEQUENCES

3.1 Definition of a Multiplexed Sequence

Let SR1 and SR2 be two linear feedback shift registers with m and n stages respectively where $m>1$, $n>1$, $(m,n) = 1$. Denote the stages of SR1 by $A_0, A_1, \ldots, A_{m-1}$ and those of SR2 by $B_0, B_1, \ldots, B_{n-1}$ so that $A_i(t)$ and $B_j(t)$ are the contents of A_i and B_j respectively at time t. SR1 has primitive characteristic polynomial $f(x)$ over GF(2) and generates a PN sequence (a_t) of period 2^m-1. SR2 has primitive characteristic polynomial $g(x)$ over GF(2) and generates a PN sequence (b_t) of period 2^n-1. A multiplexer is used to produce a sequence, which we call a <u>multiplexed sequence</u>, related to the states of SR1 and SR2 as follows.

First choose an integer k in the range $1 \leq k \leq m$. We can only choose $k = m$ if $2^m-1 \leq n$ and if $k \neq m$, then k must also satisfy $2^k \leq n$. Next choose k stages $A_0, A_{\tau_1}, \ldots, A_{\tau_{k-1}}$ where $0<\tau_1<\ldots<\tau_{k-1}$. At any time t, the binary k-tuple $(A_0(t), A_{\tau_1}(t), \ldots, A_{\tau_{k-1}}(t))$ is interpreted as the binary representation of a natural number which we denote by N_t. Clearly $0 \leq N_t \leq 2^k-1$ but if $k = m$, then since the binary m-tuple $(0,0,\ldots,0$ is never a state, we can improve inequality slightly to $1 \leq N_t \leq 2^m-1$.

If $k<m$, choose an injective mapping $\gamma : \{0,1,\ldots,2^k-1\} \to \{0,1,\ldots,n-1\}$. If $k = m$, restrict the domain of γ to $\{1,2,\ldots,2^m-1\}$. (Note the bounds imposed on k guarantee the existence of such a mapping.) With these choices of $k, \tau_1, \tau_2, \ldots, \tau_{k-1}$ and γ, we define a <u>multiplexed sequence</u> (u_t) by

$$u_t = B_{\gamma(N_t)}(t).$$

Since $B_j(t) = B_0(t+j) = b_{t+j}$, we may write

$$u_t = b_{t+\gamma(N_t)}.$$

N.B. We choose A_0 as one of our k stages from SR1 without loss of generality. Any arbitrary selection of k stages is equivalent to the above choice with a different initial state, since $A_i(t) = A_0(t+i)$ for $1 \leq i \leq m-1$.

<u>Example</u> The following is an illustration of a multiplexed sequence. Let $m = 3$, $n = 4$, $f(x) = 1+x+x^3$ and $g(x) = 1+x^3+x^4$. We take $k = 2$ and select the two stages A_0 and A_1 from SR1.

Let $\gamma : \{0,1,2,3\} \to \{0,1,2,3\}$ be the injective mapping defined by

$$\gamma(0) = 2,\ \gamma(1) = 3,\ \gamma(2) = 0,\ \gamma(3) = 1.$$

Suppose SR1 and SR2 are given the initial states 100 and 1000 respectively. The first seven states of the system are shown below. The binary digits forming the multiplexed sequence are underlined.

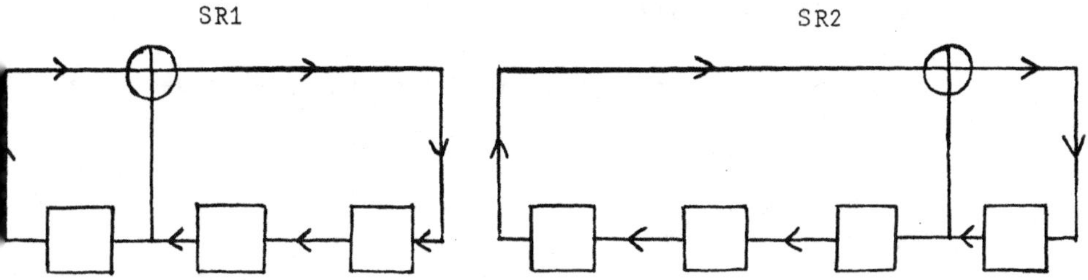

A_0	A_1	A_2	B_0	B_1	B_2	B_3	
1	0	0	$\underline{1}$	0	0	0	
0	0	1	0	0	$\underline{0}$	1	STATES
0	1	0	0	0	1	$\underline{1}$	
1	0	1	$\underline{0}$	1	1	1	
0	1	1	1	1	1	$\underline{1}$	
1	1	1	1	$\underline{1}$	1	0	
1	1	0	1	$\underline{1}$	0	1	

It is seen that

$N_0 = 2,\quad \gamma(N_0) = 0 \quad$ and $u_0 = B_0(0) = 1;$

$N_1 = 0,\quad \gamma(N_1) = 2 \quad$ and $u_1 = B_2(1) = 0;$

$N_2 = 1,\quad \gamma(N_2) = 3 \quad$ and $u_2 = B_3(2) = 1;$

and so on.

The first 120 terms of the sequence (u_t) are given by

1 0 1 0 1 1 1 1 0 1 0 0 0 0 0 0 1 0 1 1 1 1 1 1 1 0 1 0 0 0 0 0 1 1
1 1 0 0 0 1 1 1 1 1 0 1 1 0 1 1 1 1 1 1 0 1 1 0 0 0 0 0 0 0 1 0 1 0
1 0 0 0 1 0 0 0 0 0 1 1 1 1 0 1 1 1 0 1 0 1 0 0 1 1 1 0 1 0 0 1 0 1
1 0 1 1 0 1 0 1 1 1 1 0 1 0 0 0 0 0.

3.2 The General Term of a Multiplexed Sequence

The general term of the multiplexed sequence (u_t) can be expressed explicitly in terms of (a_t) and (b_t) :-

Definition We define $P_0(t), P_1(t), \ldots, P_{2^k-1}(t)$ to be the 2^k functions of t (t a non-negative integer) with values in GF(2), formed by taking all 2^k possible products of the terms $a_t, a_{t+\tau_1}, \ldots, a_{t+\tau_{k-1}}$, so that $P_0(t) = 1$ (the empty product) and if $i<j\leq 2^k-1$, $P_j(t)$ is the product of at least as many terms as $P_i(t)$.

Theorem 4 If $1\leq k<m$, the general term of the multiplexed sequence (u_t) can be expressed as

$$u_t = \sum_{\ell=0}^{2^k-1} P_\ell(t) b_{t+\nu_\ell}$$

where $\nu_0, \nu_1, \ldots, \nu_{2^k-1}$ are completely determined by $\gamma(0), \gamma(1), \ldots, \gamma(2^k-1)$ and the 2^k sequences $_{\nu_\ell}(b_t)$ $(\ell = 0,1,\ldots,2^k-1)$ are linearly independent in $\Omega(g)$.

Proof We describe the general term u_t of the multiplexed sequence by a table with 2^k entries arranged as follows.

a_t	$a_{t+\tau_1}$		$a_{t+\tau_{k-1}}$	u_t
0	0	. . . .	0	$b_{t+\rho_0}$
1	0	. . . .	0	$b_{t+\rho_1}$
0	1	. . . .	0	$b_{t+\rho_2}$
.	.			.
.	.			.
0	0	. . . .	1	$b_{t+\rho_k}$
1	1	. . . .	0	$b_{t+\rho_{k+1}}$
.	.			.
.	.			.
.	.			.
1	1	. . . .	1	$b_{t+\rho_{2^k-1}}$

The first row defines the term u_t when the binary k-tuple is all zeros. The next k rows correspond to all binary k-tuples with exactly one one; the next $\binom{k}{2}$ rows correspond to all binary k-tuples with two ones, and so on. $\rho_0,\rho_1,\ldots,\rho_{2^k-1}$ is the appropriate reordering of $\gamma(0),\gamma(1),\ldots,\gamma(2^k-1)$. For $t = 0,1,2,\ldots$, let $\bar{a}_t$ denote the binary complement of a_t, so that $\bar{a}_t = 1+a_t \pmod 2$. We can express the general term of the sequence (u_t) as a sum of 2^k product terms, one for each row of the table. That is,

$$u_t = \bar{a}_t\bar{a}_{t+\tau_1}\cdots\bar{a}_{t+\tau_{k-1}}\, b_{t+\rho_0} + a_t\bar{a}_{t+\tau_1}\cdots\bar{a}_{t+\tau_{k-1}}\, b_{t+\rho_1}$$
$$+\bar{a}_t a_{t+\tau_1}\cdots\bar{a}_{t+\tau_{k-1}}\, b_{t+\rho_2} + \ldots + a_t a_{t+\tau_1}\cdots a_{t+\tau_{k-1}}\, b_{t+\rho_{2^k-1}},$$

since for any assignment of values for $a_t, a_{t+\tau_1},\ldots,a_{t+\tau_{k-1}}$, all but one of the 2^k product terms will be identically zero. Replacing $\bar{a}_t$ by $1+a_t$ and expanding each term according to the distributive law, we have

$$u_t = \sum_{j=0}^{2^k-1} Q_j(t) b_{t+\rho_j} \qquad \text{where } Q_{2^k-1}(t) = P_{2^k-1}(t)$$

and for $j = 0,1,\ldots,2^k-2$, $Q_j(t) = P_j(t)$ + some linear combination over GF(2) of $P_{j+1}(t), P_{j+2}(t), \ldots, P_{2^k-1}(t)$. (We may assume that binary k-tuples with the same number of ones are arranged in the table so that this is so.) Thus for $j = 0,1,\ldots,2^k-1$ we may write

$$Q_j(t) = \sum_{\ell=j}^{2^k-1} c_{j\ell} P_\ell(t) \quad \text{where } c_{jj} = 1.$$

Therefore $u_t = \sum_{j=0}^{2^k-1} \left(\sum_{\ell=j}^{2^k-1} c_{j\ell} P_\ell(t) \right) b_{t+\rho_j}$. We can write this as

$$u_t = \sum_{j=0}^{2^k-1} \sum_{\ell=0}^{2^k-1} c_{j\ell} P_\ell(t) b_{t+\rho_j} \quad \text{where } c_{j\ell} = 0 \text{ if } \ell<j.$$

Changing the order of summation we get

$$u_t = \sum_{\ell=0}^{2^k-1} P_\ell(t) \left(\sum_{j=0}^{\ell} c_{j\ell} b_{t+\rho_j} \right), \text{ since } c_{j\ell} = 0 \text{ if } j>\ell.$$

But $c_{\ell\ell} = 1$ for $\ell = 0,1,\ldots,2^k-1$ and so

$$u_t = P_0(t) b_{t+\rho_0} + \sum_{\ell=1}^{2^k-1} P_\ell(t) \left(b_{t+\rho_\ell} + \sum_{j=0}^{\ell-1} c_{j\ell} b_{t+\rho_j} \right).$$

The 2^k sequences $_{\rho_\ell}(b_t)$ $(\ell=0,1,\ldots,2^k-1)$ are a subset of the n sequences $(b_t), {}_1(b_t), \ldots, {}_{n-1}(b_t)$ which are linearly independent in $\Omega(g)$.

Now let $\nu_0 = \rho_0$ and for $\ell = 1,2,\ldots,2^k-1$

$$_{\nu_\ell}(b_t) = {}_{\rho_\ell}(b_t) + \sum_{j=0}^{\ell-1} c_{j\ell}\, {}_{\rho_j}(b_t).$$

Then for $t = 0,1,2,\ldots$

$$u_t = \sum_{\ell=0}^{2^k-1} P_\ell(t) b_{t+\nu_\ell}$$ and the 2^k sequences $_{\nu_\ell}(b_t)$ $(\ell=0,1,\ldots,2^k-1)$ are also linearly independent in $\Omega(g)$. ¤

3.3 The Minimum Polynomial

We first introduce the concept of linear disjointness which we need in order to discuss the minimum polynomial. Let R be a ring containing a field F and such that the identity 1 of F is also the identity of R. Then R is a vector space over F and in this sense we speak below of subspaces of R.

Definition Two subspaces L and L' of R are said to be linearly disjoint over F if the following condition is satisfied : whenever $x_1,x_2,\ldots,x_r$ are elements of L which are linearly independent over F and $x_1',x_2',\ldots,x_s'$ are elements of L' which are linearly independent over F, then the rs products $x_i x_j'$ are also linearly independent over F.

Linear disjointness of L,L' is clearly a symmetric relationship between the two spaces and is relative to the preassigned ground field F. The following is equivalent to linear disjointness (see [Zariski & Samuel, 1958] page 109) :-

Whenever $x_1,x_2,\ldots,x_r$ are elements of L which are linearly independent over F then these elements x_i are also linearly independent over L'.

The following may easily be proved [Jennings, 1980].

Result 5 If (m,n) = 1, then regarding $GF(2^{mn})$ as a vector space over GF(2), the subspaces $GF(2^m)$ and $GF(2^n)$ are linearly disjoint over GF(2).

Let the factorization of f(x) and g(x), in $GF(2^m)$ and $GF(2^n)$ respectively, be given by

$$f(x) = \prod_{i=0}^{m-1} (x+\alpha^{2^i}), \quad g(x) = \prod_{j=0}^{n-1} (x+\beta^{2^j}).$$

(α and β are primitive elements in their respective fields.) For any non-negative integer j, define the weight of j, w(j) as the number of ones in the binary expansion of j. Before discussing the minimum polynomial of (u_t), we need a polynomial closely related to f(x) :-

<u>Definition</u> For $1 \le s \le m$, define the polynomial $F_s(x)$ of degree $\sum_{i=1}^{s} \binom{m}{i}$ over GF(2) by

$$F_s(x) = \prod_{\substack{1 \le i \le 2^m-1 \\ 1 \le w(i) \le s}} (x+\alpha^i) .$$

Without loss of generality, we will assume SR1 has initial state vector $(a_0, a_1, \ldots, a_{m-1})$ such that for $t = 0,1,2,\ldots$

$$a_t = \sum_{r=0}^{m-1} \alpha^{2^r t} \tag{3}$$

(see remark after Result 3). Then for $e = 1,2,\ldots,k-1$ and $t = 0,1,2,\ldots$

$$a_{t+\tau_e} = \sum_{r=0}^{m-1} (\alpha^{2^r})^{t+\tau_e} = \sum_{r=0}^{m-1} (\alpha^{\tau_e})^{2^r} \alpha^{2^r t} \tag{4}$$

<u>Remark</u> The functions of t given by $P_0(t), P_1(t), \ldots, P_{2^k-1}(t)$ are now defined by equations (3) and (4). We may take $P_0(t) = 1 = (\alpha^0)^t$. For $1 \le \ell \le 2^k-1$, if $P_\ell(t)$ is a product of exactly s of the terms $a_t, a_{t+\tau_1}, \ldots, a_{t+\tau_{k-1}}$, then $P_\ell(t)$ is a linear combination over $GF(2^m)$ of the t-th powers of the roots of the polynomial $F_s(x)$.

For example,

$$a_{t+\tau_1} a_{t+\tau_2} = \sum_{r_1=0}^{m-1} \sum_{r_2=0}^{m-1} (\alpha^{\tau_1})^{2^{r_1}} (\alpha^{\tau_2})^{2^{r_2}} \left(\alpha^{2^{r_1}+2^{r_2}}\right)^t \text{ and } 1 \le w\left(2^{r_1}+2^{r_2}\right) \le 2.$$

<u>Theorem 6</u> Suppose $1 \le k < m$. Then there exist uniquely determined elements η_{ij} in $GF(2^{mn})$ such that for $t = 0,1,2,\ldots$

$$u_t = \sum_{\substack{0 \le i \le 2^m-1 \\ 0 \le w(i) \le k}} \sum_{j=0}^{n-1} \eta_{ij} \left(\alpha^i \beta^{2^j}\right)^t . \tag{5}$$

Furthermore, for any i and j, $\eta_{ij} \neq 0$ if and only if at least one of the 2^k functions $P_0(t), P_1(t), \ldots, P_{2^k-1}(t)$ has a non-zero coefficient of α^{it}.

<u>Proof</u> By Theorem 4, for t = 0,1,2,..., we have

$$u_t = \sum_{\ell=0}^{2^k-1} P_\ell(t) b_{t+\nu_\ell} \tag{6}$$

where the $_{\nu_\ell}(b_t)$ (ℓ = 0,1,...,2^k-1) are linearly independent in $\Omega(g)$.

By Result 3, there exist unique elements $\xi_0,\xi_1,\ldots,\xi_{2^k-1}$ in GF(2^n) such that for ℓ = 0,1,...,2^k-1 and t = 0,1,2,...

$$b_{t+\nu_\ell} = \sum_{j=0}^{n-1} \xi_\ell^{2^j} \beta^{2^j t}. \tag{7}$$

Substituting the expressions for $a_t, a_{t+\tau_1},\ldots,a_{t+\tau_{k-1}}, b_{t+\nu_0}, b_{t+\nu_1},\ldots,$ $b_{t+\nu_{2^k-1}}$ from (3), (4) and (7) into equation (6), we have

$$u_t = \sum_{\substack{0\le i<2^m-1\\ 0\le w(i)\le k}} \sum_{j=0}^{n-1} \eta_{ij}\left(\alpha^i\beta^{2^j}\right)^t.$$

For a fixed i and j, η_{ij} has the form

$$\eta_{ij} = \sum_{\ell=0}^{2^k-1} \delta_\ell \xi_\ell^{2^j} \tag{8}$$

where each $\delta_\ell \in$ GF(2^m) and is the coefficient (possibly zero) of α^{it} in the function $P_\ell(t)$. The elements $\xi_0,\xi_1,\ldots,\xi_{2^k-1}$ are linearly independent over GF(2) since the 2^k sequences $_{\nu_\ell}(b_t)$ (ℓ = 0,1,...,2^k-1) are linearly independent in $\Omega(g)$. Therefore for j = 0,1,...,n-1, $\xi_0^{2^j},\xi_1^{2^j},\ldots,\xi_{2^k-1}^{2^j}$ are also linearly independent over GF(2), since

$$\sum_{\ell=0}^{2^k-1} d_\ell \xi_\ell^{2^j} = \left(\sum_{\ell=0}^{2^k-1} d_\ell \xi_\ell\right)^{2^j} \qquad \text{where } d_\ell \in \mathrm{GF}(2).$$

Now regarding GF(2^{mn}) as a vector space over GF(2), the subspaces GF(2^m) and GF(2^n) are linearly disjoint over GF(2), by Result 5. So for j = 0,1,...,n-1

$$\xi_0^{2^j},\xi_1^{2^j},\ldots,\xi_{2^k-1}^{2^j}$$

are linearly independent over $GF(2^m)$. Therefore from equation (8), we see that $\eta_{ij} \neq 0$ if and only if $\delta_\ell \neq 0$ for some ℓ. That is, $\eta_{ij} \neq 0$ if and only if at least one of the 2^k functions of $t, P_0(t), P_1(t), \ldots, P_{2^k-1}(t)$ has a non-zero coefficient of α^{it}. ¤

<u>Corollary 7</u> If $1 \leq k < m$ the minimum polynomial of a multiplexed sequence (u_t) is independent of the injective mapping $\gamma : \{0,1,\ldots,2^k-1\} \to \{0,1,\ldots,n-1\}$.

<u>Proof</u> From equation (5), $\alpha^i \beta^{2^j}$ is a root of the minimum polynomial of (u_t) if and only if $\eta_{ij} \neq 0$. This in turn depends only on the sequences $(a_t), \tau_1(a_t), \ldots, \tau_{k-1}(a_t)$ by way of the functions $P_0(t), P_1(t), \ldots, P_{2^k-1}(t)$.

Before proceeding further with the minimum polynomial, we require the following lemma.

<u>Lemma 8</u> Let α be a primitive element of $GF(2^m)$ and d a positive integer in the range $1 \leq d < m$. Then the m elements $\alpha^d, (\alpha^d)^2, \ldots, (\alpha^d)^{2^{m-1}}$ are all distinct.

<u>Proof</u> Suppose otherwise and $(\alpha^d)^{2^i} = (\alpha^d)^{2^j}$ where $0 \leq i < j \leq m-1$. Then $(\alpha^d)^{2^j - 2^i} = 1$ and α^d has order dividing $2^j - 2^i = 2^i(2^s-1)$ where $s = j-i < m$. Every element of $GF(2^m)$ has odd order and so α^d has order dividing 2^s-1 and is therefore an element of $GF(2^s)$. Therefore $\alpha^d \in GF(2^q)$ where $q = \text{h.c.f.}\ (s,m)$. But $q<m$ and $q|m$ implies $q \leq m/2$. Since α has order 2^m-1 we have

$$2^m-1 \mid d(2^q-1)$$

from which we conclude that

$$2^m-1 \leq d(2^q-1).$$

That is, $(2^{m/2}+1)(2^{m/2}-1) \leq d(2^q-1) \leq d(2^{m/2}-1)$. Therefore $2^{m/2}+1 \leq d$. But $d<m$ by hypothesis and $m < 2^{m/2}+1$, which is a contradiction.

Theorem 9 Let $H(x)$ denote the minimum polynomial of a multiplexed sequence.

(i) If $k = 1$, $H(x) = (f \S g).g$, of degree $n(1+m)$;

(ii) If $2 \le k < m$, and the k stages $A_0, A_{\tau_1}, \ldots, A_{\tau_{k-1}}$ are equidistant, $H(x) = (F_k \S g).g$ of degree

$$n.\sum_{i=0}^{k} \binom{m}{i}.$$

Proof Equation (5) expresses the general term of the sequence (u_t) as a linear combination over $GF(2^{mn})$ of the t-th powers of the roots of the polynomial $(F_k \S g).g$. Therefore $(u_t) \in \Omega((F_k \S g).g)$ by Result 3 and the minimum polynomial will be a divisor of $(F_k \S g).g$. By Theorem 6, $\eta_{ij} \neq 0$ if and only if at least one of the 2^k functions of t, $P_0(t), P_1(t), \ldots, P_{2^k-1}(t)$ has a non-zero coefficient of α^{it}. Since $P_0(t) = (\alpha^0)^t$ we have $\eta_{0j} \neq 0$. Now $P_1(t) = \sum_{r=0}^{m-1} \alpha^{2^r t}$ and so $\eta_{ij} \neq 0$ if $w(i) = 1$. This proves (i).

Now assume $2 \le k < m$ and $\tau_1 = d, \tau_2 = 2d, \ldots, \tau_{k-1} = (k-1)d \le m-1$. Then from equation (4) we have

$$a_{t+ed} = \sum_{r=0}^{m-1} (\alpha^{ed})^{2^r} \alpha^{2^r t}$$

for $e = 1,2,\ldots,k-1$.

We now show that if $2 \le w(i) \le k$, the η_{ij} in equation (5) are all non-zero. Suppose $i = 2^{i_1} + 2^{i_2} + \ldots + 2^{i_s}$ where $2 \le s \le k$ and $0 \le i_1 < i_2 < \ldots < i_s \le m-1$. We pick the function $P_\ell(t)$ which is the product of the s terms $a_t, a_{t+d}, \ldots, a_{t+(s-1)d}$.

Let $r_1, r_2, \ldots, r_s$ denote the r's in the summation signs for $a_t, a_{t+d}, \ldots, a_{t+(s-1)d}$ respectively. Then there are $s!$ ways of choosing

$r_1, r_2, \ldots, r_s$ in the product $P_\ell(t) = a_t a_{t+d} \cdot \ldots \cdot a_{t+(s-1)d}$ such that $2^{r_1} + 2^{r_2} + \ldots + 2^{r_s} = i = 2^{i_1} + 2^{i_2} + \ldots + 2^{i_s}$. The coefficient of α^{it} in the function $P_\ell(t)$ is therefore given by the determinant $\Delta(i)$, where

$$\Delta(i) = \begin{vmatrix} 1 & 1 & \ldots & 1 \\ (\alpha^d)^{2^{i_1}} & (\alpha^d)^{2^{i_2}} & \ldots & (\alpha^d)^{2^{i_s}} \\ (\alpha^{2d})^{2^{i_1}} & (\alpha^{2d})^{2^{i_2}} & \ldots & (\alpha^{2d})^{2^{i_s}} \\ \vdots & & & \vdots \\ (\alpha^{(s-1)d})^{2^{i_1}} & \ldots & \ldots & (\alpha^{(s-1)d})^{2^{i_s}} \end{vmatrix}$$

Since $d<m, \alpha^d, (\alpha^d)^2, (\alpha^d)^4, \ldots, (\alpha^d)^{2^{m-1}}$ are all distinct by Lemma 8. Put $\chi_1 = (\alpha^d)^{2^{i_1}}, \chi_2 = (\alpha^d)^{2^{i_2}}, \ldots, \chi_s = (\alpha^d)^{2^{i_s}}$. Then

$$\Delta(i) = \begin{vmatrix} 1 & 1 & \ldots & 1 \\ \chi_1 & \chi_2 & \ldots & \chi_s \\ \chi_1^2 & \chi_2^2 & \ldots & \chi_s^2 \\ \vdots & \vdots & & \vdots \\ \chi_1^{s-1} & \chi_2^{s-1} & \ldots & \chi_s^{s-1} \end{vmatrix} = \prod_{I<J} (\chi_I + \chi_J).$$

Since $\chi_1, \chi_2, \ldots, \chi_s$ are all different, then the Vandermonde determinant $\Delta(i) \neq 0$, (see [Peterson & Weldon, 1972], page 270). Therefore $\eta_{ij} \neq 0$ for $j = 0,1,\ldots,n-1$ and the minimum polynomial of the sequence (u_t) is $(F_k \S g).g$.

Example We refer to the multiplexed sequence which has $k = 2$,

$$f(x) = 1+x+x^3 = (x+\alpha)(x+\alpha^2)(x+\alpha^4),$$

$$g(x) = 1+x^3+x^4 = (x+\beta)(x+\beta^2)(x+\beta^4)(x+\beta^8).$$

By Theorem 9, this sequence has minimum polynomial $(F_2 \S g).g$ whose roots are given by

$$\{\alpha^i \beta^{2^j} : 0 \le i < 7, \quad 0 \le w(i) \le 2, \quad 0 \le j \le 3\}.$$

These are precisely the roots of the polynomial $(1+x^7)\S g(x) = 1+x^7+x^{28}$.

The above Theorem has been proved using alternative methods by Manfred Hain who has also studied further generalizations. Other possible approaches to determining the minimum polynomial have been developed by Tore Herlestam.

The techniques involved in Theorems 4 and 6 can be adopted with only slight modification to deal with the case $k = m$. The table defining the general term of the sequence (u_t) in terms of the state vector $(a_t, a_{t+1}, \ldots, a_{t+m-1})$ has 2^m-1 entries, since m zeros is never a state of the shift register. We can then express the general term of the sequence (u_t) by

$$u_t = \sum_{\ell=1}^{2^m-1} P_\ell(t) b_{t+\nu_\ell}$$

where $\nu_1, \nu_2, \ldots, \nu_{2^m-1}$ are completely determined by $\gamma(1), \gamma(2), \ldots, \gamma(2^m-1)$, and the 2^m-1 sequences $_{\nu_\ell}(b_t)$ $(\ell = 1,2,\ldots,2^m-1)$ are linearly independent in $\Omega(g)$. As in Theorem 6, we can find unique elements η_{ij} in $GF(2^{mn})$ such that for $t = 0,1,2,\ldots$

$$u_t = \sum_{1 \le i \le 2^m-1} \sum_{j=0}^{n-1} \eta_{ij} (\alpha^i \beta^{2^j})^t .$$

That is, we can express the general term of the sequence (u_t) as a linear combination over $GF(2^{mn})$ of the t-th powers of the roots of the polynomial $F_m \S g$. It is then a routine step to show that all η_{ij} are non-zero, since the m stages are necessarily equidistant. We therefore have the following :-

<u>Theorem 10</u> If $k = m$, the minimum polynomial of a multiplexed sequence (u_t) is $F_m \S g$ of degree $n(2^m-1)$.

If $2<k<m$ and the k stages $A_0, A_{\tau_1}, \ldots, A_{\tau_{k-1}}$ are not equidistant, then the minimum polynomial may or may not be $(F_k \S g).g$. Many examples have been found [Jennings, 1980] of primitive polynomials $f(x)$ for which the minimum polynomial is a proper divisor of $(F_k \S g).g$. For example, if $f(x) = 1+x+x^2+x^5+x^6$, $k = 3$ and $\tau_1 = 1$, $\tau_2 = 4$, the minimum polynomial has degree $40n$ (assuming $(6,n) = 1$), instead of $42n$, the degree of $(F_3 \S g).g$. However, we can guarantee that the minimum polynomial has exponent $(2^m-1)(2^n-1)$, since $\alpha\beta$ is always a root. Thus from Result 2, we derive the following :

<u>Theorem 11</u> The period of a multiplexed sequence is $(2^m-1)(2^n-1)$.

This final result may well be proved much more directly using techniques developed by Blakely and Purdy.

ON USING PRIME POLYNOMIALS IN CRYPTO GENERATORS*

Tore Herlestam

Department of Computer Engineering
University of Lund
P.O.Box 725
S-220 07 LUND/SWEDEN

bstract - In this note a primality test for polynomials over a finite field is ana-yzed. It is particularly well suited to achieve fast computations in the binary case. ots of prime polynomials which do not have to possess the maximum length property can e easily accessed by means of the test.

xamples of binary prime polynomials generated through the use of the test are given or degrees from 35 up to 55.

he computational requirements are compared with a related test for maximum length and lso with some common factorization procedures. As main application the use of prime olynomials in certain crypto generators is considered.

This research was supported in part by the National Swedish Board for Technical De-elopment under grant 81-3323 at the University of Lund.

I INTRODUCTION

The linear shift registers have long been playing a leading part as main components in pseudo random generators. When used for cryptologic purposes such generators should preferably have a controllable complexity. General results in this direction have been obtained by several investigators (cf.[Herlestam, 1982]).

It is customary to use maximum length feedback in shift registers for crypto applications. This leads however to difficulties when the feedback is to be part of the secret key, since the key production center has then to sustain a comparatively heavy computational burden.

In many instances it turns out that prime polynomials could be used as replacement for maximum length polynomials. For key production purposes it would thus be very convenient to have at hand a fast primality test for polynomials over a finite field.

Irreducibility can of course always be tested by means of a factorization procedure. For polynomials over finite fields Berlekamp´s wellknown factoring sheme or other approaches [Knuth, 1981, Sec. 4.6.2] may thus be applied. However, this way of handling primality cannot be considered particularly efficient in general.

Maximum length polynomials, often called primitive, are in particular prime. They can be generated by means of rather efficient methods, such as the procudure by Alanen and Knuth [Alanen, 1964]. An even simpler algorithm for testing only primality without requiring the maximum length property is however still lacking.

Below a primality test of this kind is described and analyzed. It turns out that, in general, the degree must be a prime power or a product of only two different primes in order that the test shall work, but also that even in the remaining cases the test can be used successfully together with some supplementary checking.

The test may be regarded as a deterministic counterpart to the probabilistic primality tests for integers by Solovay and Strassen and by Rabin (see [Williams, 1978]).

In section II an account is given of some relevant algebraic preliminaries. The primality test is described and analyzed in sections III and IV, and section V contains extensions to cover cases where the test has to be supplemented by further checking. A summary forms the concluding section VI.

A proof of a number theoretical lemma used in section III is given in the appendix.

II SOME PROPERTIES OF PRIME POLYNOMIALS OVER GF(q)

Any finite field can be identified with GF(q), q a prime power. If f(t) in the polynomial ring GF(q)[t] is prime then the residue class ring GF(q)[t]/f(t)GF(q)[t] is a representation of the field $GF(q^n)$, where n denotes the degree of f(t).

The elements of $GF(q^n)$ are the solutions of the equation $x^{q^n}=x$. Since we can identify any element x with a polynomial

$$x(t) = \sum_{0}^{n-1} a_k t^k \quad \text{modulo } f(t),$$

where the coefficients a_k belong to GF(q), and since $a^q=a$ holds in GF(q), we have

$$x(t)^{q^m} = \sum_{0}^{n-1} a_k t^{kq^m}$$

so that $x(t)^{q^m}=x(t)$ (modulo f(t)) for all x if and only if $t^{q^m}=t$ (modulo f(t)). Thus $t^{q^n}=t$ (modulo f(t)) when n=deg f, but $t^{q^m}\neq t$ (modulo f(t)) when $0<m<n$. As a consequence per f, defined as the smallest positive r such that $f(t)|(t^r-1)$, divides q^n-1 but does not divide q^m-1 for $0<m<n$. In particular, per f is a divisor of q^n-1 other than those of the form q^d-1 with $d|n$, $d\neq n$.

This forms the basis for a variant of the maximum length test by Alanen and Knuth [Alanen, 1964]:

1. check $f(x)\neq 0$ for all x in GF(q),
2. check $t^{q^n}=t$ (modulo f(t)), where n=deg f,
3. for every prime divisor p' of q^n-1
   check $t^d\neq 1$ (modulo f(t)), where $d=(q^n-1)/p'$;

if f satisfies all these checks then f is a maximum length polynomial.

Apparently the most time consuming step is the third. This step also eliminates all prime polynomials which do not possess the maximum length property. Furthermore, it presupposes that the prime decomposition of q^n-1 is known.

On the other hand, if q^n-1 is prime, i.e. q=2 and 2^n-1 is a Mersenne prime, then the third step is trivial. Moreover, in this case every prime polynomial has the maximum length property.

III A PRIMALITY TEST

Assume that

1. $f(x)\neq 0$ for all x in GF(q),
2. $t^{q^n}\equiv t$ (modulo f(t)), where n=deg f,
3. $t^{q^m}\not\equiv t$ (modulo f(t)) for 0<m<n.

From 1. we infer that f(t) contains no first degree factor.

From 2. it follows that f(t) is square free, since $t^{q^n-1}-1$ has no double zero. Hence the prime decomposition of f is

$$f = p_1 p_2 \cdots p_r,$$

where $p_1, p_2, \ldots, p_r$ are different prime polynomials and $1<d_j=\deg p_j\leq n$. Here equality holds if and only if f is prime. Further,

$$n = d_1+d_2+\ldots+d_r.$$

According to the chinese remainder theorem the residue class ring GF(q)[t]/ /f(t)GF(q)[t] is isomorphic to

$$GF(q^{d_1}) \oplus GF(q^{d_2}) \oplus \ldots \oplus GF(q^{d_r})$$

and the multiplicative group of units U(GF(q)[t]/f(t)GF(q)[t]) is isomorphic to

$$U(GF(q^{d_1})) \otimes U(GF(q^{d_2})) \otimes \ldots \otimes U(GF(q^{d_r})).$$

Hence

$$t^{q^n-1}\equiv 1 \text{ (modulo } f(t))$$

if and only if

$$t^{q^n-1}\equiv 1 \text{ (modulo } p_j(t)),\ 1\leq j\leq r.$$

Since $t^{q^{d_j}-1}\equiv 1$ (modulo $p_j(t)$), $1\leq j\leq r$, we must have

$$p_j(t) \mid \gcd(t^{q^n-1}-1, t^{q^{d_j}-1}-1),\ 1\leq j\leq r.$$

As is easily seen,

$$\gcd(t^{q^n-1}-1, t^{q^{d_j}-1}-1)=t^{\gcd(q^n-1,q^{d_j}-1)}-1=t^{q^{\gcd(n,d_j)}-1}-1,$$

which implies that $\gcd(n,d_j)=d_j$, i.e. $d_j \mid n$, since $p_j(t)$ does not not divide $t^{q^d-1}-1$ with d a proper divisor of d_j. In case f is composite this means that all d_j's in

$n=d_1+d_2+\ldots+d_r$ are proper divisors of n. We call this an <u>additive decomposition</u>. We have to distinguish between two cases:

a) $\mathrm{lcm}(d_1,d_2,\ldots,d_r) < n$ for all additive decompositions; in this case we call n <u>admissible</u>;

b) $\mathrm{lcm}(d_1,d_2,\ldots,d_r) = n$ for at least one additive decomposition; in this case we call n <u>non-admissible</u>.

When n is admissible and f is composite, then $n=d_1+d_2+\ldots+d_r$, $\mathrm{lcm}(d_1,d_2,\ldots,d_r)$ being a proper divisor of n, and thus $t^{q^m}=t$ (modulo f(t)) for some m, $0<m<n$. Consequently we have proved

<u>Theorem 1:</u> Let f(t) be a polynomial over GF(q) of degree n, and assume n admissible. Then

1. $f(x)\neq 0$ for all x in GF(q),
2. $t^{q^n}=t$ (modulo f(t)),
3. $t^{q^m}\neq t$ (modulo f(t)) when $0<m<n$

if and only if f is prime.

<u>Note</u> - In general admissibility is not only sufficient but also necessary. However, the limited supply of different prime polynomials of low degrees can make the primality test work even for non-admissible n's in some cases. Examples will be given below.

Now we are left with a number theoretical problem:

given n, decide whether n is admissible or not.

A non-admissible n can be multiplied with any factor k without achieving admissibility, for if $n=d_1+d_2+\ldots+d_r$, where $\mathrm{lcm}(d_1,d_2,\ldots,d_r)=n$, then $kn=(kd_1)+(kd_2)+\ldots+(kd_r)$, where $\mathrm{lcm}(kd_1,kd_2,\ldots,kd_r)=kn$. Thus we have

<u>Lemma 1</u>: Every multiple of a non-admissible integer is also non-admissible.

Suppose that $n=p^e$ is a prime power. Then every proper divisor of n is a divisor of p^{e-1}. In particular, when e=1 there are no proper divisors. Anyway, $\mathrm{lcm}(d_1,d_2,\ldots,d_r)$ divides p^{e-1}, implying that n is admissible.

Next, assume $n=p_1p_2$, where p_1 and p_2 are different primes. Then the only proper divisors of n are p_1 and p_2, so that every additive decomposition may be written $p_1p_2=n_1p_1+n_2p_2$, implying $n_1=p_2, n_2=0$ or $n_1=0, n_2=p_1$. Thus n is admissible. In order to show that all other n's than $n=p^e$ and $n=p_1p_2$ are non-admissible it suffices to consider the cases $n=p_1^2p_2$ and $n=p_1p_2p_3$, according to lemma 1.

Assume first that $n=p_1^2p_2$ where $p_1<p_2$. Dividing p_2 by p_1 we can write $p_2=n_2p_1+n_1$,

where n_1 and n_2 are positive. Putting $n_3=p_1-1$ we have

$$p_1^2p_2=n_1p_1+n_2p_1^2+n_3p_1p_2,$$

an additive decomposition implying that $p_1^2p_2$ is non-admissible.

Next, let $n=p_1^2p_2$ where $p_1>p_2$. Dividing p_1 by p_2 we can write $p_1=m_1p_2-n_1$, where m_1 and n_1 are positive and $m_1<p_1$. Putting $n_2=1$ and $n_3=p_1-m_1$ we have again

$$p_1^2p_2=n_1p_1+n_2p_1^2+n_3p_1p_2,$$

showing that $p_1^2p_2$ is non-admissible.

Finally, let $n=p_1p_2p_3$ where $p_1<p_2<p_3$. Dividing p_2 by p_1 we can write $p_2=m_1p_1-n_1$, where m_1 and n_1 are positive and $m_1<p_2$. Putting $n_2=1$ and $n_3=p_2-m_1$ we have

$$p_1p_2p_3=n_1p_3+n_2p_2p_3+n_3p_1p_3,$$

again an additive decomposition showing that n is non-admissible.

Summing up we have proved

<u>Theorem 2:</u> A positive integer is admissible if and only if it is a prime power or a product of only two different primes.

As numerical examples the first non-admissible integers are 12, 18, 20, 24, 28, 30, 36, 40, 42, 44, 45, 48, 50, 52, 54, 56, 60, ...

When q=2 theorem 1 works even for the non-admissible n=44, since there is only one prime polynomial over GF(2) of degree 2 and three of degree 4, so that we cannot use the additive decompositions $44=n_12+n_24+n_311+n_422$, where $(n_1,n_2,n_3,n_4)=(2k+1,5-k,0,1)$ and $(2k+1,5-k,2,0)$, $0\leq k\leq 5$, to construct a composite f(t) satisfying the test. The same holds for n=4p when p is a prime $\geq$ 11.

It is fairly obvious that similar exceptional cases exist, for instance when $n=2^kp$, p being a prime $> 2^{2^{k-1}}-1$, or, for general q, $p > (q^{2^k}-q)/2$.

IV COMPUTATIONAL SPEED

Let us first consider the case q=2. Then the initial step of the test is almost trivial: $f(0)\neq 0$ means that the constant term in the polynomial must be 1 and $f(1)\neq 0$ means that the number of non-vanishing terms must be odd.

In the second and third step we have to deal with successive squarings modulo f(t). This may of course be done very quickly on a binary machine.

Turning next to the case where q is a prime > 2, the first step now involves evaluation of f(x) in several points. Using well known procedures (see [Knuth, 1981]) this will not make said step too slow, apart from instances when q is very large.

In the remaining steps the crucial process is the computation of $x(t)^q$. As always it can be done quite efficiently by means of successive squarings and the binary representation of q (cf. [Knuth, 1981]). But some slow-down is caused by the modulo q arithmetic in the coefficients.

In the general case $q=p^e$ the field GF(q) is most efficiently implemented as the residue class ring modulo a prime polynomial over GF(p) of degree e. Evidently the multiplication has to be speeded up by means of some sort of tables, for instance logarithms (cf. [Alanen, 1964]).

When a prime polynomial has to be chosen almost at random by means of the test, it appears appropriate to start with a polynomial satisfying the first step. The number of such polynomials of degree n is $(q-1)q^{n-2}$.

The number of prime polynomials of degree n is

$$\psi(n) = \frac{1}{n} \sum_{d|n} \mu(d) q^{n/d},$$

where μ denotes Möbius' μ-function. Hence the probability of hitting a prime polynomial is $\psi(n)/(q-1)q^{n-2}$, which can be estimated roughly as $q^2/(q-1)n$. For moderately large values of n/q the chances for finding a prime polynomial by trial and error, using the test, have thus to be considered fairly good.

As a numerical example when q=2, $\psi(49)/2^{47} \approx 0.08$ so that one out of 12 polynomials of degree 49 and with f(0)=f(1)=1 will be prime.

In order to test the speed when only limited computing power is available, the algorithm has been implemented in the case GF(2) on a programmable desk calculator, a HP 9815. A mean running time of $T(n) = 0.027\, n^{2.86}$ seconds per polynomial of degree n was found empirically, i.e.

n	19	29	39	49
T(n)	2	8	18	32 minutes.

As examples of the numerical outcome the following randomly chosen prime polynomials over GF(2) may be quoted, in customary octal notation.

n	prime polynomial of degree n over GF(2)
35	40 40000 02101
37	360 14310 02551
38	427 44643 77763
39	1200 00135 77767
41	6003 02002 06001
43	23276 72037 73773
44	60030 50320 00401
46	3 77777 77025 27777
47	5 46711 41777 44035
49	25 40000 00041 10005
51	101 62002 10020 02143
52	200 44000 23004 20001
53	402 60022 10064 01541
55	3310 54314 43320 07201

V NON-ADMISSIBLE AND RESTRICTED CASES

Let n be non-admissible and let

$$n=n_{k1}d_{k1}+n_{k2}d_{k2}+\ldots+n_{kr}d_{kr},\quad r=r(k),\ k=1,2,\ldots,s,$$

be all the additive decompositions with $d_{k1}<d_{k2}<\ldots<d_{kr}$, $n_{kj}>0$, and $\mathrm{lcm}(d_{k1},d_{k2},\ldots,d_{kr})=n$. If f(t) satisfies the primality test of theorem 1 without being prime, it has to be divisible by some prime polynomial of degree d_{k1}, $1\le k\le s$. Thus primality can be inferred after checking those possible prime divisors.

Since all prime polynomials of degree d are factors of $t^{q^d-1}-1$ we may take advantage of a reduction modulo $t^{q^d-1}-1$ before trying to decide whether the polynomial under test has any prime factor of degree d.

As an example the non-admissible n=12 has 2,3,4 and 6 as proper divisors. Any additive decomposition $12=n_1 2+n_2 3+n_3 4+n_4 6$ implying non-admissibility must have $n_3\neq 0$ and n_2 or $n_4\neq 0$. The only solutions are $(n_1,n_2,n_3,n_4)=(1,0,1,1)$ and $(1,2,1,0)$. Hence, a polynomial of degree 12 satisfying the conditions of theorem 1 and, in addition, not divisible by any second degree prime polynomial, must be prime. Even with this supplementary checking the test is evidently a substantial improvement over the exhaustive checking of all possible prime divisors of up to the sixth degree, and also over other general factorization procedures.

For some applications it is desirable to impose, in addition to primality, some lower bound on the period of the polynomial under test. This can be done as follows.

Assume that of all the divisors of q^n-1 other than those of the form q^d-1, where d divides n, only $D_1,D_2,\ldots,D_m$ are less than a certain tolerable bound B. If $t^D \neq 1$ (modulo f(t)), where $D=\mathrm{lcm}(D_1,D_2,\ldots,D_m)$, and if f(t) is prime, then the period of f(t) is at least B.

Presuming B moderately large, the computational effort to attain per $f \geq B$ by means of the described procedure will of course be much less than that required for testing the maximum length property when q^n-1 is large and composite.

VI SUMMARY

In the preceding sections we have seen that it is possible to derive a very simple primality test for polynomials over GF(q) when the degree is a prime power or a product of only two different primes. We have also noticed that the test can be supplemented by fairly simple checks in order to cover other cases and to impose restrictions on the period of the polynomial.

Particularly in the binary case very fast computations can be achieved. This is especially welcome in applications where prime polynomials, possibly with restricted periods, have to be generated more or less randomly for use as feedback polynomials in pseudo random generators with controllable complexity, based on nonlinear functions of linear shift register sequences.

APPENDIX

In section III the following number theoretical lemmas were used. They are certainly not new, but since it is much easier to prove them than to find the most appropriate reference, they are presented here with proofs but without references.

Lemma A: Over any field, $\gcd(t^m-1,t^n-1) = t^{\gcd(m,n)}-1$.

Proof: If $d|m$ and $d|n$ then, trivially, $(t^d-1)|(t^m-1)$ and $(t^d-1)|(t^n-1)$. Now let $d=\gcd(m,n)$. From Euclid's gcd-algorithm we get $d=mx+ny$ with $x>0$, $y<0$, i.e. $mx=d-ny$. The binomial formula can be shortened to

$$(t^s)^z = (t^s-1+1)^z = 1 + (t^s-1)K_z(t^s-1),$$

where $K_z(u)$ is a polynomial in u with integer coefficients. Applying it to $t^d(t^n)^{-y} = (t^m)^x$ we get

$$t^d-1 = (t^m-1)K_x(t^m-1) - (t^n-1)t^dK_{-y}(t^n-1)$$

and hence

$$t^d - 1 = \gcd(t^m - 1, t^n - 1).$$

Lemma B: For any positive integer q,

$$\gcd(q^m - 1, q^n - 1) = q^{\gcd(m,n)} - 1.$$

Proof: Substitute q for t in the proof of lemma A.

Section 6

Cryptography in Large Communication Systems

COMMUNICATION SECURITY IN REMOTE CONTROLLED COMPUTER SYSTEMS

M.R. Oberman
PTT Dr. Neher Laboratories
P.O. Box 421
2260 AK Leidschendam
Netherlands

ABSTRACT

Nowadays remote controlled computer systems are in widespread use. Several systems use the communication facilities offered by the public switched telephone network. In view of the public aspects of the network it is necessary that dial-up systems should have sufficient access security and communication security. In this paper it is proposed that this security be provided by the use of cryptography.

KEY WORD INDEX

Communication security, cryptography, remote control.

INTRODUCTION

Major applications of cryptography include the securing of information in information processing and in information communication systems. In this world of growing concern about privacy and integrity of information in which multi-user systems, communication systems and communication facilities are in common use, it is necessary that there should be a better protection against the several kinds of unintended use of systems and facilities.

The value of the information and the risks involved may be determinative of the level of protection of information systems. In general, the use of cryptography only is not the ultimate solution to provide security. Several other ways of protection may be involved as well. Some of the aspects involved can be determined by an adapted layered model (fig. 1).

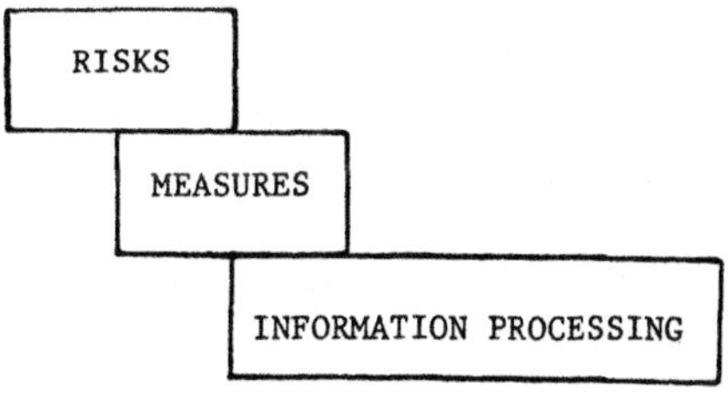

fig. 1

In a part of the present paper this layered model will be used as a guide to discuss the subject of securing a remote controlled computer system.

. RISK ANALYSIS

n general, four types of risks are involved regarding issues like:
- privacy and integrity of information
- company's reliable name
- financial risks
- material risks

n this subject of securing information for access and communication with remote con-rolled computer systems, the information communication between the terminal and the ystem is exchanged via the public switched telephone network.
herefore, the computer systems are provided with public dialling ports and can be ialled by (portable) terminals via the telephone network. In general, the controlling unction is location-independent. Unfortunately, location-independent system control ia the public switched telephone network obstructs the use of a dialling back pro-edure as a kind of confirmation. But dialling back action only provides a low level ire tapping and other methods of influencing the communication process.

2. MEASURES

From the risk analysis (fig. 1) it is clear that some measures will have to be taken to secure dial-up systems. Some possibilities will be discussed in this chapter. A simple, but not very effective way of securing dialling ports is keeping the dialled number secret.

However, since most telephone numbers are published in the telephone directory, and since the first digits are assigned to certain areas, only a few unknown digits have to be discovered. This is fairly simple. In general a computer modem will answer within two seconds or less; a human subscriber will not be so very quick. So this method does not provide sufficient protection.

Often, access control to a system is achieved by passwords. This is a rather low level of protection. In general, very common passwords are used; these can easily be checked out by a microcomputer, which may contain a kind of password dictionary.

Furthermore, for human factor purposes a password must be smaller than four characters and, or easy to remember.

For security purposes the length should be larger than six characters and purely random composed.

Hence, an ideal password does not exist.

Therefore securing information by the use of cryptography may be a (user friendly!) solution to the problem.

3. INFORMATION PROCESSING

In the third layer information processing is dealt with. For this purpose it is necessary to have a look at the terminals which are involved in the communication process.

In general, for a proper analysis is needed, then the model (fig. 1) has to be extended to the receiving party (fig. 2).

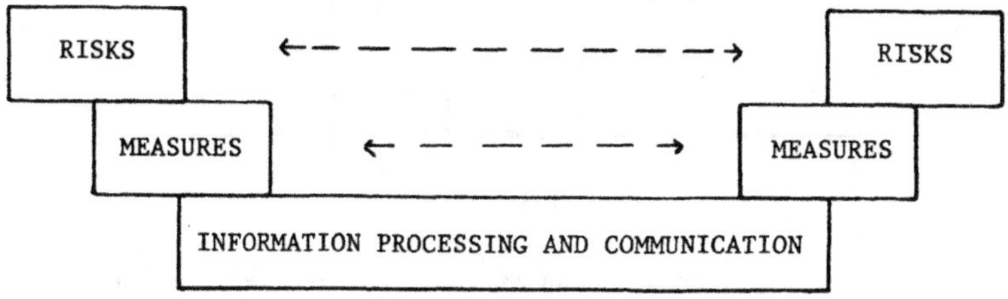

fig. 2

Every level has a peer entity at both ends. If a (distributed) system needs security, an equal evaluation is necessary in order to avoid weak spots in the security environment.

This paper will be focused on the cryptographic aspects of the communication security.

4. ENCRYPTION

Several ways of encrypting information are available. In this application a cipher-feedback blockmode encryption has been selected (fig. 3).

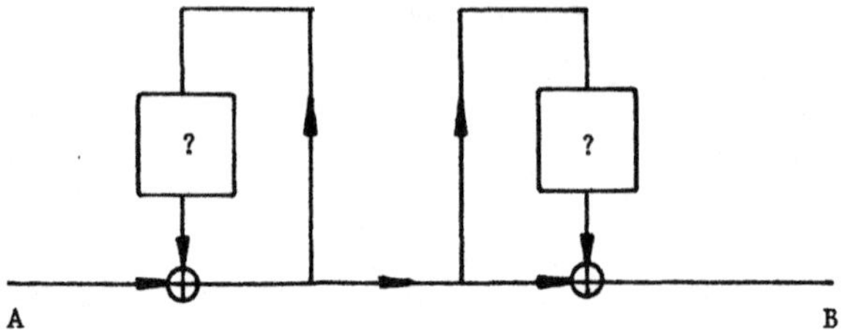

fig. 3

The reason why this mode has been chosen is found in the flat statistics for this mode in comparison with straightforward encryption.
Iterative loops and fault divergent properties in autokey modes are not very favourable for extensive use either.
In the prototype version the Data Encryption Standard (DES) may be used, but it is possible to use different compositions due to the greater processing speed in several of the DES integrated circuits.
Multi-encryption, in contrast with double encryption will be discussed in chapter 5.
First of all, the communication between user A and the system B has to be defined.
The procedure for communication between A and B may be as follows, when for example, A talks to B.

- A unlocks his terminal
- A dials the system and synchronizes with B
- A says to B: Hello I am terminal number X
- B chooses the corresponding key which X will use.
- B send the message (N) Ex to A. In which N is a random number. Ex is the key which may be used for encryption/decryption for the communication with the supposed terminal X.
- A decrypts the message and computes (N+terminal id. X) Ex and sends the message to B
- B decrypts the message and subtracts the terminal identification number which he supposes. The number left over together with the original N sent by B provides the check on the terminal identity.

The conversation between A and B is basically defined by two sets of services primitives.

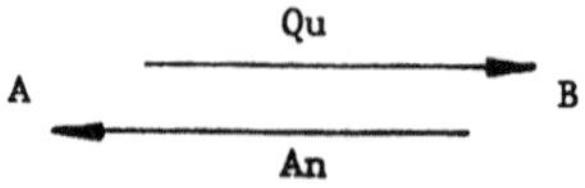

fig. 4

in which Qu = Question and An = Answer (Acknowledge).
Because of the two way operation (full duplex connection), both ends need an encryption buffer (E),/decryption buffer (D) (fig. 5).

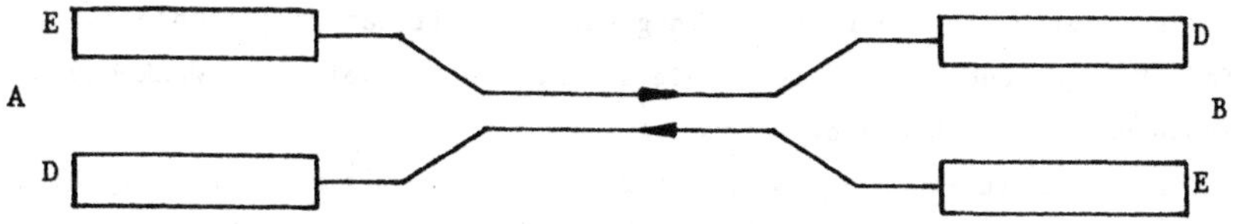

fig. 5

he buffers A, E and B, D used in the ciphertext-feedback mode may
ccasionally differ from their corresponding contents. This may have the following auses:

- A and B lost synchronisation
- transmission errors
- somebody tries to inject or modify information !!

ue to the composition of the communication protocol, A or B will detect large errors n the decrypted message. In view of the ciphertext chaining at least one block is istorted.
 will notify A, or A will notify B the error state. As a result an error and identi-y recovery procedure will be started. By the time the buffers are reloaded according o an error recovery procedure A, buffer E and B, buffer D contain new values, unknown o third parties.
he buffer contents will continue to proceed after the Question/Answer procedure has een re-established.
f a restart seems to be impossible, a disconnect will occur.
n this case the length of the blockcipher provides the length of the discarded mes-age.
 longer length indicates an easier detection if errors are introduced or information s injected into the communication channel. This advantage will be offered by the multi-ncryption scheme, which is discussed in the next chapter.
f course the keys which are used in this system are available at both communication nds. Several keys may be loaded for use. The changes may be effected by an internal imer, keys may be stored in CMOS with battery back-up.
ampering with a terminal automatically deletes the keys by means of the battery backup. ccess to operating the terminal may be provided by a physical key which (un)locks the eyboard or a password which provides access to the terminal only.

5. MULTI- ENCRYPTION

Because of the fact that a more extensive block length encryption has certain advantages (also disadvantages) over smaller block lengths and also considering that there is a surplus of cryptographic transformation speed in most DES chips available, it will be possible to strengthen the encryption. In general in literature a double encryption is advised for stronger encryption, but these schemes do not solve the weak-key problem which is introduced with double encryption.

The main principle of multi-encryption is found in a better mixing of the key bits with the data bits. An example is given in fig. 6. which is a simple but effective revision of the well-known double encryption scheme! This scheme will not give known results with weak and semi-weak keys.

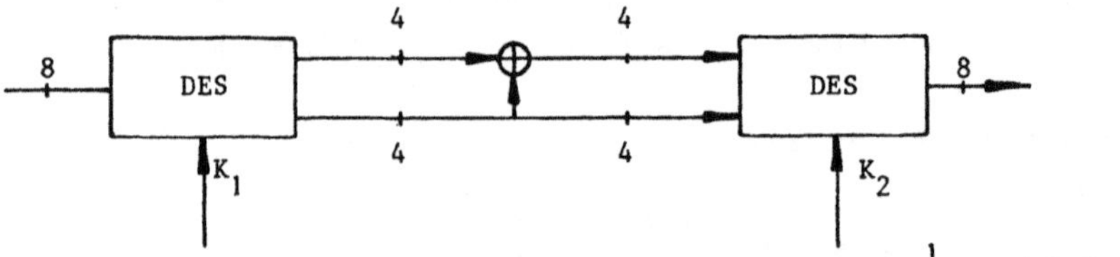

fig. 6

Fig. 7 shows a multi-encryption scheme. The key length is 112 bits. This scheme resists the weak keys. It is also much harder to break than a single encryption scheme or the double encryption scheme.

The reason is that a mixing of all key bits with all the different data bits simulates the use of encryption data with a larger key.

This may mean that the key is not so easy to break, even if the key bits are randomly selected from ASCII characters only.

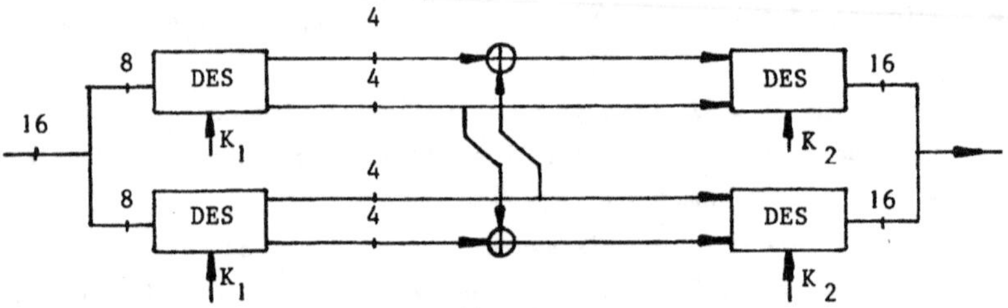

fig. 7

Different schemes are possible. This scheme enables the use the standard-defined DES modes as autokey feed-back and ciphertext feedback.

Then, only a larger block is required in the feedback loop.

Multi-encryption schemes are in general more complex than the single encryption schemes. The multi-encryption schemes solve the (semi) weak key problem. The decryption by unauthorised persons will be considerably more complex due to a longer key and perhaps because the encryption scheme is not known.

Privacy and Data Protection in Medicine

Lothar Horbach
Institute for Medical Statistics and Documentation
University of Erlangen-Nürnberg

Privacy as an elementary individual right is legally based in paragraph 203 of the German penal code (3).

Misuse of informations relating to the private life or the business of a person known by a physician practising his profession is punished by imprisonment up to one year or by fine. Similar professional groups are also cited in paragraph 203. Certainly it is not by chance that medical doctors are noted in the first place. In the precomputer - era this was the only legal base concerning privacy.

Every young doctor entering a clinic was informed about some basic rules already in former times: No information about a patient should be given by phone: He may be asked for the state of disease of the mother named X by a person who is not the daughter but a curious neighbour.

There are plenty of data gathered for every patient in a modern clinic. Medical records at the end of a treatment are still nowadays remoted into a record office by systems varying from clinic to clinic. E.g. in systems where records are arranged in alphabetic order the char-women has no difficulty to look in a given moment for the diagnosis of some known person.

Both examples were and are still typical as violations of medical professional discretion. They represent hurts of single persons' privacy. No curious person would be able to take away all or big parts of the tons of paper of a medical record office.

This situation has completely changed with the introduction of computers into medical services. Taking into account the growing mass of data in modern clinics, e.g. by investigations in different laboratories, the handling of data by computers has become a necessity. But which is the cause for these large discussions about medical data banks managed by the aid of computers which generally only store a part of medical informations about patients. The old record offices are persisting.

A first cause of this apprehension in public life and the development of laws is the facilitated handling of masses of data, its transfer and the possibilities of evaluations by the computer. In this situation the consciousness of the population and the legal authorities have changed.

Since the 28th April 1978 a bavarian data protection law exists which is - like in other German Länder - closely related to the general German law of the protection of person - related data (2). In this new law reference is made to a lot of technical details of data handling by computers: control of entering, delivery, storage, use, access, transfer, ordering, organization of data etc. in computer systems.

This workshop deals with cryptographical methods supporting protection of data. I feel the necessity to add to your technical devices of Crypthography some remarks of quite another point of view of the problem. There is a big lack of legal indications for the different procedures of data protection. In reverse by this legal uncertainty in many fields medical research is obstructed by the new laws of data protection, expecially in epidemiology. In the same time I'll try to turn out some problems calling for technical solutions deriving from these considerations.

Lawyers in a conference about "Privacy-Data Bank-Data Protection" organized by the Society for Legal and Admistration Informatics held in Bad Homburg v.d.H. in February 1982 took reference to the classical relation physician to patient. In a modern university clinic patients are often presented to very different clinical offices of diagnosis and/or therapy and in the same time to different physicians. Generally a 1 to n relationship with perhaps different levels of privacy exists. What are the consequences of data handling by a computer?

In order to highlight the arising difficulties I will take the example of the development of our Clinical Information System in Erlangen where our Medical Faculty is equiped by a computer of the type SIEMENS 7.541 which is installed in the Institute of Medical Documentation and Statistics. In a first stage we are about to implement a cancer registry including identification, diagnosis, histological characterization of the tumour and some data of follow-up. There are patients only documented by one clinic, others treated and documented by different clinics.

There ist no doubt about the fact that the record linkage of data arising at different places and at different times is only possible if they can be related to the identification of a given person by name, number or other identifyers. We are not legitimated to implement a common data banc for all participating clinics if we follow the old rule that only those data should be available for a physicion and/or a clinic, if they are related to a patient treated by the physician repectively the clinic.

The question deturning from this situation is how to admit an access to particular patient files but prevent the access to the others. Besides privacy the interest of clinicians is for example to prevent that collegues may use data of their own for scientific investigations. Sometimes it is a question of bilateral convention if physicians from different clinics have access to all data concerning patients treated in at least one of these clinics for the sake of a quick access to data in emergency cases, e.g. between internal medicine and surgery.

If we take into consideration only the access of physicians to patient-related data in a university clinic data protection laws of to-day are not restrictive. The only question should be cleared that those who supervise and handle data - generally medical informaticians and their personnel - have to be associates to the staff of physicians. In the case of the cancer registry in Erlangen which is supported by a fund of the Federal Government the issue was that the chief supervisor should be a doctor.

But following the law of data protection the patient entering a clinic has to give his consent by signature that his data are stored and handled by a computer. If he refuses he should not have any personal disadvantage as it is postulated by lawyers. But in modern clinical laboratories there are computers fullfilling routine work in on line registering, correcting and transferring data. Refusing patients would necessarily have disadvantages because computers are involved in modern clinica investigation techniques.

In my opinion the legitimate postulation of the law is the protection of data against use for other than medical purposes. There is a catalogue of technical and organisatorial measures in the interest of data protection according to paragraph 6 of the Federal data protection law (BDSG) respectively article 15 of the Bavarian law (BayDSG). Patient-related medical data in the schedule of stages of growing safety from A to E are situated in the 4th position (D). Here the data are classed the misuse of which can essentially impair the social or the economic situation of a person. Organisatorial measures, hardware devices, numerous software strategies - which should be user-isolated - and access control measures are prescribed. Lawyers admit a certain cost-benefit-relationship of measures to be taken (1). The procedures of data protection and securing from the standpoint of the informaticians are discussed by WEDEKIND (4). I cannot enter into the details within the frame of my exposure.

But I'll try to point out the difficulties arisen by the laws of data protection for the German medical research of to-day, especially for epidemiology.

In the last years we carried out the statistical evaluation of a professional cancer study in the heavy chemical industry in Germany. We had to link data from different places and institutionswithin and outside the factories to files of persons dead by cancer or other causes within a certain interval of time in the considered factories.

The identification of the person was only necessary in the working phase of data linkage. We got the person files without identification: after the linkage of data this identification for the statistician was without any importance; anonymized data were sufficient for the evaluation of the working histories concerning exposure to chemical agents and its statistical association with the cause of death. The gathering of these data was organized by physicians belonging to the factories. In the early 70th they had no difficulties to get data describing chemical exposure, but already minor problems to have informations concerning the cause of death by general practitioners, clinics or boards of health which gather the coroner's inquests.

Today the carrying out of such a study would be impossible because modern laws of data protection have lead to an awarenes of the problem of privacy together with legal uncertainty to which extent person-related data, even data of dead persons, should be protected. Only if laws are more precisely formulated the procedures of protection - expecially those of Cryptography discussed in this workshop - can be applied in an effective and usefull manner.

Literatur

1) ANGERMANN, A., THOME, R. — Ansätze für eine Kosten-Nutzen-Analyse des Datenschutzes
data report 8, 18 - 22 (1973)

2) DAMMANN, U., SIMITIS, SP. — Bundesdatenschutzgesetz (BSSG)
Textausgabe mit Auszügen aus der Gesetzgebungsdokumentation und den Verwaltungsvorschriften der Länder
Nomos Verlagsgesellschaft, 4. Aufl., Baden-Baden 1981

3) DESCHEK, H.-H. — Strafgesetzbuch
Textausgabe mit ausführlichem Sachregister und einer Einführung
dtv., 19. Auflage, München 1980

4) WEDEKIND, H. — Zur Durchführung des § 6,1 BDSG
Datenschutz und Datensicherung, 4, 181-185 (1978)

Section 7

The Data Encryption Standard

Cryptanalysis of the Data Encryption Standard by the Method of Formal Coding

by

Ingrid Schaumüller-Bichl

VOEST - ALPINE AG
A-4010 Linz
AUSTRIA

ABSTRACT:

The "Method of Formal Coding" consists in representing each bit of a DES ciphertext block as an XOR-sum-of-products of the plaintext bits and the key bits. Subsequent introduction of the "MFC-complexity measure" yields interesting results on the security of the DES and the influence of various parameters.

I) Introduction:

In January 1977 the US National Bureau of Standards published the specifications for the Data Encryption Standard (DES for short), that is "to be used by US Federal organizations when these organizations specify that cryptographic protection is to be used for sensitive or valuable computer data" ([NBS, 1977])

In its basic form the algorithm enciphers and deciphers blocks of data consisting of 64 bits under control of a 64 bit key performing 16 rounds.

After being subjected to an initial permutation IP the plaintext block P is devided into a left half L_o and a right half R_o. In each of the 16 rounds

$$L_i := R_{i-1}$$

and

$$R_i := L_{i-1} \oplus f(R_{i-1}, K_i)$$

are computed (here i runs from 1 to 16, K_i consists of 48 bits selected from the key K, the "cipher function" f is a concatenation of substitution and permutation). Subjecting the result to the inverse initial permutation IP^{-1} yields the ciphertext C.

Knowledge of the DES is prerequisite for this paper. A detailed description of the algorithm can be found in [NBS, 1977] We shall use the terminology given there with the two slight exceptions of the expansion function E and the permutation P that will be designated EXP and PER in this paper in order to prevent confusion with the commonly used abbreviations for "encipherment" and "plaintext" respectively.

Yet before adopted as an US standard the DES aroused a lot of discussions and disputes about its security that did not cease up to this day. But although the algorithm was subjected to thorough examinations no method was published until now to solve for a single key bit in a time acceptable for practical purposes.

Also the Method of Formal Coding , a short cut attack against which the DES is not unconditionally secure, should not be expected to be able to actually break the DES in the near future because of the enormous amount of computer memory needed. But guided by it the "MFC-complexity measure" can be introduced that proves to be quite adequate to meet the needs of cryptocomplexity Introducing also a complexity measure adequate for S-boxes (called S-complexity) renders possible to analyse the influence of various parameters of the DES on the security of that cipher system and to make frequently used, but rather vague propositions such as "using linear S-boxes weakens the DES considerably", "raising the number of rounds raises the security" or "multiple encryption guarantees multiple security" more precise.

II) The Method of Formal Coding

Although not necessary in principle all considerations in this paper are based on a known plaintext attack, that means, that the cryptanalyst has not only full knowledge about the cipher system, but also knows any amount of plaintext and corresponding ciphertext he needs. His task is to determine the key in use.

One possible method to compute the key at least in principle is the Method of Formal Coding.

The main idea was suggested in [Hellman, 1976]: every bit of the ciphertext is represented as a term in XOR-sum-of-products-form (XOR-sop-form) of the 64 (known) plaintext bits and the 64 (unknown) key bits. To accomplish that, the unknown key bits are put up by the literal expressions $k_1, k_2, \ldots k_{64}$. Then the very same algorithm as for encipherment is performed with the only exception that computation is not done in $\mathbb{Z}_2$, but in $\mathbb{Z}_2[k_1, k_2, \ldots k_{64}]$ (the ring of polynomials in the variables $k_1, k_2, \ldots k_{64}$ with coefficients in $\mathbb{Z}_2$).

It is obvious how to perform the permutations IP,IP^{-1}, PER and the expansion function EXP in $\mathbb{Z}_2[k_1,k_2,...k_{64}]$. What remains is the computation of

$$S(EXP(R_{i-1}) \oplus K_i).$$

We shall see in chapter 3 that it is easy to represent every output variable of an S-box in XOR-sum-of-products-form of the six input variables, but that it is usually very difficult to find "minimal" representations.

Proceeding this way yields 64 terms in XOR-sop-form. As 8 bits of the key are used only for parity check and not for encipherment they will not occur in these terms. So equating each term with the corresponding bit of the ciphertext yields a system of 64 equations in 56 unknowns (the relevant key bits). The existence of a solution for this system is guaranteed, but its uniqueness is not.

III) Two Complexity Measures

Attempting to apply the Method of Formal Coding to actually break the DES we are soon faced with the following practical difficulties: the terms occuring in computations become "big", "complicated" or however one likes to express it. In order to make this statement more precise we need some definitions:

Definition 1:

a) Let $n \in \mathbb{N}$, $p \in \mathbb{Z}_2[x_1,...x_n]$ be in XOR-sop-form with

$$p = a_o \oplus \sum_{j=1}^{n} \sum_{1 \leq i_1 ... i_j \leq n} a_{i_1...i_j} x_{i_1} \cdots x_{i_j}$$

then

$$|\{a_{i_1...i_j} \mid a_{i_1...i_j} = 1\}| =: L_p$$

is the length of the polynomial p.

b) Let $p,q \in \mathbb{Z}_2[x_1,\ldots x_n]$, $\bar{p},\bar{q}$ be the induced polynomial functions.

p and q are <u>equivalent</u>: <=>

$$:\Leftrightarrow \quad \bar{p}(a_1,\ldots a_n) = \bar{q}(a_1,\ldots a_n) \qquad (\forall\ (a_1,\ldots a_n) \in (\mathbb{Z}_2)^n)$$

c) p is <u>simpler</u> than q: <=> $L_p < L_q$

d) A polynomial in $\mathbb{Z}_2[x_1,\ldots x_n]$ is called <u>MFC-minimal</u>, if there exists no simpler equivalent polynomial.

For simplicity we shall abbreviate "p is equivalent to q" "p=q" from now on.

It is easy to show that for every term occuring during computation in the MFC there exists an equivalent MFC-minimal polynomial, but the task always to find one with justifiable expense of time and memory seems to be unsolved until today. In [Schaumüller, 1981] two algorithms are presented both based on well known rules of calculation in $\mathbb{Z}_2$ and both often considerably simplifying a polynomial in $\mathbb{Z}_2[k_1,\ldots k_n]$ with respect to definition 1.c., but both not guaranteeing to yield an MFC-minimal polynomial.

Nevertheless the concept of MFC-minimal polynomials makes it possible to define a complexity measure for the DES that seems to be quite adequate to the needs of cryptocomplexity:

<u>Definition 2:</u>

Let

P and $C \in (\mathbb{Z}_2)^{64}$ be a corresponding plaintext-ciphertext pair,

$$T_1'(k_1,\ldots k_{64}) = c_1$$
$$\vdots$$
$$T_{64}'(k_1,\ldots k_{64}) = c_{64}$$

the system of equations obtained by the Formal Coding of P, and let

$$T_i(k_1,\ldots k_{64}) \qquad (i\in\{1,\ldots 64\})$$

be an MFC-minimal term equivalent to

$$T_i'(k_1,\ldots k_{64})$$

Then
$$\sum_{i=1}^{64} L_{T_i}$$

is the MFC-complexity of the DES with respect to the plaintext P.

Although the length of each term - and consequently the MFC-complexity of the DES, which is the sum of the lengths of the individual terms - depends on the specific plaintext, we often relinguish accurateness and speak simply of "the MFC-complexity of the DES" as we are mainly interested in orders of magnitude and it may be assumed that they are approximately equal for every plaintext with other parameters remaining unchanged.

The complexity measure just introduced is one out of many possible. It meets the demands we have to put to such a measure in a high degree: the higher the MFC-complexity the more difficult it is firstly to actually compute the system of equations and secondly to solve this system, i.e. to compute the key in use thus breaking the Data Encryption Standard.

It is not possible at present to specify the actual MFC-complexity of the DES. We only can give an upper bound of

$$64.\sum_{i=0}^{56}\binom{56}{i} = 64.2^{56} \approx 5.10^{18} \qquad (*)$$

This is a big number indeed. But, as mentioned above, it is an upper bound, while the actual MFC-complexity of the DES might be by far smaller (compare the special case of linearized DES-versions!).

Moreover the main object of the Method of Formal Coding is to investigate the influence of the individual parameters on the security of the DES, something that can be accomplished at least partly also by considering simplified versions.

To begin with we have to put the question which items of the DES influence its MFC-complexity at all.
It is easy to see that these are

- ◊ the block length
- ◊ the key length
- ◊ the number of rounds
- ◊ IP, PC-1, PC-2, EXP, PER
- ◊ the S-boxes
- ◊ the plaintext

The effect of each of these parameters can be investigated by changing it while all other parameters remain fixed and observing the changes in the MFC-complexity.

Simple considerations show that the influences of IP, PC-1, PC-2, EXP, PER, the block length and the plaintext are rather small, as long as "pathological" cases like

$$\text{PC-2} = \begin{pmatrix} 1 & 1 & 1 & \dots & 1 \\ \vdots & & & & \vdots \\ 1 & 1 & 1 & \dots & 1 \end{pmatrix}$$

are avoided.

Of central importance for the security of the DES against an MFC-attack are:

- ◊ the key length
- ◊ the number of rounds
- ◊ the S-boxes

We see that these are the very same parameters that one would specify intuitively if asked what parameters of the DES are most important for its security. This indicates again that the MFC-complexity measure is quite adequate for the analysis of the DES.

The effects of reducing the key length and the number of rounds are obvious. What remains to be investigated is the effect of a "simplification" of the S-boxes. For that purpose we have to lay down first when an S-box is to be called "simpler" or "more complicated" than a second one.

Viewing an S-box as a table with 4 times 16 elements from $\mathbb{Z}_{16}$ like in [NBS, 1977], this seems to be impossible. Nevertheless everyone might intuitively call linear S-boxes simpler than affine ones and these again by far simpler than those used in the DES.

In order to make these ideas more precise we use the binary versions of S-boxes, that means, we represent them as functions

$$S_i : (\mathbb{Z}_2)^6 \longrightarrow (\mathbb{Z}_2)^4 \qquad (i \in \{1,\ldots 8\})$$

$$(x_1,\ldots x_6) \longmapsto ({}_iy_1,\ldots {}_iy_4)$$

As every ${}_iy_j$ can be represented by an element in $\mathbb{Z}_2[x_1,\ldots x_6]$ (we call $({}_iz_1,\ldots {}_iz_4)$ $({}_iz_j \in \mathbb{Z}_2[x_1,\ldots x_6])$ an MFC-representation of an S-box) we are lead to the following definition:

<u>Definition 3:</u>

Let S be an S-box,

$(z_1,\ldots z_4)$ an MFC-representation of S,

r_k the number of summands in $(z_1,\ldots z_4)$ with strictly k variables.

Then

$$Com(S) := (r_6, r_5, \ldots r_1, r_o)$$

is the <u>S-complexity</u> of the given MFC-representation of S.

If there is no danger of confusion we shall often speak simply of the S-complexity or merely the complexity of an S-box.

Introducing lexicographic order it is possible to compare the complexities of different MFC-representations of the same S-box as well as different S-boxes.

It is of central importance to find MFC-representations of S-boxes which are minimal in respect to the S-complexity measure just introduced (we shall call them <u>S-minimal</u>).

For that purpose the following lemma proves useful:

Lemma:

a) For every S-box there exists an MFC-representation with complexity

$$(128,0,0,0,0,0,0)$$

b) For every linear resp. affine S-box there exists an S-minimal MFC-representation with complexity

$$(0,0,0,0,0,r_1,0) \quad \text{resp.} \quad (0,0,0,0,0,r_1,r_o)$$

c) For every S-box there exists an MFC-representation with complexity

$$(0,r_5,r_4,r_3,r_2,r_1,r_o)$$

Sketches of proofs:

a) Compute the disjunctive canonical form and replace "$\vee$" by "$\oplus$"

b) As in linear S-boxes

$$S(a \oplus b) = S(a) \oplus S(b)$$

must hold true, every z_i must be a sum of merely linear expressions x_j.

Affine S-boxes differ from linear ones only in that the constant 1 may be added to one or several z_i.

c) Proceeding from the representation described in a) we may represent every

$$\bar{x}_j \quad \text{by} \quad x_j \oplus 1$$

and multiply out.

The result contains the product

$$x_1 x_2 x_3 x_4 x_5 x_6$$

32 times, all other summands have less than 6 factors.

(The same result was presented by R.Schroeppel in [Hellman, 1976] but proved differently.)

It was not yet possible to find MFC-representations of the S-boxes used in DES that are guaranteed to be S-minimal. But applying different methods that are not contained in this paper, we succeeded in computing representations with at least "rather small" complexities. These representations are summarized in the appendix.

IV) Implementing the Method of Formal Coding for Special Cases

The Method of Formal Coding was implemented on a minicomputer for two special cases:

a) an algorithm similar to the DES in its basic features but strongly simplified (it was called VDES and is described in its details in [Schaumüller, 1981]).

b) DES-versions with linear or affine S-boxes.

The corresponding computer programs were called FCVDES and FCLDES respectively.

The plaintext-ciphertext-pairs needed for the Method of Formal Coding were computed by the program "DES" that is presented in [Biermeier, 1980]. This program was not only designed for enciphering and deciphering under the Data Encryption Standard, but also gives the user the opportunity to change all relevant parameters of the algorithm.

While FCVDES was used only for demonstration FCLDES yielded some interesting results, among them:

1) Computation speed:

   Of course in this special case the Method of Formal Coding yields the required key by far faster than a brute force attack that indeed does not take advantage of the special structure of linear S-boxes. But it seems to be even faster than computing the key from the equation

$$C = AP+BK \qquad (A\in(\mathbb{Z}_2)^{64}_{64}\ ,\ B\in(\mathbb{Z}_2)^{56}_{64}\ )$$

   by computing

$$K = B^{-1}(C-AP)$$

2) The maximal MFC-complexity of a DES-version with linear or affine S-boxes is

$$56.64 = 3584$$

Computation of several examples yielded that the actual complexity (which, by the way, depends merely on the S-boxes, but not on the plaintext in this special case) is about half as big on an average.

V) The Influence of the Parameters

a) Key length vs maximal MFC-complexity of corresponding DES-versions:
As obvious from (*) in chapter 3 the maximal MFC-complexity is reduced by a factor of 2 when the key length is diminished by 1.
(Note that this result is similar to that one derived in the entirely different case of brute force attacks.)

b) Maximal and average actual MFC-complexity vs number of rounds:
At present this connection can be stated only for linearized DES-versions:

The maximal MFC-complexity rises strongly in the first three rounds. Here the same percentages are valid as given in [Meyer, 1978] for the cipher text/key intersymbol dependence vs number of rounds. This implies that the upper bound of the MFC-complexity is reached after 5 rounds.
Evaluation of the results obtained from a number of examples yielded that the average actual complexity in every round is about half as high.

c) S-complexity vs MFC-complexity:
With the exception of the key length the S-boxes are the item most essential to the MFC-complexity of the DES (and

incontestedly also to its security).
One possible way to estimate the actual MFC-complexity of the DES is the analysis of DES-versions with S-boxes of smaller S-complexity.
Starting from linear and affine S-boxes S-boxes with complexity $(0,0,0,0,r_2,r_1,r_o)$, subsequently $(0,0,0,r_3,r_2,r_1,r_o)$ and so on will have to be investigated, whereat there is hope that conclusions on the actual complexity of the DES can be drawn.

A lot of other questions arise in this context, but it is hardly possible to answer them by merely theoretical considerations. What is rather needed are the results of actual experiments, but they can be obtained only after implementing the Method of Formal Coding on a large special purpose computer.

VI) How to raise the security of the DES:

Competent experts agree that the DES will yield to a brute force attack in a future not too far away though vehement disputes about the exact date arouse.

In order to increase security it is often suggested (cf [Hellman, 1976]) to use a 128 bit key.

There are a lot of possibilities to realize such a doubling of key length. The preceding considerations give a hint how to accomplish that very effectively: instead of merely providing a new algorithm for the generation of partial keys selecting 48 bits from 128 in every round it would be better whether to replace the 8 S-boxes by four S-boxes each having 12 inputs and 8 outputs or by additionally doubling the block length and using 8 S-boxes with 12 inputs and 8 outputs each. As such S-boxes may have an S-complexity up to

$$(0,r_{11},r_{10},\ldots r_o)$$

the MFC-complexity of a corresponding DES-version may increase considerably.

VII) Can the Method of Formal Coding Be Used to Actually Break DES ?

It must be doubted that the Method of Formal Coding as it was presented in chapter 2 will ever be employed to break the Data Encryption Standard. For as soon as there exist computers that are able to perform a successful MFC-attack the very same computers may be used for a brute force attack also. Nevertheless if some efficient algorithm for the minimization of polynomials in $\mathbb{Z}_2[x_1,...x_n]$ is found successful cryptanalysis of the DES might be accomplished by the following slight modification of the Method of Formal Coding: instead of starting only from the plaintext and computing the polynomials corresponding to the ciphertext bits by performing 16 rounds, we can "start from both sides", i.e., the plaintext as well as the ciphertext are enciphered resp. deciphered "formally" (that means, computation is done in $\mathbb{Z}_2[k_1,...k_{64}]$) in 8 rounds. Subsequently the corresponding terms in L_8 and R_8 are equaled. Again a system of 64 equations in 56 unknowns is to be solved, but now the computations for deriving as well as for solving this system should be by far simpler.

Appendix:

S-boxes, their MFC-representations and S-complexities:

S1:

Table of S1:

14	4	13	1	2	15	11	8	3	10	6	12	5	9	0	7
0	15	7	4	14	2	13	1	10	6	12	11	9	5	3	8
4	1	14	8	13	6	2	11	15	12	9	7	3	10	5	0
15	12	8	2	4	9	1	7	5	11	3	14	10	0	6	13

MFC-representation:

$$y_1 = x_1x_2\bar{x}_3\bar{x}_4x_6 \oplus x_1x_2\bar{x}_3\bar{x}_5x_6 \oplus \bar{x}_1\bar{x}_2x_3\bar{x}_4 \oplus \bar{x}_1\bar{x}_3\bar{x}_4\bar{x}_5 \oplus$$
$$x_1\bar{x}_2x_4\bar{x}_5 \oplus \bar{x}_1\bar{x}_3x_4\bar{x}_6 \oplus x_4x_5\bar{x}_6 \oplus x_3\bar{x}_5 \oplus \bar{x}_4x_6 \oplus x_2$$

$$y_2 = x_1x_2\bar{x}_3x_5\bar{x}_6 \oplus x_1\bar{x}_2x_3\bar{x}_4\bar{x}_6 \oplus \bar{x}_1\bar{x}_3\bar{x}_4\bar{x}_5x_6 \oplus \bar{x}_1\bar{x}_2\bar{x}_4x_5x_6 \oplus$$
$$x_2x_4\bar{x}_5\bar{x}_6 \oplus \bar{x}_1\bar{x}_4x_5 \oplus \bar{x}_1x_2\bar{x}_6 \oplus \bar{x}_2x_5x_6 \oplus \bar{x}_2x_3x_6 \oplus x_1x_4x_6 \oplus \bar{x}_3\bar{x}_5$$

$$y_3 = \bar{x}_1\bar{x}_2\bar{x}_3\bar{x}_4\bar{x}_6 \oplus \bar{x}_1x_2x_4x_5\bar{x}_6 \oplus x_1x_3\bar{x}_4\bar{x}_5x_6 \oplus x_1\bar{x}_2\bar{x}_3x_5x_6 \oplus$$
$$\bar{x}_1\bar{x}_2x_3x_5 \oplus x_4\bar{x}_5x_6 \oplus \bar{x}_2\bar{x}_4x_5 \oplus x_1\bar{x}_4\bar{x}_6 \oplus x_1\bar{x}_3\bar{x}_5 \oplus x_2 \oplus x_3$$

$$y_4 = \bar{x}_1x_2\bar{x}_4\bar{x}_5\bar{x}_6 \oplus \bar{x}_1\bar{x}_2x_4x_5x_6 \oplus x_1\bar{x}_3\bar{x}_4x_5\bar{x}_6 \oplus x_1\bar{x}_2\bar{x}_3\bar{x}_4\bar{x}_6 \oplus$$
$$\bar{x}_1\bar{x}_2x_3\bar{x}_5x_6 \oplus x_3\bar{x}_5\bar{x}_6 \oplus x_4x_5x_6 \oplus \bar{x}_2x_5x_6 \oplus \bar{x}_2x_4 \oplus x_3 \oplus x_1$$

S-complexity:

$$\mathrm{Com}(S1) = (0,15,6,13,4,5,0)$$

S2:

Table of S2:

15	1	8	14	6	11	3	4	9	7	2	13	12	0	5	10
3	13	4	7	15	2	8	14	12	0	1	10	6	9	11	5
0	14	7	11	10	4	13	1	5	8	12	6	9	3	2	15
13	8	10	1	3	15	4	2	11	6	7	12	0	5	14	9

MFC-representation:

$$y_1 = x_1\bar{x}_2\bar{x}_4x_5\bar{x}_6 \oplus \bar{x}_1x_2\bar{x}_3\bar{x}_6 \oplus x_1x_3x_5x_6 \oplus \bar{x}_2\bar{x}_4\bar{x}_5 \oplus x_1\bar{x}_2\bar{x}_5 \oplus x_2x_5 \oplus x_3 \oplus x_4 \oplus x_6$$

$$y_2 = x_1x_2x_4x_5\bar{x}_6 \oplus x_1x_2x_3x_5\bar{x}_6 \oplus \bar{x}_3x_4x_5x_6 \oplus x_2x_4\bar{x}_6 \oplus \bar{x}_3x_6 \oplus x_2\bar{x}_3 \oplus x_1 \oplus x_4 \oplus \bar{x}_5$$

$$y_3 = x_1x_2\bar{x}_3x_5\bar{x}_6 \oplus \bar{x}_1x_2\bar{x}_4\bar{x}_5x_6 \oplus x_1x_2\bar{x}_3\bar{x}_4 \oplus \bar{x}_1x_3\bar{x}_4\bar{x}_5 \oplus \bar{x}_1x_3x_4x_6 \oplus x_1x_4x_5 \oplus x_2\bar{x}_3x_6 \oplus x_1x_5x_6 \oplus x_1 \oplus x_2 \oplus x_3 \oplus x_4 \oplus \bar{x}_5$$

$$y_4 = \bar{x}_1\bar{x}_2\bar{x}_3\bar{x}_5\bar{x}_6 \oplus \bar{x}_1x_2\bar{x}_4x_6 \oplus x_1x_2x_3\bar{x}_5 \oplus x_2\bar{x}_4\bar{x}_5\bar{x}_6 \oplus \bar{x}_1x_4x_5x_6 \oplus \bar{x}_3\bar{x}_5x_6 \oplus \bar{x}_2x_3\bar{x}_6 \oplus \bar{x}_1x_5 \oplus \bar{x}_2x_4 \oplus x_3$$

S-complexity:

$$Com(S2) = (0,6,10,8,5,12,0)$$

S3:

Table of S3:

10	0	9	14	6	3	15	5	1	13	12	7	11	4	2	8
13	7	0	9	3	4	6	10	2	8	5	14	12	11	15	1
13	6	4	9	8	15	3	0	11	1	2	12	5	10	14	7
1	10	13	0	6	9	8	7	4	15	14	3	11	5	2	12

MFC-representation:

$$y_1 = \bar{x}_1\bar{x}_2x_4x_5\bar{x}_6 \oplus \bar{x}_1x_3\bar{x}_4x_5x_6 \oplus \bar{x}_1\bar{x}_2\bar{x}_3\bar{x}_4 \oplus \bar{x}_2x_3\bar{x}_5\bar{x}_6 \oplus \bar{x}_1\bar{x}_4\bar{x}_6 \oplus x_2x_3x_6 \oplus x_1x_4 \oplus \bar{x}_3\bar{x}_6 \oplus x_5$$

$$y_2 = x_1\bar{x}_3x_4x_5x_6 \oplus \bar{x}_1x_2\bar{x}_3\bar{x}_5\bar{x}_6 \oplus \bar{x}_1x_2\bar{x}_3x_4 \oplus x_2x_4x_6 \oplus x_4\bar{x}_5\bar{x}_6 \oplus x_3\bar{x}_5 \oplus x_1 \oplus x_2 \oplus x_4 \oplus x_6$$

$$y_3 = \bar{x}_1\bar{x}_2\bar{x}_3\bar{x}_4\bar{x}_6 \oplus x_1x_3x_4\bar{x}_5\bar{x}_6 \oplus x_1\bar{x}_2x_4x_5\bar{x}_6 \oplus \bar{x}_1\bar{x}_3x_5\bar{x}_6 \oplus \bar{x}_1\bar{x}_3x_4x_5 \oplus \bar{x}_3x_4x_5x_6 \oplus \bar{x}_1\bar{x}_2\bar{x}_4x_5 \oplus \bar{x}_1\bar{x}_2x_5x_6 \oplus x_1x_2\bar{x}_3\bar{x}_6 \oplus x_1x_3\bar{x}_4x_6 \oplus x_2\bar{x}_4x_6 \oplus x_1x_2x_6 \oplus \bar{x}_1x_3 \oplus x_5$$

$$y_4 = x_1x_2x_3\bar{x}_4x_6 \oplus x_1x_2\bar{x}_5x_6 \oplus x_1\bar{x}_2\bar{x}_3\bar{x}_5 \oplus \bar{x}_1x_4\bar{x}_5 \oplus x_1\bar{x}_4\bar{x}_6 \oplus x_3x_5 \oplus x_1 \oplus x_2 \oplus x_6$$

S-complexity:

Com(S3) = (0,8,12,8,5,9,0)

S4:

Table of S4:

7	13	14	3	0	6	9	10	1	2	8	5	11	12	4	15
13	8	11	5	6	15	0	3	4	7	2	12	1	10	14	9
10	6	9	0	12	11	7	13	15	1	3	14	5	2	8	4
3	15	0	6	10	1	13	8	9	4	5	11	12	7	2	14

MFC-representation:

$$y_1 = x_1\bar{x}_3\bar{x}_4\bar{x}_5\bar{x}_6 \oplus x_1x_2\bar{x}_3x_4\bar{x}_6 \oplus \bar{x}_1\bar{x}_2\bar{x}_3\bar{x}_5x_6 \oplus \bar{x}_1x_2\bar{x}_3\bar{x}_4x_6 \oplus \bar{x}_2x_4\bar{x}_5x_6 \oplus \bar{x}_1x_3x_5\bar{x}_6 \oplus \bar{x}_1x_2x_3\bar{x}_5 \oplus \bar{x}_1\bar{x}_2\bar{x}_4x_5 \oplus x_1\bar{x}_4x_5x_6 \oplus x_1\bar{x}_2x_3 \oplus x_4\bar{x}_5 \oplus x_2x_6$$

$$y_2 = x_1\bar{x}_2\bar{x}_3x_4x_6 \oplus x_1x_3\bar{x}_4x_5x_6 \oplus \bar{x}_1x_2x_3x_5\bar{x}_6 \oplus \bar{x}_1x_2\bar{x}_3x_4\bar{x}_6 \oplus \bar{x}_2\bar{x}_4\bar{x}_5\bar{x}_6 \oplus \bar{x}_1x_2x_4x_5 \oplus x_1\bar{x}_2x_5\bar{x}_6 \oplus \bar{x}_1\bar{x}_2\bar{x}_3x_5 \oplus \bar{x}_3x_6 \oplus \bar{x}_2x_3 \oplus x_1\bar{x}_5 \oplus x_4$$

$$y_3 = x_1x_2x_3\bar{x}_5x_6 \oplus x_1x_2x_3\bar{x}_4x_6 \oplus \bar{x}_1x_3x_4\bar{x}_5\bar{x}_6 \oplus \bar{x}_1\bar{x}_2x_3\bar{x}_4\bar{x}_6 \oplus x_2x_4x_5x_6 \oplus x_1\bar{x}_2x_4\bar{x}_5 \oplus x_1\bar{x}_2\bar{x}_3\bar{x}_5 \oplus x_1\bar{x}_4\bar{x}_5x_6 \oplus \bar{x}_2\bar{x}_5x_6 \oplus \bar{x}_4x_6 \oplus \bar{x}_3\bar{x}_6 \oplus \bar{x}_4x_5 \oplus \bar{x}_2\bar{x}_3 \oplus \bar{x}_1$$

$$y_4 = x_1x_2\bar{x}_3x_4\bar{x}_6 \oplus x_1\bar{x}_2x_3x_5x_6 \oplus \bar{x}_1\bar{x}_3x_4x_5x_6 \oplus \bar{x}_1x_2x_3\bar{x}_4x_6 \oplus x_1\bar{x}_3\bar{x}_5\bar{x}_6 \oplus x_1\bar{x}_2x_4x_6 \oplus x_1x_2\bar{x}_4x_5 \oplus \bar{x}_2\bar{x}_4x_5\bar{x}_6 \oplus \bar{x}_1x_2\bar{x}_3 \oplus \bar{x}_1x_5 \oplus \bar{x}_2\bar{x}_6 \oplus \bar{x}_4\bar{x}_6 \oplus \bar{x}_3$$

S-complexity:

Com(S4) = (0,16,17,3,12,3,0)

S5:

Table of S5:

2	12	4	1	7	10	11	6	8	5	3	15	13	0	14	9
14	11	2	12	4	7	13	1	5	0	15	10	3	9	8	6
4	2	1	11	10	13	7	8	15	9	12	5	6	3	0	14
11	8	12	7	1	14	2	13	6	15	0	9	10	4	5	3

MFC-representation:

$$y_1 = \bar{x}_1\bar{x}_2\bar{x}_4\bar{x}_5\bar{x}_6 \oplus \bar{x}_1\bar{x}_3x_4\bar{x}_5\bar{x}_6 \oplus x_1x_3\bar{x}_4\bar{x}_5x_6 \oplus x_1\bar{x}_2x_3\bar{x}_4 \oplus x_1x_2\bar{x}_3\bar{x}_6 \oplus x_2x_4x_5x_6 \oplus x_2\bar{x}_3\bar{x}_5x_6 \oplus \bar{x}_1x_2x_5 \oplus \bar{x}_1\bar{x}_4x_6 \oplus x_4x_5 \oplus \bar{x}_3x_6 \oplus \bar{x}_1$$

$$y_2 = \bar{x}_1x_2\bar{x}_3\bar{x}_4\bar{x}_6 \oplus x_3\bar{x}_4\bar{x}_5x_6 \oplus x_1\bar{x}_4x_5x_6 \oplus x_1\bar{x}_3x_4x_5 \oplus x_2\bar{x}_4x_6 \oplus x_2\bar{x}_3\bar{x}_4 \oplus \bar{x}_1x_2\bar{x}_4 \oplus x_1 \oplus x_2 \oplus x_3 \oplus x_4 \oplus x_5 \oplus x_6$$

$$y_3 = \bar{x}_1\bar{x}_2\bar{x}_3\bar{x}_5\bar{x}_6 \oplus \bar{x}_1x_2\bar{x}_3\bar{x}_4\bar{x}_6 \oplus \bar{x}_1x_3\bar{x}_4\bar{x}_5\bar{x}_6 \oplus x_1x_2\bar{x}_4\bar{x}_5x_6 \oplus x_1\bar{x}_2x_3\bar{x}_5 \oplus x_1\bar{x}_4\bar{x}_5 \oplus \bar{x}_1\bar{x}_3x_6 \oplus \bar{x}_2\bar{x}_4\bar{x}_5 \oplus \bar{x}_3x_5 \oplus x_4x_6 \oplus x_1\bar{x}_6 \oplus x_2x_5 \oplus 1$$

$$y_4 = \bar{x}_1x_3x_4\bar{x}_5\bar{x}_6 \oplus x_1x_2\bar{x}_3\bar{x}_5\bar{x}_6 \oplus \bar{x}_1\bar{x}_2x_4x_5 \oplus x_1\bar{x}_2\bar{x}_3x_4 \oplus x_2\bar{x}_4\bar{x}_5\bar{x}_6 \oplus \bar{x}_1x_3\bar{x}_6 \oplus \bar{x}_3x_5\bar{x}_6 \oplus x_2\bar{x}_3x_5 \oplus x_3x_4 \oplus x_1x_6 \oplus \bar{x}_2\bar{x}_5 \oplus 1$$

S-complexity:

Com(S5) = (0,10,11,11,9,7,2)

S6:

Table of S6:

12	1	10	15	9	2	6	8	0	13	3	4	14	7	5	11
10	15	4	2	7	12	9	5	6	1	13	14	0	11	3	8
9	14	15	5	2	8	12	3	7	0	4	10	1	13	11	6
4	3	2	12	9	5	15	10	11	14	1	7	6	0	8	13

MFC-representation:

$$y_1 = x_1\bar{x}_2x_4\bar{x}_5x_6 \oplus \bar{x}_1x_2x_3x_4x_6 \oplus x_1\bar{x}_2x_3\bar{x}_5x_6 \oplus \bar{x}_3\bar{x}_4\bar{x}_5\bar{x}_6 \oplus \bar{x}_1x_3\bar{x}_5 \oplus x_1x_5\bar{x}_6 \oplus x_2\bar{x}_3 \oplus \bar{x}_1x_6 \oplus x_4$$

$$y_2 = x_1\bar{x}_2x_3\bar{x}_5\bar{x}_6 \oplus x_1x_2x_3x_4x_6 \oplus \bar{x}_1x_4x_5\bar{x}_6 \oplus \bar{x}_1\bar{x}_3\bar{x}_4x_5 \oplus \bar{x}_1\bar{x}_2x_4x_5 \oplus \bar{x}_2x_4x_5\bar{x}_6 \oplus x_1\bar{x}_5 \oplus \bar{x}_2\bar{x}_4 \oplus x_3 \oplus x_6$$

$$y_3 = x_1x_2x_4x_5\bar{x}_6 \oplus x_1\bar{x}_2x_3x_5\bar{x}_6 \oplus \bar{x}_1\bar{x}_2x_3\bar{x}_5 \oplus \bar{x}_1x_4x_5x_6 \oplus x_2x_4x_5 \oplus x_1\bar{x}_3x_5 \oplus \bar{x}_1\bar{x}_3x_6 \oplus x_2x_5x_6 \oplus x_1x_2 \oplus x_3\bar{x}_6 \oplus x_4$$

$$y_4 = \bar{x}_1x_2x_4\bar{x}_5x_6 \oplus \bar{x}_1\bar{x}_3x_4\bar{x}_5\bar{x}_6 \oplus x_2\bar{x}_3x_4\bar{x}_6 \oplus x_1x_2\bar{x}_3x_6 \oplus \bar{x}_1\bar{x}_4\bar{x}_6 \oplus x_1x_3x_5 \oplus \bar{x}_2x_3 \oplus \bar{x}_4x_5 \oplus \bar{x}_6$$

S-complexity:

Com(S6) = (0,9,9,8,8,5,0)

S7:

Table of S7:

4	11	2	14	15	0	8	13	3	12	9	7	5	10	6	1
13	0	11	7	4	9	1	10	14	3	5	12	2	15	8	6
1	4	11	13	12	3	7	14	10	15	6	8	0	5	9	2
6	11	13	8	1	4	10	7	9	5	0	15	14	2	3	12

MFC-representation:

$$y_1 = x_1\bar{x}_3\bar{x}_4x_5\bar{x}_6 \oplus \bar{x}_1x_2x_3\bar{x}_4\bar{x}_6 \oplus x_1\bar{x}_2\bar{x}_4\bar{x}_5 \oplus x_1x_2\bar{x}_3x_5 \oplus x_3x_4x_5\bar{x}_6 \oplus x_1x_3\bar{x}_5x_6 \oplus \bar{x}_1x_6 \oplus \bar{x}_1\bar{x}_5 \oplus x_2x_4 \oplus \bar{x}_3$$

$$y_2 = \bar{x}_1\bar{x}_2x_4\bar{x}_5x_6 \oplus x_1\bar{x}_3x_4x_5 \oplus x_1x_2x_3\bar{x}_4 \oplus x_1x_2\bar{x}_3\bar{x}_6 \oplus \bar{x}_3x_4x_5x_6 \oplus x_1x_4\bar{x}_5\bar{x}_6 \oplus \bar{x}_1\bar{x}_2x_6 \oplus \bar{x}_2x_4\bar{x}_6 \oplus x_1\bar{x}_3 \oplus x_2\bar{x}_3 \oplus x_5 \oplus \bar{x}_6$$

$$y_3 = x_1\bar{x}_2x_3\bar{x}_5\bar{x}_6 \oplus \bar{x}_1x_2x_3x_4x_6 \oplus \bar{x}_1x_3x_4\bar{x}_5x_6 \oplus x_1x_2x_4\bar{x}_5 \oplus \bar{x}_2x_4x_5\bar{x}_6 \oplus \bar{x}_1x_5\bar{x}_6 \oplus x_1\bar{x}_3x_6 \oplus x_3\bar{x}_6 \oplus x_2 \oplus x_4$$

$$y_4 = x_1\bar{x}_3x_4\bar{x}_5x_6 \oplus x_2x_4\bar{x}_5x_6 \oplus x_1x_2x_5x_6 \oplus x_1x_2\bar{x}_4x_6 \oplus x_1x_2\bar{x}_3x_6 \oplus \bar{x}_3x_4\bar{x}_5 \oplus \bar{x}_2\bar{x}_3 \oplus x_1 \oplus x_4 \oplus x_5 \oplus \bar{x}_6$$

S-complexity:

Com(S7) = (0,7,15,5,7,9,0)

S8:

Table of S8:

13	2	8	4	6	15	11	1	10	9	3	14	5	0	12	7
1	15	13	8	10	3	7	4	12	5	6	11	0	14	9	2
7	11	4	1	9	12	14	2	0	6	10	13	15	3	5	8
2	1	14	7	4	10	8	13	15	12	9	0	3	5	6	11

MFC-representation:

$$y_1 = \bar{x}_1\bar{x}_2\bar{x}_3x_4\bar{x}_6 \oplus x_1x_2\bar{x}_3\bar{x}_5x_6 \oplus x_1\bar{x}_2\bar{x}_4\bar{x}_5\bar{x}_6 \oplus \bar{x}_1x_2\bar{x}_4\bar{x}_5 \oplus \bar{x}_1x_2x_4\bar{x}_6 \oplus x_1\bar{x}_3\bar{x}_6 \oplus \bar{x}_4\bar{x}_5x_6 \oplus \bar{x}_2x_5x_6 \oplus x_1\bar{x}_3\bar{x}_5 \oplus \bar{x}_2\bar{x}_4\bar{x}_6 \oplus x_2x_4 \oplus \bar{x}_1x_6 \oplus x_3 \oplus x_5$$

$$y_2 = x_1\bar{x}_2x_3x_4\bar{x}_6 \oplus x_1\bar{x}_3x_5\bar{x}_6 \oplus \bar{x}_1x_2\bar{x}_4\bar{x}_5 \oplus \bar{x}_1\bar{x}_2\bar{x}_3 \oplus x_1x_4\bar{x}_6 \oplus \bar{x}_3\bar{x}_5 \oplus x_1\bar{x}_5 \oplus x_2 \oplus x_4 \oplus \bar{x}_6$$

$$y_3 = x_1x_2\bar{x}_3x_5\bar{x}_6 \oplus \bar{x}_1\bar{x}_2\bar{x}_4x_5x_6 \oplus x_2\bar{x}_3\bar{x}_4x_6 \oplus \bar{x}_1\bar{x}_3x_5 \oplus \bar{x}_4x_5x_6 \oplus x_1x_4\bar{x}_6 \oplus \bar{x}_1x_4x_5 \oplus x_1 \oplus x_2 \oplus x_3$$

$$y_4 = x_1\bar{x}_2\bar{x}_3\bar{x}_5\bar{x}_6 \oplus x_1\bar{x}_2\bar{x}_3\bar{x}_4x_6 \oplus \bar{x}_1\bar{x}_2\bar{x}_4\bar{x}_5 \oplus x_1\bar{x}_4\bar{x}_5\bar{x}_6 \oplus x_3\bar{x}_4\bar{x}_5x_6 \oplus \bar{x}_2\bar{x}_5\bar{x}_6 \oplus \bar{x}_2\bar{x}_3x_6 \oplus \bar{x}_2\bar{x}_4 \oplus x_4\bar{x}_6 \oplus x_1 \oplus x_3 \oplus x_5$$

S-complexity:

Com(S8) = (0,8,8,13,6,11,0)

ARE BIG S-BOXES BEST?

J A Gordon and H Retkin, Hatfield Polytechnic, England.

Abstract

Various probabilities of accidental linearities occurring in a random, reversible substitution lookup table (S-box) with m address and m contents bits are calculated. These probabilities decrease very dramatically with increasing m. It is conjectured that good S-boxes may be built by choosing a random, reversible table of sufficient size.

Introduction

Many encryption techniques employ nonlinear lookup tables to substitute one binary vector for another. The technique may be identified in schemes as far removed from each other as the simple monoalphabetic substitution cipher, and the NBS Data Encryption Standard (FIPS-46).

Shannon [2] uses the term confusion to denote the process of substituting one byte for another. The current jargon is to describe a device which substitutes one byte for another according to a fixed table as a substitution box or S-box. An S-box has an input and an output, each of which is a binary vector. Since an S-box is essentially a read-only-memory the input may be termed the address, and the output the contents. An S-box with m address and n contents bits for each substitution will be called an (m,n) S-box.

The FIPS-46 algorithm contains eight (6,4) S-boxes. It turns out to be convenient to regard each of these S-boxes as a collection of four (4,4) S-boxes, each one making a 4 to 4 bit substitution, with the other two bits being used to make a 1-in-4 choice between the four S-boxes. When viewed in this way, each of the (4,4) S-boxes in fact contains each of the 16 possible entries 0000 thru 1111 exactly once in its set of outputs. This is an example of an important class of S-boxes to which we address our attention, namely S-boxes with the same number of address bits as contents bits, and with every possible contents vector occurring exactly once. S-boxes in this class will be called reversible.

Design techniques for 'good' S-boxes are somewhat sparse in the open literature, and here we focus attention on the statistical properties of random, reversible S-boxes, and begin to answer the question how good an S-box do you get if you choose the contents as a random permutation of the set of all possible outputs? Preliminary work seems to show that a variety of desirable properties are likely to be found in such a randomly chosen S-box if the number of entries is made large enough.

S-box criteria

The sort of properties which might be considered desirable are

* Absence of any linearity between input and output bits.
* Each output bit should depend upon each input bit. In other words, for each i, j less than m (the number of address or contents bits) there exists at least one pair of entries whose inputs differ only in bit i while their outputs differ in at least bit j.
* The average number of output bits which change when one input bit is changed should be reasonably large.
* Given total uncertainty of address, there should be total uncertainty of contents. This is achieved if each possible contents vector 00...00 thru 11...11 occurs exactly the same number of times; when the number of address and contents bits are equal, then each possible contents vector occurs exactly once.

The S-boxes used in the FIPS-46 algorithm pass all these criteria with flying colours, and exceed statistical expectations in these respects to such an extent that these criteria were probably considered important by the designers.

In this paper we focus attention on the first of these criteria, namely linearity of entries, and it will emerge that as the number of bits in the address and contents of a certain class of random S-box are increased, so the probability of an accidental and unintentional linearity becomes exceedingly small.

This work was motivated, inter alia by the observation that there are only 2 possible (1,1) reversible S-boxes and both are linear; that there are 24 possible (2,2) reversible S-boxes and all are linear; that of the 40320 possible (3,3) reversible S-boxes 43.3% have at least one linear output bit, and 3.3% have all three output bits linear; and that (4,4) is the chosen dimension for the S-boxes used in the FIPS-46 algorithm. It was decided to investigate how the proportion of linear boxes in the population of all reversible S-boxes behaves with increasing number of entries.

Reversible m-bit to m-bit S-Boxes

We shall use the expression (m,n) S-box to denote a binary substitution box (i.e. a lookup table) with m address bits and n data bits. Such a device consists of an ordered list of 2^m n-bit bytes, the x th of with is said to have address (or input) x, and contents (or output) y, where x and y are integers in the range $(0,2^m-1)$ and $(0,2^n-1)$ respectively. A corresponding pair (x,y) will be termed an entry. We shall restrict attention to reversible s-boxes. These must of necessity satisfy the condition m = n, and in addition each possible value of y must occur exactly once over the set of all addresses. In other words, the outputs consist of a permutation of the inputs. The number of possible reversible (m,m) S-boxes is clearly $2^m!$.

We shall concern ourselves with the number of reversible (m,m) S-boxes for which some or all of the output bits are linear functions or partly-linear functions of some or all of the address bits. For brevity we shall describe such outputs are being 'linear'. Alternatively it may be viewed that our concern is regarding the probability of such linearities occurring by chance in a randomly chosen (m,m) S-box. Such a device may be conceptually generated by placing all the numbers 0 thru 2^m-1 in a hat, stirring well and then drawing them at random without replacement. It might be that the occurrence of such linearities would be considered undesirable for some cryptological applications, and some overbounds on the probabilties of occurrence could be useful.

We begin by addressing ourselves to the question, how many distinct, reversible (m,m) S-boxes exist for which k or more output bits are linear functions of the input bits? In order to answer this question we firstly simplify it and enquire how many, distinct reversible (m,m) S-boxes exist for which a particular output bit (say bit number 0) is a linear function of the address bits. The method we shall use is to enumerate the number of distinct ways which exist for carrying out a particular construction guaranteed to generate an S-box of the specified type, and then to use the observation - that although the constructions are distinct the resulting S-boxes are not necessarily distinct, - to declare the result to be an overbound.

The linear function of interest is

$$y_o = \sum_j a_j x_j + b$$

where x_j is the jth bit of x.

There are 2 choices for b and 2^m-1 choices for the a's, yielding altogether $2.(2^m-1)$ linear relationships for y_0. For any such linear relationship for y_0, we must still assign the remaining output bits y_1 thru y_{m-1} such that each such (m-1) tuple is assigned exactly twice, once to a value of x for which y_0 is 0, and once for a value of x for which y_0 is 1. There are 2^{m-1} distinct (m-1)-tuples and we have in effect to permute them twice, one permutation forming the assignment to x's yielding y_0 =0 and the other forming the assignment ot x's yielding y_0 =1. Thus the number of distinct, reversible (m,m) S-boxes for which y_0 is linear is

$$S(m,\{y_0\}) = 2(2^m - 1)(2^{m-1}!)^2$$

where the symbol $S(m,\{y_0\})$ denotes the number of (m,m) S-boxes for which y_0, or more precisely, the set consisting of the single element y_0 is some linear function of the address bts, and this number includes those S-boxes for which additional output bits are linear. In the same way, if Y is any subset of $\{y_0,y_1,...,y_m\}$ then S(m,Y) may be used to denote the number of (m,m) S-boxes having the property that EVERY output bit of Y is linear. Again this does not preclude those S-boxes in which additional output bits are linear.

We now generalise y_0 to y_i (in other words we are no longer concerned about which bit is the linear one), thus increasing the number of ways in which the above construction may be performed by a factor m, to

$$S(m,\{y_0\}) + s(m,\{y_1\}) +\ldots+ S(m,\{y_{m-1}\})$$

$$\text{i.e.} \quad 2m(2^m-1)(2^{m-1}!)^2,$$

since the value of $S(m,\{y_i\})$ is independant of i. Now the above is an enumeration of the number of ways in which a specific constructional technique could be used to generate a reversible (m,m) S-box for which one output bit is a linear function of the input bits. It is clear that some S-boxes will be generated more than once by this procedure, i.e. there is no guarantee that these will be distinct S-boxes, and so the bound, which we shall denote be B(m,1) is an upper one.

In addition there is no guarantee that ONLY one output bit is linear, and indeed the procedure will generate all reversible S-boxes for which 1,2,3,...,m bits are linear functions of the input bits. Also, some linear functions involve a relatively small subset (i.e. perhaps only one) of the input bits. Thus the formula above is an overbound on the number of distinct, reversible (m,m) S-boxes for which one or more output bits are linear functions of one or more of the input bits.

We are now in a position to widen the discussion. Consider now the question, how many distinct, reversible (m,m) S-boxes are there such that k or more bits are linear functions of one or more of the input bits? The linear relationship now becomes

$$y_i = \sum_j a_{ij} x_j + b_i = A.x + B$$

where x,A and B are matrices of dimensions (m,1), (k,m) and (k,1) respectively. The rows of A must be independant for reversibility, thus

row 1 of A may be chosen from $2^m - 2^0$ values

row 2 of A may be chosen from $2^m - 2^1$ values

row 3 of A may be chosen from $2^m - 2^2$ values

and so on until

row k of A may be chosen from $2^m - 2^{k-1}$ values

i.e. the 1st row must be nonzero, the 2nd row must be nonzero and distinct from the 1st. The 3rd must be nonzero and not any of the 4 linear functions of the earlier ones and so on. Therefore the number of choices for A is

$$(2^m-2^o)(2^m-2^1)\ldots(2^m-2^{k-1})$$

Also B may be chosen in 2^k ways.
The number of distinct linear relationships for any specified k-subset Y of the output bits in terms of input bits, is thus

$$S(m,Y) = 2^k(2^m-2^o)(2^m - 2)\ldots(2^m-2^{k-1}),$$

and by taking the sum of such expressions for all k-subsets of Y we get

$$2^k(2^m - 2^0)\ldots.(2^m - 2^{k-1})C(m,k)$$

where C(m,k) is the number of selections of k from m objects =m!/(k!(m-k)!). This last term enters since we are not concerned about exactly which set of k output bits are the linear ones.

For any given linear relationship we can partition the inputs x into 2^k distinct sets. All x's in a given set are assigned the same common value of the k linear bits of y. We still need to assign the remaining m-k output bits for each x. Clearly for reversibility, each x within a given set must be assigned a distinct (m-k) tuple of the remaining output bits. Each set may thus be assigned in $2^{m-k}!$ ways, so each of the linear relationships may have the remaining bits assigned in

$$(2^{m-k}!)^{2^k} \quad \text{ways.}$$

The required bound is altogether

$$B(m,k) = 2^k C(m,k)(2^m-1)(2^m-2)\ldots(2^m-2^{k-1})(2^{m-k}!)^{2^k}$$

Similar remarks regarding overbounding apply equally to the above formulae.

This result accords in a satisfying way with other, established results. Thus when k = 1 it reduces to

$$B(m,1) = 2m(2^m - 1)(2^{m-1}!)^2$$

When k = m the bound becomes

$$B(m,m) = 2^m (2^m-1)(2^m-2)\ldots(2^m-2^{m-1})$$

which is precisely the number of distinct, reversible and wholly linear (m,m) S-boxes.

Finally when k=0 we get

$$B(m,0) = 2^m!.$$

which is just the number of distinct, reversible (m,m) S-boxes.

Now, by applying the inclusion/exclusion principle we may turn the above bounds into exact values, and we find that if L(r) (r=0,1,...,m) denote the number of (m,m) S-boxes that are linear in exactly r output bits then

$$L(r) = \sum_i (-1)^i C(i,r)B(m,i);$$

in particular, by putting r=0 we obtain the number of (m,m) S-boxes which are totally nonlinear, namely

$$L(0) = B(m,0) - B(m,1) + B(m,2) - \ldots + (-1)^m b(m,m)$$

hence the probability that a random (m,m) reversible S-box will be linear in just one bit is $1 - L(0)/B(m,0)$.

We may convert these results to probabilities of occurrence by dividing in each case by the number of distinct, reversible (m,m) S-boxes, namely $2^m!$. It is clear from the formulae, and intuitively satisfying that the most probable linearity is that one or more outputs are linear, this probability being given by

$$\frac{2m(2^m-1)(2^{m-1}!)^2}{2^m!}$$

This result is illustrated in figure 1. The reduction in probability with increasing value of m is seen to be most dramatic. The overbound when m = 4 (as in FIPS-46) is around 1%, while when m = 8 the bound has reduced to 10^{-72}.

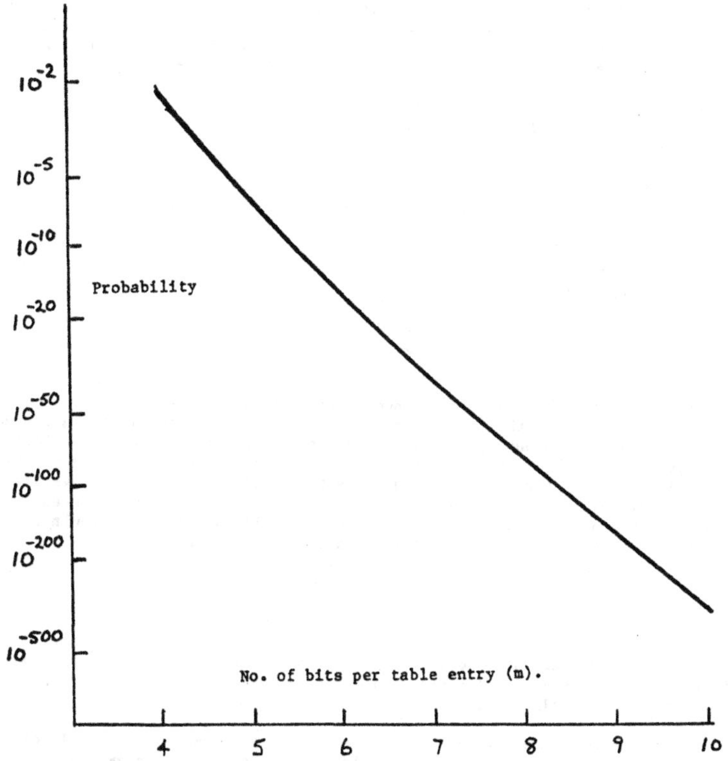

Figure 1

Overbound on the probability that one or more bits of a random reversible S-box will be linear functions of the address bits.

Now that we know an overbound to the number of distinct, reversible (m,m) S-boxes with various numbers of linear bits we may extend this result to what we shall call partly-linear relationships. In other words, we shall overbound the number of distinct, reversible S-boxes for which a significant fraction of the entries exhibit such a linear relationship among k or more output bits. We will define a measure of linearity as follows. Let f be the greatest fraction such that there exist a k by m matrix A, a k by 1 matrix B, and a subset of k bits of y, denoted y*, with the property that a fraction f of the S-box entries satisfy

$$y^* = A.x + B.$$

Such an S-box will be said to exhibit a linearity f over k output bits. We shall now derive an overbound on the the number of distinct, reversible (m,m) S-boxes which exhibit a linearity f or greater over k or more output bits. We begin by taking a reversible (m,m) S-box with the property that exactly k of its output bits are linear functions of the input bits. We retain exactly $f.2^m$ of the 2^m entries and permute the remaining outputs.

Clearly every distinct, reversible (m,m) S-box for which a fraction f or greater of the entries have k or more outputs linear, will be generated at least once by this procedure. For any given starting S-box, the number of ways we can choose the initial fraction f of retained entries is $C(2^m,f.2^m)$, and the number of ways of permuting the remaining entries is $((1-f).2^m)!$

The resulting product is $2^m!/(f.2^m)!$

In addition we already have an overbound on the number of starting S-boxes. In the interests of simplicity we shall limit discussion to the case where k=1. Thus the number of distinct, reversible (m,m) S-boxes for which a fraction f or more of the entries have the property that one or more of the output bits are linear functions of one or more of the input bits is overbounded by

$$\frac{2m(2^m-1)(2^{m-1}!)^2\,2^m!}{(f.2^m)!}$$

Expressed as a probability of occurrence, we obtain

$$\frac{2m(2^m-1)(2^{m-1}!)^2}{(f.2^m)!}$$

Now as before this is an overbound since the original number of starting S-boxes was overbounded. Now especially for small values of f - the retained fraction of entries, it is likely that some permutations will by chance generate other, partly-linear relationships for different matrices A and B than those appropriate to the starting S-box, and that these matrices exhibit a greater fraction than f of entries satisfying the new linearity. Thus we assert that this is an overbound on the number of distinct, reversible (m,m) S-boxes for which a fraction f OR MORE of the entries have one or more output bits which are linear functions of the input bits. A similar result could be derived for the case of k or more output bits by using the appropriate formula.

Conclusion

As far as accidental linearity is concerned it would appear that by choosing a large enough S-box, the probability of building a bad table may be reduced to acceptable levels by choosing the entries to be a random permutation of all possible outputs.

The rate of change of probability of linearity with address size m is so dramatic that it is clear that some considerable care must be taken when constructing S-boxes of dimension say (4,4) - as used in FIPS-46, and indeed this accords with claims.

We are at present looking into how the other S-box criteria check out for random reversible S-boxes, but preliminary results look equally hopeful.

References

[1] Federal Information Processing Standard Publication no 46. Department of Commerce, National Bureau of Standards, Gaithersburg, Md, USA.

[2] Shannon, C.E. "A Mathematical theory of Secrecy Systems" Bell System Technical Journal 1948.

THE AVERAGE CYCLE SIZE OF THE KEY STREAM IN OUTPUT FEEDBACK ENCIPHERMENT

D. W. Davies and G. I. P. Parkin
National Physical Laboratory
Teddington, Middlesex,
U.K.

Output feedback is a method of using the 'Data Encryption Standard' (DES), and it is defined in Federal Information Processing Standards Publication 81 produced by the US National Bureau of Standards. The principle is shown in Figure 1. Its purpose is to provide a method of using the DES without error extension, since both encipherment and decipherment consist of adding a 'key-stream' modulo 2 to the data stream. It has been defined for the values m = 1, 2, 3 .... 64 of the parameter m, which is the feedback width.

The key-stream generator contains a 64 bit register R which is initialised by placing in it the initialising variable (IV) possibly padded out on the left with zeros if it contains less than 64 bits. For each step of operation, R is the data input of the DES algorithm which produces, by encipherment, Ek(R) using the key k. Only the left hand m bits of the output (bits 1, 2 .... m) are used, and these become the next m bits of the key-stream. They are also placed in the right hand m bit positions of the R register for the next step of operation, shifting the contents of that register left by m bits to make room for them.

This kind of stream cipher depends for its security on the unpredicability of the key-stream. Being a finite state machine with 2^{64} states it must enter a repetitive cycle of 2^{64} states or less. If a cycle can be found (ie there are two identical segments of key-stream of non-trivial extent) messages M_1 and M_2 enciphered with identical segments provide, from the modulo 2 addition of their ciphertexts, the value of $M_1 + M_2$, and this allows M_1 and M_2 to be discovered if there is enough redundancy. Therefore repetition of the key-stream must be prevented, which implies that the stream must not be allowed to continue long enough, with a given key, that a repeat has more than a very low probability. There are similar dangers when one key value is used for an excessive amount of data even if the generator is re-initialised from time to time by randomly chosen IVs. Therefore a good key-stream generator should have an average cycle length which is very large, preferably comparable with 2^{64}, the maximum value it can have for the OFB key-stream generator.

In this paper we calculate the average cycle lengths for each value of m. The case m = 64 is a well known result in the theory of permutations. For the other values, an estimate of average cycle length can be made only by using an approximate mathematical model of the generator which is rather difficult to justify. Therefore we have carried out an experiment with an 8 bit register in place of R and randomly chosen permutations of the 256 states in place of DES. The results of the experiment confirm the theory and encourage us to apply it to the actual OFB configuration. The broad conclusion is reached that OFB with m = 64 is reasonably secure but OFB with any other value of m is of greatly inferior security. Since OFB with values of m other then 64 has no advantages we propose that the only recognised OFB mode of operation should be m = 64

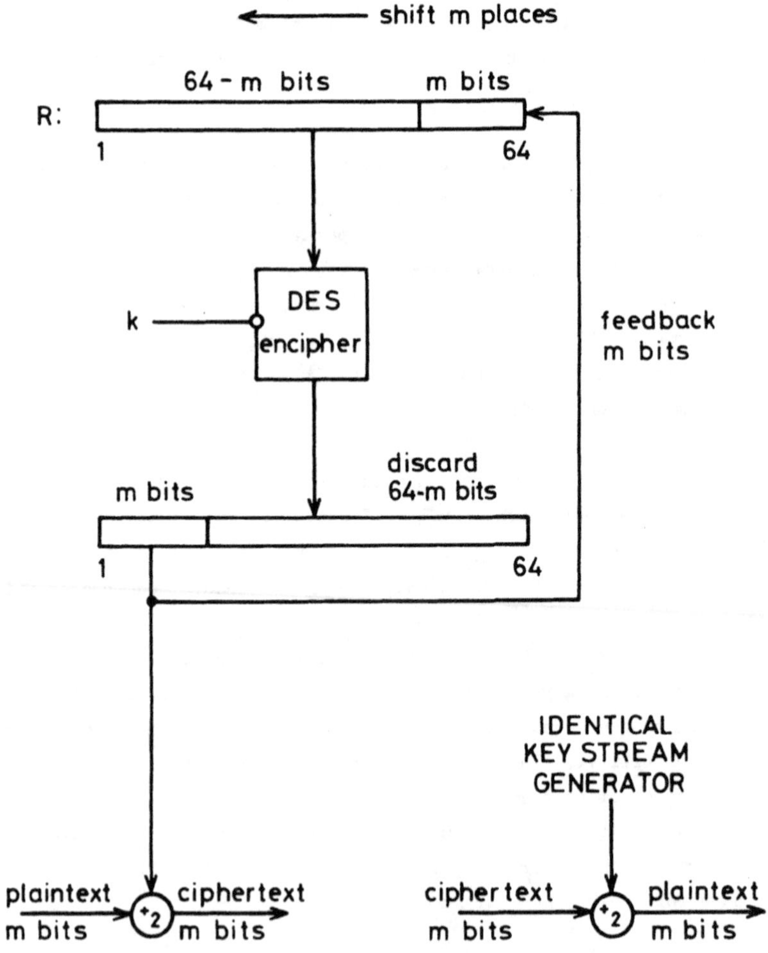

Figure 1 Output feedback

The state transition graph of OFB

For each state of R (a number R in the domain $0 \leq R < 2^{64}$) a single cycle of OFB operation produces a new state $R' = f(R)$ where f is defined by the OFB method of operation, described above. In particular, for m = 64, f(R) = Ek(R). The function f is apparently random and the main difference between m = 64 and other values is that, for m = 64, f(R) has a inverse, the function Dk(R').

From any given starting value (IV) such as R_o, the operation f(R) produces in turn the values R_1, R_2, R_3 .... until after some step (the bth step) the register R contains a value R_b equal to an earlier value R_a which was reached after the ath step. This is described by saying that starting value R_o produces a cycle of length b-a after a tail of length a. The graph produced by these edges R-R' consists of a collection of cycles and some 'trees' rooted on the members of the cycle. Figure 2(a) illustrates the form of the state transition graph and Figure 2(b) illustrates the states reached from a typical starting state with a = 4 and b = 9. Our problem is to calculate the mean value of the cycle size, averaging over all the 2^{64} starting states. This is not the same as the average length of the cycles in the graph. (Generally, large cycles are accessible from more starting points, so they are weighted more heavily in our distribution.)

For the case m = 64 the graph contains no trees but only cycles because f(R) has a unique inverse. The cycle begins when the state R returns to the initial value R_o. If it returned to a later value, that state would have two predecessors which is impossible when f(R) has a unique inverse.

Average cycle length for m = 64

For each value of the key k, the DES defines a permutation of the R values R'= Ek(R). This is a permutation of the 2^{64} objects R. The cycle structure of permutations has been well studied and it is known that within the n! permutations of n objects the combined cycles of size c number exactly n!/c and therefore contain n! objects (note that here we are counting in total n.n! objects in the n! permutations).

If we assume that the DES functions are a randomly chosen set from among the $(2^{64})!$ permutations, it follows that the cycle length from a randomly chosen starting state will take any of the values 1, 2, ... 2^{64} with equal probability 2^{-64}.

Measured in this way (from a random starting state), the average cycle length for m = 64 is $2^{63} + \frac{1}{2}$, a large enough value for all practical purposes. Although small cycles are possible, they are improbable and a cryptanalyst could not afford to wait long enough for a cycle of useful size to appear. For example, cycles of 10^6 or less (2^{20} approximately) occur with probability 2^{-44}. In this respect, 64 bit OFB is safe, assuming the cycle distribution of DES is that of randomly chosen permutations on 2^{64} objects.

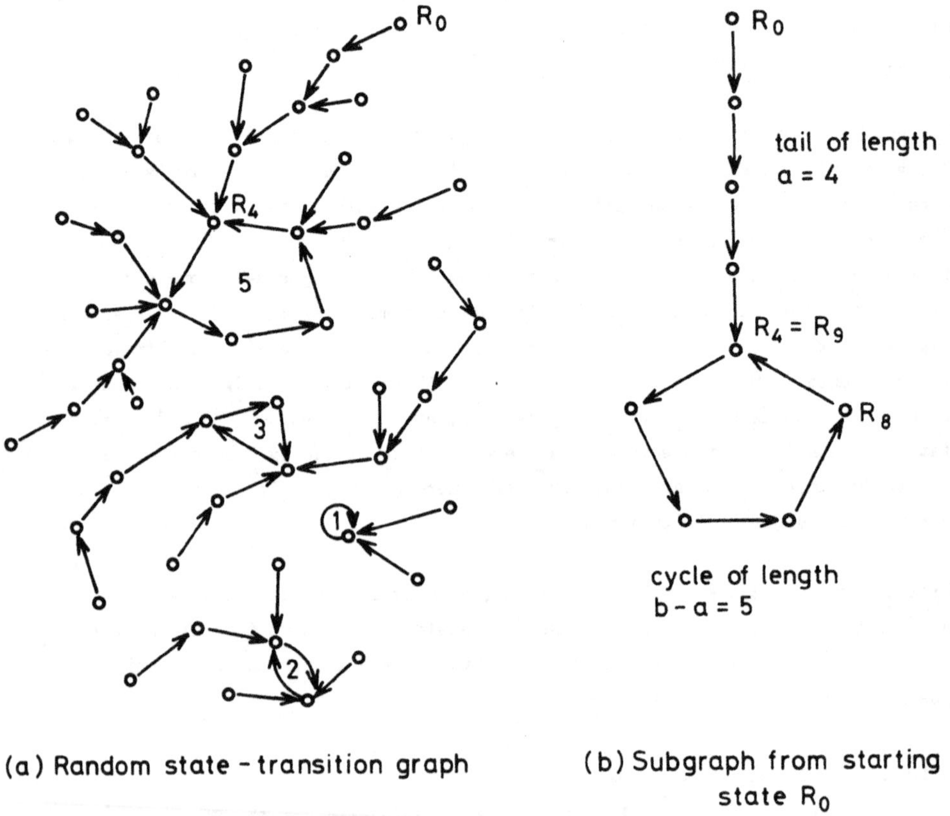

Figure 2 The state transition graph

A theory for average cycle length when $m \neq 64$

The success with random permutations suggest that for $m \neq 64$ we assume that $R' = f(R)$ is a random function in which R' is chosen at random for each of the 2^{64} values of R. This assumption is difficult to justify since R and R' are closely related, having 64–m bits in common (shifted). Later we shall show that the assumption gives reasonably accurate results, except when m or 64 – m is small.

The cycle structure of random functions was studied by Knuth [Knuth 1969] in connection with random number generators and by Brent and Pollard [Brent 1981] in connection with factorisation and we shall use their results. Knuth obtains an average cycle length, for a random function over n values, of $(\pi n/8)^{\frac{1}{2}} + \frac{1}{3}$ and an average tail length of $(\pi n/8)^{\frac{1}{2}} - \frac{2}{3}$. The near equality arises from the random way in which the point of re-entry is chosen from the states already visited. If the midpoint of an odd numbered chain were chosen, there would be one more state in the cycle than in the tail, as in Figure 2(b).

The $n^{\frac{1}{2}}$ relationship is related to the 'birthday problem'. This asks how many randomly chosen samples of n objects are needed to give a probability greater than $\frac{1}{2}$ of two or more samples being identical (how many people in a room to make it likely that two or more have the same birthday, n = 365). For large n, the answer is approximated by $n^{\frac{1}{2}}$; the actual value for n = 365 is 23.

A random function $R' = f(R)$ is characterised by the number of values of R which exist as inverses of a given R'. For each state in the state transition graph the number of its inverses is the number of states having transitions leading into it, called by Brent and Pollard the 'in-degree'. For a random function, when the number of states n is large, the in-degree has a Poisson distribution with average 1 and variance 1. The probabilities of in-degrees of values 0, 1, 2 .... are the co-efficients of 1, x, x^2, ... in the series -

$$e^{-1}\left(1 + x + \frac{x^2}{2!} + \frac{x^3}{3!} + \ldots\right)$$

For values of m such as 1, 2, 3 and 61, 62, 63 the distribution of in-degrees can be shown to depart from Poisson and for these cases Brent and Pollard conjecture that the average cycle length is $(\pi n/8V)^{\frac{1}{2}} + \frac{1}{3}$ where V is the variance of the in-degree. We have added the $\frac{1}{3}$ to agree with Knuth's result when n is not very large.

Calculation of the in-degree distribution for m = 1, 2 ....

Given R', the normal OFB operation can be put into reverse to calculate the values of R, if any, which satisfy $R' = f(R)$. This reverse OFB is illustrated in Figure 3 for m = 1. The value in R' is shifted right by one bit, the right most bit y becoming the new value of bit 1 of the DES output. The new DES input is fully specified by R', except for the first bit x which can be varied to give two possible solutions for R.

To find the in-degree of R' (the number of R solutions), try x = 0 and x = 1 and for each value check whether bit 1 of Ek(R) has the correct value y. There are four cases, shown in Figure 3, which have equal probability $\frac{1}{4}$. Hence the probabilities of in-degree values 0, 1 and 2 are $\frac{1}{4}$, $\frac{1}{2}$, $\frac{1}{4}$ respectively, giving variance $V = \frac{1}{2}$.

By a similar argument for m = 2 there are 4 values which the two left hand bits of

R can take and each case has a probability $\frac{1}{4}$ of generating the two bits of DES output correctly. The number of correct solutions in the in-degree and its values 0, 1, 2, 3 or 4 are distributed in a Binomial fashion with average value 2 and variance $V = 0.75$. Their probabilities are the coefficient of x^0, x^1 .... x^4 in the expansion of $(\frac{3}{4} + \frac{1}{4} x)^4$.

shift right 1 bit

R: x

DES encipher

k

"reverse feedback" 1 bit

y

x, ✓ = y incorrect/ correct

in-degree

x	0	1	1	2
0	x	✓	x	✓
1	x	x	✓	✓

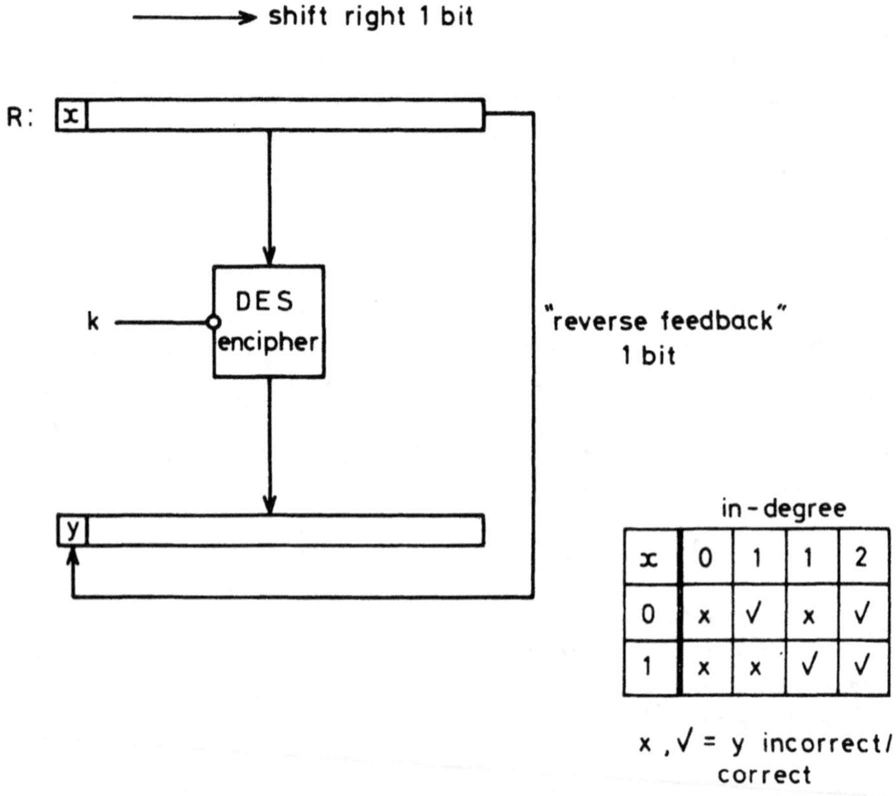

Figure 3 Probability of indegree = 0, 1, 2 for m = 1

For general m, using this argument, $V = 1 - 2^{-m}$. For m = 1, 2, 3 .... this takes values $\frac{1}{2}$, $\frac{3}{4}$, $\frac{7}{8}$, $\frac{15}{16}$ .... which closely approach 1 for moderate m. The argument loses validity for values of m near to 63 and for these a different argument is used.

Calculation of the in-degree for m = 63, 62 ....

For m = 63, to find the number of inverse value of R' by reversing OFB, 63 bits of R' are shifted right and taken into the DES output register as shown in Figure 4. Only one bit of DES output, shown as y, has to be found. The check to be made is whether,

For either value, $y = 0$ or 1, the inverse DES function Dk maps this value into an R value with the correct value of bit 64 (shown as x) which was derived from bit 1 of R′. The probability calculation is exactly as before, showing that $m = 1$ and $m = 63$ have similar in-degree distributions. The same similarity exists for $m = 2, 62$ etc and in general m, $64 - m$ have similar properties. For $m > 32$ we can use $V = 1 - 2^{m-64}$ as the best approximation for the variance of the in-degree.

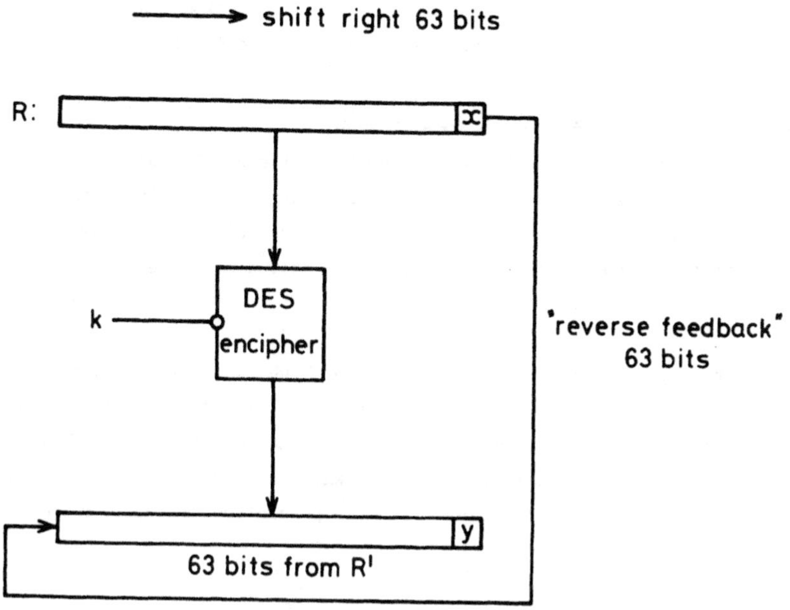

Figure 4 Probability of indegree = 0, 1, 2 for m = 63

<u>Average cycle length for m = 1, 2 ....63</u>

The random function assumption ($V = 1$) gives an average cycle length $(\pi n/8V)^{\frac{1}{2}} + \frac{1}{3}$ equal to 0.6267×2^{32} or 2^{31} approximately. This assumption is valid, according to our theory, for values of m not close to 1 or 63. The largest values of average cycle length are those for $m = 1$, $m = 63$, with $V = \frac{1}{2}$ which are only $\sqrt{2}$ larger, ie 0.8862×2^{32}. All the other values of m, except $m = 64$, have intermediate values. This kind of OFB operation greatly inferior (by a factor 2^{32} or more) compared with $m = 64$.

Another characteristic of these random functions is the relatively small average number of distinct cycles, about $\frac{1}{2} \ln n$ which is 22. This comes about because each cycle has a dense growth of attached trees leading into it. The very small proportion of states which are in the cycles might make it practicable for a cryptanalyst to store the cycles and search for their occurrence statistically. Averages give a misleading impression of the state graph of random functions because of the wide variations of form. For example any large cycles (for example those greater than twice the average) tend to be associated with nearly all the starting states, so the eventual output pattern is very predictable if large cycles occur.

The arguments we have used, in which R′ = f(R) has been assumed to be a random function, do not give great confidence because the actual function f(R) is certainly not random. In order to check our results we have carried out a statistical experiment.

Experimental calculation of average cycle length

Working with DES to discover cycles of order of magnitude 2^{32} would be too slow, so we used for the experiment a register size of 8 binary digits, giving the set of R values: 0, 1 .... 255. With this size, the function which represents the cipher (the DES substitute) and the function f(R) can be stored as tables of 255 x 8 bits in a small computer.

In place of the cipher functions Ek(R) for random k we used a randomly chosen permutation of the 256 values. The runs were carried out with 10,000 different permutations for each value of m. For each permutation and m value, each of the 256 starting values was explored and the size of cycle c to which it led was determined, then the cycle length distribution was calculated for the population of 10,000 x 256 (for each m value).

The process of finding a random permutation began with a table of 256 values consisting of the numbers 0, 1, 2 .... 255. The principle used was to transpose the value in address i with the value in address j for i = 0, 1 .... 255 and corresponding values of j given by a pseudo-random source of numbers. In order to make all the permutations different, i = 0 and i = 1 were permuted with j addresses which were a different pair on each occasion. Then the subsequent permutations left the values in i = 0 and i = 1 unchanged.

From the permutation, for each value of m, f(R) was calculated by shifting the R value m bits to the left and entering the left hand m bits of the permuted value of R. This table of f(R) was the basis for the cycle length determination. Although the permutations were distinct, this was not necessarily true of the f(R) tables, since some bits of the permuted values of R were discarded. A table c(R) is formed giving the cycle length c to which the state R leads. As each new starting state R_0 is explored, the states it leads to are marked 1, 2, 3 .... until either it re-cycles or it leads to an R value for which c(R) is known. The new cycle, if any, is given a cycle length by comparison of the sequence numbers. Then all the states R_0, R_1 .... are marked with that cycle length.

During this process, a count is made of the number of states leading to each cycle length c. When a new trial leads to the value c, the count for c is incremented by the number of new states that have been identified with it. At the end of the entire calculation for each m value, the average of c was determined, with the following results, compared here with the theoretical values.

m =	1	2	3	4	5	6	7	8
Average cycle length	15.22	12.17	11.46	11.26	11.42	12.09	14.33	128.65
Theoretical value	14.51	11.91	11.05	10.69	11.05	11.91	14.51	128.5

Figures 5-12 give the distribution of cycle length for m = 1, 2 .... 8. The agreement p with theory for m = 8 is, of course, excellent. The agreement for the other values of m shows that Brent and Pollard's conjecture works well, even for these rather unlikely functions. The similarity of m with 8-m is well illustrated by the results, except that m = 1 gives a higher average cycle length than m = 7.

In the cycle length distributions for m = 1 to m = 3 there are apparent departures from the regular curve at small cycle lengths. These can be explained by enumerating the state values which enter into these cycles and estimating the probability of transitions between them. For example, the relative incidence of the first 7 cycle length values for m = 1 are estimated to be 1, $\frac{1}{2}$, $\frac{3}{4}$, $\frac{3}{4}$, $\frac{5}{16}$, $\frac{27}{32}$ and $\frac{63}{64}$, which is in reasonable agreement with the experimental results. Similar predictions partly explain the values obtained for cycle length c when $mc < 8$.

For m = 2, the ratios 1, $\frac{3}{4}$, $\frac{5}{16}$ are obtained. For m = 3, the ratio 1, $\frac{7}{8}$ is not in good agreement.

The high incidence of cycles of length 2 for m = 8 is still unexplained. It may be a consequence of the pseudo-random number generator or the way it was used to produce the permutations. Some further tests will be made in an attempt to resolve this.

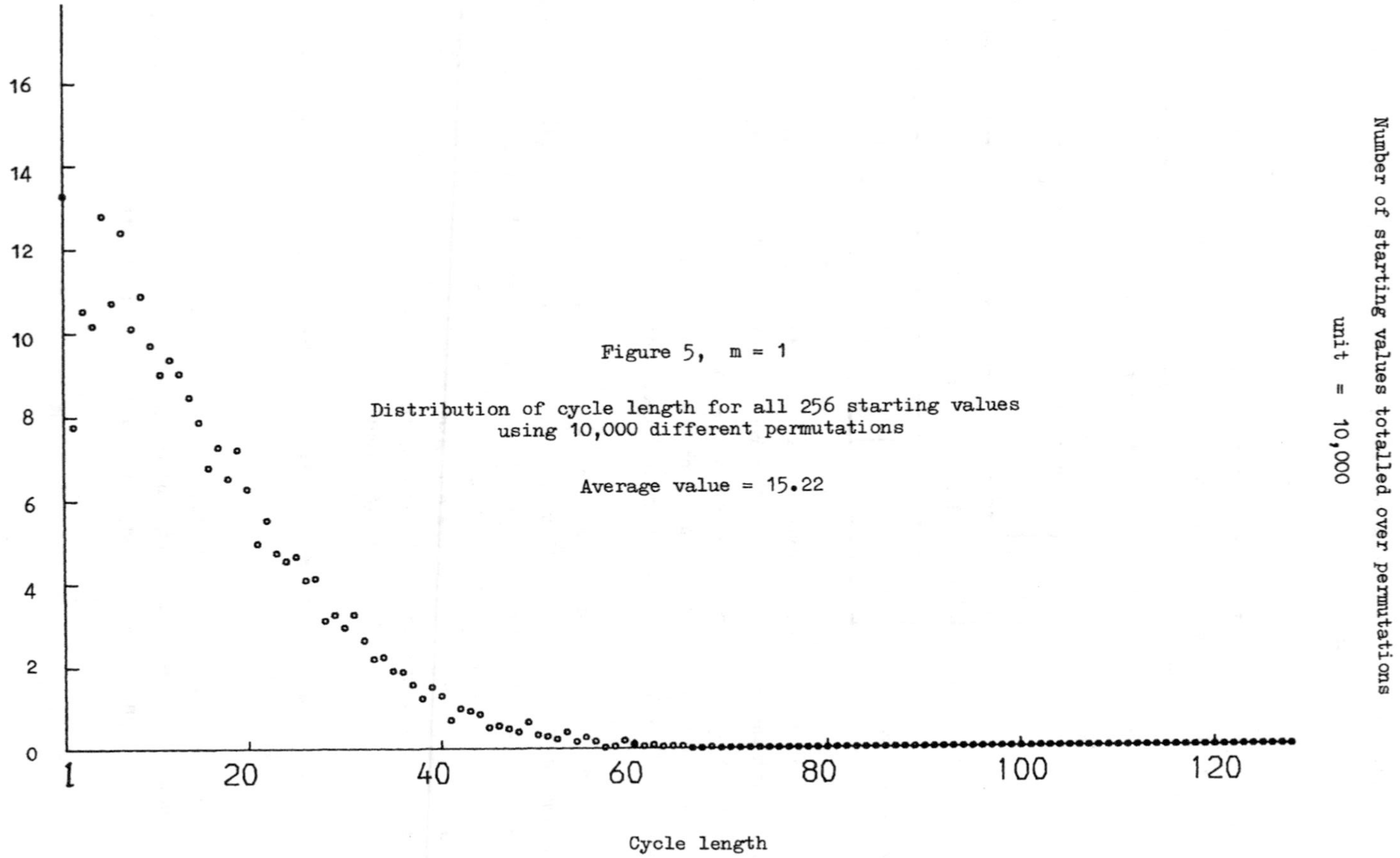

Figure 5, m = 1

Distribution of cycle length for all 256 starting values using 10,000 different permutations

Average value = 15.22

Number of starting values totalled over permutations

unit = 10,000

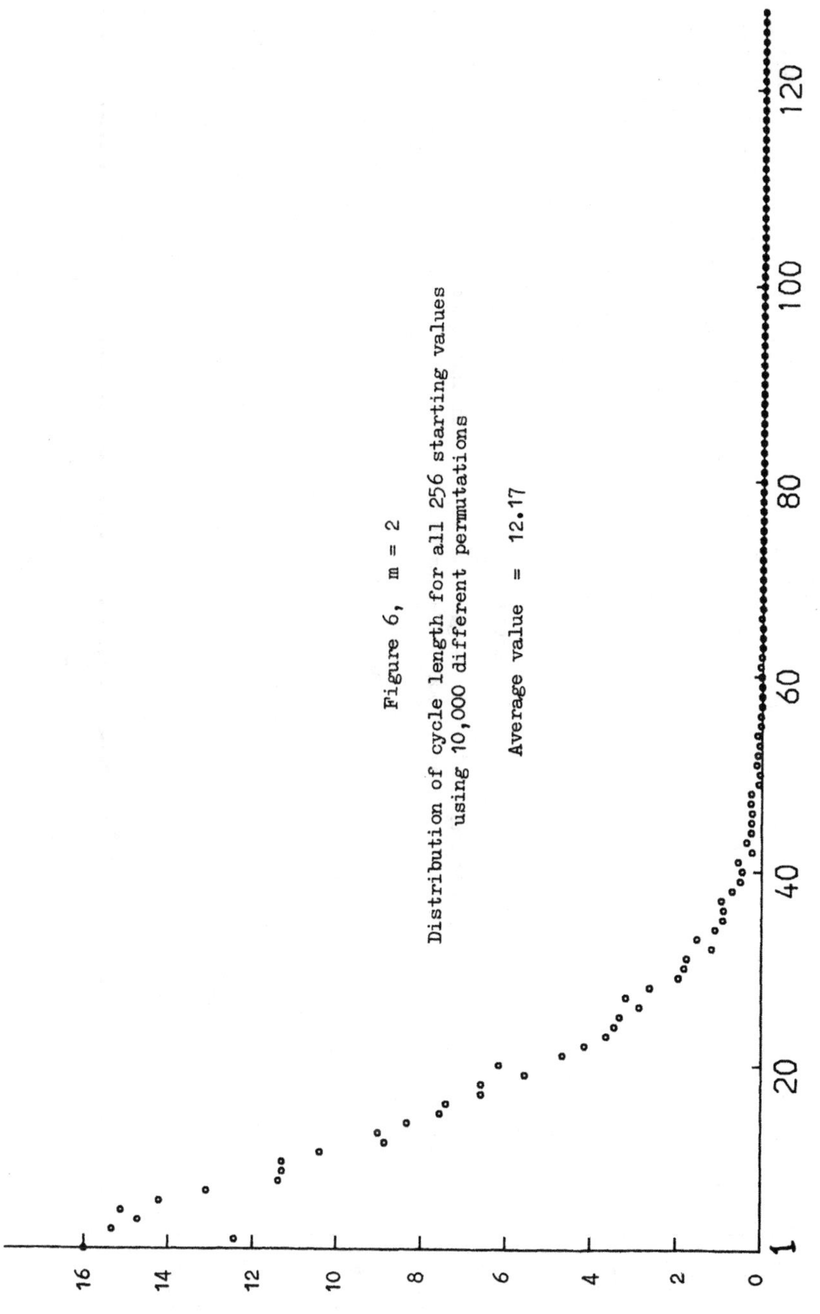

Figure 6, m = 2

Distribution of cycle length for all 256 starting values using 10,000 different permutations

Average value = 12.17

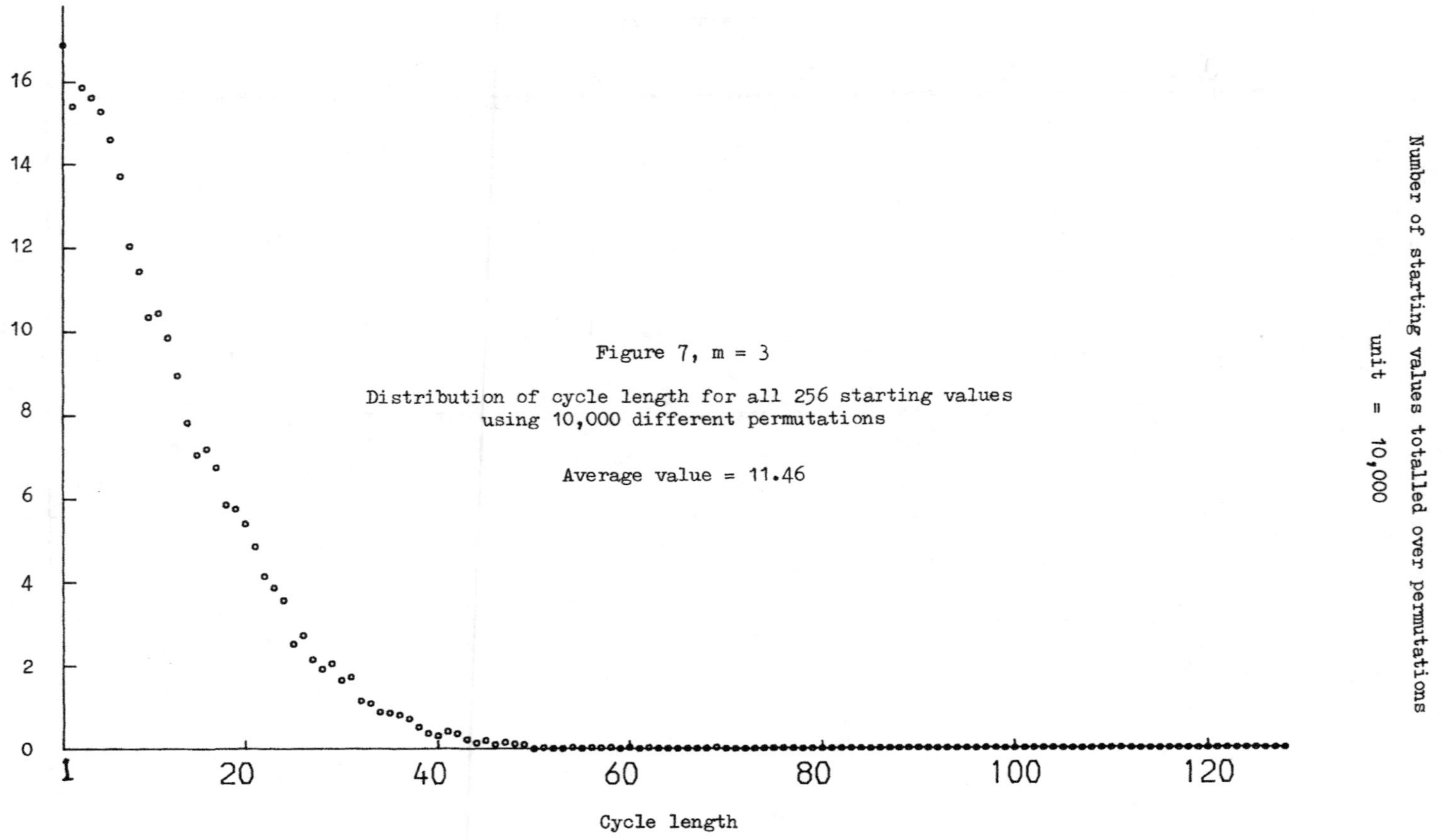

Figure 7, m = 3

Distribution of cycle length for all 256 starting values using 10,000 different permutations

Average value = 11.46

Number of starting values totalled over permutations
unit = 10,000

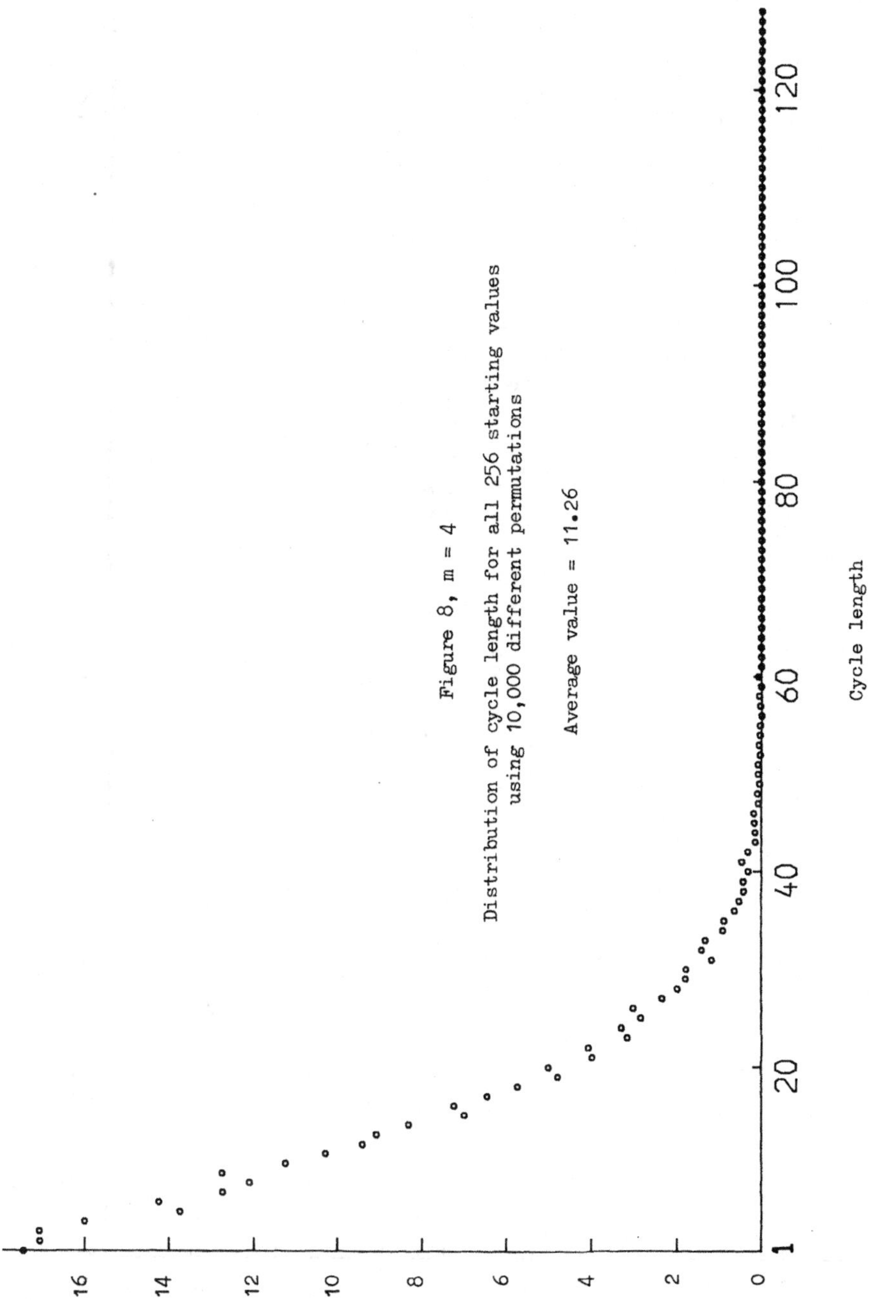

Figure 8, m = 4

Distribution of cycle length for all 256 starting values
using 10,000 different permutations

Average value = 11.26

Number of starting values totalled over permutations
unit = 10,000

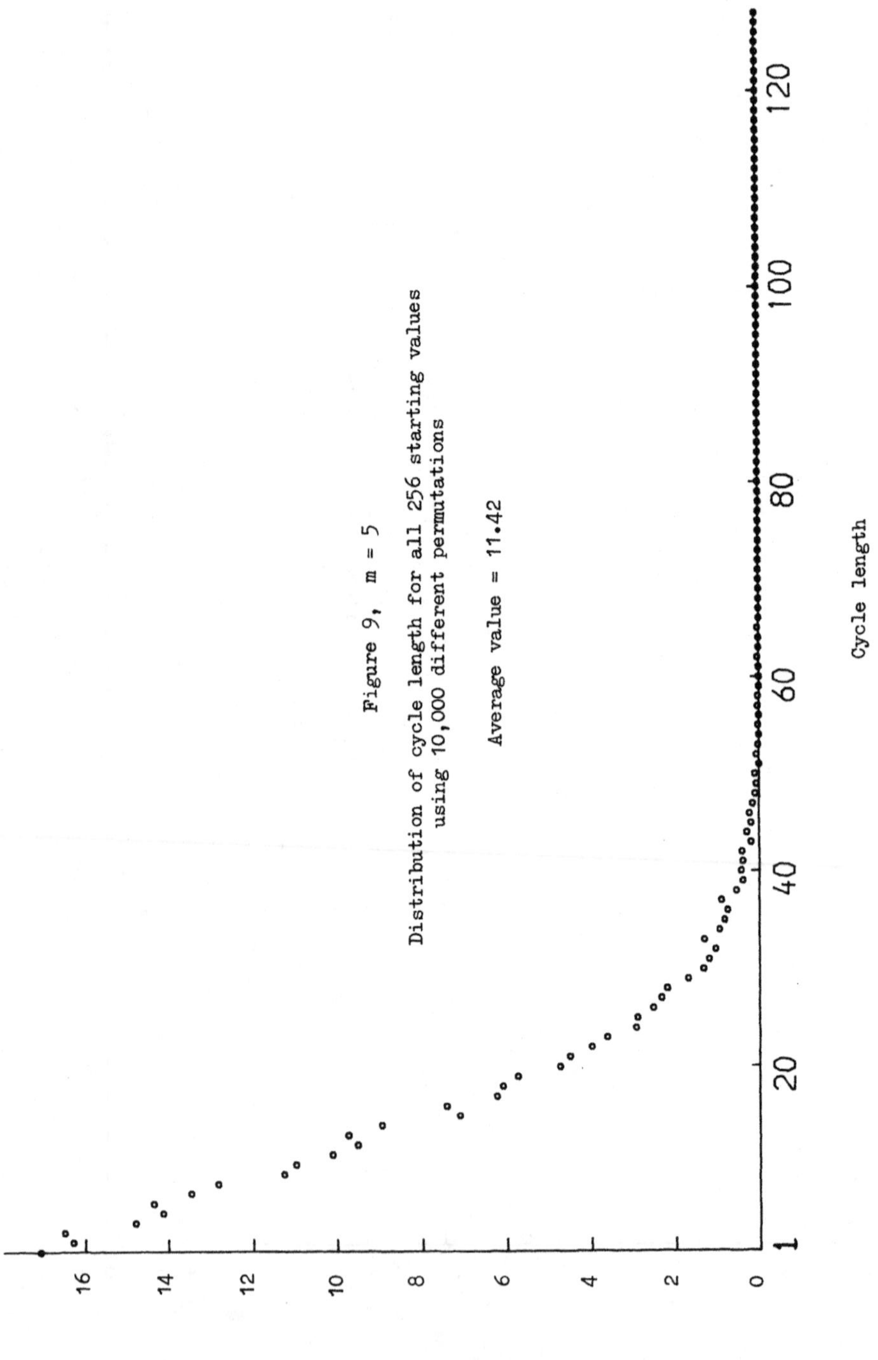

Figure 9, m = 5

Distribution of cycle length for all 256 starting values
using 10,000 different permutations

Average value = 11.42

Cycle length

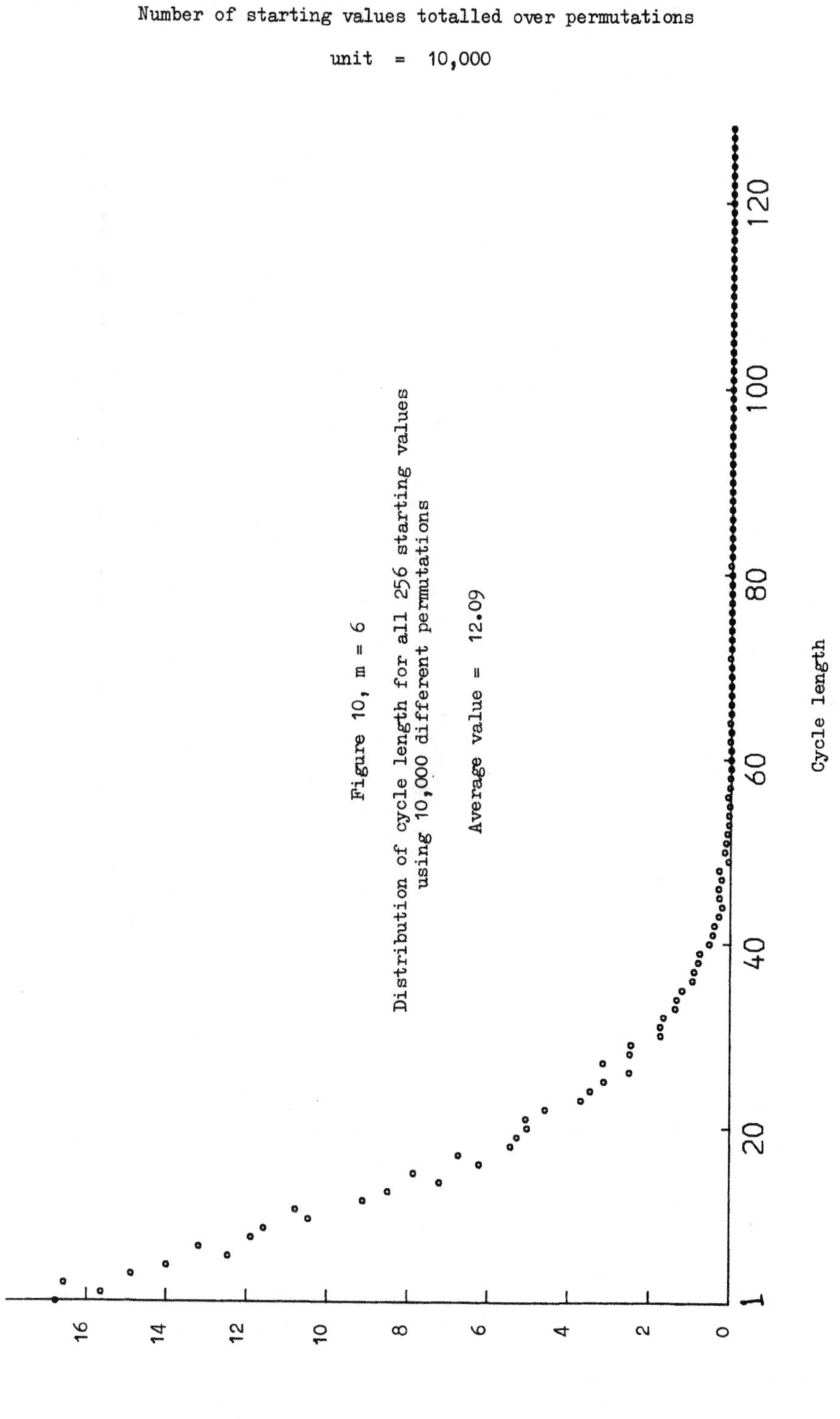

Figure 10, m = 6

Distribution of cycle length for all 256 starting values using 10,000 different permutations

Average value = 12.09

Number of starting values totalled over permutations

unit = 10,000

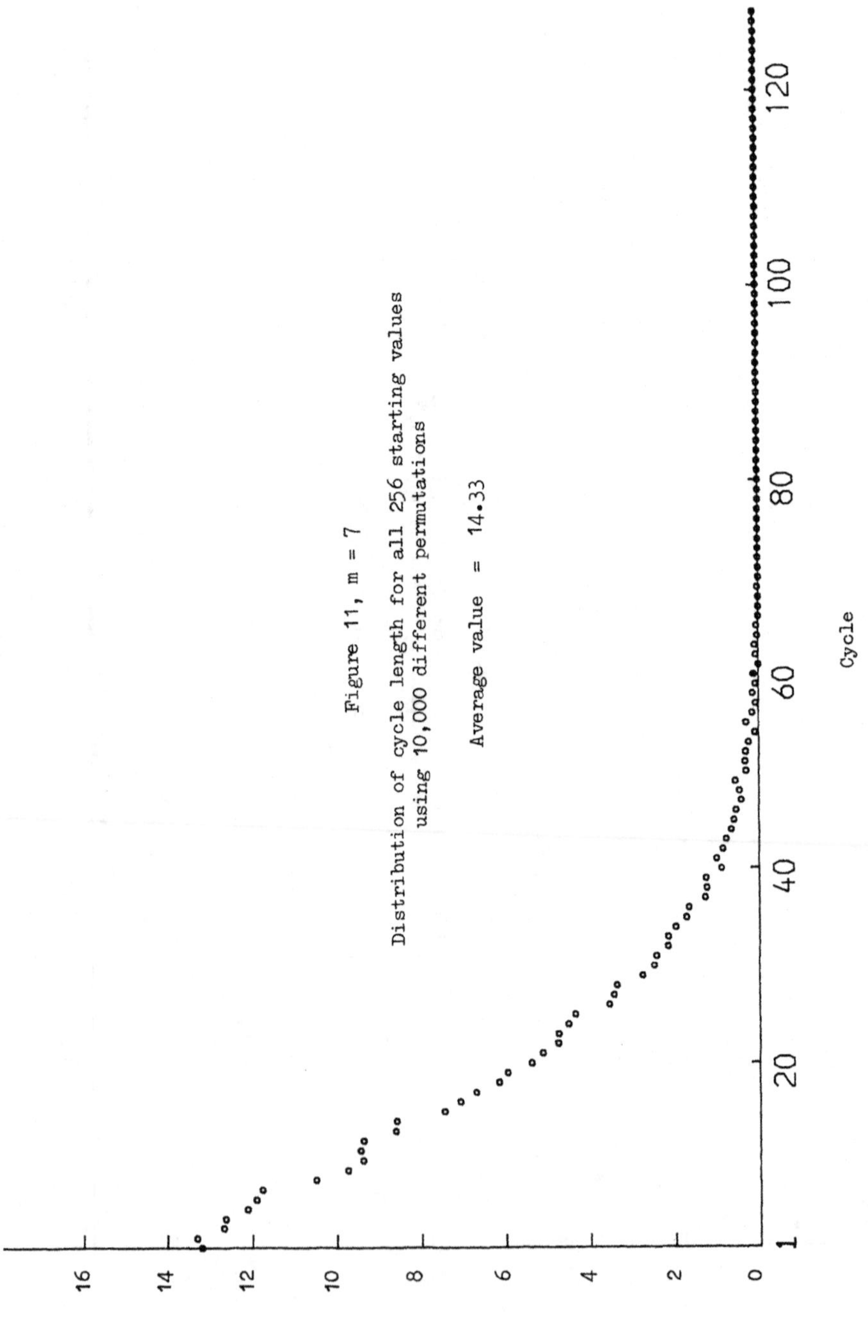

Figure 11, m = 7

Distribution of cycle length for all 256 starting values using 10,000 different permutations

Average value = 14.33

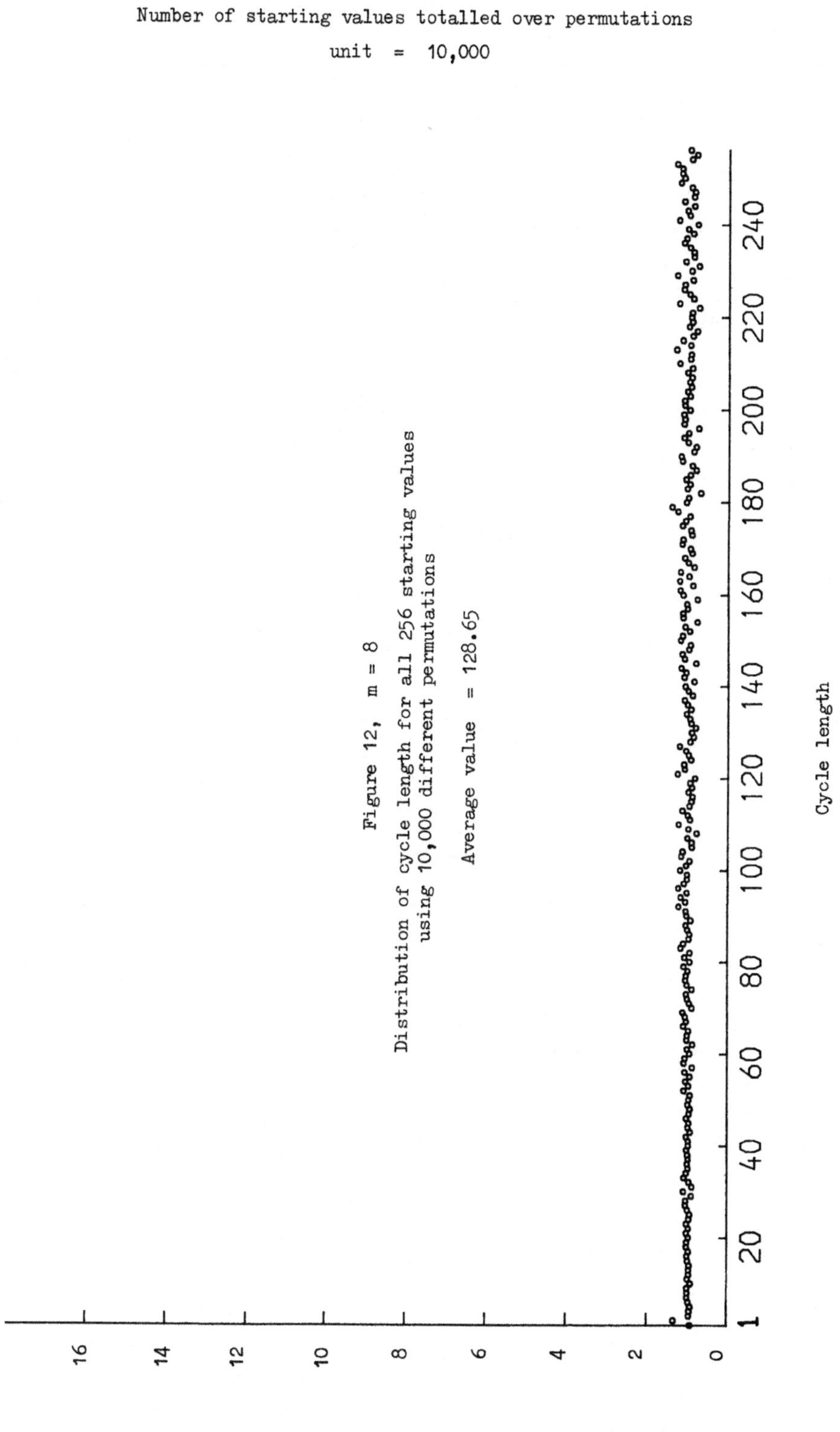

Figure 12, m = 8

Distribution of cycle length for all 256 starting values using 10,000 different permutations

Average value = 128.65

Section 8

Authentication Systems

Authentication Procedures.

M. Davio, J.-M. Goethals and J.-J. Quisquater.

Philips Research Laboratory,

Ave. van Becelaere, 2, Box 8,
B 1170, Brussels, Belgium.

Abstract

The purpose of this paper is to illustrate the use of one-way functions and public-key algorithms in some authentication procedures. Special emphasis is given to the problem of mutual authentication of a card and a point-of-sale terminal in an off-line situation.

1. Introduction.

Cryptographic transformations provide solutions to two major problems of data security : the ***privacy problem***, preventing an opponent from extracting confidential information from intercepted material, and the ***authentication problem***, preventing an opponent from altering messages or injecting false information into a communication system. More generally in the latter problem, one would like to prevent an intruder from impersonating an authorized user of a system. Thus there are two aspects involved in authentication problems. One is concerned with checking the authenticity of constant quantities, like passwords, authorizations or keys, and the other is concerned with the authenticity or integrity of variable quantities, like messages.

In this paper we shall only be concerned with the former aspect of the authentication problem. Clearly, to ensure the security of a system, it should not be possible for an intruder to subvert or bypass the authentication procedure. Another remark which should be made is that any authentication procedure will require a reference value to be available, either stored or dynamically generated. In a computer network this reference might be stored at a central location and made available through a communication medium at a remote mode of the network where the authentication procedure takes place. This is the on-line situation. In an off-line situation when direct communication with a central authority is not possible one has to rely on reference values which are locally, dynamically generated.

In this paper, we briefly discuss some authentication procedures involving the use of one-way functions and public-key algorithms and then examine in more details a possible solution in an off-line situation.

2. Authentication using stored passwords.

This is the classical situation of the "login" problem, discussed in [Diffie-Hellman, 1976]. When a new user is authorized to access a multiuser computer system, he is asked to choose a password which is entered into the system's password directory. Each time he logs in, a user is asked to provide his password which is then compared to the value stored in the password directory. The access to this directory must be protected from all users in order to prevent forged logins. Clearly exposure of the password directory is a serious threat. A very simple countermeasure to that threat is provided by the use of a one-way function f.

A *one-way function* is a function f with the property that, given x in its domain, it is easy to compute the value $f(x)$, but, for almost all y in its range, it is computationally infeasible to solve the equation $y = f(x)$ for x. Thus, if one does not store in the password directory the password PW, but merely its image $f(PW)$ by the one-way function f, it is impossible for anyone who has access to this directory to derive the password PW from the stored value $f(PW)$. Therefore exposure of the password directory is no longer a serious threat. Moreover since $f(PW)$ is easily computed from PW, the additional cost due to the computations which need to be performed each time a user logs in is not significant.

3. The challenge and response procedure.

Password logins are vulnerable to eavesdropping, even when a one-way function is used to protect the password directory. As printed out in [Diffie-Hellman, 1979] it is possible to foil eavesdropping by use of a challenge and response procedure in which the user to be authenticated is asked to perform a task that no one else can perform.

This task can be for example the computation of the response $f(x)$ to the challenge x by use of a secret function f known only to the user. The challenge x must be variable and preferably never repeat in order to foil eavesdropping.

If the secret function f is not known to the system, it will be necessary to use as reference value a list of potential challenges x_i and of the corresponding responses $f(x_i)$, in which the system will select at random a challenge each time the user logs in. If the function f is known to the system, the challenge can be totally random, as then the system can compare the response to its own computation.

A very elegant solution was proposed by Shamir [Shamir, 1980] in which the system doesn't need to know the secret function and yet can use a totally random challenge. The only requirement is that the system S can select at random a function f_S which commutes with the secret function f_U of the user U. Commutativity means that, for any argument x in the common domain of f_S and f_U, the following holds :

$$f_S(f_U(x)) = f_U(f_S(x)).$$

It is also assumed that a reference value consisting of a pair $(r, f_U(r))$ is available to the system. The authentication procedure then goes as follows. To challenge the user U, the system selects at random a function f_S, computes $f_S(r)$, and asks U to apply his function f_U to it. The result is easily verified since S can compare it with $f_S(f_U(r))$ which he can obtain from the reference value. The challenge is random due to the random selection of f_S by S.

Another solution allowing a random challenge is possible with a public-key cryptosystem [Diffie-Hellman, 1976] in which the public enciphering function E and the secret deciphering function D commute, that is, satisfy for any r in their domain,

$$E(D(r)) = D(E(r)) = r.$$

Here we assume that the public function E_U of any user U is available to the system. The authentication procedure then goes as follows. The system selects at random a value r and asks U to apply his secret function D_U to it. After having received the response $D_U(r)$ the system then applies the public function E_U to it and checks if $E_U(D_U(r)) = r$.

4. Off-line authentication.

In this section we briefly discuss a possible solution to the authentication problem in an off-line situation. The situation we consider more specifically is that of a point-of-sale where an intelligent card is used for payment. By an ***intelligent card*** we mean a card containing a microprocessor with some computing power. Prior to being able to make any transaction, the card needs to be authenticated by the point-of-sale terminal, and conversely, the terminal should be authenticated by the card. We shall make the following assumptions :

(i) the system as a whole is run by some authority, and the authentication problem can then be formulated as follows : the two parties have to convince themselves that the other party is an actual member of the general system ;

(ii) the two parties are provided with some computing power embedded either in an intelligent card or in a terminal, and the authentication procedure takes place between these two devices ;

(iii) the authentication procedure is an off-line process, i.e. is made without resorting to the authority. Thus the authentication problem can be reformulated as follows : each of the two parties should convince himself that the other one owns a valid "signature" of the authority.

The system should be protected against the possibilities offered by repeated wiretapping. This requires that no confidential information be circulated in the clear at the interface and that the dialog between a specific card and a specific terminal varies at each execution. Thus some randomization should be introduced in the procedure.

The system should also be protected against the possibility for an opponent to get physical access to some confidential information. Here it may be assumed that the technological skill required is so high that it is practically equivalent to the possibility for the opponent to produce replicas of the card or of the terminal. A reasonable protection countermeasure consists of imposing a validity period shorter than the replication time. Finally it is advisable to provide each card and terminal with a sufficient level of personification in order to reduce the vulnerability of the system to compromission of one of its elements.

The solution described here makes use of a public-key cryptosystem with the signature feature, like the RSA system proposed in [Rivest, Shamir, Adleman, 1978]. It was previously described in [Davio, Quisquater, 1982]. A very similar solution was proposed in [Simmons, 1981].

As above, we use the notation D for the secret function, and E for the public function, of the public scheme. In addition we use the subscripts C and T to refer to the card and the terminal, respectively. As suggested in the previous discussion, the card and the terminal should bear a ***signature*** of the ***authority*** which they should be able to check for authenticity. This signature is an encrypted form of some ***identifier*** which, among other things, could contain the following :

- some information about the validity period, e.g. issue and / or expiration dates
- some personification, e.g. an account or serial number
- a personal identification number (in encrypted form)
- and, in any case, a great deal of redundancy.

When issuing a card C or validating a terminal T, the authority :

- assigns identifiers i_C and i_T;
- computes $s_C = D_C(i_C)$, $s_T = D_T(i_T)$ using distinct secret functions D_C and D_T;
- finally distributes s_C and E_T to the card C and s_T and E_C to the terminal T, where E_C and E_T are the public functions associated to D_C and D_T, respectively.

In addition the card and the terminal are provided with some information regarding the validity of the identifier of the other party which, as well as the redundant part of this identifier, they should be able to check.

The ***authentication protocol*** itself consists of the following steps :

- C sends s_C to T;
- T computes $E_C(s_C) = i_C$ and checks that it satisfies certain tests (as indicated above);
- then T sends s_T to C which similarly computes $E_T(s_T) = i_T$ and checks its validity.

At this point both C and T may ascertain, up to some confidence level, that they are not dealing with impostors, and the transaction can proceed.

However, in order to foil wiretapping, it would be advisable to randomize the dialog. Thus s_C and s_T should be sent in encrypted form using a key which varies at each session. So, prior to the exchange of s_C and s_T, the card and the terminal should establish a ***session key***. To do this T generates a random number R and sends R and $f_T(R)$ to C, where f_T is a one-way function commuting with the function f_C of the card. The card C then computes $f_C(R)$ which is returned to T. They both use

$$K = f_T(f_C(R)) = f_C(f_T(R))$$

as the key for the session. This key can be used to encrypt s_C and s_T as well as any subsequent messages using some standard cipher.

References.

- M. Davio, J. J. Quisquater (1982), "Methodology in information security. Mutual authentication procedures. Application to access control", *Proc. 1982 International Zurich Seminar on Digital Communications (Zurich, March 9-11, 1982)*, pp. 87-92.
- W. Diffie, M. Hellman (1976), "New directions in cryptography", *IEEE Transactions on Information Theory*, **IT-22**, 6, pp. 644-654.
- W. Diffie, M. Hellman (1979), "Privacy and authentication : an introduction to cryptography", *Proc. IEEE*, **67**, 3, pp. 397-427.
- R. L. Rivest, A. Shamir, L. Adleman (1978), " A method for obtaining digital signatures and public-key cryptosystems", *Communications of the ACM*, **21**, 2, pp. 120-126.
- A. Shamir (1980) "On the power of commutativity in cryptography", in "Automata, languages and programming", ICALP80, *Lecture Notes in Computer Science*, 85, Springer Verlag, Berlin, 1980, pp. 582-595.
- G. J. Simmons (1981), "A system for point-of-sale or access, user authentication and identification", *IEEE Workshop on Communications Security*, Santa Barbara, CA., August 24-26, 1981.

FAST AUTHENTICATION IN A TRAPDOOR-KNAPSACK PUBLIC KEY CRYPTOSYSTEM

P. Schöbi
Institute of Communication Technology
ETH-Zentrum
CH-8092 Zürich

J.L. Massey
Institute of Telecommunications
ETH-Zentrum
CH-8092 Zürich

ABSTRACT

Public Key Cryptosystems based on the trapdoor knapsack method proposed y Merkle and Hellman are not well suited to provide authentication in the sense of ublic key authentication because only a small fraction of all possible message words f a typical length lead to a binary solution of the knapsack problem. In this paper, new method is discussed which provides a nonbinary solution for the knapsack problem f a Merkle/Hellman scheme. The algorithm works for any message word with a compara- ively short computation time. Thus, the solution can be used as a secure authenti- ation pattern.

I INTRODUCTION

In a public key cryptosystem (PKC), each user deposits his enciphering lgorithm in a public directory but keeps secret the corresponding deciphering algo- ithm [Diffie/Hellman, 1976]. When user A wishes to send a secret message to user B, e encrypts the plaintext M using B's public encryption algorithm E_B; B then decrypts he resulting cryptogram $E_B(M)$ using his secret decryption algorithm D_B. In contrast o a conventional cryptosystem in which only A and B would jointly know some secret ey so that the ability to form a cryptogram would identify the sender as A, in the KC user B cannot be sure that the cryptogram came from A as its header or part of the laintext might suggest. Any other user besides A could just as easily have formed $_B(M)$. Thus, message authentication is an essential problem in a PKC.

In [Diffie/Hellman, 1976], the authors suggest the authentication procedure diagrammed in Fig. 1 for use in a PKC. After sending the cryptogram $E_B(M)$ to user B, user A forms a 'pre-signature' S as some prescribed function of the plaintext M, say as a one-way hash of it [Merkle/Hellman, 1978]. User A then transforms this pre-signature using his own secret deciphering algorithm D_A to form the actual signatur $X = D_A(S)$, which he then transmits to B. User B can validate the signature by applying the public enciphering algorithm E_A to obtain $S = E_A(X)$ (under the proviso soon to be stated), which he then compares to the prescribed function of the plaintext M that he already possesses. User B can then be certain that the prior cryptogram came from A as no other user could form $X = D_A(S)$ even if he knew M. Not even user B could have produced X so user A cannot later deny that he sent the prior cryptogram. Thus the procedure for Fig. 1 produces unforgeable and irrevocable signatures in a PKC. The only problem, as Merkle and Hellman clearly mention in [Merkle/Hellman, 1978], is that the procedure of Fig. 1 will work if and only if S is a valid cryptogram from A's enciphering algorithm, i.e. is in the range of the function E_A.

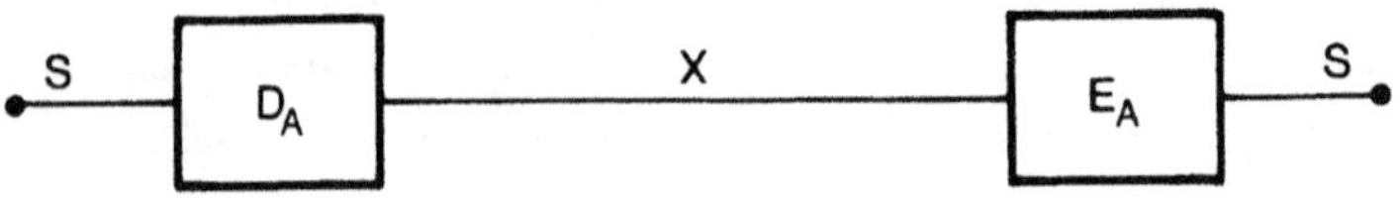

Fig. 1: The Diffie/Hellman authentication procedure.

The condition that S be in the range of E_A can be a serious shortcoming of the authentication procedure in Fig. 1 when the enciphering algorithm E_A causes an expansion of the plaintext when both the cryptogram and the plaintext are represented by binary strings, since then only a small fraction of the binary strings whose length equals that of the cryptogram will in fact be valid cryptograms. Thus the probability, p, will be small that the pre-signature S is a valid cryptogram. This can be partially remedied (as suggested by Diffie and Hellman) by including a 'random tail' in the string S, then varying this tail until S is a valid cryptogram, as user A can check by applying first D_A and then E_A to see if S again results. However, on the average, 1/p of such trials would be required, which is prohibitively large when p is very small.

The trapdoor knapsack (TK) PKC proposed by Merkle and Hellman [Merkle/Hellman, 1978] is a PKC in which the enciphering algorithm expands the plaintext, and hence which is subject to the authentication shortcoming described above. In this paper, we propose a new solution to the authentication problem for the TK-PKC. In section II, we give a brief description of the TK-PKC and its specific authentication problem. In section III, we offer out proposed solution to the authentication problem by showing how to modify the TK-PKC so that every pre-signature becomes effectively a valid cryptogram. Finally, in section IV, we discuss system performance and security.

II THE TK-PKC AND ITS AUTHENTICATION PROBLEM

A vector $\underline{b} = [b_1, b_2, \ldots, b_n]$ with positive integer components is said to be 'superincreasing' if each component in the vector exceeds the sum of the previous components. In the TK-PKC each user, say user A, would independently form his public enciphering algorithm E_A and his secred deciphering algorithm D_A (which, hereafter, are denoted simply as E and D) as follows:

(1) Randomly choose a superincreasing vector $\underline{b} = [b_1, b_2, \ldots, b_n]$ of length n.

(2) Choose the vector $\underline{a}^{(k)} = [a_1^{(k)}, \ldots, a_n^{(k)}]$ as a random permutation of $\underline{b}$. Set $i = k-1$.

(3) Randomly choose an integer $m^{(i)}$ such that

$$m^{(i)} > \sum_{j=1}^{n} a_j^{(i+1)} \qquad (1)$$

and randomly choose a second integer $w^{(i)}$ such that $0 < w^{(i)} < m^{(i)}$ and such that $w^{(i)}$ and $m^{(i)}$ are relatively prime. Calculate $u^{(i)}$ such that $0 < u^{(i)} < m^{(i)}$ and

$$w^{(i)}\, u^{(i)} = 1 \pmod{m^{(i)}}. \qquad (2)$$

(4) Calculate the vector $\underline{a}^{(i)} = [a_1^{(i)}, \ldots, a_n^{(i)}]$, where $0 < a_j^{(i)} < m^{(i)}$, as

$$a_j^{(i)} = w^{(i)}\, a_j^{(i+1)} \pmod{m^{(i)}} \qquad (3)$$

for $j = 1, 2, \ldots, n$.

(5) If $i > 0$, reduce i by 1 and return to step (3). Otherwise stop.

The public enciphering algorithm E consists of the 'knapsack vector' $\underline{a}^{(0)} = [a_1^{(0)}, \ldots, a_n^{(0)}]$ together with the specification that the plaintext is to be a vector $\underline{x} = [x_1, \ldots, x_n]$ where $x_i \in \{0,1\}$, and that the corresponding cryptogram S is to be the integer

$$S = \sum_{i=1}^{n} x_i\, a_i^{(0)} \qquad (4)$$

which we shall, when convenient, also write as the 'dot product'

$$S = \underline{x} \cdot \underline{a}^{(0)}.$$

The secret deciphering algorithm begins with $S^{(0)} = S$, then recursively calculates $S^{(k)}$, $0 \leq S^{(k)} < m^{(k)}$ in the manner

$$S^{(i+1)} = u^{(i)}\, S^{(i)} \pmod{m^{(i)}} \qquad (5)$$

for $i = 0, 1, \ldots, k-1$. Because of (1) and (2), it follows that

$$S^{(k)} = \sum_{j=1}^{n} x_j \, a_j^{(k)} = \sum_{j=1}^{n} x_{i_j} \, b_j \tag{6}$$

here i_j is the index (known to user A who made the permutation in step (2)) such hat $a_{i_j}^{(k)} = b_j$. Because the sequence $\underline{b}$ is superincreasing, (6) can easily be solved or the components of $\underline{x}$ to complete deciphering using the following algorithm:

lgorithm I:

Begin with $j = n$.

a) If $S^{(k)} \geq b_j$, set $x_{i_j} = 1$ and then reduce $S^{(k)}$ by b_j. Otherwise set $i_j = 0$.

b) If $j \geq 2$, reduce j by 1 and return to step a).

c) If $S^{(k)} = 0$, announce that an apparently valid deciphering has been ompleted. Otherwise announce that the original S could not have been a valid cryptoram.

The reason for the terminology 'apparently valid' in step c) is that it s possible for an invalid cryptogram S (i.e. an integer such that there is no $\underline{x}$ for hich (4) is satisfied) to be transformed via (5) to an $S^{(k)}$ such that there is an $\underline{x}$ atisfying (6) and hence that will be found by algorithm I; this property will be exloited in section III. To be sure that the 'apparently valid' deciphering was in fact alid, the resulting $\underline{x}$ must be enciphered with the public knapsack vector $\underline{a}^{(0)}$ to conirm that the resulting cryptogram is the original S.

The purpose of the iterations (3) is to disguise the easy knapsack problem 6) so that it appears as a hard knapsack problem (4) for all users except user A, who lone can undo these iterations by the inverse operations of (5). For guidance on the hoice of the various parameters in the TK-PKC and the advisability of choosing $k > 2$, he reader is referred to [Merkle/Hellman, 1978], [Shamir/Zippel, 1980] and [Shamir, 982].

Define $S_{max}^{(i)}$ as the sum of the elements of the vector $\underline{a}^{(i)}$. Then, from (4) e see that the largest integer which is a valid cryptogram (or 'valid knapsack') n the TK-PKC is

$$S_{max}^{(0)} = \sum_{i=1}^{n} a_i^{(0)} \tag{7}$$

hile the smallest such integer is 0. In general, any integer S such that

$$0 \leq S \leq S_{max}^{(0)} \tag{8}$$

s a candidate for a valid knapsack, and hence is a candidate for the pre-signature n the authentication scheme of Fig. 1 until it is rejected because, when the deciphersng algorithm D is applied to S, either $S^{(k)} \neq 0$ in step c) of algorithm I or an apparently valid' deciphering results but the resulting S' when encrypted with E gives cryptogram different from S. As there must be precisely 2^n valid knapsacks, it is natural to call the fraction

$$\rho = 2^n / (S_{max}^{(0)} + 1) \qquad (9)$$

of integers S satisfying (8) that are valid knapsacks the *density* of valid knapsacks. Notice that ρ coincides with the probability p that a pre-signature S is a valid cryptogram when the pre-signature is equally likely to take on any value in the range specified by (8), and ρ can be expected to be a good approximation to p even when the maximum value of a pre-signature is much smaller than $S_{max}^{(0)}$. Thus, for the authentication scheme of Fig. 1 to be practicable for a TK-PKC, the density must be fairly high, say $\rho \simeq 1/10$ or greater.

The smallest possible value of $S_{max}^{(0)}$ is that which gives $\rho = 1$ in (9), namely $S_{max}^{(0)} = 2^n - 1$. It can be seen by a simple induction on n that in this case the public knapsack vector $\underline{a}^{(0)}$ must be a permutation of the superincreasing vector $[1, 2, 4, 8, .., 2^{n-1}]$. Thus, the cryptogram S can be as easily solved for the plaintext $\underline{x}$ by any user as by the legitimate receiver, the system is totally insecure ! Shamir [Shamir, 1979] has given compelling arguments that in fact any TK-PKC with high density is insecure. Thus, the TK-PKC must be modified to some extent if the above-mentioned probability p is to be made high without compromising security.

III A PROPOSED NEW AUTHENTICATION PROCEDURE FOR THE TK-PKC

A. Pseudo-Density of Trapdoor Knapsacks

We define an integer S in the range (8) to be a *pseudo-valid knapsack* f application of the deciphering algorithm D to S results in an 'apparently valid' eciphering in step c) of algorithm I. Note that any valid knapsack is also a pseudo-alid knapsack. Note also that if S is a valid knapsack and $S' = S + m^{(0)}$ with $' \leq S^{(0)}_{max}$, then S' is a pseudo-valid knapsack (but not a valid knapsack), since both and S' would when D is applied yield the same $S^{(1)}$ as a result of (5). Thus, there enerally are many pseudo-valid knapsacks that are not also valid knapsacks. Defining ne *pseudo-density*, ρ', as the fraction of integers S in the range (8) which are pseudo-alid knapsacks, we have immediately

$$\rho' \geq \rho \ . \tag{10}$$

We now state the following result as being of some possible general inter-st, even though we shall make no direct later use of it:

emma 1

ne pseudo-density of valid knapsacks, when $k > 1$ and $m^{(0)} \gg m^{(k-1)}$, is in general ell-approximated by

$$\rho' \approx 2^n / m^{(k-1)} . \tag{11}$$

ecause of (5), $S^{(k)}$ will always satisfy

$$0 \leq S^{(k)} < m^{(k-1)} \tag{12}$$

nen D is applied to any integer S. Thus for S choosen uniformly and randomly from the ange (8), the operations (5) will result in $S^{(k)}$ being nearly uniformly distributed ver the range (12). But exactly 2^n values of $S^{(k)}$ will result in an 'apparently valid' eciphering in step c) of algorithm I, namely the 2^n possible values of the sum in (6) orresponding to the 2^n different values of $\underline{x}$. This establishes (11).

We note that (11) can generally be expected to be a good approximation to he pseudo-density even when S is restricted to lie in a much smaller range than that iven by (8), as might well be the case for allowable pre-signatures S in the authenti-ation scheme of Fig. 1.

B. A nonbinary TK-PKC with high density

We begin from the TK-PKC as described in section II, but we now modify the deciphering algorithm so that any nonnegative integer S [in particular any S in the range (8)] will lead to an 'apparently valid' deciphering. To this end, we first replace algorithm I with the following algorithm:

Algorithm II: [Produces $\underline{x}$ such that $\underline{x}\cdot\underline{a}^{(k)} = S^{(k)}$.]

Begin with j = n.

a) If $S^{(k)} \geqq b_j$, set $x_{i_j} = q$, where q is the largest integer such that $S^{(k)} \geqq q\, b_j$, and then reduce $S^{(k)}$ by $q\, b_j$. Otherwise , set $x_{i_j} = 0$.

b) If $j \geqq 2$, reduce j by 1 and return to step a).

c) If $S^{(k)} = 0$, announce that an apparently valid deciphering has been completed, otherwise, announce that the original S could not have been a valid cryptogram.

Notice, that when S is in fact a valid cryptogram, then this new deciphering algorithm, which we shall denote by D', will lead to the same $\underline{x}$ as the previous D, i.e., to the correct binary plaintext vector. However, when S is not a valid cryptogram, D' can lead to 'apparent' plaintext vectors $\underline{x}$ with nonbinary components as well as to binary plaintexts. In fact, upon defining for convenience

$$b_{n+1} = \max S^{(k)} + 1$$

where $\max S^{(k)}$ here denotes the largest input value to D' that might be used [which could be larger than $S^{(k)}_{max}$], we can state the following two results.

Lemma 2:

The integers x_{i_j} computed by algorithm II [regardless of whether step c) results in $S^{(k)} = 0$] satisfy

$$0 \leqq x_{i_j} < b_{j+1}/ b_j \ , \quad j = 1,2,..,n, \tag{13}$$

when the algorithm is applied to any nonnegative integer S in the range $0 \leqq S \leqq \max S^{(k}$ moreover, for each j, any value of x_{i_j} satisfying (13) is possible.

Lemma 3:

The necessary and sufficient condition such that every integer S in the range (8) when deciphered by D' yields an 'apparently valid' deciphering [i.e., results in $S^{(k)}=0$ is that $b_1 = 1$.

Proofs:

We begin by noting that, in step a) of algorithm II, q and the new value of $S^{(k)}$ are the quotient and remainder, respectively, when the present value of $S^{(k)}$ is divided by

j. Thus, the value of $S^{(k)}$ [which initially is smaller than b_{n+1}] will always be less than b_{j+1} when step a) is entered and hence $x_{i_j} = q$ will satisfy (13). Moreover, if initially $S^{(k)} = Q\, b_J$ for $0 \leq Q < b_{J+1}/ b_J$, then $S^{(k)} < b_{J+1}$, so that step a) will give $x_{i_j} = 0$ for $j > J$ followed by $x_{i_J} = Q$. This proves Lemma 2. Because the final value of $S^{(k)}$ will be the remainder after a division by b_1, this final value must be zero when $b_1 = 1$. But if $b_1 \geq 2$, the initial value $S^{(k)} = 1$ will be unchanged in each pass through step a) so the final value of $S^{(k)}$ will also be 1. This proves Lemma 3.

For convenience, we now define

$$m'^{(-1)} = S_{max}^{(0)} + 1 \tag{14}$$

so that the inequality

$$0 \leq \underline{x}\cdot\underline{a}^{(i)} < m^{(i-1)} \tag{15}$$

holds for $0 \leq i \leq k$ whenever $\underline{x}$ has *binary* components. More generally, if the components of $\underline{x}$ are integers (possibly negative) such that

$$|x_j| \leq \beta, \quad 1 \leq j \leq n \tag{16}$$

then (15) can be replaced by

$$|\underline{x}\cdot\underline{a}^{(i)}| < \beta\, m^{(i-1)}, \qquad 0 \leq i \leq k. \tag{17}$$

We next note that (3) implies that typically

$$\sum_{j=1}^{n} a_j^{(i)} \simeq (n/2)\; m^{(i)}$$

so (1) further implies that typically

$$m^{(i-1)} \simeq (n/2)\; m^{(i)} \tag{18}$$

Thus, there entails virtually no loss of generality when we assume hereafter that the integers $m^{(i)}$ are further required to satisfy

$$m^{(i-1)} > m^{(i)}, \quad 1 \leq i \leq k. \tag{19}$$

With these preliminaries, we can now state the following lemma that will be the basis for our subsequent authentication procedure.

Lemma 4:

If $\underline{x}$ is a vector with integer components satisfying (16) such that

$$\underline{x}\cdot\underline{a}^{(i+1)} = \Sigma^{(i+1)} \tag{20}$$

then

$$\underline{x}\cdot\underline{a}^{(i)} = \Sigma^{(i)} + L\, m^{(i)} \tag{21}$$

for some integer L satisfying

$$|L| < (\beta+1)\, m^{(i-1)} \,/\, m^{(i)} \tag{22}$$

where $\Sigma^{(i)}$ $[0 \leq \Sigma^{(i)} \leq m^{(i)}]$ is defined by

$$\Sigma^{(i)} = w^{(i)} \Sigma^{(i+1)} \pmod{m^{(i)}}. \tag{23}$$

Proof:

Multiplying both sides of (20) by $w^{(i)}$ and then reducing modulo $m^{(i)}$, we see by virtue of (3) and (23) that

$$\underline{x} \cdot \underline{a}^{(i)} = \Sigma^{(i)} \pmod{m^{(i)}},$$

which is equivalent to (21) holding for some integer L. But by definition

$$0 \leq \Sigma^{(i)} < m^{(i-1)},$$

which together with (17) gives

$$|\underline{x} \cdot \underline{a}^{(i)} - \Sigma^{(i)}| \leq |\underline{x} \cdot \underline{a}^{(i)}| + \Sigma^{(i)} < (\beta+1)\, m^{(i-1)}.$$

Inequality (22) now follows from this inequality and (21).

Notice that when $\Sigma^{(i)} = 0$ in Lemma 4, the corresponding $\underline{x} \cdot \underline{a}^{(i)}$ is some integer multiple of $m^{(i)}$ according to (21). We shall make use of such vectors $\underline{x}$ in our authentication procedure to 'correct' for discrepancies between $\underline{x} \cdot \underline{a}^{(i)}$ and $S^{(i)}$ at each step in the deciphering process. Toward this end, we write $\underline{t}(i,L)$ to denote a vector with integer components such that

$$\underline{t}(i,L) \cdot \underline{a}^{(i)} = L\, m^{(i)}, \tag{24}$$

and we call $\underline{t}(i,L)$ an i-th level *correction vector with multiplicity L*. It follows from (24) that

$$[N_1\, \underline{t}(i,L_1) + N_2\, \underline{t}(i,L_2)] \cdot \underline{a}^{(i)} = [N_1 L_1 + N_2 L_2]\, m^{(i)}; \tag{25}$$

this linear relationship can be used to combine correction vectors so as to produce further correction vectors. Notice in particular that we can choose $-\underline{t}(i,L)$ as the correction vector of multiplicity -L without altering the magnitudes of the components We now state an authentication procedure in which we assume the availability of $\underline{t}(i,L)$ for $0 \leq i < k$ and for all necessary positive multiplicities L. In the next section, we will determine the necessary multiplicities and show how to find such correction vectors whose components have small magnitude, as required for the authentication procedure to be secure. We also hereafter assume that $b_1 = 1$ so that, according to Lemma 3, every pre-signature S is an apparently valid knapsack for the deciphering algorithm D'.

Signature-Forming Algorithm for TK-PKC:

a) Set $S^{(0)}$ equal to the given pre-signature S. Compute the integer

$$S^{(i+1)} = u^{(i)} S^{(i)} \pmod{m^{(i)}}$$

for $i = 0,1,\ldots,k$.

b) Apply Algorithm II to $S^{(k)}$ to produce a vector $\underline{x}$ such that

$$\underline{x}\cdot\underline{a}^{(k)} = S^{(k)}.$$

et i = k-1.

c) Calculate the integer $L = [\underline{x}\cdot\underline{a}^{(i)} - S^{(i)}] / m^{(i)}$

d) If $L \geq 0$, replace $\underline{x}$ by $\underline{x} - \underline{t}(i,L)$. If $L < 0$, replace $\underline{x}$ by $\underline{x} + \underline{t}(i,-L)$.

e) If $i = 0$, stop; $\underline{x}$ is the desired signature satisfying $\underline{x}\cdot\underline{a}^{(0)} = S$.

therwise, decrement i by 1 and return to step c).

That the above algorithm does indeed form a signature $\underline{x}$ such that $\cdot\underline{a}^{(0)} = S^{(0)}$ follows from Lemma 4, which asserts that the number L computed in step) is indeed an integer and satisfies (21) with $\Sigma^{(i)} = S^{(i)}$ so that, when $L \neq 0$, tep d) gives

$$[\underline{x} \mp \underline{t}(i,\pm L)]\ \underline{a}^{(i)} = S^{(i)} + L\ m^{(i)} - L\ m^{(i)} = S^{(i)}$$

or i = k-1, k-2, ..., 0.

To determine the computational effort required by the Signature-Forming lgorithm, we first note that step a) requires k multiplications whose two factors are ntegers of about n bits each. Step b) requires at most n subtractions, which is about quivalent to one further such multiplication. Because the L found in step c) will lways be a small integer (as will be shown in the next section), the total effort or steps c), d) and e) will be only a small fraction of that required for steps a) nd b). Thus, the total computational effort is about that required for k+1 multipli-ations of n-bit integers, which is roughly equal to the effort required for a single eciphering by Algorithm D'. This is certainly an acceptable small amount of computation o produce signatures in most applications. It remains to show, however, that the ecessary correction vectors can realistically be formed and stored.

C. Formation of the correction vectors

The key to generating the necessary correction vectors lies in Lemma 4. f for some given integer h, we can randomly produce a vector $\underline{x}$, whose components ave small magnitude, such that

$$\underline{x}\cdot\underline{a}^{(i+1)} = h\ m^{(i)}, \tag{26}$$

en Lemma 4 assures us that for some integer L

$$\underline{x}\cdot\underline{a}^{(i)} = L\ m^{(i)} \tag{27}$$

that, according to (24), $\underline{x}$ is a possible choice for $\underline{t}(i,L)$. We will need to choose ndomly enough such different $\underline{x}$ until we have choosen $\underline{t}(i,L)$ for all (positive) mul-plicities that have high probability of occurrence when the Signature-Forming Algo-thm of the previous section is applied to an allowable pre-signature S. Suppose that multiplicities for $1 \leq L \leq \mu$ suffice for the correction vectors. Postponing temporarily the discussion of how μ is chosen, we now show how the desired correction vectors can be found. For the sake of specificity, we describe the procedure for a TK-PKC where the knapsack vector has been chosen so that $b_1 = 1$ and

$$b_{j+1}/\, b_j \leq 5 \tag{28}$$

for $j = 1, 2, \ldots, n-1$; the necessary modifications for the general situation will be obvious.

1. The Correction Vectors $t(k-1,L)$:

We begin by randomly choosing a vector $\underline{x}' = [x_1', x_2', \ldots, x_n']$ so that the components are independently selected and so that each component is equally likely to have magnitude 0, 1, 2 or 3 and is equally likely to be positive or negative if non-zero. Thus,

$$|x_j'| \leq 3 \tag{29}$$

so that each component is a 3-bit signed integer. We next compute $\underline{x}'\cdot\underline{a}^{(k-1)}$, replacing $\underline{x}'$ by $-\underline{x}'$ if this quantity is negative, thus assuring that

$$\underline{x}'\cdot\underline{a}^{(k-1)} \geq 0.$$

This assures that we can now use Algorithm II with h = 0 to find $\underline{x}''$ such that

$$\underline{x}''\cdot\underline{a}^{(k)} = \underline{x}'\cdot\underline{a}^{(k)} + h\, m^{(k-1)} \tag{30}$$

where, because of (13) and (28), the components of $\underline{x}''$ satisfy

$$0 \leq x_j'' \leq 4. \tag{31}$$

Now defining

$$\underline{x} = \underline{x}'' - \underline{x}', \tag{32}$$

we see from (30) that

$$\underline{x}\cdot\underline{a}^{(k)} = h\, m^{(k-1)}. \tag{33}$$

We can now apply Lemma 4 (with $\Sigma^{(k)} = h\, m^{(k-1)}$ so that $\Sigma^{(k-1)} = 0$) to conclude that

$$\underline{x}\cdot\underline{a}^{(k-1)} = L\, m^{(k-1)}$$

for some integer L. If $L < 0$, we replace $\underline{x}$ by $-\underline{x}$, thus assuring that

$$\underline{x}\cdot\underline{a}^{(k-1)} = L\, m^{(k-1)} > 0. \tag{34}$$

Thus, we see that we may now choose

$$\underline{t}(k-1,L) = \underline{x} \tag{35}$$

as our (k-1)-level correction vector with positive multiplicity L. Moreover, it follows from (29), (31) and (32) that the components of this correction vector satisfy

$$|x_j| \leq 7. \tag{36}$$

Next, using a new random $\underline{x}'$, we repeat the above steps but this time sing h = 1 in (30) to obtain a second correction vector for a possibly different ositive multiplicity.

We shall call the correction vectors obtained as above (with h = 0 or = 1) class-1 correction vectors. Each time, we obtain a class-1 correction vector y this process with a previously unobtained multiplicity μ or less, we form its sum nd difference with all previously obtained class-1 correction vectors to generate, ccording to (25), new correction vectors that we shall call class-2 correction vectors. f these class-2 correction vectors have a previously unobtained positive multiplicity f μ or less, they are included in the set of correction vectors. Likewise, each lass-1 correction vector is combined by sum and difference with the previously formed lass-2 correction vectors to form class-3 correction vectors that are included in the et of correction vectors if they have a previously unobtained positive multiplicity f μ or less. All of the correction vectors so formed have components guaranteed to atisfy

$$|t_j(k-1,L)| \leq 3*7 = 21 \tag{37}$$

ut the maximum magnitudes will generally be considerably smaller.

The above process is repeated by further random choices of $\underline{x}'$ until a orrection vector $\underline{t}(k-1,L)$ has been formed for $1 \leq L \leq \mu$.

. The Correction Vectors $\underline{t}(k-2,L)$:

We begin by random choosing $\underline{x}'$, in exactly the same manner as just explai-ed, so that $\underline{x}'\cdot\underline{a}^{(k-1)} > 0$, but we then use Algorithm II to find $\underline{x}''$ such that

$$\underline{x}''\cdot\underline{a}^{(k)} = \underline{x}'\cdot\underline{a}^{(k)} + h\, u^{(k-1)}\, m^{(k-2)} \pmod{m^{(k-1)}} \tag{38}$$

ather than to satisfy (30). Applying Lemma 4 to

$$(\underline{x}'' - \underline{x}')\cdot\underline{a}^{(k)} = h\, u^{(k-1)}\, m^{(k-2)} \pmod{m^{(k-1)}},$$

here now $\Sigma^{(k)} = h\, u^{(k-1)}\, m^{(k-2)} \pmod{m^{(k-1)}}$ so that

$$\begin{aligned}\Sigma^{(k-1)} &= h\, w^{(k-1)}\, u^{(k-1)}\, m^{(k-2)} \pmod{m^{(k-1)}}\\ &= h\, m^{(k-2)},\end{aligned} \tag{39}$$

hus gives

$$(\underline{x}'' - \underline{x}')\cdot\underline{a}^{(k-1)} = h\, m^{(k-2)} + L'\, m^{(k-1)}$$

or some integer L'. Using the previously formed correction vector $\underline{t}(k-1,L')$, we can ow form

$$\underline{x} = \underline{x}'' - \underline{x}' - \underline{t}(k-1,L') \tag{40}$$

which will satisfy

$$\underline{x}\cdot\underline{a}^{(k-1)} = h\ m^{(k-2)}.$$

Again we invoke Lemma 4, now to obtain

$$\underline{x}\cdot\underline{a}^{(k-2)} = L\ m^{(k-2)}$$

for some integer L. If $L < 0$, we replace $\underline{x}$ by $-\underline{x}$ to obtain a vector $\underline{x}$ such that

$$\underline{x}\cdot\underline{a}^{(k-2)} = L\ m^{(k-2)} > 0, \qquad (41)$$

so that we may now choose

$$\underline{t}(k-2,L) = \underline{x} \qquad (42)$$

as a (k-2)-level correction vector of class 1 with positive multiplicity L. It follows from (29), (31) and (37) that the components of $\underline{x}$ satisfy

$$|x_j| \leq 28.$$

Choosing both $h = 0$ and $h = 1$, and forming also class-2 and class-3 correction vectors by sums and differences as before, we continue with further choices of $\underline{x}'$ until $t(k-2,L)$ has been obtained for all L, $1 \leq L \leq \mu$. The components of these (k-2)-level correction vectors are guaranteed to satisfy

$$|t_j(k-2,L)| \leq 3*28 = 84 \qquad (43)$$

but the maximum components will generally be considerably smaller.

3. The Remaining Correction Vectors :

To find the correction vectors $\underline{t}(k-i,L)$ for $i > 2$, we again choose $\underline{x}'$ exactly as before, but then use Algorithm II to find $\underline{x}''$ such that

$$\underline{x}''\cdot\underline{a}^{(k)} = \underline{x}'\cdot\underline{a}^{(k)} + h\ u^{(k-1)} \ldots [u^{(k-i+2)} (\ u^{(k-i+1)}$$
$$m^{(k-i)} \bmod m^{(k-i+1)}\ ) \bmod m^{(k-i+2)}] \ldots \bmod m^{(k-1)}. \qquad (44)$$

We then use $\underline{x}'' - \underline{x}'$ with the correction vectors obtained at the previous levels to obtain finally a vector $\underline{x}$ such that

$$\underline{x}\cdot\underline{a}^{(k-i)} = L\ m^{(k-i)} > 0$$

which we may then choose as a (k-i)-level correction vector of class 1 with positive multiplicity L. Choosing both $h = 0$ and $h = 1$, and forming also clas-2 and class-3 correction vectors by sums and differences as before, we continue with further choices of $\underline{x}'$ until $\underline{t}(k-i,L)$ has been formed for all L , $1 \leq L \leq \mu$. It can readily be checked that the components of these (k-i)-level correction vectors are guaranteed to satisfy

$$|t_j(k-i,L)| \leq (4)^{i-1} * 21 \qquad (45)$$

.e., at most two more bits are required to represent the components of the correction ctors at each successive level], but again the maximum components will generally be nsiderably smaller.

This process is iterated with increasing i until finally the 0-level rrection vectors $\underline{t}(0,L)$ have been formed for $1 \leq L \leq \mu$. These complete the set of rrection vectors required to carry out the Signature-Forming Algorithm.

As an indication of the actual complexity of forming the set of correction ctors, the above process was implemented for a TK-PKC system of practical size, mely $n = 200$, $k = 3$ and $\mu = 3/2\ n = 300$ [the choice of which will soon be explained]. enty random choices of $\underline{x}'$ sufficed to generate all $\mu = 300$ level 2 correction vecrs; 34 choices of $\underline{x}'$ were needed for level 1 and 29 choices of $\underline{x}'$ were required for vel 0. Modular multiplications similar to that in (5) dominate the effort in the rrection Vectors Forming Algorithm and , to compute $\underline{t}(k-i,L)$, $i-1$ such multiplitions have to be performed. In our example, 34 multiplications were necessary for vel 1 while for level zero 2*29 = 58 multiplications were necessary. Counting the uivalent of one further multiplication for each of the (20 + 34 + 29) applications Algorithm II to a new $\underline{x}'\cdot a^{(k)}$, one finds a total of 175 multiplications required ich is about the same effort as needed for deciphering about 44 cryptograms in this stem. It was found that 5, 7 and 8 bits sufficed to represent the components of e level 2, 1 and 0 correction vectors, respectively, rather than the 6, 8 and 10 t maximums that are guaranteed to be sufficient by (45). Since each correction ctor has $n = 200$ components, it follows that 300 * 200 * (5+7+8) bits, or 150 kilote of storage would be required for storing the correction vectors in the $k = 3$, $= 200$ system. This would appear to be an acceptable memory requirement for an authentition system for a TK-PKC.

It remains to explain the choice $\mu = 3/2\ n$ and the reason for using both $= 0$ and $h = 1$ in the process of forming the correction vectors.

From (19) and (22), we see that the necessary multiplicity L that could required is bounded by

$$L < (\beta + 1)\ n/2$$

ere β is the maximum magnitude among the components of the vector being corrected. is extremely unlikely, however, (as can be deduced from the proof of Lemma 4) that ch a large multiplicity will be required. Experimentation with $k = 3$, $n = 200$ -PKC's revealed that the probability was less than 1 % that a randomly chosen pregnature would require a correction vector with multiplicity of magnitude greater an $\mu = 3/2\ n$; the probability rises to about 20 % for $\mu = n$. For other values of k d n, some experimentation would be rquired to determine a satisfactory choce of μ.

The choice $h = 0$ in (26), (38) or (44) was found to yield correction ectors with an average multiplicity of about $n/4$, whereas the average was about $3n/4$

for h = 1. When h = 0 only was used, the necessary number of random choices of $\underline{x}'$ required to obtain all correction vectors with multiplicities up to $\mu = 3n/2$ was greatly more than when both h = 0 and h = 1 were used.

D. Security of the Proposed Authentication System

Based on the knowledge of a large set Ω of signatures, the following attack could reveal $m^{(0)}$:

a) Find a subset A of Ω such that all elements of A use the same correction vector at level 0 by checking the correlation $\rho = \underline{x} \cdot \underline{x}' / |\underline{x}||\underline{x}'|$ for each pair $\underline{x}$ and $\underline{x}'$ in A.

b) Sum the vectors in Ω and in A and divide each sum by the number of terms to obtain the 'average' vectors $\underline{t}_\Omega$ and $\underline{t}_A$, respectively.

c) Take the difference $\underline{t} = \text{int}[\underline{t}_A - \underline{t}_\Omega]$, where $\text{int}[\underline{v}]$ denotes the vector whose components are the integer parts of the components of the vector $\underline{v}$, as the estimate for the correction vector common to the elements of A.

d) Form the dot-product $\underline{t} \cdot \underline{a}^{(0)}$ to obtain a multiple of $m^{(0)}$.

e) Perform steps a)..d) for another set A' of signatures. Taking the greatest common divisor of the two multiples of $m^{(0)}$ that have been found will now give $m^{(0)}$ with a high probability.

The method works as described because $\underline{t}_A$ is the sum of the common level-0 correction vector and some average 'noise vector' whose components are determined by the bias introduced by Algorithm II in step b) of the Signature-Forming Algorithm and by the bias in the elements of the correction vectors of the other levels. The central limit theorem implies that $\underline{t}_\Omega$ is close to this average noise vector if enough signatures were summed to produce $\underline{t}_A$. On the other hand, if the standard deviation of the elements of the components of $\underline{t}_A$ is *greater* than 1/2, then the estimate in step c) above will be correct with probability less than 2^{-n}. This fact can be used to give a maximum number of signatures that should be formed using the same set of correction vectors to foil the above attack. In the specific example given in the previous section the standard deviations of the components of the signatures were found to be greater than 10 in almost all components. Thus, when A contains less than 400 elements, then the standard deviation of the components of $\underline{t}_A$ will be greater than 1/2. It is very unlikely - as our simulations confirmed - that in a set Ω of less than about 5'000 elements more than 400 elements use the same level-0 correction vector. Therefore, we propose to foil the above attack by changing the set of correction vectors after having produced 5'000 signatures, a task which is easier than computing 50 signatures, as we have shown in the previous section.

There are two further objections to the security of the proposed authentication system:

1) The system can accept virtually all pre-signatures, which is a weakness because high density knapsacks are not secure [Shamir/Zippel, 1980], [Shamir, 1979].

2) Because nonbinary solutions are allowed, security will be reduced in the sense that signatures can be easily forged.

To the above objections, we make the following replies:

To 1: One possible starting point for an attack on high density knapsacks is the presence of small elements in the original superincreasing vector. However, the published attacks based on this property work exclusively for systems with one [Shamir/Zippel, 1980] of at most two iterations [Shamir, 1982]. The attack of [Shamir, 1979] applies to systems where (almost) all knapsacks have a *unique* solution. In the proposed system, many solutions exist for every knapsack, which foils this attack.

To 2: Allowing multivariate solutions presumably increases the possibility to forge a signature because it is normally easier to find one of many possible solutions than to find a unique solution. In fact, given any two relatively prime components, say $a_i^{(0)}$ and $a_j^{(0)}$, of the public knapsack vector, one can always find (by using Euclid's greatest common divisor algorithm) integers m_1 and m_2 such that

$$1 = m_1 a_i^{(0)} + m_2 a_j^{(0)} .$$

Hence for any presignature S,

$$S = (S\, m_1)\, a_i^{(0)} + (S\, m_2)\, a_j^{(0)}$$

so that the vector $\underline{x}$ which is zero in all components except the i-th and j-th where it equals $S\, m_1$ and $S\, m_2$, respectively, is a valid non-binary signature that can easily be forged - however, its non-zero components are enormously large. In a secure system, the maximum allowable size of the elements of a valid signature must be held as small as possible. Obviously there is a relation between this maximum size and the dimension of vectors for a secure system in this sense that a high dimension will permit larger vector components for the same security. On the other hand, the magnitude of the components in the proposed system increases slowly with the dimension. This ensures a secure system when the dimension is sufficiently large. Although dimension n = 200 seems to be quite secure, it is not clear as yet how much smaller an n could be tolerated in a secure system.

IV REMARKS

An authentication procedure producing digital signatures for the TK-PKC has been proposed. In comparison with an authentication system proposed in [Merkle/ Hellman, 1978], our system requires a smaller computational effort but requires significantly more memory to store the necessary correction vectors. The computational effort for signing a message in our proposed system is about the same as that for deciphering in a TK-PKC as proposed in [Merkle/Hellman, 1978]. Shamir [Shamir, 1978] has proposed a different knapsack-based authentication scheme. Using a system of this kind and of comparable security to the dimension 200 system proposed here would require the storage of a binary 200*400 matrix - a storage requirement that is indeed smaller than that for the correction vectors in our system. On the other hand, Shamir' system cannot be used for enciphering messages, whereas our system allows enciphering and authentication on the basis of one single knapsack vector, which has clear implementation advantages.

ACKNOWLEDGMENT

The authors are grateful to Dr. A. Shamir of the Weizmann Institute, Rehovot for some helpful suggestions as to Prof. Dr. P. Leuthold of the Swiss Federal Institute of Technology, Zürich, for his encouragement and support of this research.

Section 9

The Merkle - Hellman - Scheme

A NEW ALGORITHM FOR THE SOLUTION OF THE KNAPSACK PROBLEM

Ingemar Ingemarsson
Linköping Inst. of Technology
Dept. of Electrical Engineering
S-581 83 Linköping
SWEDEN

Abstract

A new algorithm for the solution of the knapsack problem is described. The algorithm is based upon successive reductions modulo suitably chosen integers. Thus the original knapsack problem is transformed into a system of modified knapsack problems. Very often a partial solution to the system can be found. The system and the original knapsack can then be reduced to a lower dimensionality and the algorithm repeated.

So far we have not been able to characterize the class of knapsack problems for which the algorithm is effective. There are indications, however, that most knapsack problems for which we know that there is one and only one solution may be solved fast by the use of the new algorithm.

1. Introduction

The knapsack problem and the fact that it is in general difficult to solve has been used by Merkle and Hellman [Merkle, 1978] to define a public key crypto system. It is, however, in this context not possible to use a general knapsack problem. We are limited to an array of integers that is an integer multiple (mod p) of a super-increasing [Merkle, 1978] sequence. This particular class of knapsack problems may allow faster algorithms than those for general knapsack problems.

In this paper a new algorithm is presented. The algorithm transforms the original knapsack problem into a system of modified knapsack problems by successive reductions modulo suitably chosen integers. In some cases the system is easier to solve, at least partially, than the original knapsack problem. Thereby the number of unknowns in the problem is reduced and the algorithm may be used again.

2. The Algorithm

The knapsack problem is to solve for the unknown binary vector $\bar{x}$ in (1)

$$S_0 = \sum_{j=0}^{n} k_{0j}\, x_j \qquad (1)$$

where $x_j \in \{0,1\}$

and $\bar{k}_0 = (k_{01}, \ldots, k_{n1})$

is an integer vector.

In general (1) may have any number of solutions for $\bar{x}$. We will, however, limit ourself to the case where (1) has one and only one solution.

Equation (1) is reduced modulo an integer ℓ_{11} of our choice. We obtain:

$$S_1 = S_0 - \lfloor \frac{S_0}{\ell_{11}} \rfloor \ell_{11} = \sum_{j=0}^{n} k_{1j} x_j + \ell_{11} \cdot y_1$$

where y_1 is the integer:

$$y_1 = \sum_{j=0}^{n} x_j \lfloor \frac{k_{0j}}{\ell_{11}} \rfloor - \lfloor \frac{S_0}{\ell_{11}} \rfloor$$

Here $\lfloor\ \rfloor$ denotes the integer part.

By successive further reductions we obtain the system of equations:

$$S_i = \sum_{j=0}^{n} k_{ij} x_j + \sum_{j=1}^{i} \ell_{ij} y_i \tag{2}$$

where: $S_i = S_{i-1} \bmod \ell_{ii}$ for $i > 0$

$k_{ij} = k_{i-1,j} \bmod \ell_{ii}$ for $i > 0$

$\ell_{ij} = \ell_{i-1,j} \bmod \ell_{ii}$ for $j < i$

$\ell_{ij} = 0$ for $j > i$

and $$y_i = \sum_{j=1}^{i-1} \lfloor \frac{\ell_{i-1,j}}{\ell_{ij}} \rfloor \cdot y_j + \sum_{j=0}^{n} \lfloor \frac{k_{i-1,j}}{\ell_{ii}} \rfloor x_i - \lfloor \frac{S_{i-1}}{\ell_{ii}} \rfloor \tag{3}$$

Note that the integers ℓ_{ii} are independent variables.

We now solve for y_i in (2):

$$y_i = -\sum_{j=0}^{n} b_{ij} x_j + z_i \quad \text{for } i > 0 \tag{4}$$

where $b_{ij} = \frac{k_{ij}}{\ell_{ii}} - \sum_{v=1}^{i-1} \frac{\ell_{iv}}{\ell_{ii}} \cdot b_{vj}$

and $z_i = \frac{S_i}{\ell_{ii}} - \sum_{v=1}^{i-1} \frac{\ell_{iv}}{\ell_{ii}} z_v$

Even though (1) has only one solution, (2) and (4) may mave more than one integer solution for y_i with $x_j \in \{0,1\}$. Only one of these solutions, however, will also satisfy (3).

The idea of the algorithm is to use the fact that x_j is bound to the interval [0,1] (in fact $x_j \in \{0,1\}$) to bound y_i using (3) and (4). If we are lucky there is only one integer y_i (for some i) in the interval so found. The derived y_i are inserted in (4) and some x_j are found using the same bounding technique. Then the number of unknown variables x in (1) is reduced. The knapsack problem is then reformulated to one of lesser dimensionality and the algorithm is repeated.

From (4) we can derive a recursive relation for y_i. We multiply (4) by ℓ_{iv}/ℓ_{ii} and sum over v from 1 to i-1. This yields:

$$\sum_{v=1}^{i-1} \frac{\ell_{iv}}{\ell_{ii}} y_v = -\sum_{j=0}^{n} \left(\sum_{v=1}^{n} \frac{\ell_{iv}}{\ell_{ii}} b_{vj} \right) x_j + \sum_{v=1}^{i-1} \frac{\ell_{iv}}{\ell_{ii}} z_v$$

We now observe that:

$$\sum_{v=1}^{i-1} \frac{\ell_{iv}}{\ell_{ii}} b_{vj} = \frac{k_{ij}}{\ell_{ii}} - b_{ij}$$

and

$$\sum_{v=1}^{i-1} \frac{\ell_{iv}}{\ell_{ii}} z_v = \frac{S_i}{\ell_{ii}} - z_i$$

Thus:

$$\sum_{v=1}^{i-1} \frac{\ell_{iv}}{\ell_{ii}} y_v = -\sum_{j=0}^{n} \frac{k_{ij}}{\ell_{ii}} + \sum_{j=0}^{n} b_{ij} x_j - z_i + \frac{S_i}{\ell_{ii}}$$

We recognize y_i from (4) in the right part of the above relation. This finally yields:

$$y_i = -\sum_{j=0}^{n} \frac{k_{ij}}{\ell_{ii}} \cdot x_j + \frac{S_i}{\ell_{ii}} - \sum_{v=1}^{i-1} \frac{\ell_{iv}}{\ell_{ii}} y_v \qquad (5)$$

As we have noted before, (5) might have multiple solutions (integers y_i and $x_j \in \{0,1\}$) due to the modulo reductions leading to (2). To obtain a unique solution we have to use both (5) and (3).

3. Bounding of y_i

We will now bound y_i using the fact that $x_j \in \{0,1\}$. We observe that k_{ij} and ℓ_{ij} are non-negative for all i and j while b_{ij} can have any sign. This observation used in (3), (4) and (5) yields:

$$\max y_i = \left\lfloor \min \left\{ \begin{array}{l} z_i - \sum\limits_{j \text{ such that } b_{ij} < 0} b_{ij} \\[2ex] \dfrac{S_i}{\ell_{ii}} - \sum\limits_{v=1}^{i-1} \dfrac{\ell_{iv}}{\ell_{ii}} \min y_v \\[2ex] \sum\limits_{v=1}^{i-1} \left\lfloor \dfrac{\ell_{i-1,j}}{\ell_{ii}} \right\rfloor \max y_i + \sum\limits_{j=0}^{n} \left\lfloor \dfrac{k_{i-1,j}}{\ell_{ii}} \right\rfloor - \left\lfloor \dfrac{S_{i-1}}{\ell_{ii}} \right\rfloor \end{array} \right. \right\rfloor$$

$$\min y_i = \left\lceil \max \left\{ \begin{array}{l} z_i - \sum\limits_{j \text{ such that } b_{ij} > 0} b_{ij} \\[2ex] - \sum\limits_{j=0}^{n} \dfrac{k_{ij}}{\ell_{ii}} + \dfrac{S_i}{\ell_{ii}} - \sum\limits_{v=1}^{i-1} \dfrac{\ell_{iv}}{\ell_{ii}} \max y_v \\[2ex] \sum\limits_{v=1}^{i-1} \left\lfloor \dfrac{\ell_{i-1,j}}{\ell_{ii}} \right\rfloor \min y_i - \left\lfloor \dfrac{S_{i-1}}{\ell_{ii}} \right\rfloor \end{array} \right. \right\rceil$$

Here $\lceil x \rceil$ denotes the integer $\geq x$

The most important part in the bounding above, is the one based on (4) using the coefficient b_{ij}. To obtain tight bounds we use the following rule:

Choose ℓ_{ii} to minimize $\sum\limits_{j=0}^{n} \lvert b_{ij} \rvert$

How well the algorithm works using this rule is still an open question. Experience indicates, however, that the bounds for y_i often embraces just one integer for i from 4-5 on upwards.

Once a number of y_i are found they can be used in (4) to give a system of equations. From this system the same number of x_j may be solved using the same bounding technique as when deriving y,

4. Geometric interpretation

The system of equations (2) (for i > 0) may be written in matrix form:

$$\bar{S} = K\bar{x} + L\bar{y} \tag{6}$$

If (which often turns out to be advantageously) ℓ_{ii} is chosen amongst $\{k_{i-1,j}\}_{j=0}^{n}$ then the columns of the matrix K may be rearranged (i.e. x_j renumbered) so that K is upper triangular. The matrix L is by definition lower triangular.

Using (6) we can rewrite (4) yielding:

$$\bar{y} = -B\bar{x} + \bar{z} \tag{7}$$

where

$$B = L^{-1}K$$

Since $x_j \in \{0,1\}$ the possible vectors $\bar{x}$ terminate in the corners of the n-dimensional hypercube with one corner at the origin. This hypercube is transformed by the matrix B into the integer lattice formed by all possible vectors $\bar{y}$. The efficiency of the algorithm relies upon that not more than one lattice point is located in or on the transformed cube. The volume of the tranformed cube is equal to the determinant of the matrix B. With the above mentioned choice of ℓ_{ii} (yielding a triangular matrix K) the determinant of B is:

$$\det B = \frac{\det K}{\det L} = \frac{\sum_{i=1}^{n} k_{1i}}{\sum_{i=1}^{n} \ell_{ii}} = \frac{k_{nn}}{k_{01}}$$

Due to the modulo reductions, k_{nn} is very small, in fact often less than 10. Thus the volume of the transformed cube is small, in the order of the inverted value of an element in $\{k_{0j}\}$. This should guarantee a single lattice point within or on the transformed hypercube if B is orthogonal or close to orthogonal. The problem is that the algorithm can not guarantee this. How to make the matrix B to our advantage is still an open problem.

Reference

[Merkle, 1978] R.C. Merkle and M.E. Hellman: "Hiding Information and Signatures in Trap-Door Knapsacks", IEEE Trans. on Information Theory, Vol. IT-24, pp. 525-530, September 1978.

Trapdoors in Knapsack Kryptosystems

Prof. Dr. R. Eier — Institut für Datenverarbeitung, Technische Universität Wien

Dipl.-Ing. H. Lagger — Forschungslaboratorien der Siemens AG., München

Abstract

A way to attack public-key cryptosystems based on the knapsack problem is proposed. The basic idea of the approach described is to find pairs of natural numbers, namely values for a modulus $\bar{m}$ and a multiplier $\bar{w}$, which reduce the knapsack elements simultaneously by modular multiplication. The ratio $\bar{r}=\bar{w}/\bar{m}$ plays an overriding role.

Introduction

In the last years a new kind of cryptographic system, the public-key system, has been introduced [Diffie, Hellman, 1976]. This system uses different keys for encryption and decryption. The key used to encrypt a message can be made public. There is no longer any need to transmit keys through secure channels.

Some of these public-key systems are based on the knapsack problem. In the following, some aspects associated with the security of such systems will be discussed.

A knapsack is mathematically represented by a vector A of n natural numbers $(a_1 \ldots\ldots a_n)$. The knapsack problem is to find a binary vector $(x_1 \ldots . x_n)$ for a given sum S, such that

$$S = \sum_{i=1}^{n} a_i \, x_i \tag{1}$$

holds, if such an X does exist [Merkle, Hellman, 1979].

Almost n additions are needed to compute the sum S for a given vector X, yet finding a vector X corresponding to a known sum S grows exponentionally with the dimension of n.

This property can be used to construct a public-key system. The public-key in such a cryptosystem is given by the vector A and the message to be transmitted is represented by the binary vector X. The cryptogram $S = \sum a_i \, x_i$ is sent to the intended receiver. Only this person knows the hidden structure and is thus in the position to reconstruct the information X.

There exist various structures of knapsacks which allow for a fast computation of the vector X. R.C. Merkle and M.E. Hellman originally proposed using a superincreasing sequence $(a'_1 \ldots a'_n)$ with the property

$$\sum_{i=1}^{k} a'_i < a'_{k+1} \tag{2}$$

To hide this structure they suggested to use a modulus m and a multiplier v, such that

$$\sum_{i=1}^{n} a'_i < m \qquad \text{and} \qquad (3)$$

$$\gcd(v, m) = 1.$$

Instead of publishing the elements a'_i, the system is published according to

$$a_i = a'_i * v \qquad (\text{mod } m). \qquad (4)$$

On the premises that gcd (v, m) = 1, a natural number w exists, which fulfills the property

$$w * v = 1 \qquad (\text{mod } m). \qquad (5)$$

This number w can be used together with the modulus in order to recover the hidden structure and thus to decrypt the transmitted cryptogram.

The Cryptanalytic Attack

A cryptanalyst is not in the possession of the secret parameters m, w. However, he may try to find other pairs of natural numbers $\bar{m}$, $\bar{w}$, which fulfill the following properties:

$$\bar{a}_i = a_i * \bar{w} \qquad (\text{mod } \bar{m}) \qquad (6)$$

$$\sum_{i=1}^{n} \bar{a}_i < \bar{m} \qquad (7)$$

The problem of this kind of analysis is to find appropriate pairs of natural numbers $\bar{m}$, $\bar{w}$, which reduce the elements a_i simultaneously by modular multiplication. The probability that two randomly chosen numbers have this property is very small [Shamir, 1980]. As will be shown later, the knowledge of a correct pair of integers is almost equivalent to the knowledge of the original trapdoor information. We call such pairs knapsack trapdoors. An exhaustive search for correct parameters $\bar{m}$, $\bar{w}$ seems to be computationally unfeasible. One has two degrees of freedom, namely the selection of the integers $\bar{m}$ and $\bar{w}$. To narrow down the number of possible candidates we first study the effect of the operation denoted by (6).

Equivalently one can write

$$\bar{a}_i/\bar{m} = a_i * \bar{w}/\bar{m} \qquad (\text{mod } 1) \qquad (8)$$

or with the ratio $\bar{r} = \bar{w}/\bar{m}$

$$\bar{a}_i/\bar{m} = a_i * \bar{r} \qquad (\text{mod } 1) \qquad (9)$$

The function represents a sawtooth like curve starting at the origin with an ascent a_i. Upon reaching 1 the function falls back and starts from the zero line again.

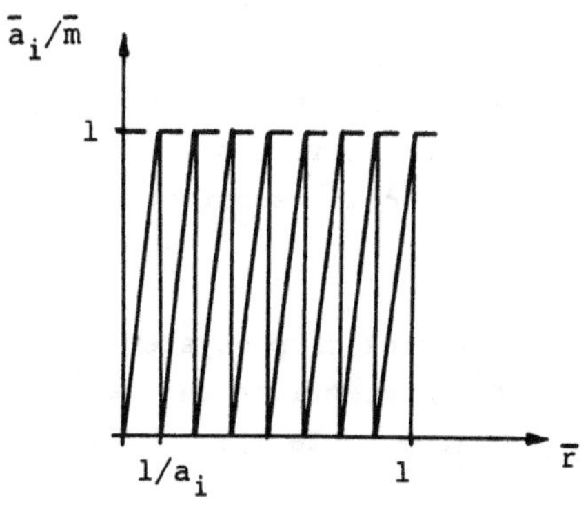

This function therefore consists of a set of parallel lines. The length of one period is given by $1/a_i$. As noted above, a cryptanalyst has to find paris of natural numbers $\bar{m}$, $\bar{w}$, which fulfill the property

$$\sum_{i=1}^{n} a_i * \bar{r} \pmod 1 < 1 . \qquad (10)$$

This means he has to search for one characteristic rational parameter $\bar{r}$ instead of two parameters $\bar{m}$, $\bar{w}$. If one adds together all the sawtooth like curves with the frequencies a_i, the resulting curve will be in general greater than one. There must however be at least one small interval $[r_1, r_2]$ where this function is less than one.

If this interval has once been found one has no difficulty to compute appropriate natural numbers $\bar{m}$, $\bar{w}$, with a ratio $\bar{r} = \bar{w}/\bar{m}$ lying in the interval $r_1 < \bar{r} < r_2$.

If knapsack systems with large numbers are considered, there remains the problem how to find the small intervals according to the knapsack trapdoors.

To simplify the solution we propose to shift the interval of the function by a factor of 0.5 in the direction of negative values:

$$\hat{a}_i/\bar{m} = (\bar{a}_i/\bar{m} + 0.5) \pmod 1 - 0.5 \qquad (11)$$

To derive an equation instead of a congruence, now the sum of all absolute values $\hat{a}_i/\bar{m}$ must be smaller than 1. Graphically this is equivalent to a superposition of n triangular like curves with the frequencies a_i. The advantage of this is, that the number of intervals where the resulting curve is less than one as well as the width of these intervals becomes substantionally increased.

If one choses for example the small knapsack cryptosystem published in [Hellman 1979], intervals for appropriate ratios $\bar{w}/\bar{m}$ are found by a short computer program (see table 1).

Public-Key:

$a_1=2292$	$a_3=211$	$a_5=1283$	$a_7=759$	$a_9=2597$
$a_2=1089$	$a_4=1625$	$a_6=599$	$a_8=315$	$a_{10}=2463$

$0.175370 < \bar{r} < 0.175395$

$0.350785 < \bar{r} < 0.350790$

$0.412305 < \bar{r} < 0.412405$

Table 1: Intervals for appropriate ratios $\bar{r}=\bar{w}/\bar{m}$

Because all triangular curves ly symmetrically about the value $r = 0.5$, all derived intervals can be found between $r = 0.5$ and $r = 1$ as well.

In order to analyze knapsack systems with more and larger elements, one has to take measures to diminish the computational effort. For example the periodic structure of the elementary functions can be used to iteratively restrict the regions where the minima for the resulting function must be located.

Discussion

The described algorithm indicates one way to find knapsack trapdoors. Using these trapdoors, a cryptanalyst may attack a cryptosystem in various ways.

As discussed by A. Shamir, he may try to find n linearly independent equations in n unknowns x_i. This attempt need not be successful in each case. In contrast to [Shamir, 1980] we found that not all resulting equations are linearly independent. If a large knapsack system is considered such as proposed in [Merkle, Hellman, 1979], there exists only one linearly indepent solution. Another method of attack may prove to be more successful. Here the salient point is to find a pair of integers with a ratio $\bar{r}=\bar{w}/\bar{m}$ lying very close to the ratio r=w/m, so that the first transformed element becomes very small. Using this type of trapdoor, the hidden structure is likely to reappear. In our example a modulus $\bar{m}$ = 1701559 and a multiplier $\bar{w}$ = 1000000 lead to a superincreasing sequence as well as the original used parameters m=2731 an w=1605. In addition one can find the region of the original modulus m by summing all elements a_i and by dividing the sum by n/2.

Yet another attack would be to look for partially solvable knapsacks [Ingmarsson, 1980]. This method may prove quite efficient using the above mentioned trapdoors.

Finally one can state that the difficulty of attacking such a cryptosystem does not consist of applying the trapdoors, but in finding them. The time needed to find such trapdoors depends crucially on the magnitude of the knapsack elements used.

Section 10

The Rivest - Shamir - Adleman - Scheme

Is the RSA - Scheme safe?

(Abstract)

C.P. Schnorr

Fachbereich Mathematik

Universität Frankfurt

Summary: We present a new factoring algorithm which under reasonable assumptions and for $r \geq 2$ will factor about $n(r-2)^{-(r-2)}$ integers in $[1,n]$ within $n^{1/2r}$ multiplications in G(-n). Here G(-n) is the group of equivalence classes under $SL_2(\mathbb{Z})$, of primitive, positive forms $ax^2 + bxy + cy^2$ with discriminant $-n = b^2 - 4ac$. Let $h(-n) = |G(-n)|$ be the class number. Then n will be factored within this time bound if

(1) the largest prime divisor of h(- n) is $\leq n^{1/r}$

(2) the second largest prime divisor of h(- n) is $\leq n^{1/2r}$.

So far it is unpredictable which integers n satisfy these conditions.

Stage 1 of the algorithm

$H \in G(-n)$ is called ambiguous if $H^2 = 1$ is the unit in G(- n). It is well known that the ambiguous classes correspond to the factorizations $n = n_1 \cdot n_2$ of n with $\gcd(n_1, n_2) = 1$. Our method of factoring n is to construct an ambiguous class in G(- n) as follows:

begin input n,r

form the list $p_1 = 2, p_2 = 3, \ldots$ of all primes $p_i < n^{1/2r}$

stage 1 choose $H_0 \in G(-n)$ arbitrarily, $i := 2$, $H := H_0$

while $p_i < n^{1/2r}$ **do**

$$\left[\begin{array}{l} e_i := \max \{ \nu \mid p_i^{\nu} < n^{1/2r} \} \\ H := H^{p_i^{e_i}}, \; i := i + 1 \end{array}\right]$$

$\nu := 1, \quad e_* := \log_2 \sqrt{n}, \quad \bar{H} := H$

__while__ $\nu \leq e_* \wedge H \neq 1$ __do__ $[S := H, H := H^2, \nu := \nu + 1]$

__if__ $H \neq 1$ __then goto__ stage 2

S is ambiguous and yields some divisor t of n

if $t \in \{1,n\}$ __then__ return to stage 1 and choose another independent H_0

__end__

__Fact 1__ Suppose $h(-n) \mid \prod_{p_i < n^{1/2r}} p_i^{e_i}$ and $\mathrm{ord}(H_0)$ even, then stage 1 generates an ambiguous class $S \neq 1$.

In case $-n \equiv 1 \bmod 4$ every ambiguous class $S \neq 1$ yields a proper factor of n. In particular, when n has d distinct prime factors, then $2^{d-1} \mid h(-n)$, and there are exactly 2^{d-1} ambiguous classes corresponding to the 2^{d-1} pairs (n_1, n_2) with $n_1 \cdot n_2 = n$, $n_1 < n_2$, $\gcd(n_1, n_2) = 1$. Moreover, when n is composite and $H_0 \in G(-n)$ is chosen at random, then prob $[\mathrm{ord}(H_0)$ even $] \geq 1/2$. Hence stage 1 has a chance $\geq 1/2$ to find a proper factor of n provided $h(-n) \mid \prod_{p_i < n^{1/2r}} p_i^{e_i}$. A few repetitions of stage 1 almost surely generate a proper factor of n provided $h(-n) \mid \prod_i p_i^{e_i}$ and n is composite:

__Fact 2__ Suppose $h(-n) \mid \prod_i p_i^{e_i}$ and n is composite.
If stage 1 is passed with H_0 chosen independently k times, then with probability $\geq 1 - 2^{-k}$ a proper factor of n has been found.

Next we consider the chance that

$$h(-n) \mid \prod_{p_i < n^{1/2r}} p_i^{e_i}, \quad e_i := \lfloor \log n^{1/r} / \log p_i \rfloor$$

for random n. Siegel (1936) proved

$$\forall \varepsilon : \exists n_\varepsilon : \forall n \geq n_\varepsilon : h(-n) \in [n^{1/2-\varepsilon}, n^{1/2+\varepsilon}].$$

We will assume the following

Hypothesis 4 for all r and sufficiently large n:

$$\#\{ m \le n: h(-m) \mid \prod_{p_i \le n^{1/2r}} p_i^{e_i} \} / n \ge \#\{ \bar{m} \le \sqrt{n}: \bar{m} \mid \prod_{p_i < n^{1/2r}} p_i^{e_i} \} / \sqrt{n}.$$

Conclusion By Hypothesis 4 stage 1 factors about one out of r^r integers n in about $\lesssim 4.6\, n^{1/2r}$ G(- n) - multiplications.

Using a Pollard - Brent recursion in stage 2

If $h(-n) \nmid \prod_i p_i^{e_i}$ with $e_i = \lfloor \log n / \log p_i \rfloor$ for $p_i \le n^{1/2r}$ then stage 1 fails to factor n and computes

$$\bar{H} := H_0^{\prod_{2 \nmid p_i} p_i^{e_i}} , \qquad H := H_0^{\prod_i p_i^{e_i}} = \bar{H}^{2^{e_*}} .$$

Stage 2 uses H, $\bar{H}$ and will most likely find a proper divisor of n within $O(n^{1/2r})$ steps provided $\mathrm{ord}(H) \le n^{1/r}$.

Stage 2 generates a random walk through the cyclic group $< \bar{H} >$ with generator $\bar{H}$. With some function $f : < \bar{H} > \longrightarrow < \bar{H} >$ let

$$\bar{H}_1 := \bar{H} , \quad \bar{H}_{i+1} := f(\bar{H}_i) .$$

The function f must be chosen such that

(1) f is easy to compute

(2) f is sufficiently random

(3) every relation $\bar{H}_j = \bar{H}_k$ with $j \neq k$ yields an ambiguous class S, depending on $\bar{H}$, f, j, k.

It is known (see Knuth(1981), exercise 3.1.12) that some $k < j \lesssim \sqrt{\frac{\pi}{2}}\, n^{1/2r}$ with $\bar{H}_j = \bar{H}_k$ can be expected if f is sufficiently random.

<u>Stage 2:</u> For some random function $g : \langle H \rangle \longrightarrow \{2,3\}$ let

(4) $$H_1 = H \quad , \quad H_{i+1} = H_i^{g(H_i)} .$$

Find some $k < j$ with $H_k = H_j$, and then start a similar recursion on $\bar{H}$:

(5) $$\bar{H}_1 = \bar{H} \quad , \quad \bar{H}_{i+1} = \begin{cases} \bar{H}_i & i < k \wedge g(H_i) = 2 \\ \bar{H}_i^{g(H_i)} & \text{otherwise} \end{cases}$$

We have

$$\mathrm{ord}(H_k) \mid T \qquad \text{with} \qquad T = \prod_{i=k}^{j-1} g(H_i) - 1$$

$$H = \bar{H}^{2^{e_*}} \qquad \text{with} \qquad e_* = \lfloor \log n^{1/r} / \log 2 \rfloor .$$

$$H_k = H^{2^{\bar{k}}} = \bar{H}^{2^{e_*+\bar{k}}} \quad , \quad \bar{H}_k = \bar{H}^{3^{k-\bar{k}}}$$

with $\bar{k} = \# \{ i < k \mid g(H_i) = 2 \}$.

Now suppose

(6) $$\mathrm{ord}(H) \equiv 1 \bmod 2, \qquad T \equiv 1 \bmod 2$$

which will almost surely be the case, and let

$$\mathrm{ord}(\bar{H}) \equiv 2^e \bmod 2^{e+1}.$$

Then

$$\mathrm{ord}(\bar{H}_k) = 2^e \, \mathrm{ord}(H_k)$$

$$\mathrm{ord}(\bar{H}_k) \mid 2^e \, T \quad , \quad \bar{H}_k^{\,T} = \bar{H}_j \cdot \bar{H}_k^{-1} .$$

Hence (6) implies

<u>Fact 5</u> $\mathrm{ord}(\bar{H}_j \; \bar{H}_k^{-1}) = 2^e$

and therefore $S := (\bar{H}_j \bar{H}_k^{-1})^{2^{e-1}}$ is an ambiguous class S with $S \neq 1$ whenever $e \geq 1$.

Let $F(n,r) \cdot n$ be the number of integers in $[1,n]$ which will be factored by stage 2. By heuristical arguments we obtain the following lower bound on $F(n,r)$:

n	r	$n^{1/2r}$	r^{-r}	$F(n,r)$
2^{100}	4	$5.8 \cdot 10^{4}$	$4 \cdot 10^{-3}$	$3.4 \cdot 10^{-2}$
2^{200}	5	$1 \cdot 10^{6}$	$3.2 \cdot 10^{-4}$	$3.8 \cdot 10^{-3}$
2^{300}	6	$3.3 \cdot 10^{7}$	$2 \cdot 10^{-5}$	$3.6 \cdot 10^{-4}$
2^{400}	7	$4 \cdot 10^{8}$	$1.2 \cdot 10^{-6}$	$2.6 \cdot 10^{-5}$
2^{500}	7.6	$8 \cdot 10^{9}$	$2 \cdot 10^{-7}$	$5.2 \cdot 10^{-6}$

EIN EFFIZIENZVERGLEICH DER FAKTORISIERUNGSVERFAHREN VON MORRISON-BRILLHART UND SCHROEPPEL*)

(EXTENDED ABSTRACT)

J. Sattler
C.P. Schnorr

Fachbereich Mathematik
Universität Frankfurt

Abstrakt Die Algorithmen von Morrison-Brillhart und Schroeppel sind für große natürliche Zahlen (allgemeiner Gestalt und bezügl. der worst-case-Rechenzeit) die effizientesten aller bis heute bekannten Faktorisierungsalgorithmen. Der vorgelegte Effizienzvergleich basiert auf einer theoretischen Analyse, deren Annahmen experimentell verifiziert wurden. Wegen der übergroßen Rechenzeiten ist nämlich ein experimenteller Vergleich der Laufzeiten beider Algorithmen für Zahlen $n > 10^{50}$ zur Zeit technisch sehr schwierig. Die der Analyse zugrunde gelegten Annahmen betreffen das Verhalten der zahlentheoretischen Funktion

$$\psi(n,v) := \#\{x \in [1,n] \mid (p \text{ prim} \wedge p|x) \Rightarrow p \leq v\}$$

sowie damit verwandter Funktionen. Entgegen den bisherigen Vermutungen können wir zeigen, daß der Morrison-Brillhart-Algorithmus dem Schroeppel-Algorithmus für Zahlen aller Größenbereiche überlegen ist.

*) Diese Arbeit wurde im Rahmen des Forschungsprojektes SICHERHEIT KRYPTOGRAPHISCHER VERFAHREN angefertigt, welches vom BMFT unter dem Förderungskennzeichen 08 30108 gefördert wird.

Einleitung

Hintergrund dieses Vergleichs der beiden asymptotisch schnellsten Faktorisierungsverfahren ist, daß die Sicherheit des RSA-Schemas [RSA 78] als öffentliches Kryptosystem weitgehend darauf beruht, daß es keine schnellen Verfahren gibt, um große Zahlen in ihre Primfaktoren zu zerlegen. In den am MIT hergestellten Chips zum RSA-Schema werden je zwei Primzahlen $p,q \approx 2^{250} \approx 10^{75}$ zufällig gewählt. Ihr Produkt $n = p \cdot q$ ist der öffentliche Schlüssel zum Kodieren, während die Dekodierung nur unter Kenntnis der geheim gehaltenen Primzahlen p und q gelingt. In der Tat führen die bisher bekannten Ansätze zum Brechen des RSA-Schemas alle zur Zerlegung von n in die Faktoren p und q. Damit stellt sich die Frage nach schnellen Faktorisierungsverfahren.

Bei der Diskussion der Sicherheit des RSA-Schemas beziehen sich Rivest et alii auf den unpublizierten Algorithmus von Schroeppel als den asymptotisch schnellsten Faktorisierungsalgorithmus. Seine Laufzeit geben sie mit $e^{\sqrt{\ln n \ \ln\ln n}}$ Makroschritten ($\approx$ arithmetische Operationen in $\mathbb{Z}_n$) an, dies bedeutet für $n \approx 10^{150}$ etwa 10^9 Jahre, sofern ein Makroschritt 10^{-3} Sek. erfordert.

Eine detaillierte Analyse des Schroeppel-Algorithmus zeigt, daß die Laufzeit asymptotisch stärker und zwar fast wie $e^{\frac{3}{2}(\sqrt{\ln n \ \ln\ln n} - \ln\ln n - \ln\ln\ln n)}$ wächst. Damit ist der Schroeppel-Algorithmus sogar langsamer als der Morrison-Brillhart-Algorithmus mit $e^{\sqrt{\frac{3}{2}\ln n \ \ln\ln n} - \frac{3}{2}(\ln\ln n + \ln\ln\ln n)}$ Makroschritten.

Um die im RSA-Schema verwendeten Zahlen $n \approx 10^{150}$ zu zerlegen, benötigt der Morrison-Brillhart-Algorithmus voraussichtlich ca. $9 \cdot 10^8$ Jahre und ca. 10^{13} Bit Speicherplatz, der Schroeppel-Algorithmus dagegen etwa 10^{13} Jahre und ca. 10^{16} Bit Speicherplatz (jeweils unter der Annahme, daß eine Multiplikation in $\mathbb{Z}_n$ ca. 10^{-3} Sek. kostet). Dies bedeutet auch, daß beim Einsatz einer hochleistungsfähigen Arithmetik bei der eine Multiplikation in $\mathbb{Z}_n$ etwa 10^{-6} Sek. kostet (dies erscheint technisch möglich) und wenn ca. 10^4 dieser Multiplikations-Prozessoren zur Parallel-Ausführung des Morrison-Brillhart-Algorithmus eingesetzt werden, dann können Zahlen $n \approx 10^{150}$ in etwa 90 Jahren zerlegt werden. Allerdings dürfte es schwierig sein, den dazu erforderlichen Speicherplatz von 10^{13} Bit zu beschaffen.

Wir beschreiben vorweg die den Faktorisierungsverfahren von Morrison, Brillhart und Schroeppel zugrunde liegende Methode. Um eine natürliche Zahl n zu zerlegen, reicht es aus, ganze Zahlen x,y zu berechnen mit

$$x^2 = y^2 \bmod n \ , \ x \not\equiv \pm y \bmod n \qquad (1.1)$$

Aus $x^2 = y^2 \bmod n$ folgt nämlich $(x-y)(x+y) = 0 \bmod n$ und $x \not\equiv \pm y \bmod n$ impliziert, daß $ggT(x \pm y, n)$ nicht triviale Teiler von n sind.

Beide Faktorisierungsverfahren gehen so vor, daß man Zahlen $x,y \in \mathbb{Z}$ mit (1.1) konstruiert, indem man für ein geeignetes v etwa O(v) Zahlen T_i der Größe $T_i \leq 2\sqrt{n}$ erzeugt derart, daß die T_i nur Primfaktoren $\leq v$ haben.

Morrison, Brillhart sammeln Kongruenzen vom Typ

$$T_i = A_i^2 \bmod n \qquad (1.2)$$

und wählen T_i als geeignete Kontinuanten der Kettenbruchentwicklung von $\sqrt{n}$. Dabei nutzen sie aus, daß die T_i Quadrate in $\mathbb{Z}_n$ sind, deren Wurzel A_i durch die Kettenbruch-Rekursion mitgeliefert wird. Zum Auffinden der Primfaktoren $\le v$ von T_i setzen wir die Pollard'sche Faktorisierungsmethode ein und kommen damit zu einer erheblichen Verbesserung des Verfahrens. Schroeppel sammelt etwa $O(v)$ Kongruenzen vom Typ

$$T_{a,b} = (\sqrt{n} + a)\cdot(\sqrt{n} + b) \bmod n \qquad (1.3)$$

mit $|a|, |b| = o(n)$, so daß $T_{a,b}$ nur Primteiler $\le v$ hat. Schroeppel nutzt aus, daß die $T_{a,b}$ bei festem a einer linearen Progression genügen und man daher die Primteiler der $T_{a,b}$ mit Siebmethoden relativ schnell findet.

In beiden Verfahren erhält man schließlich x und y, indem man Kongruenzen des Typs (1.2) bzw. (1.3) multiplikativ kombiniert. Die geeignete Kombination dieser Kongruenzen erhält man durch Lösen eines linearen Gleichungssystems im Raum der Exponentenvektoren $(z_{i,p} | p \le v, p \text{ prim})$ der Primfaktorzerlegung $T_i = \prod_{\substack{p \le v \\ p \text{ prim}}} p^{z_{i,p}}$

Die Rechenzeit, die in diesen Algorithmen bei der Suche nach den T_i mit (1.2) (bzw. nach den $T_{a,b}$ mit (1.3)) anfällt, hängt von der zahlentheoretischen Funktion

$$\psi(n,v) = \#\{x \in [1,n] \mid (p \text{ prim} \wedge p|x) \implies p \le v\}; \; n,v \in \mathbb{N}$$

ab. Wir vergleichen die beiden Algorithmen unter folgender

Annahme 1: $\psi(n,n^{1/r}) \approx n \cdot r^{-r}$ für $r \sim \frac{\ln n}{\ln\ln n}$ (1.4)

Diese Annahme haben wir für $n \le 10^{30}$ und für $r \le 6$ experimentell gestützt (vgl. hierzu die ausführliche Version der vorliegenden Arbeit).

Pomerance [POM 81] hat einen Beweis geliefert für

$$\psi(n,n^{1/r}) = n\cdot r^{r+o(r)} \quad \text{für } r \le \frac{\ln n}{(1+\varepsilon)\ln\ln n}$$

Unabhängig von der vorliegenden Arbeit kam auch Pomerance in [POM 81] zu dem Schluß, daß der Morrison-Brillhart-Algorithmus dem Schroeppel-Algorithmus asymptotisch überlegen ist.

2. Der Algorithmus von Morrison-Brillhart

Algorithmus "Morrison-Brillhart"

<u>begin</u> input n,r

comment [n ist die zu faktorisierende Zahl; die optimale Wahl von r entnehme man der Rechenzeitanalyse]

<u>Stufe ∅</u> $v = \lfloor n^{1/r} \rfloor$

Es sei $\overline{\pi}(v) := \{p \le v : p \text{ prim} \wedge (\frac{n}{p}) = 1\}$. Lege die Liste $\overline{P}_r := \{p_1,\dots,p_{\overline{\pi}(v)}\}$ der Primzahlen $p \le v$ mit $(\frac{n}{p}) = 1$ an. Mit $p_o := -1$ setze $\overline{P}_r := \overline{P}_r \cup \{p_o\}$.

comment [Da nur Primzahlen mit $(\frac{n}{p}) = 1$ als Teiler der in Stufe 1 zu faktorisierenden Zahlen w auftreten, wählen wir eine ausgedünnte Primzahlbasis]

$B = \emptyset$

$i := 0$

<u>Stufe 1</u> <u>while</u> $\# B \le \overline{\pi}(v)+1$ <u>do</u>

<u>begin</u>

erzeuge gemäß der Rekursion (IO) - (I5) das i-te Glied $w := (-1)^i Q_i = A_{i-1}^2 \bmod n$ der Kettenbruchfolge von $\sqrt{n}$.

Berechne $\underline{a} = (a_k \mid k = 0,\dots,\overline{\pi}(v))$ und w^* mit

$w = w^* \prod_{k=o}^{\overline{\pi}(v)} p_k^{a_k}$ und $w^* \in (\mathbb{N} \setminus \bigcup_{k=1}^{\overline{\pi}(v)} p_k \mathbb{N})$

<u>Test</u> <u>if</u> $w^* = 1$ <u>then</u> $[B := B \cup \{\underline{a}\},\ w_{\underline{a}} := Q_i,\ z_{\underline{a}} := A_{i-1}]$

$i := i+1$

<u>end</u>

<u>Stufe 2</u> Suche eine nichttriviale Lösung von

$\Sigma_{\underline{a}\in B} f_{\underline{a}} \cdot \underline{a} = \underline{0} \bmod 2$, $\quad f_{\underline{a}} \in \{0,1\}$

und setze

$x := \Pi_{f_{\underline{a}}=1} z_{\underline{a}}$, $y := \Pi_{k=0}^{\pi(v)} p_k^{(\Sigma_{f_{\underline{a}}=1} a_k)/2}$

<u>comment</u> [wegen $w_{\underline{a}} = z_{\underline{a}}^2 = \Pi_{k=0}^{\pi(v)} p_k^{a_k} \bmod n$ gilt

$x^2 = y^2 = \Pi_{f_{\underline{a}}=1} w_{\underline{a}} \bmod n$; falls $x \not\equiv \pm y \bmod n$ ist,

so sind $ggT(x \pm y, n)$ nichttriviale Faktoren von n]

<u>end</u>

2.1 Die Struktur der Kettenbruchfolge zu $\sqrt{n}$

Bei der Entwicklung von $\sqrt{n}$ in einen Kettenbruch

$$\sqrt{n} = [q_0, \ldots, q_{i-1}, \frac{\sqrt{n}+P_i}{Q_i}]$$

(vgl. [KNU 81]) sind die Werte $q_i, i \geq 0$, und $P_i, Q_i, i \geq 1$, gemäß folgender Iterationsformeln zu berechnen:

(I0) $\quad q_0 = \lfloor \sqrt{n} \rfloor, \; P_1 = q_0, \; Q_1 = n - q_0^2$

(I1) $\quad q_{i-1} = \left\lfloor \frac{\sqrt{n}-P_{i-1}}{Q_{i-1}} \right\rfloor, \; i \geq 2$

(I2) $\quad P_i = q_{i-1} \cdot Q_{i-1} - P_{i-1}, \; i \geq 2$

(I3) $\quad Q_i = \frac{n - P_i^2}{Q_{i-1}}, \; i \geq 2$

Wir schätzen zunächst ab, von welcher Größenordnung die in Stufe 1 des Morrison-Brillhart-Algorithmus über $\overline{P}_r$ zu faktorisierenden Zahlen sind, d.h. wir zeigen

$$\forall i \geq 1: Q_i \leq 2 \cdot \sqrt{n} \qquad (2.1)$$

Setzt man (I1) in (I2) ein, so erhält man

$$\forall i \geq 2: P_i = \left\lfloor \frac{\sqrt{n}+P_{i+1}}{Q_{i-1}} \right\rfloor \cdot Q_{i-1} - P_{i-1}$$

$$\leq \sqrt{n}$$

Daher folgt aus (I2):

$$\forall\, i \geq 2:\ Q_{i-1} = \frac{P_i + P_{i-1}}{q_i} \leq \frac{2\sqrt{n}}{q_i} \leq 2\sqrt{n}$$

und damit ist (2.1) gezeigt. Außerdem ist $(-1)^i Q_i$ ein Quadrat in $\mathbb{Z}_n$ und wir benötigen Quadratwurzeln von $(-1)^i Q_i$. Mit

(I4) $\quad A_{-1} = 1,\ A_o = q_o$ und $A_i = q_i A_{i-1} + A_{i-2},\ i \geq 2$

(I5) $\quad B_{-1} = 0,\ B_o = 1$ und $B_i = q_i B_{i-1} + B_{i-2},\ i \geq 2$

kann man durch vollständige Induktion zeigen (vgl. [WUN 79]):

$$\forall\, i \geq 1:\ A_{i-1}^2 - nB_{i-1}^2 = (-1)^i Q_i \qquad (2.2)$$

Daraus folgt

$$\forall\, i \geq 1:\ (-1)^i Q_i = A_{i-1}^2 \bmod n \qquad (2.3)$$

d.h. daß $(-1)^i Q_i$ ein Quadrat in $\mathbb{Z}_n$ ist, von dem die Wurzel A_{i-1} schnell berechnet werden kann.
Außerdem haben wir (vgl. [KNU 81]):

$$\forall\, i \geq 1:\ \mathrm{ggt}(A_i, B_i) = 1 \qquad (2.4)$$

Der folgende Fakt rechtfertigt, daß nur Primzahlen p mit $(\frac{n}{p}) = 1$ in die Primzahlbasis $\overline{P}_r$ aufgenommen werden:

<u>Fakt 1:</u>

$p \mid Q_i \Rightarrow (\frac{n}{p}) = 1 \ \vee\ p \mid n$

<u>Beweis</u>

Aus $p \mid Q_i$ folgt wegen (2.2)

$$n = \frac{A_{i-1}^2}{B_{i-1}^2} \bmod p$$

Daher ist $(\frac{n}{p}) = 1$ oder es gilt $p \mid n$.

In Stufe 1 des Morrison-Brillhart-Algorithmus werden $\overline{\pi}(v) + 2$ Elemente $(-1)^i Q_i$ gesucht, welche über der Primzahlbasis $\overline{P}_r$ in Faktoren zerfallen. Um eine Rechenzeitabschätzung für Stufe 1 geben zu können, benötigt man daher eine Abschätzung für die Dichte

$$\overline{\psi}(n,r) := \lim_{m\to\infty} \frac{\#\{i \leq m \mid (p \text{ prim} \wedge p \mid Q_i) \Rightarrow p \in \overline{P}_r\}}{m}$$

der über $\overline{P}_r$ zerfallenden Elemente der Kettenbruchfolge zu $\sqrt{n}$. Wir wollen einen Zusammenhang zwischen $\overline{\psi}(n,r)$ und $\psi(n,n^{1/r})$ herstellen und daher beweisen wir den folgenden Fakt:'

Fakt 2

Sei p prim und es gelte $(\frac{n}{p}) = 1$. Falls die Reste (A_i mod p, B_i mod p) gleichverteilt in $\mathbb{Z}_p^2 \setminus \{(0,0)\}$ sind, dann haben wir

$$Ws(p \mid Q_i) = \frac{2}{p+1}$$

Beweis:

Sei p prim und es gelte $(\frac{n}{p}) = 1$. Wegen (2.2) gilt:

$$\forall i \in \mathbb{N}: \ (p \mid Q_i \iff A_{i-1}^2 \equiv n\, B_{i-1}^2 \bmod p) \qquad (2.5)$$

Zu jedem $a \in [1,p-1]$ gibt es wegen $(\frac{n}{p}) = 1$ genau zwei Elemente $b \in [0,p-1]$ mit

$$a^2 \equiv nb^2 \bmod p$$

Falls ($A_i$mod p, $B_i$mod p) gleichverteilt in $\mathbb{Z}_p^2 \setminus \{(0,0)\}$ ist (beachte: ($A_i$mod p, $B_i$mod p) $\neq$ (0,0) gilt wegen (2.4)), folgt daher aus (2.5)

$$\forall i \in \mathbb{N}: \ Ws(p \mid Q_i) = \frac{\#\{(a,b) \in \mathbb{Z}_p^2 \setminus \{(0,0)\} \mid a^2 \equiv nb^2 \bmod p\}}{p^2-1}$$

$$= \frac{2(p-1)}{p^2-1}$$

$$= \frac{2}{p+1} \qquad (2.6)$$

Für ein zufällig gewähltes $a \in [1, 2\cdot\sqrt{n}]$ ist jedes Element der Primzahlbasis

$$P_r = \{p \in [1, n^{1/r}] \mid p \text{ prim}\}$$

mit Wahrscheinlichkeit $\frac{1}{p}$ ein Teiler von a. Unter der Annahme, daß die Reste ($A_i \bmod p, B_i \bmod p$) gleichverteilt in $\mathbb{Z}_p^2 \setminus \{(0,0)\}$ sind, ist nach Fakt 2 jedes $p \in (\bar{P}_r \setminus \{-1\})$ mit Wahrscheinlichkeit $\frac{2}{p}$ ein Teiler von Q_i. Wegen $\#P_r \approx 2\cdot\#\bar{P}_r$ ist es daher sinnvoll anzunehmen (vgl. auch [WUN 79]):

<u>Annahme 2</u> $\quad \exists n_0 \in \mathbb{N}\, \forall n \geq n_0\, \forall r \geq 0: \bar{\Psi}(n,r) \approx \dfrac{\Psi(2\sqrt{n}, n^{1/r})}{2\sqrt{n}}$ (2.7)

2.2 Rechenzeitanalyse des Morrison-Brillhart-Algorithmus

Wir können die Rechenzeit des Morrison-Brillhart-Algorithmus asymptotisch wie folgt abschätzen:

<u>Satz 1</u>

Unter den Annahmen (1.4) und (2.7) gilt für die Rechenzeit $T_{MB}(n)$ des Morrison-Brillhart-Algorithmus:

$$T_{MB}(n) = O(e^{\sqrt{\frac{3}{2}\ln n \ln\ln n} - \frac{3}{2}(\ln\ln n + \ln\ln\ln n)})$$

<u>Beweis:</u>

Zur Faktorisierung der $(-1)^i Q_i$ in Stufe 1 des Morrison-Brillhart-Algorithmus bietet sich der Pollard-Algorithmus an (vgl. [SCH 81]). Zur Auffindung aller Primfaktoren $\leq p$ der eingegebenen Zahl n benötigt der Pollard-Algorithmus erfahrungsgemäß etwa $\sqrt{p}$ viele Makroschritte (vgl. [GUY 75]). Da in Stufe 1 des Morrison-Brillhart-Algorithmus nur nach dem Auftreten von Primfaktoren $\leq n^{1/r}$ in $(-1)^i Q_i$ gesucht wird, kann diese Stufe daher so realisiert werden, indem man den Pollard-Algorithmus etwa $n^{1/2r}$ viele Makroschritte auf jedem $(-1)^i Q_i$ rechnen läßt. Da wir $\pi(n^{1/r})+1$ viele über P_r zerlegbare Zahlen finden müssen, ergibt sich daher für Stufe 1 eine Gesamtrechenzeit $T_{MB,1}(n,r)$ von

$$T_{MB,1}(n,r) \approx \frac{\overline{\pi}(n^{1/r})\cdot n^{1/2r}}{\overline{\Psi}(n,r)}$$

vielen Makroschritten. Wegen $\overline{\pi}(n^{1/r}) \approx \frac{r}{2\cdot\ln n}\, n^{1/r}$ und wegen (1.4) folgt aus Fakt 2

$$T_{MB,1}(n,r) \approx \frac{r\cdot n^{3/2r}\cdot 2\sqrt{n}}{2\cdot\ln n\cdot(2\sqrt{n},n^{1/r})}$$

$$\approx \frac{r\cdot n^{3/2r}\cdot(\frac{r}{2})^{\frac{r}{2}}}{2\cdot\ln n} \qquad (2.8)$$

Die Lösung des linearen Gleichungssystems in Stufe 2 des Morrison-Brillhart-Algorithmus erfordert

$$T_{MB,2}(n,r) = (\overline{\pi}(n^{1/r}))^3$$

$$\approx \frac{r^3}{(2\cdot\ln n)^3}\cdot n^{3/r} \qquad (2.9)$$

viele Bitoperationen.

Um die asymptotische Rechenzeit des Algorithmus durch eine günstige Wahl von r optimieren zu können, minimieren wir

$$n^{3/2r}\cdot r^{\frac{r}{2}} + n^{3/r}$$

Mit dem Ansatz

$$r(n) = c\sqrt{\frac{\ln n}{\ln\ln n}}$$

ist in erster Näherung der Ausdruck

$$e^{(\frac{3}{2c}+\frac{c}{4})\sqrt{\ln n\ \ln\ln n}} + e^{\sqrt{\frac{3}{c}\ln n\ \ln\ln n}}$$

zu minimieren. Daher wählen wir $c = \sqrt{6}$ und durch Einsetzen von

$$r(n) = \sqrt{\frac{6\ln n}{\ln\ln n}} \qquad (2.10)$$

in (2.8), (2.9) erhalten wir für die Gesamtrechenzeit $T_{MB}(n)$ des Morrison-Brillhart-Algorithmus

$$T_{MB}(n) = T_{MB,1}(n,r(n)) + T_{MB,2}(n,r(n))$$

$$= O\left(\frac{r(n)}{\ln n} \cdot n^{3/2r} \cdot \left(\frac{r(n)}{2}\right)^{\frac{r(n)}{2}} + \left(\frac{r(n)}{\ln n}\right)^3 \cdot n^{3/r(n)}\right)$$

$$= o\left(\frac{e^{\frac{3}{2\sqrt{6}}\sqrt{\ln n \,\ln\ln n}} * \left(\sqrt{\frac{3}{2}\,\frac{\ln n}{\ln\ln n}}\right)^{\sqrt{\frac{3}{2}\,\frac{\ln n}{\ln\ln n}}}}{(\ln\ln n)^{1/4} * (\ln n)^{1/2}} + \frac{e^{\sqrt{\frac{3}{2}\ln n \,\ln\ln n}}}{(\ln n \,\ln\ln n)^{3/2}}\right)$$

$$= o\left(\left(e^{-\sqrt{\frac{3}{2}\,\frac{\ln n}{\ln\ln n}}\left(\frac{1}{2}\ln\ln\ln n - \frac{1}{2}\ln \frac{3}{2}\right)} + e^{-\frac{3}{2}(\ln\ln n + \ln\ln\ln n)}\right) * e^{\frac{3}{2}\sqrt{\ln n \,\ln\ln n}}\right)$$

$$= O\left(e^{\sqrt{\frac{3}{2}\ln n \,\ln\ln n} - \frac{3}{2}(\ln\ln n + \ln\ln\ln n)}\right)$$

Die Abschätzung zeigt, daß für die asymptotische Rechenzeit der Aufwand zur Auflösung des linearen Gleichungssystems dominierend ist. ∎

3. Der Algorithmus von Schroeppel

Algorithmus "Schroeppel"

<u>begin</u> input n,r,t

<u>comment</u> [n ist die zu faktorisierende Zahl; die optimale Wahl von r,t entnehme man der Rechenzeitanalyse]

<u>Stufe Ø</u> $v := \lfloor n^{1/r} \rfloor$

$s := \min\{m \in \mathbb{N} \mid m \geq n^{1/t}$ und m gerade$\}$

Bilde die Liste $P = \{p_1, \ldots, p_{\pi(v)}\}$ aller Primzahlen $\leq v$

Mit $p_o := -1$ setze $P := P \cup \{p_o\}$

$B = \emptyset$

<u>Stufe 1</u> für $i = 0, \ldots, 2s$ sei $Q_i := \lfloor \sqrt{n} \rfloor - \frac{s}{2} + i$

für alle $(i,j) \in [0,s]^2$

<u>do</u> $T_{ij} := Q_i * Q_{i+j} - n$

und berechne $\underline{a} = (a_k \in \mathbb{N} \mid 0 \leq k \leq \pi(v))$ und w^* mit

$$T_{ij} = w^* \prod_{k=1}^{\pi(v)} p_k^{a_k} \wedge w^* \in \left(\mathbb{N} \setminus \bigcup_{k=1}^{\pi(v)} p_k \mathbb{N}\right)$$

<u>"Test":</u> <u>if</u> $w^* = 1$ <u>then</u> $[\underline{b} := e_i \oplus e_{i+j}$

$B := B \cup \{(\underline{a}, \underline{b})\}]$

<u>comment</u> [Dabei ist $e_i \in \{0,1\}^{2s+1}$ der i-te Einheitsvektor und $\oplus$ die bitweise Vektoraddition modulo 2]

<u>Stufe 2</u> Suche eine nichttriviale Lösung von

$$\Sigma_{(\underline{a},\underline{b}) \in B} f_{(\underline{a},\underline{b})} \cdot (\underline{a},\underline{b}) = \underline{0} \bmod 2, \qquad f_{(\underline{a},\underline{b})} \in \{0,1\}$$

Setze

$$x := \prod_{k=1}^{\pi(v)} p_k^{(\Sigma_{f_{(\underline{a},\underline{b})}=1} a_k)/2}$$

$$y := \prod_{l=o}^{2s} Q_l^{(\Sigma_{f_{(\underline{a},\underline{b})}=1} b_l)/2}$$

<u>comment</u> [Es ist $x^2 = y^2 \bmod n$; falls $x \neq \pm y \bmod n$ ist, so sind $ggT(x \pm y, n)$ nichttriviale Faktoren von n]

<u>end</u>

3.1 Verwendbarkeit von Siebmethoden im Schroeppel-Algorithmus

Die entscheidende Eigenschaft des Schroeppel-Algorithmus besteht darin, daß bei der Suche nach den über der Primzahlbasis P zerlegbaren Elemente des Feldes T Siebmethoden angewendet werden können. Bevor wir die Rechenzeit des Schroeppel-Algorithmus analysieren, geben wir daher an, wie die Berechnung der Vektoren $\underline{a}$ in Stufe 1 unter Verwendung von Siebmethoden realisiert werden kann.

<u>Stufe 1</u> <u>for</u> i = 0 <u>to</u> 2s <u>let</u> $Q_i := \lfloor \sqrt{n} \rfloor - \frac{s}{2} + i$

<u>for</u> i = 0 <u>to</u> s <u>do</u>

<u>for</u> j = 0 <u>to</u> s <u>do</u>

$T_{i,j} = Q_i * Q_{i+j} - n$

<u>comment:</u> [Für festes i bildet $(T_{i,j})_{0 \leq j \leq s}$ wegen $T_{i,j+1} = T_{i,j} + Q_i;\ 0 \leq j \leq s-1$ eine arithmetische Folge]

$a_{j,k} := 0$ <u>for</u> $j = 0,\ldots,2s+1, k = 0,\ldots,\pi(v)$

<u>comment:</u> [Die $(s+1, \pi(v)+1)$-Matrix $(a_{j,k})$ dient im folgenden Siebverfahren zur Speicherung der $a_{j,k} := \max\{\varepsilon : P_k^{\varepsilon} | T_{i,j}\}$]

"Sieb": $\underline{\text{if}}\ T_{i,j} < 0\ \underline{\text{then}}\ a_{j,o} = 1$

$T_{i,j} = -T_{i,j}$

$\underline{\text{for}}\ k = 1\ \underline{\text{to}}\ \pi(v)\ \underline{\text{do}}$

$\underline{\text{case 1}}\ p_k | Q_i \wedge p_k | T_{i,o}$

$\underline{\text{for}}\ j = 0\ \underline{\text{to}}\ s\ \underline{\text{do}}$

$[a_{j,k} := \max\{\varepsilon : p_k^{\varepsilon} | T_{i,j}\}$

$T_{i,j} := T_{i,j} / p_k^{a_{j,k}}]$ (3.1)

$\underline{\text{comment}}\ [p_k | Q_i \wedge p_k | T_{i,o} \Rightarrow \forall j : p_k | T_{i,j}]$

$\underline{\text{case 2}}\ p_k \nmid Q_i$

$j_o := -T_{i,o} * Q_i^{-1} \bmod p_k$ mit $j_o \in [0, p_k - 1]$

$\underline{\text{for}}\ j = j_o\ \underline{\text{to}}\ s\ \underline{\text{step}}\ p_k\ \underline{\text{do}}$

$a_{j,k} = \max\{\varepsilon : p_k^{\varepsilon} | T_{i,j}\}$

$T_{i,j} = T_{i,j} / p_k^{a_{j,k}}$ (3.2)

$\underline{\text{comment}}$ [Aus $p_k \nmid Q_i$ folgt:

$p_k | T_{i,j} \iff T_{i,o} + jQ_i = 0 \bmod p_k$

$\iff j = -T_{i,o} * Q_i^{-1} \bmod p_k]$

$\underline{\text{case 3}}\ p_k | Q_i \wedge p_k \nmid T_{i,o}$

continue

$\underline{\text{comment}}\ [p_k | Q_i \wedge p_k \nmid T_{i,o} \Rightarrow \forall j : p_k \nmid T_{ij}]$

$\underline{\text{end}}$

$\underline{\text{for}}\ j = 0\ \underline{\text{to}}\ s\ \underline{\text{do}}$

$\underline{\text{if}}\ T_{i,j} = 1\ \underline{\text{then}}\ [\underline{a} := (a_{j,k} | k = 0, \ldots, \pi(v))$

$\underline{b} := e_i \oplus e_{i+j}$

$B := B \cup \{(\underline{a}, \underline{b})\}]$

3.2 Rechenzeitanalyse des Schroeppel-Algorithmus

Beim Sieben in Stufe 1 fallen für jedes p_k mit $p_k\ T_{i,j}$ in (3.1) bzw. (3.2)

$$a_{j,k} := \max\{\varepsilon : p_k^{\varepsilon} | T_{i,j}\} + 1$$

Makroschritte an. Die Gesamtzahl dieser Makroschritte ist höchstens

$$2s^2 * \sum_{k=1}^{\pi(v)} \sum_{\nu : p_k^\nu \leq n^{1/r}} p_k^{-\nu}$$

$$= 2s^2 * (\sum_{k=1}^{\pi(v)} p_k^{-1} + O(1))$$

$$= 2s^2 * (\ln\ln n + O(1))$$

Dabei gilt die letzte Gleichung nach Hardy, Wright (vgl. Theorem 427 in [HW 60]). Alle übrigen Rechenschritte in Stufe 1 etwa zur Bildung der $T_{i,j}$ sind demgegenüber vernachlässigbar. Auch den Faktor 2 in der obigen Abschätzung kann man unterdrücken, wenn man die Primzahlpotenzen in derselben Weise wie die Primzahlen durchsiebt. In Stufe 1 müssen etwa $\pi(n^{1/r})+2s+1$ Kongruenzen erzeugt werden, damit das lineare Gleichungssystem in Stufe 2 eine nicht triviale Lösung hat. Mit $s = n^{1/t}$ gilt wegen (1.4):

$$\frac{2s \cdot \sqrt{n}}{\psi(2s\sqrt{n}, n^{1/r})} \approx \frac{n^{\frac{1}{2}+\frac{1}{t}}}{\psi(n^{\frac{1}{2}+\frac{1}{t}}, n^{\frac{1}{r}})} \approx \left(\frac{r}{2}+\frac{r}{t}\right)^{\left(\frac{r}{2}+\frac{r}{t}\right)}$$

Damit mindestens $\pi(n^{1/r})+2s \approx \frac{r}{\ln n} n^{1/r} + 2n^{1/t}$ Kongruenzen erzeugt werden, müssen r und t so gewählt werden, daß

$$s^2 = n^{2/t} \gtrsim \left(\frac{r}{\ln n} \cdot n^{1/r} + 2n^{1/t}\right) \cdot \left(\frac{r}{2}+\frac{r}{t}\right)^{\frac{r}{2}+\frac{r}{t}} . \quad (3.3)$$

Für die Anzahl $T_{Sch,1}(n,r,s)$ der Makroschritte in Stufe 1 gilt damit die Abschätzung:

$$T_{Sch,1}(n,r,s) = \left(\frac{r}{\ln n} n^{1/r} + 2n^{1/t}\right)\left(\frac{r}{2}+\frac{r}{t}\right)^{\left(\frac{r}{2}+\frac{r}{t}\right)} \ln\ln n \quad (3.4)$$

$$\lesssim n^{2/t} \ln\ln n .$$

Die Lösung des linearen Gleichungssystems in Stufe 2 erfordert

$$T_{Sch,2}(n,r,s) = (\pi(n^{1/r})+2\cdot s)^3$$

$$\approx(\frac{r}{\ln n}\, n^{1/r}+2\cdot n^{1/t})^3 \qquad (3.5)$$

viele Bitoperationen.

Indem man die Parameter r,t gemäß

$$r(n) := 2\cdot\sqrt{\frac{\ln n}{\ln\ln n}} \qquad (3.6)$$

$$t(n) := \frac{2\,\ln n}{\sqrt{\ln n\,\ln\ln n} - \ln\ln n - \ln\ln\ln n} \qquad (3.7)$$

wählt, kann man die Rechenzeit des Schroeppel-Algorithmus etwas besser als mit $O(e^{1.5\cdot\sqrt{\ln n\,\ln\ln n}})$ abschätzen:

<u>Satz 2</u>

Unter der Annahme (1.4) und sofern in Stufe 2 das Gauß'sche Eliminationsverfahren verwendet wird, gilt für die Rechenzeit $T_{Sch}(n)$ des Schroeppel-Algorithmus:

$$T_{Sch}(n) = O(e^{1.5(\sqrt{\ln n\,\ln\ln n} - \ln\ln n - \ln\ln\ln n)})$$

■

Rivest, Shamir und Adleman [RSA 78] sehen die Hauptgefahr für das RSA-Schema in dem Schroeppel-Algorithmus, für den sie eine Laufzeit von $O(e^{\sqrt{\ln n \ \ln\ln n}})$ angeben. Diese obere Schranke für die Laufzeit des Schroeppel-Algorithmus steht bis heute unwidersprochen im Raum. Eine solche Laufzeitschranke läßt sich jedoch nach unseren Erkenntnissen nur unter Verletzung von Bedingung (3.3) beweisen. Da (3.3) jedoch eine notwendige Bedingung für die Korrektheit des Schroeppel-Algorithmus ist, können wir eine asymptotisch stärkere untere Schranke für die Laufzeit des Schroeppel-Algorithmus beweisen, denn es gilt:

Satz 3

Unter Annahme (1.4) gilt für die Rechenzeit des Schroeppel-Algorithmus:

$$T_{Sch}(n)=\Omega(e^{1.5\sqrt{\ln n \ \ln\ln n} - \sqrt{\frac{\ln n}{\ln\ln n}} \ln\ln\ln n - \ln\ln n - \ln\ln\ln n}) \ ^{*)}$$

■

4. Vergleich der beiden Algorithmen

In diesem Kapitel wollen wir die beiden Algorithmen für Zahlen n fester Größenordnungen miteinander vergleichen. Hierbei muß im Gegensatz zu der asymptotischen Analyse aus den Kapiteln 2 und 3 berücksichtigt werden, daß ein (in Stufe 1 anfallender) Makroschritt wesentlich mehr Rechenzeit erfordert als eine (in Stufe 2 anfallende) Bitoperation. Die folgenden Vergleichswerte sind daher nicht aus den asymptotischen Rechenzeitabschätzungen der Sätze 1 und 2, sondern aus den (ebenfalls auf der Annahme (1.4) basierenden) Formeln (2.8) und (2.9) bzw. (3.4) und (3.5) berechnet worden.

---

*) Für Abbildungen $f: \mathbb{N} \to \mathbb{R}$, $g: \mathbb{N} \to \mathbb{R}$ schreiben wir $f(n) = \Omega(g(n))$ genau dann, wenn gilt:
$\exists c \in \mathbb{N} \ \exists n_0 \in \mathbb{N} \ \forall n \geq n_0 : f(n) \geq c \cdot g(n)$

Aufgrund der Laufzeiten unserer Unterprogramme für die Arithmetik in $\mathbb{Z}_n$ haben wir für $n \in [10^{20}, 10,^{50}]$ (bzw. für $n \approx 10^{150}$) für jeden in Stufe 1 anfallenden Makroschritt 10^{-5} Sek. (bzw. 10^{-3} Sek.) angesetzt (Hinweis: Im Falle $n \leq 10^{40}$ sind die in Stufe 1 der Algorithmen zu zerlegenden Zahlen $\leq 2 \cdot 10^{20}$ und daher kann in diesem Falle bei allerdings gleichem Aufwand die auf nahezu allen Rechnern zur Verfügung stehende Multiplikation von 72-Bit-Zahlen ausgenutzt werden). Außerdem sind wir davon ausgegangen, daß eine Addition von 36-Bit-Zahlen 10^{-6} Sek. erfordert. Sofern die Lösung des linearen Gleichungssystems in Stufe 2 der Algorithmen in ASSEMBLER programmiert wird, so kann jede Spalte der Matrix durch ein einzelnes Bit repräsentiert werden. Daher erfordert jede Bitoperation aus Stufe 2 etwa $(36 \cdot 10^6)^{-1}$ Sek.

In den folgenden Tabellen geben wir auch den Parameter r an, um zu verdeutlichen, daß die optimale Rechenzeit in der Praxis für ein anderes als das in der asymptotischen Analyse gewählte r erzielt wird.

4.1 Die Leistungsgrenze der Algorithmen

Zunächst vergleichen wir die Algorithmen in den Bereichen $n \approx 10^{20}$, $n \approx 10^{30}$, $n \approx 10^{40}$ und $n \approx 10^{50}$. Die dabei erhaltenen Rechenzeiten zeigen, daß der Morrison-Brillhart-Algorithmus dem Schroeppel-Algorithmus in diesen Bereichen eindeutig überlegen ist.

n =	10^{20}	10^{30}	10^{40}	10^{50}
Morrison-Brillhart				
r	7.3	8.8	9.9	10.9
Rechenzeit	1 Sek.	5 Sek.	29 Min.	10 Std.
Speicherplatzbedarf (in Bit)	$1.1*10^4$	$2,6*10^4$	$3.5*10^5$	$3.3*10^6$
Schroeppel				
r	5.5	6.6	8	9
t	8.1	9.6	10.6	11.4
Rechenzeit	22 Min.	2,5 Tage	100 Tage	14 Jahre
Speicherplatzbedarf (in Bit)	$1,2\ 10^6$	$3,6*10^7$	$4,2*10^8$	$5,8*10^9$

Tabelle 1

Aufgrund unserer (unter der Annahme (1.4) erzielten) Rechenzeitabschätzung benötigt der Morrison-Brillhart-Algorithmus für $n \approx 10^{40}$ etwa $10^{8.2} \approx n^{0.2}$ Makroschritte. Gemäß den praktischen Erfahrungen von Wunderlich ([WUN 79]) benötigt der Morrison-Brillhart-Algorithmus im Bereich $n \approx 10^{40}$ etwa $n^{0.21}$ arithmetische Operationen.

4.2 Die Algorithmen und das RSA-Schema

Alle bis heute bekannten Ansätze zum Brechen des RSA-Schemas führen zur Zerlegung des geheimen Schlüssels m in seine Faktoren p und q. Es ist daher interessant, die Laufzeiten der Algorithmen von Morrison-Brillhart und Schroeppel für n in der von Rivest, Shamir, Adleman für das RSA-Schema vorgeschlagenen Größenordnung $n \approx 2^{500} \approx 3.27*10^{150}$ zu vergleichen:

	$n \approx 10^{150}$
Morrison-Brillhart	
r	19.1
Rechenzeit	$9*10^8$ Jahre
Speicherplatzbedarf (in Bit)	$1,5*10^{13}$
Schroeppel	
r	15.1
t	17.9
Rechenzeit	$2*10^{13}$ Jahre
Speicherplatzbedarf (in Bit)	$7.2*10^{17}$

Tabelle 2

Wie bereits in der Einleitung erwähnt, stellt der Schroeppel-Algorithmus keine Gefahr für das RSA-Schema dar. Um die Sicherheit des RSA-Schemas auch gegen eine Implementierung des Morrison-Brillhart-Algorithmus bei parallelem Einsatz von ca. 10^4 hochleistungsfähigen Multiplikationsprozessoren zu gewährleisten, sollte eine Vergrößerung des Schlüssels auf etwa 600 Bit in Betracht gezogen werden.

Acknowledgement

Die statistische Analyse der Funktion Ψ wurde auf der DEC-10 der Universität Frankfurt durchgeführt. Die Programme hierzu wurden von H.G.Franke und H.P.Stein erstellt.

Literatur

[GUY 75] : R.K. Guy: How to factor a number, Proc. Fifth Manitoba Conference on Numerical Math. 1975, pp. 49-89

[HW 60] : G.H. Hardy, E.M. Wright: Zahlentheorie, Oldenbourg Verlag, 1958

[KNU 76] : D.E. Knuth: Analysis of a simple Factorization Algorithm, TCS 3 (1976), pp.321-348

[KNU 81] : D.E. Knuth: The art of computer programming, Vol.2, Addison Wesley, 1981

[LP 31] : D.H. Lehmer, R.E. Powers: On factoring large numbers Amer. Math. Soc. 37 (1931), 770-776

[MB 75] : M.A. Morrison, J. Brillhart: A method of factoring and the factorization of F_7, Math. Comp. 29 (1975), 183-205

[MON 81] : L. Monier: Algorithmes de Factorisation d'Entiers, Thèse, Paris 1980

[POM 81] : C. Pomerance: Analysis and comparison of some integer factoring algorithms, Preprint, University of Georgia (1981)

[RSA 78] : R.L. Rivest, A. Shamir, L. Adleman: A method for obtaining digital signatures and public-key cryptosystems, CACM 1978(2),pp.120-126

[SCH 81a]: C.P. Schnorr: Refined analysis and improvements on some factoring algorithms, Preprint, Frankfurt 1981

[WUN 79] : M.L. Wunderlich: A running time analysis of Brillhart's continued fraction factoring method, Number Theory, Carbondale 1979 Lecture Notes 751, pp. 328-342

FINITE SEMIGROUPS AND THE RSA-CRYPTOSYSTEM

A. Ecker
Hahn-Meitner-Institut für Kernforschung Berlin GmbH
Bereich Datenverarbeitung und Elektronik
Glienicker Str. 100, 1000 Berlin 39/FRG

1. Introduction

A closer look at the RSA-cryptosystem reveals that its main feature are permutation-polynomials $x^c (c>1)$ over the multiplicative semigroup Z_m of integers modulo m. Thus it is quite natural to see whether there are other finite semigroups S for which permutation polynomials exists. It is quite clear from Z_m that one has to put certain restrictions on S to guarantee the existence of permutation-polynomials x^c. This problem is closely related to that of the ideal generalization of the Euler-Fermat theorem studied recently by [Ecker, 1980] and [Schwarz, 1981] . Section 2. of this paper gives for reasons of completeness a description of the structure of finite semigroups from [Hewitt and Zuckerman, 1960] and [Lyapin, 1974]. In section 3. the Euler-Fermat theorem in S is treated as in [Ecker, 1980]. In section 4. polynomial-functions x^c over S are considered and necessary and sufficient conditions are given for the existence of permutation-polynomials x^c. Besides that fixed points or alternatively solutions of $x^c=x$ are treated. In section 5. we look at $S=Z_m$ from the point of view underlying sections 2.-4. For this approach although with a quite different motivation see also [Hewitt and Zuckerman, 1960] and [Schwarz, 1981]. In section 6. three examples of finite semigroups are studied that might serve as a basis for an extended RSA-cryptosystem. We show that the most promising of those semigroups is the multiplicative semigroup of matrices over Z_m.

2. Periodic Semigroups

Let S be a semigroup and x be an element of S. We shall say that x is of finite order if there exists two integers h>0, d>0 such that $x^{h+d}=x^h$. It is easy to see that all elements of a finite semigroup are of finite order. We now list some well-known simple properties of elements of finite order (see [Lyapin, 1974] Chapter III.3.).

If x is of finite order, the sequence

$x, x^2, x^3, \ldots$

contains at most h+d-1 distinct elements. If t is the smallest integer such that $x^t=x^s$, $1 \le s < t$, we let $h=h_x=s$, $d=d_x=t-s$. What we just described is the structure of the cyclic semigroup S_x generated by $x \in S$. The ordered pair (h,d) of positive integers is called the type of S_x. It is well-known that $x^h, \ldots, x^{h+d-1}$ is a cyclic group of order d. Hence it contains a unique idempotent $e=x^r$ and the least number $r=r_x$ having this property is uniquely determined by $h \le r \le h+d-1$ and $d|r$. It is easy to see that x^{r+1} is one of the generators of the group $\{x^h, \ldots, x^{h+d-1}\} = \{xe, x^2 \cdot e, \ldots, x^d \cdot e=e\}$. S_x is a group if and only if h=1, in this case r=d and $x^{d+1}=x$. S_x has a zero if and only if d=1 and $z=x^h$ is that zero; r=h and $e=z=x^h$.

Remark. A cyclic semigroup S_x has a nice visualization as a digraph.

We next give a list of some useful properties of elements of finite order in a semigroup. Proofs are obvious or may be found in one of the following papers [Hewitt and Zuckerman, 1960], [Lyapin, 1974], [Vandiver and Weaver, 1958]. We suppose $x \in S$, S any semigroup and (h,d) the type of S_x if $x \in S$ is of finite order.

Lemma 2.1

(1) If x is of finite order, then $x^{t+s}=x^t$ if and only if $t \ge h$ and $d|s$.

(2) If x is of finite order, then $(x^m)^2=x^m$ if and only if $d|m$, $m \ge h$ holds

(3) If $(x^m)^2=x^m$ for some $m \ge 1$, then x is of finite order.

(4) If $(x^m)^2=x^m$ and $(x^n)^2=x^n$, then $x^m(x^m)^n=(x^n)^m=x^n$.

(5) If x is of finite order and $h_x=1$, then $(x^d)^2=x^d$.

(6) If S is a semigroup all of whose elements are of finite order and if S has a left unit e and S has just one idempotent element, then S is a group.

Definition 2.1 A semigroup S is said to be periodic if all its cyclic subsemigroups are finite.

Theorem 2.1 Suppose that S is a commutative periodic semigroup. If $h_x=1$ for all $x \in S$, then S consists of a set of disjoint groups.

Theorem 2.2 If S is a commutative periodic semigroup, then $S^o = \{x | x \in S,$

$_x=1\}$ is a subsemigroup of S. For each $e\in E_S$ we take $K_e=\{x|x\in S,\ x^m=e$ for some integer $m\geq 1\}$. Then is each K_e a semigroup and

$$S=\bigcup_{e\in E_S} K_e,\quad K_e\cap K_f=\phi\,(e\neq f)$$

and $K_e\cap S^o=G_e$ is a group and $G_e=e\cdot K_e$. E_S is the set of idempotent elements of S.

Remark. If S contains an identity element 1, then $G_1=K_1$.

In the preceding theorems we have dealt only with commutative semigroups. We now drop that restriction but add other conditions.

Definition 2.2 An element a of a semigroup S is regular if a=axa for some $x\in S$. A semigroup is regular if every element of S is regular. If in addition ax=xa the element a is called completely regular. A semigroup S is completely regular if all its elements are completely regular.

Remark. The concepts of regularity and complete regularity coincide for commutative semigroups.

Proposition 2.1 Let $e\in E_S$ be an idempotent of a semigroup S. Then

$$G_e=\{a|a\in S,\ a=e\cdot a=a\cdot e,\ e=a\cdot a'=a'\cdot a \text{ for some } a'\in S\}$$

is the greatest subgroup of S having e as its identiy.

Corollary 2.1.2 An element $a\in S$ is contained in some subgroup of S iff a is completely regular.

Definition 2.3 If S is a semigroup with identity 1, then G_1 is the group of units of S. The elements of G_1 are called the invertible elements or units of S.

Theorem 2.3 A semigroup S is completely regular if and only if S is a union of (disjoint) groups.

Corollary 2.3.1 Suppose S is a periodic semigroup. Then $h_x=1$ for all $x\in S$ iff S consists of a union of (disjoint) groups.

Theorem 2.4 The ensemble of elements of a periodic semigroup S may be divided into pairwise disjoint classes K_e, $e\in E_S$, such that each class contains a single idempotent e:

$$S=\bigcup_{e\in E_E} K_e,\quad K_e\cap K_f=\phi\,(e\neq f).$$

Theorem 2.5 Suppose S is a periodic semigroup $e\in E_S$, then

$$G_e = e\cdot K_e = K_e\cdot e \subset K_e.$$

If S contains an identity element 1, then $G_1 = K_1$.

3. The Euler-Fermat Theorem in Finite Semigroups

In this section S denotes a finite semigroup. Thus S is periodic but not necessarily commutative.

Definition 3.1 If S is a finite semigroup, we define the integers H, D and R in the following way:

$$H = \max\{\, h_x \mid x\in S\}$$

$$D = \ell.c.m.\{d_x \mid x\in S\},$$

R is the unique integer satisfying $H\le R<H+D$ and $D\mid R$.

Remark. What concerns the definition of H and D see [Ecker, 1980] and [Schwarz, 1981] (in [Schwarz, 1981] K is used instead of H). R seems to appear for the first time in [Schwarz, 1981].

Theorem 3.1 Let S be a finite semigroup and H, D as in Definition 3.1. Then

$$x^{t+s} = x^t$$

for all $x\in S$ if and only if $t\ge H$ and $D\mid s$. For any $x\in S$ the element x^r is an idempotent,

$$(x^r)^2 = x^r$$

if and only if $H\le r$ and $D\mid r$.

Corollary 3.1.1 Let S be a finite semigroup and let $H=H_S$ and $D=D_S$ be as above. Then

$$x^{H+D} = x^H$$

for all $x\in S$. H and D are the least positive integers having this property.

Corollary 3.1.2 Let S be a finite semigroup and R be defined as in Definition 3.1. Then x^R is an idempotent for all x in S and $R=R_S$ is the least positive integer having this property.

Remark. Note that we know from section 2. Theorems 2.2, 2.4, 2.5 any finite semigroup to be an union of (disjoint) sets $K_e (e\in E_S)$ and $G_e \subset K_e$ the maximal group with e as its unit. If K_e is a subsemigroup of S we can restrict Definition 3.1 to K_e. Thus we obtain local versions of Theorem 3.1 and its corollaries. [Schwarz, 1981] calls Corollary 3.1.1 the global Euler-Fermat theorem and the restriction to the semigroup K_e the local Euler-Fermat theorem.

Example A simple example is S=G, where G is a finite group. We define exp G the exponent of G to be the ℓ.c.m. of the orders for all elements of G. If $x\in G$, then we know G_x is of type $(1, d_x)$ for all $x\in G$ where d_x is the order of x in G. Hence D = exp G and especially if G is a finite abelian group exp G is the maximum order of all $x\in G$. Note that in this case there exists at least one $a\in G$ with $d_a = \exp G$. The Euler-Fermat theorem in a finite group thus becomes

$$x^{\exp G+1} = x \ , \quad \text{for all } x\in G.$$

Lemma 3.1 Let S be a finite semigroup, then

$$D = \ell.c.m.\{\exp G_e \mid e\in E_S\}.$$

Proposition 3.1 Let S be a completely regular semigroup. Then

$$x^c = x \ (c>1)$$

for all $x\in S$ iff $D\mid(c-1)$. The least exponent c having this property is c=D+1.

Proposition 3.2 Let S be a finite semigroup and $a\in S$. Then $a^{D+1}=a$ holds if and only if $a\in G_e$ for some $e\in E_S$.

Proposition 3.3 The relation $x^c=x$ with some integer $c>1$ holds for all $x\in S$ if and only if S is completely regular. The least c having this property is c=D+1.

Proof Half of the proof is obtained from Proposition 3.1. Now suppose there exists some integer $c>1$ and $x^c=x$ for all $x\in S$.

Then $x^{c^n}=(\ldots(x^c)^c)^c\ldots)^c=x$ for all $n\geq 1$. Hence there exists an integer $n_o>1$ with $c^{n_o}>H$. We conclude $x=x^{c^{n_o}}\in G_e$ if $x\in K_e$ and thus $K_e=G_e$ for all $e\in E_S$. S is a union of disjoint groups and from Theorem 2.3 we see that S is completely regular.

Remark. An alternative proof of Proposition 3.3 can be derived from Lemma 2.1(1) and Corollary 2.3.1.

Lemma 3.2 If S is a completely regular semigroup and x any element of S, then the relation $x^c=x^d$ with $1\leq c<d$ holds iff the relation $x^{d-c+1}=x$ holds.

Proof Any element $x\in S$ is contained in some group, where $x^c=x^d$ is clearly equivalent with $x^{d-c+1}=x$.

Theorem 3.2 A finite semigroup S is completely regular if and only if $H_S=1$.

Proof $H_S=1$ is equivalent to $h_x=1$ for all $x\in S$. From Corollary 2.3.1 and Theorem 2.3 we see that this is equivalent for S to be completely regular.

4. Polynomial-functions over Semigroups.

We consider polynomial-functions $p_c(x)=x^c$, $p_d(x)=x^d$ $(c,d\geq 1)$ over S with respect to the operation "o" of composition of functions defined by : $(p_c o p_d)(x)=p_c(p_d(x)=x^{c\cdot d}$. The set of all polynomial-functions $p_c(x)=x^c$, $c\geq 1$ is denoted by T. Note that (T,o) is an abelian semigroup. $\tilde{T}$ denotes the subgroup of all permutations in T.

Proposition 4.1 Suppose S is completely regular. Then

(i) T is isomorphic with the semigroup Z_D (the multiplicative semigroup of integers modulo D),

(ii) $\tilde{T}$ is isomorphic with the group Z_D^* of units of Z_D.

Theorem 4.1 The polynomial-function x^c, $c>1$ over S, S a finite semigroup is a permutation-polynomial if and only if the following conditions hold simultaneously:

(i) S is completely regular,

(ii) g.c.d.$\{c,D_S\}= 1$.

Proof If S is completely regular this follows immediately from Proposition 4.1.

x^c is a permutation iff x^{c^n} is a permutation for all $n\geq 1$. Therefore as in the proof of Proposition 3.3 an integer n_o exists with $x^{n_o}\in G_e$ for some $e\in E_S$ and any $x\in S$. Hence $K_e\setminus G_e=\phi$ for all $e\in E_S$. We conclude that S necessarily is completely regular.

Remark. Proposition 4.1 can be easily extended to arbitrary (finite) S by means of Corollary 3.1.1. We note that $\tilde{\mathbb{T}} =\{p_1\}$ if $H>1$ as follows from Theorem 4.1.

Definition 4.1 Given two integers c,d, $1\leq c<d$ we denote with $L(M)=L(c,d,M)$ the set of all solutions of $x^c=x^d$ in $M\subset S$. If $M=S$ then $L=L(S)$. Clearly $E_S\subset L$ and if S is commutative L is a subsemigroup of S.

Proposition 4.2 Let S be a finite semigroup and $1\leq c<d$, the number of solutions of $x^c=x^d$ is given by the formula.

$$|L| = \sum_{e\in E_S} (|L(K_e\setminus G_e)| + |L(G_e)|).$$

If $a\in K_e\setminus G_e$ for some $e\in E_S$, then $a\in L$ iff $h_a\leq c$ and $d_a|(d-c)$. If $a\in G_e$, $e\in E_S$, then $a\in L$ iff $d_a|(d-c)$. If S is isomorphic to the (external) direct product $S_1\oplus S_2\oplus\ldots\oplus S_n$ of semigroups $S_i\,(i=1,\ldots,n)$, then

$$|L(S)| = \prod_{i=1}^{n} |L(S_i)|.$$

Proof The first formula follows from theorems obtained in section 2. Lemma 2.1(1) gives the next part of Proposition 4.2. The last statement is quite clear.

Corollary 4.2.1 If G_e is a finite cyclic group of order $|G_e|$, then $|L(G_e)|=$g.c.d.$\{|G_e|,d-c\}$.

Lemma 4.1

(1) $x^c=x^d$, $1\leq c<d$ holds for all $x\in S$ iff $c\geq H$ and $D|(d-c)$.

(2) $x^c=x$, $c>1$ has only idempotent solutions if g.c.d.$\{D,c-1\}=1$.

Remark. Note that $E_S \subset L(c,d,S)$ is always true and hence $|E_S| \le |L|$.

Lemma 4.2 If S is a completely regular semigroup, then $L=L(1,d-c+1,S)$ or the set of all solutions of $x^c=x^d$ in S $(1\le c<d)$ is just the set of all fixed points of x^{d-c+1} in S.

Proof This follows from Lemma 3.2.

Definition 4.2 Let $P\subset N$, $P\neq\phi$ a set of natural numbers, then $Fix(P,S)=\{x \mid x\in S \text{ and } x^c=x^d \text{ for all } c,d\in P\}$. If $P=\{c\}$, $c\in N$ we write $Im\ x^c=Fix(\{c\},S)$, the image of S under x^c. If $P=\{1,c\}, c>1$ we write $Fix(c,S)=Fix(\{1,c\},S)$ and this is the set of fixed points of the polynomial-function $p_c(x)=x^c$. $Fix_1(P,S)=Fix(P\cup\{1\},S)$.

Remark. Note that we can assume without loss of generality $P\subset[1,D+H-1]$ if S is a finite semigroup.

If $1\in P$, then $Fix_1(P,S)=Fix(P,S)$ is the set of common fixed points of polynomial-functions $p_c(x)=x^c$ for all $c\in P$. If $|P|=2$, then $Fix(P,S)=L(c,d,S)$, where $P=\{c,d\}$. We have always $E_S\subset Fix_1(P,S)$ for any $P\subset N$ and $Fix_1(P,S)\subset Fix(P,S)$.

Proposition 4.3 Let S be a finite semigroup and $P\subset N$, $P\neq\phi$.

(i) If $2\in P$, then $Fix_1(P,S)=E_S$.

(ii) If all $c\in P$ are odd, then $Fix(3,S)\subset Fix_1(P,S)$, equality holds if $3\in P$.

Corollary 4.3.1 Let $3\in P$ and all $c\in P$ be odd, then $Fix_1(P,S)=Fix(3,S)=E_S$ if D_S is odd.

Proof See Lemma 4.1(2).

5. The Multiplicative Semigroup Z_m

The first problem to be solved is: identify the idempotents of Z_m and the sets K_e, G_e if $S=Z_m$ is the multiplicative semigroup of integers modulo $m(m>1)$. The second problem to be solved is: compute H and D for that semigroup. We note that Z_m is a semigroup with unit $\bar{1}$ and zero $\bar{0}$. Let $\bar{a}$ denote the residue class of $a\in Z$. Thus $K_{\bar{1}}=G_{\bar{1}}$, $G_{\bar{0}}=\{\bar{0}\}$ and $K_{\bar{0}}$ is just the subsemigroup of all nilpotent elements in Z_m, that is $\bar{a}\in K_{\bar{0}}$ iff $a^n\equiv 0$

(mod m) for some integer $n\geq 1$. The next proposition gives a characterization of the nilpotent, idempotent and invertible elements of the semigroup Z_m.

Proposition 5.1 Let $m=\prod_{i=1}^{k} p_i^{\alpha_i}$, $\alpha_i\geq 1$ be the factorization of a given integer $m>1$ into the product of different primes. Then the following statements hold in Z_m:

1. An idempotent element different from zero cannot be nilpotent.
2. If no zero-divisor exists, there are no idempotent elements $\neq\bar{0},\bar{1}$ (that means m=p, p a prime number).
3. The following two conditions are equivalent:
   (i) $\bar{a}^2=\bar{0} \Rightarrow \bar{a}=\bar{0}$ $(\bar{a}\in Z_m)$
   (ii) Zero is the only nilpotent element of Z_m.
4. $\bar{a}\in Z_m$ is idempotent $\Leftrightarrow \bar{a}^2=\bar{a}$
   $\Leftrightarrow$ Either $a\equiv 0 \pmod{p_i^{\alpha_i}}$
   or $a\equiv 1 \pmod{p_i^{\alpha_i}}$ for all $i=1,\ldots,k$.
5. $\bar{a}\in Z_m$ is nilpotent $\Leftrightarrow \bar{a}^n=\bar{0}$ $(n\geq 1)$
   $\Leftrightarrow$ if $p|m$ (p any prime) then $p|a$.
6. $\bar{a}\in Z_m^* \Leftrightarrow$ g.c.d. $\{a,m\}=1$.
7. $\bar{e}\in Z_m$ is idempotent $\Leftrightarrow$ $e=r\cdot c$ or $e=t\cdot d$, where $c\cdot d=m$, g.c.d. $\{c,d\}=1$ and $1=r\cdot c+t\cdot d$.

Corollary 5.1.1 The multiplicative semigroup Z_m, $m=\prod_{i=1} p_i^{\alpha_i}$ has 2^k idempotent elements and $m/p_1\cdot p_2\cdots p_k$ nilpotent elements. There are $\varphi(m)$ units, where $\varphi(\cdot)$ is Euler's function.

Corollary 5.1.2 There exists no non-zero nilpotent elements in Z_m iff m is square-free.

Remark. $\nu(m)=2^k$ is a multiplicative number-theoretic function, we have

$$\nu(m) = \sum_{d|m}\mu^2(d).$$

Definition 5.1 Let $a\in Z$, and let $m=m_1\cdot m_2$ with g.c.d. $\{m_1,m_2\}=1$, and where each prime divisor of m that divides one of the pair a,m_1 divides the other also. In consequence of this $(a_1,m_2)=1$. The nildegree n_a of a modulo m_1 is the least positive integer such that $a^n \equiv 0 \pmod{m_1}$. The order t_a of a modulo m_2 is the least positive integer t with $a^t \equiv 1 \pmod{m_2}$. If g.c.d.$\{a,m\}=1$, then $n_a=1$ and t_a is the order of a modulo m. If $m_1=m$, then $t_a=1$ and n_a is the nildegree of a modulo m. If $a\equiv 0 \pmod m$, this means $n_a=t_a=n_o=t_o=1$.

Remark. $m_1(\cdot)$ is a number-theoretic function, multiplicative worth to be studied for its own sake. If $a\equiv b \pmod m$ then $m_1(a)=m_1(b)$. Thus we can associate uniquely the pair of numbers $m_1(\bar{a})$, $m_2(\bar{a})$ with each $\bar{a}\in Z_m$. Note that $m_1(a)=m_1(a^n)$ for all $n\geq 1$.

Theorem 5.1 Let $\bar{a}\in Z_m$ and $m=m_1\cdot m_2$ as in Definition 5.1; then $S_{\bar{a}}$ is of type $(h_{\bar{a}}, d_{\bar{a}})=(n_a,t_a)$.

Corollary 5.1.1 Let $r=r_{\bar{a}}$ be the least number that has the property that $\bar{a}^r=\bar{e}$ is the unique idempotent of $S_{\bar{a}}$. Then r is the least integer with $a^r\equiv 0 \pmod{m_1}$ and $a^r\equiv 1 \pmod{m_2}$.

Lemma 5.1 Let m be as in Proposition 5.1, then we have the following alternative characterizations:

1) $\bar{a}\in Z_m$ is nilpotent $\Leftrightarrow m_1(\bar{a})=m$.
2) $\bar{a}\in Z_m^* \Leftrightarrow m_1(\bar{a})=1$.
3) $\bar{a}\in Z_m$ is idempotent $\Leftrightarrow m_1(a)\mid a$ and $m_2(a)\mid (a-1)$.

Theorem 5.2 $\bar{a}^n=\bar{e}$ for some $n\geq 1$, $\bar{a}\in Z_m$ and $\bar{e}\in E_S$ iff $m_1(\bar{a})=m_1(\bar{e})$.

Corollary 5.2.1

$$K_{\bar{e}} = \{\bar{a} \mid \bar{a}\in Z_m,\ m_1(\bar{a}) = m_1(\bar{e})\},\quad \bar{e}\in E_S.$$

Theorem 5.3

$$G_{\bar{e}}=\{\bar{a} \mid \bar{a}\in Z_m, m_1(\bar{a})=m_1(\bar{e}) \text{ and } m_1(\bar{e})\mid a\},\ \bar{e}\in E_S.$$

Proposition 5.2 The mapping $f_{\bar{e}}: G_{\bar{1}}\to G_{\bar{e}}$ defined by $f_{\bar{e}}(\bar{x})=\bar{e}\cdot\bar{x}\ (\bar{e}\in E_S)$ is a homomorphism of $G_{\bar{1}}$ onto $G_{\bar{e}}$ with kernel $\mathrm{Ker}_{\bar{e}} = \{\bar{x} \mid \bar{x}\in G_{\bar{1}},\ m_2(e)\mid (x-1)\}$. $G_{\bar{e}}$ is isomorphic to $Z^*_{m_2(e)}$.

Lemma 5.2 $\exp G_{\bar{e}} = \exp Z^*_{m_2(e)} = \lambda(m/m_1(e))$, $\bar{e}\in E_S$.

Proof This is a well-known fact from number-theory, $\lambda(m)$ denotes the "universal exponent" of m (also called the Carmichael-function), for further information see LeVeque: Topics in Number Theory Vol. I (1956), Chapter 4.

Proposition 5.3 If $S=Z_m (m>1)$ is the multiplicative semigroup of integers modulo m, then

$$D=D_S=\ell.c.m.\{\exp G_{\bar{e}} \mid \bar{e} \in E_S\}=\lambda(m).$$

Lemma 5.3 Let $N_{\bar{e}} = \max\{n_{\bar{a}} \mid \bar{a} \in K_{\bar{e}}\}$, $\bar{e} \in E_S$ and define $\varepsilon(a)=\max\{1\} \cup \{\alpha \mid p^{\alpha} \| m\}$ $(a \in Z)$. Then we get $N_{\bar{e}} = \varepsilon(m_1(e))$.

Proposition 5.4 If $S=Z_m (m>1)$, then $H=H_S=\varepsilon(m)$.

Theorem 5.4

If Z_m is the finite multiplicative semigroup of integers modulo $m (m>0)$, then

$$\bar{x}^{t+s} = \bar{x}^{t}$$

for all $\bar{x} \in Z_m$ if and only if $t \geq \varepsilon(m)$ and $\lambda(m) \mid s$.

Proof This is a special case of Theorem 3.1 if we take $S=Z_m$ and use Proposition 5.3 and Proposition 5.4.

Corollary 5.4.1 (The global Euler-Fermat-theorem)

$$\bar{x}^{\varepsilon(m)+\lambda(m)} = \bar{x}^{\varepsilon(m)}$$

for all $\bar{x} \in Z_m$. Alternatively in terms of congruences,

$$x^{\varepsilon(m)+\lambda(m)} \equiv x^{\varepsilon(m)} \pmod{m}$$

for all $x \in Z$.

Corollary 5.4.2 If m is a positive integer and t is a non-negative integer, then

$$x^{t+\varphi(m)} \equiv x^{t} \pmod{m} \quad (m>1)$$

for all integers x iff m is (t+1)th power-free.

Proof See [Ecker, 1980] Corollary 3.3.

Proposition 5.5 (The local Euler-Fermat-theorem)

Let $\bar{e}\in E_S$, $S=Z_m(m>1)$. We have

$$\bar{x}^{\varepsilon(m_1)} = \bar{x}^{\varepsilon(m_1)+\lambda(m/m_1)}$$

for all $\bar{x}\in K_{\bar{e}}$, where $m_1=m_1(e)$.

Proof Note that $K_{\bar{e}}$ is a semigroup and Lemma 5.2 and Lemma 5.3 completes the proof.

Remark. The exponents in the foregoing theorems are the best possible if one insists on idependence of the special choice of $\bar{x}\in Z_m$ or $\bar{x}\in K_{\bar{e}}$ or $\bar{x}\in K_{\bar{e}}$ ("for all $\bar{x}$").

Lemma 5.4

(i) $\varepsilon(m)\leq\varphi(m)$ for all integers $m>1$ and $\varepsilon(m)=\varphi(m)$ holds iff $m=2,4$.

(ii) If $m\neq 8,24$, then $\varepsilon(m)\leq\lambda(m)$.

Proposition 5.6 Let $m>1$, then for all $\bar{x}\in Z_m$ $\bar{x}^{\varphi(m)}$ is an idempotent of Z_m or alternatively $x^{\varphi(m)}\equiv x^{2\varphi(m)} \pmod{m}$ for all $x\in Z$.

Proposition 5.7 $\bar{a}\in Z_m(m>1)$ is regular if and only if one of the following conditions is fulfilled:

(i) $m_1(a)|a$,

(ii) $\text{g.c.d.}\{a,m\} = \text{g.c.d.}\{a^2,m\}$.

Theorem 5.5 $S=Z_m(m>1)$ is completely regular iff m is square-free.

Proof If m is square-free then Proposition 5.7(i) and Theorem 5.1 gives $h_{\bar{a}}=1$ for all $\bar{a}\in Z_m$. Hence $H_S=1$ and from Theorem 3.2 we see that $S=Z_m$ is completely regular.

Now suppose that $S=Z_m$ is completely regular and thus $H_S=1$ (Theorem 3.2). This means $h_{\bar{a}}=1$ for all $\bar{a}\in Z_m$, hence $m_1(a)|a$ for all $a\in Z$ (Proposition 5.7 (i), Theorem 5.1). It is easily seen that this is only possible if m is square-free.

Corollary 5.5.1 $S=Z_m$ is completely regular iff there exists no none-zero nilpotent element in Z_m.

Proof Corollary 5.1.2 of Proposition 5.1.

emark. Note that Z_m is a commutative semigroup, hence there is no dif-
erence between "regular" and "completely regular". Proposition 5.7 and
heorem 5.5 were first proved by [Morgado, 1974] within the framework
f elementary number-theory.

roposition 5.8 Let $\bar{a} \in Z_m (m>1)$, then

$$a \equiv a^{1+\lambda(m)} \pmod m$$

olds iff $\bar{a}$ is regular.

roof See Proposition 3.2 and Corollary 2.2.1.

orollary 5.8.1

$$a \equiv a^{1+\varphi(m)} \pmod m$$

olds iff $\bar{a}$ is regular.

roposition 5.9 The relation $\bar{x}^c = \bar{x}$ with some integer $c>1$ holds for all
$\in Z_m$ if and only if m is square-free and $\lambda(m) \mid (c-1)$. The least c having
his property is $c=1+\lambda(m)$.

roof Take $S=Z_m$ in Proposition 3.1 and see what we proved in Proposition
.3 and Theorem 5.5.

heorem 5.6 The polynomial-function x^c, $c \geq 1$ over Z_m is a permutation-
olynomial if and only if m is square-free and $\text{g.c.d.}\{c,\lambda(m)\}=1$.

roof This is Theorem 4.1 for $S=Z_m$ (see Proposition 5.3 and Theorem 5.5).

emark. Theorem 5.6 can be treated from different point of views; as a
roblem of number theory it has been solved in [Cordes, 1976] and [Small,
977]. In connection with the uniform distribution of polynomials modu-
o m [Zane, 1964] proved Theorem 5.6. For a more general question see
Kuipers and Niederreiter, 1974] Chap. 5.

learly the polynomial-function $\bar{a}x^c$, $c>1$ $(\bar{a} \in Z_m)$ is a permutation-polyno-
ial over Z_m iff m is square-free and $\text{g.c.d.}\{c,\lambda(m)\}=\text{g.c.d.}\{a,m\}=1$.

roposition 5.10 Let $m=p^\alpha$, p a prime and $\alpha \geq 1$. The number of solutions
f $x^c=x^d$, $1 \leq c < d$ in Z_m is given by the formula:

(i) If p is odd or m=2,4

$$|L(c,d,Z_m)| = m/g + \text{g.c.d.}\{d-c, \lambda(m)\}$$

(ii) $m=2^\alpha$, $\alpha \geq 3$.

$$|L(c,d,Z_m)| = m/g + \text{g.c.d.}\{d-c, 2\} \cdot \text{g.c.d.}\{d-c, \lambda(m)\}$$

g is equal to p^γ, where

$$\gamma = \begin{cases} \alpha/c, & \text{if } c \mid \alpha, \\ [\alpha/c]+1, & \text{if } c \nmid \alpha. \end{cases}$$

Remark. Note that $\gamma=1$ if $c \geq \alpha$, especially m=p gives always m/g=1.

<u>Theorem 5.7</u>([Schwarz, 1981]) Let $m = \prod_{i=1}^{n} p_i^{\alpha_i}$ and $1 \leq c < d$. Then the number of solutions of $x^c = x^d$ in Z_m is given by the formula

$$|L(c,d,Z_m)| = \prod_{i=1}^{n} (m/g_i + \ell_i).$$

Here $g_i = p_i^{\gamma_i}$ and γ_i is defined as γ in Proposition 5.10 but with respect to $p_i^{\alpha_i}$, and

$$\ell_i = \begin{cases} \text{g.c.d.}\{d-c, \lambda(p_i^{\alpha_i})\}, & \text{if } p_i \text{ is odd or } p_i^{\alpha_i} = 2,4; \\ \text{g.c.d.}\{d-c, 2\} \cdot \text{g.c.d.}\{d-c, \lambda(p_i^{\alpha_i})\}, & \text{if } p_i^{\alpha_i} = 2^\alpha, \alpha \geq 3. \end{cases}$$

<u>Corollary 5.7.1</u> The number of solutions of $x^c = x$, $c > 1$ in Z_m is given by the formula

$$|Fix(c, Z_m)| = \prod_{i=1}^{n} (1+\ell_i),$$

where ℓ_i is as in Theorem 5.7.

<u>Corollary 5.7.2</u> Let m be square-free, then the number of solutions of $x^c = x^d$, $1 \leq c < d$ is given by the formula

$$|L(c,d,Z_m)| = \prod_{i=1}^{n} (1 + \text{g.c.d}\{d-c, p_i - 1\}).$$

<u>Corollary 5.7.3</u> Let m be square-free, then the number of solutions of $x^c = x, c > 1$ is given by the formula

$$|Fix(c, Z_m)| = \prod_{i=1}^{n} (1 + \text{g.c.d.}\{c-1, p_i - 1\}).$$

Remark. Corollary 5.7.1 is Theorem 3, p. 174 in [Blakley and Borosh, 1979]. But note that the formula given by Blakley and Borosh is only true if $8 \nmid m$ is assumed.

Proposition 5.11 $E_S = \mathrm{Fix}(c, Z_m), 1 < c \le \lambda(m)$ iff g.c.d.$\{c-1, \lambda(m)\} = 1$.

Proof Half of the proof is given by Lemma 4.1(2). Suppose g.c.d.$\{c-1, \lambda(m)\} = d > 1$, then there exists an element of Z_m^* with order $\lambda(m)$. Hence an element $\bar{a} \neq \bar{1}$ of order $\lambda(m)/d$ exists in Z_m^* with $\bar{a}^c = \bar{a}$.

Proposition 5.12 Let $m>1$ be odd and square-free and g.c.d.$\{c, \lambda(m)\} = 1$, $c>1$. Then the permutation-polynomial x^c over Z_m has at least 3^n fixed-points, where $n>0$ is the number of different prime divisors of m. We have $|\mathrm{Fix}(c, Z_m)| = 3^n$ iff g.c.d.$\{c-1, \lambda(m)\} = 2$.

Proposition 5.13 Let $m>2$ be an integer and d any integer with g.c.d.$\{d, \lambda(m)\} = 1$. Then we define

$$C_d = \{c \mid 1 \le c \le \lambda(m), \text{g.c.d.}\{c, \lambda(m)\} = 1 \text{ and g.c.d.}\{c-d, \lambda(m)\} = 2\},$$

and have

$$|C_d| = \lambda(m)/f \prod_{\substack{p \mid \lambda(m) \\ p \neq 2}} (1 - 2/p),$$

where the product is taken over all different prime divisors of $\lambda(m)$, with

$$f = \begin{cases} 4, & \text{if } 4 \mid \lambda(m), \\ 2, & \text{if } 4 \nmid \lambda(m). \end{cases}$$

Corollary 5.13.1([Blakley and Borosh, 1979])

Let d=1, then we obtain the same formula as in Proposition 5.13 and if $m>2$ then always $|C_1| \ge 1$. Whether m is square-free or not makes no sense.

Proposition 5.14 Let $m>1$ be square-free and odd, then

$$|\mathrm{Fix}_1(C_1, Z_m)| = 3^n,$$

where n is the number of different prime divisors of m.

6. Some other Semigroups.

Given a finite semigroup it is tedious to computer H and D. We consider some further examples.

a. The semigroup of binary relations on a finite set. By an $n\times n$ Boolean matrix ($n>1$) we mean an $n\times n$ matrix over the set $\{0,1\}$ under the operations $a+b=\sup(a,b)$, $a\cdot b=\min(a,b)$. Denote by B_n the multiplicative semigroup of all Boolean matrices. Clearly $|B_n| = 2^{n^2}$ and B_n is isomorphic to the multiplicative semigroup of all binary relations on a finite set with n elements. In this case it is known that $H_{B_n} = (n-1)^2+1$, D_{B_n} is a function of n which can be computed in the following way. Let $n=n_1+\ldots+n_k$ be a partition of n. Then $D_{B_n} = \max\{\ell.c.m.\{n_1,\ldots,n_s\}\}$ where $(n_1,\ldots,n_k)$ runs through all possible partitions of n, or otherwise expressed: D_{B_n} is the largest order of an element in S_n (the symmetric group on n elements).

b. The multiplicative semigroup of certain finite rings.

The approach taken in Section 5 of this paper can be generalized to a class of rings containing Z_m. Let R be a principal ideal domain; if (m) $(m\in R)$ is an ideal of R with $\overline{R}=R/(m)$ a finite ring, we can get an Euler-Fermat theorem and most of the theorems and propositions in the foregoing section can be taken over to the multiplicative semigroup of $\overline{R}$.

A ring of special interest is the polynomial ring K[x], where K is a finite field. Instead of m we take $m(x)\in K[x]$, and if φ denotes the generalized φ-function of Dedekind we have a new kind of RSA-cryptosystem. Instead of m we take $m(x)\in K[x]$ and $\varphi(m(x))$ is known if the factorization of m(x) as a product of irreducible polynomials over K is known. But polynomial factoring can be done in polynomial time, hence the proposed system is unsafe.

c. Matrices over Z_m.

In a paper of [Davis, 1951] the following Euler-Fermat theorem for matrices is proved:

<u>Theorem 6.1</u> ([Davis, 1951]) Let $m=p_1^{\alpha_1}\ldots p_s^{\alpha_s}$ be an arbitrary number with s distinct prime divisors $p_1,\ldots,p_s$, $n>1$ an arbitrary integer, $p_i^{r_i}$ the least power of p_i greater than or equal to n, $q_i=\ell.c.m.\{p_i^{r_i}, p_i^{n}-1,\ldots,p_i-1\}$, and finally let

$$w = \ell.c.m.\{q_1 p_1^{\alpha_1 - 1}, \ldots, q_s p_s^{\alpha_s - 1}\}.$$

If A is a matrix of order n whose determinant is prime to m and I is the unit matrix, then

$$A^w \equiv I \pmod{m}$$

and w is the least exponent for which this is true.

If M_n denotes the multiplicative semigroup of all n×n matrices over Z_m, then $w=\exp(M_n^*)$ is just the exponent of the group of all non-singular matrices M_n^* over Z_m. We note that a factorization of m is needed to compute w. A (generalized) RSA-cryptosystem seems to be possible in M_n, if the following two problems were solved:

The structure of M_n has to be determined completely (H_{M_n}, D_{M_n}), especially the completely regular M_n have to be singled out.

HOW TO SHARE A SECRET

Maurice Mignotte, Strasbourg

I. Introduction.

We consider the following problem.

Let S be some secret. A collection of n people E_j share this secret in such a way that

- each E_j knows some information x_j ,
- for a certain fixed integer k , $2 \le k \le n$, the knowledge of any k of the x's enables to find S easily,
- the knowlegde of less than k of the x's leaves S undetermined.

This problem was considered first by A. Shamir [79] and he calls such a scheme a (k, n) threshold scheme.

The practical interest of this problem is obvious and is discussed in Shamir [79] .

Shamir gives a solution using interpolation of polynomials over a finite field, the secret being some polynomial. We give here a more elementary solution in which the secret is an integer. These two solutions are particular cases of the use of the Chinese Remainder Theorem. So we study this theorem in the following section.

II. Chinese Remainder Theorem.

Our problem is to cut some secret into pieces. An usual way in mathematics to "divide" a set into simpler pieces is to replace it by a product of simpler sets. A typical example of this situation is given by the

Chinese Remainder Theorem. Moreover, and this is essential in our application, the isomorphisms which occur in this theorem are easily computable for the two cases we consider.

The general version of the Chinese Remainder Theorem is the following.

THEOREM. - Let A be a ring. Let $I_1, \ldots, I_m$ be ideals of A such that

(1) $\quad I_j + I_{j'} = A \quad \text{for} \quad 1 \le j < j' \le m$.

Then, if $I = \bigcap_{j=1}^{m} I_j$, the function

$$f : A/I \to A/I_1 \times \ldots \times A/I_m$$
$$x \mapsto (x \bmod I_1, \ldots, x \bmod I_m)$$

is an isomorphism of rings.

Moreover, if $z_1, \ldots, z_m \in A/I$ satisfy

$$z_i \equiv \delta_{ij} \bmod I_j \quad , \quad 1 \le i, j \le m$$

(where δ_{ij} = if $(i = j)$ then 1 else 0) then

$$f^{-1}(y_1, \ldots, y_m) = y_1 z_1 + \ldots + y_m z_m .$$

► Taking the product of relations (1) for $j = i$ and $j' \neq i$ we get

$$I_i + \bigcap_{\substack{1 \le j \le m \\ j \neq i}} I_j = A \quad , \quad 1 \le i \le m .$$

The previous relation implies that there exist z'_i and z''_i, for $1 \le i \le m$, such that

$$1 = z'_i + z''_i \quad , \quad z'_i \in I_i \quad , \quad z''_i \in \bigcap_{\substack{1 \leq j \leq m \\ j \neq i}} I_j \,.$$

Then

$$z''_i \equiv \delta_{ij} \mod I_j \,.$$

If we put $z_i = z''_i \bmod I$ and define

$$g : A/I_1 \times \ldots \times A/I_m \to A/I$$
$$(y_1, \ldots, y_m) \mapsto y_1 z_1 + \ldots + y_m z_m$$

it is easily verified that f and g are reciprocal homomorphisms.◄

In our problem we take

secret : $S \in A/I$,

informations : $x_j = S \bmod I_j$.

III. Shamir's example.

In our formulation, Shamir's solution can be seen as follows. He chooses $A = F[X]$, where $F = \mathbb{Z}/p\mathbb{Z}$ is a finite field (p is a prime member), and

$$I_j = \{Q \in F[X] \,;\, Q(a_j) = 0\} \quad , \quad 1 \leq j \leq n$$

where $a_1, \ldots, a_n$ are distinct points of F .
The secret is some polynomial $S \in F[X]$ of degree smaller than k and the x_j are

$$x_j = S(a_j) \quad , \quad 1 \leq i \leq n \,.$$

In this case the Chinese Remainder Theorem is the Legendre Theorem on interpolation of polynomials.

IV. An arithmetical solution.

We take now

- $A = \mathbb{Z}$,
- $I_j = d_j \mathbb{Z}$, $1 \le j \le n$, where $d_1, \ldots, d_n$ are coprime in pairs (the d's may be public)
- the secret is some integer S, $a \le S \le b$, where a and b are given integers, $0 < a < b$.
- the informations x_j are

$$x_j = S \bmod d_j \quad , \quad 1 \le j \le n .$$

To get a (k, n) threshold scheme we take $d_1, \ldots, d_n$ so that

- the product of any k of the d_j is bigger than b
- the product of any k-1 of the d_j is smaller than a.

When k of the x_j are known, say $x_1, \ldots, x_k$, then S is given by the formula

$$S = x_1 z_1 + \ldots + x_k z_k \bmod d_1 \ldots d_k ,$$

and the z's are obtained by the (extended) euclidean algorithm. Moreover the z's have to be computed only once and one may take them so that

$$z_i \equiv \delta_{ij} \bmod d_j \quad , \quad 1 \le j \le n$$

and then

$$S \equiv x_1 z_1 + \ldots + x_n z_n \bmod d_1 \ldots d_n .$$

When only k-1 of the x_j are known, say $x_1, \ldots, x_{k-1}$ then

$$S \equiv x_1 z_1 + \dots + x_{k-1} z_{k-1} \mod d_1 \dots d_{k-1}$$

so that the interval $[a, b]$ contains at least $c = [\frac{b-a}{d_1 \dots d_{k-1}}]$ values which satisfy this condition and are equally possible values of S. If c is large enough (for example $c = 10^6$) then it is practically impossible to find S.

A possible choice is

- $d_j \simeq 10^{\ell}$, $1 \leq j \leq n$
- $a = 5.10^{k\ell-1}$, $b = 10^{k\ell}$,

where ℓ is some positive integer (for example $\ell = 6$).
Then when only $k-1$ orfew of the x's are known there are at least about $5.10^{\ell-1}$ candidates for S.

List of talks for which there was no paper submitted

Wolfgang Bitzer: A Two - Dimensional Method For Speech Scrambling

Wolfgang Bitzer: A Key - Distribution System For A Switched Communication Network

Donald Davies: The Incorporation of Cryptography in Teletex Protocols

Whitfield Diffie: A Taxonomy of Certain Cryptographic Systems

Manfred Hain: Pseudo - Random Generators with High Complexity and Good Statistics

Ernst Henze: The Solution of a General Equation for the Public Key Distribution System

Alan G.Konheim: A One - Way Sequence for Transaction Verification

Winfried Müller: Permutation Polynomials and Public-Key Cryptosystems

Tibor Nemetz: Comments on Linear Encoding

Adi Shamir: A New Cryptanalytic Attack Against Merkle - Hellman Keys

Kjell-O.Widman: The "Kryha - Machine"

Bibliography

The names written in italic letters refer back to the articles in which these references are quoted.

References:

Abramowitz, M. / Stegun, I.A. (1972), Handbook of Mathematical Functions, National Bureau of Standards Applied Math. Series 55, U.S. Dept. Commerce, Washington, D.C. / *Sloane*

Aho, A.V. / Hopcroft, J.E. / Ullman, J.D. (1974), The design and analysis of computer algorithms, Addison-Wesley / *Beth*

Ahrens, J.H. / Dieter, U. (1972), Computer methods for samling from the exponential and normal distributions, Commun. ACM, 15, 873-882 / *Sloane*

Ahrens, J.H. / Dieter, U. (1973), Extensions of Forsythe's method for random sampling from the normal distribution, Math. Comp., 27, 927-937 / *Sloane*

Alanen, J.D. / Knuth, D.E. (1964), Tables of finite fields, Synkhyā (A), 26, 305-328 / *Herlestam*

Albert, A.A. (1941), Some mathematicals aspects of cryptography, AMS 382nd Meeting / *Beth*

Angermann, A. / Thome, R. (1973), Ansätze für eine Kosten-Nutzen-Analyse des Datenschutzes, data report 8, 18-22 / *Horbach*

Atkinson, A.C. / Pearce, M.C. (1976), The computer generation of beta, gamma and normal random variables, J. Royal Statist. Soc., A139, 431-461 / *Sloane*

Auerbach, H. (1933-34), Sur les groupes lineaires bornes, Studia Math., 4, 113-127, 158-166; 5, 43-49 / *Sloane*

Ayoub, F. (1981) Encryption with keyed random permutations, Electronics Letters, 17, 583-585 / *Sloane*

Baer, R.M. / Brock, P. (1968), Natural sorting over permutation spaces, Math. Comp., 22, 385-410 / *Sloane*

Bazeries, E. (1901), Les chiffres secrets dêvoilês, Fasquelle, Paris / *Bauer*

Beesley, P. (1977), Very Special Intelligence, Hamish, London / *Bauer*

Beker, H.J. / Mitchell, C.J., Permutations with restricted displacement, to be submitted / *Beker*

Beker, H.J. / Piper, F.C. (1982), Cipher Systems: The protection of communications, Norhtwood Books / *Beker, Beth, Jennings, Piper*

Berlekamp, E.R. (1968), Algebraic Coding Theory, McGraw-Hill, N.Y. / *Sloane*

Berlekamp, E.R. / McEliece, R.J. / van Tilborg, H., On the inherent intractability of certain coding problems, IEEE Trans. Inf. Theory, IT-24, 384-386 / *Beth*

Bernhard, R. (1982), Breaching system security, IEEE Spectrum, 19 (No. 6), 24-31 / *Sloane*

Beth, T. (1982), Kryptographie als Instrument des Datenschutzes, Informatik Spektrum, 5, 82-96 / *Beth*

Beth, T. / Heß, P. / Wirl, K. (1983), Kryptographie, Leitfäden der ang. Informatik, Teubner, Stuttgart / *Beth, Heß, Wirl*

Beth, T. / Strehl, V. (1981) Materialien zur Codierungstheorie, Berichte des IMMD Erlangen, 11 (No. 14) / *Beth*

Biermeier, J. (1980), Ein Dialogprogramm des DES-Algorithmus zur Kryptanalyse, Diplomarbeit, Linz / *Schaumüller-Bichl*

Blakely / Borosh (1979), Rivest-Shamir-Adleman public key kryptosystems do not always conceal messages, Comp. & Maths. with Appls. 5, 169-178 / *Ecker*

Blakely, G.R. / Purdy, G.B. (1981), A necessary and sufficient condition for fundamential periods of cascade machines to be products of the fundamental periods of their constituent finite state machines, Information Sciences 24, 71-91 / *Jennings*

Bloomfield, P. (1976), Fourier Analysis of Time Series: An Introduction, Wiley, N.Y. / *Sloane*

Blum, L. / Blum, M. / Shub, M. (1982), A simple secure pseudo-random number generator, presented at "Crypto 82", Univ. of Calif., Santa Barbara, August 1982 / *Sloane*

Boothby, W.M. / Weiss, G.L., eds. (1972), Symmetric Spaces, Dekker, N.Y. / *Sloane*

Bourbaki, N. (1968), Groupes et algebras de Lie, Chap. 4-6, Hermann, Paris / *Sloane*

Bovey, J.D. (1980), The probability that some power of permutation has small degree, Bull. London Math. Soc. 12, 47-51 / *Sloane*

Bovey, J.D. / Williamson, A. (1978), The probability of generating the symmetric group, Bull. London Math. Soc., 10, 91-96 / *Sloane*

Box, G.E.P. / Muller, M.E. (1958), A note on the generation of normal debiates, Annals Math. Stat., 29, 610-611 / *Sloane*

Brent, R.P. (1974), A Gaussian pseudo-random number generator, Commun. ACM, 17, 704-706 / *Sloane*

Brent, R.P. / Pollard, J.M. (1981), Factorisation of the eight Fermat number, Mathematics of computation, 36 (No. 154), p. 628 / *Davies*

Brigham, E.O. (1974), The Fast Fourier Transform, Prentice-Hall, Englewood Cliffs, N.J. / *Sloane*

Bright, H.S. / Ension, R.L. (2979), Quasi-random number sequences from a long-period TPL generator with remarks on application to crpytography, Computing Surveys, 11, 357-370 / *Sloane*

Brillinger, D.R. (1975), Time Series: Data Analysis and Theory, Holt, Rinehart and Winston, N.Y. / *Sloane*

Bromfield, A.J. / Mitchell, C.J., Permutation selector for a sliding window time element scrambler, to be submitted / *Beker*

Brown, G.W. (1956), Monte Carlo methods, in Modern Mathematics for the Engineer, edited E.f. Beckenbach, McGraw-Hill, N.Y., 279-303 / *Sloane*

Brown, M. / Solomon, H. (1979), On combining pseudorandom number generators, Ann. Statistics, 7, 691-695 / *Sloane*

Cartan, E. (1966), The Theory of Spinors, Hermann, Paris, Reprinted by Dover Publications, N.Y., 1981 / *Sloane*

Chambers, R.P. (1967), Random-number generation, IEEE Spectrum, 4 (No. 2), 48-56 / *Sloane*

Chatfield, C.(1975), The Analysis of Time Series: Theory and Practice, Chapman and Hall, London / *Sloane*

Chomsky, N. / Halle, M. (1968), The Sound Pattern of English, N.Y. / *Timmann*

Cohen, D.I.A. (1976), An explanation of the first digit phenomenon, JCT (A) 20, 367-370 / *Beth*

Cook, J.M. (1959), Remarks on a recent paper, Commun. ACM, 2 (No. 10), p. 26 / *Sloane*

Cook, J.M. (1957), Rational formulae for the production of a spherically symmetric probability distribution, Math. Tables Other Aids Comp., 11, 81-82 / *Sloane*

Conway, J.H. / Parker, R.A. / Sloane, N.J.A. (1982), the covering radius of the Leech lattice, Proc. Royal Soc. London, A 380, 261-290 / *Sloane*

Coppersmith, D. / Grossman, E. (1975), Generators for certain alternating groups with applications to cryptography, SIAM J. Applied Math., 29, 624-627 / *Sloane*

Cordes, (1976), Permutation mod m in the form x^n , Amer. Math. Monthly 83, 32-33 / *Ecker*

Coxeter, H.S.M. (1973), Regular Polytopes, Dover, N.Y., third edition/ *Sloane*

Dammann, U. / Simitis, Sp. (1981), Bundesdatenschutzgesetz (BSSG), Textausgabe mit Auszügen aus der Gesetzgegungsdokumentation und den Verwaltungsvorschriften der Länder, Nomos Verlagsges., 4. Auflage, Baden-Baden / *Horbach*

Davio, M. / Quisquater, J.J. (1982), Methodology in information security, Mutual authentication procedures, Application to access control, Proc. 1982 International Zurich Seminar on Digital Communications (Zurich, March 9-11, 1982), 87-92 / *Davio, Goethals*

Davis, (1951), The Euler-Fermat theorem for matrices, Duke Math. J., 18, 613-617 / *Ecker*

Davis, R.M. (1978), The Data Encryption Standard in perspecitve, IEEE Communications Society Magazine, 16 (November), 5-9 / *Sloane*

Deak, I. (1979) Comparison of methods for generating uniformly distributed random points in and on a hypersphere, Problems of Control and Information Theory, 8, 1o5-113 / *Sloane*

Delastelle, F. (1902), Traité élémentaire de cryptographie, Gautier-Villars, Paris / *Bauer*

Delattre, P. (1965), Comparing the Phonetic Features of English, French German and Spanish, Heidelberg / *Timmann*

Denning, D. (1982), Cryptography and Data Security, Addison-Wesley, Reading, Mass. / *Bauer*

Deschek, H.-H. (1980), Strafgesetzbuch, Textausgabe mit ausführlichem Sachregister und einer Einführung, dtv, 19. Auflage, München / *Horbach*

Diaconis, P. (1980), Average running time of the Fast Fourier transform, J. Algorithms, 1, 187-208 / *Sloane*

Diaconis, P. (1982), Group Theory in Statistics, lecture notes, Harvard University / *Sloane*

Diaconis, P. / Graham, R.L. (1977), Spearman's footrule as a measure of disarray, J. Royal Stat. Soc., B 39, 262-268 / *Sloane*

Diaconis, P. / Graham, R.L. / Kantor, W.M. (1982), The mathematics of perfect shuffles, Advances in Applied Math., in press. / *Sloane*

Diaconis, P. / Shahshahani, M. (1981), Generating a random permutation with random transpositions, Z. Wahrscheinlichkeitstheorie, 57, 159-179 / *Sloane*

Diaconis, P. / Shahshahani, M. (1982), Factoring probabilities on compact groups, preprint / *Sloane*

Dieter, U. / Ahrens, J.H. (1973), A combinatorial method for the generation of normally distributed random variables, Computing, 11, 137-146 / *Sloane*

Diffie, W. / Hellman, M.E. (1976), A critique of the proposed Data Encryption Standard, Commun. ACM, 19, 164-165 / *Sloane*

Diffie, W. / Hellman, M.E. (1976), New Directions in Cryptography, IEEE Transactions on Information Theory, IT-22 (No. 6), 644-654 / *Bauer, Beth, Davies, Eier, Goethals, Lagger, Schöbi*

Diffie, W. / Hellman, M.E. (1977), Exhaustive cryptanalysis of the NBS data encryption standard, Computer 10, 74-84 / *Beth, Sloane*

Diffie, W. / Hellman, M.E. (1979), Privacy and authentication: an introduction to cryptography, Proc. IEEE, 67, (No. 3), 397-427 / *Davio, Goethals*

Dixon, J.D. (1969), The probability of generating the symmetric group, Math. Zeit., 110, 199-205 /*Sloane*

Dornhoff, L. / Hohn, F. (1978), Applied modern algebra, MacMillan, N.Y. / *Beth*

Durstenfeld, R. (1964), Random permutation, Commun. ACM, 7, p.420 / *Sloane*

Dym, H. / MacKean, H.P. (1972), Fourier series and integrals, Academic Press, London, N.Y. / *Beth*

Eaton, M.L. / Perlman, M. (1977), Generating O(n) with reflections, Pacific J. Math., 73, 73-80 / *Sloane*

Ecker, (1980), Comment on the note: The congruence $a^{r+s} \equiv a^{r}$ (mod m) by A.E. Livingston and M.L. Livingston, Amer. Math. Monthly 87, 811-814 / *Ecker*

Ehlers, C.Th. (1981), Probleme des Datenzugangs in der medizinischen Forschung, Tech. Lit. Ges. / *Beth*

Einarsson, G. (1980), Address Assignment for a Time-Frequency-Coded, Spread-Spectrum System, B.S.T.J., 59, 1241-1255 / *Györfi*

Even, S. / Goldreich, O. (1981), The minimum-lenght generator sequence problem is NP-hard, J. Algorithms, 2, 311-313 / *Sloane*

Eyraud, C. (1951), Précis de cryptographie moderne, Editions Raoul Tari (2nd edition), Paris / *Bauer*

Federal Information Processing Standard Publication No. 46, Department of Commerce, National Bureau of Standards, Gaithersburg, Md, USA / *Gordon*

Federal Register, (1975), August 1 / *Beth*

Feistel, H. (1973), Cryptography and computer privacy, Scientific American, 228 (May), 15-23 / *Sloane*

Feistel, H. / Notz, W.A. / Smith, J.L. (1975), Some cryptographic techniques for machine-to-machine data communications, Porc. IEEE, 63, 1545-1554 / *Sloane*

Feller, W. (1957), An Introduction to Probability Theory and Its Applications, Volume I, Wiley, N.Y. (2nd edition) / *Sloane*

Fellner, H. (1982), Master Thesis (in German), Institut für Systemwissenschaften, Universität Linz / *Pichler*

Fienberg, S.E. (1971), Randomization and social affairs: the 1970 draft lottery, Science, 167 (22 January), 255-261 / *Sloane*

Figl, A. (1926), Systeme des Chiffrierens, Moser, Graz (3rd edition) / *Bauer*

Fino, B.J. / Algazi, V.r. (1976), Unified matrix treatment of the fast Walsh-Hadamard transform, IEEE Trans. Computers, C-25, 1142-1146 / *Sloane*

Fox, P.A. ed. (1976), The PORT Mathematical Subroutine Library, Bell Laboratories, Murray Hill, N.J. / *Sloane*

Franke, H.W. (1982), Die geheime Nachricht, Umschau-Verlag, Frankfurt / *Beth*

Furstenberg, H. (1980), Random walks on Lie groups, in Harmonic Analysis and Representations of Semisimple Lie Groups, edited by J.A. Wolf et. al., Reidel Publ., Dordrecht, Holland, 467-489 / *Sloane*

Furrer, F.J. (1981), Fehlerkorrigierende Block-Codierung für die Datenübertragung, Birkhäuser, Basel, Boston, Stuttgart / *Beth*

Gaines, H.F. (1956), Cryptanalysis, Dover, N.Y. / *Bauer*

Garey, M.R. / Johnson, D.S. (1979), Computers and intractability, Freeman, Oxford / *Beth*

Geffe, P.R. (1967), An open letter to communication engineers, Proc. IEEE, 55, 2173 / *Sloane*

Geramita, A.v. / Seberry, J. (1979), Orthogonal Designs, Dekker, N.Y. / *Sloane*

Gilbert, E.N. / MacWilliams, F.J. / Sloane, N.J.A. (1974), Codes which detect deception, Bell Syst. Tech. J. 53, 405-424 / *Beth*

Girsdansky, M.B. (1971), Data privacy-cryptology and the computer at IBM Research, IBM Research Reports, 7, (No. 4), 12 pages /*Sloane*

Givierge, M. (1925), Cours de Cryptographie, Berger-Levrault, Paris / *Bauer*

Golomb, S.W. (1964), Random permutation, Bull. Amer. Math. Soc., 70, 747 / *Sloane*

Golomb, S.W. (1967), Shift Register Sequences, Holden-Day / *Beth, Jennings, Piper*

Goncharov, V. (1944), Du domaine d'analyse combinatoire, (Russian, French summary), Bull. de l'Académie URSS, Sér. Math. 8, 3-48, English translation in Amer. Math. Soc. Translations, (2) 19, 1-46 / *Sloane*

Good, I.J. (1958), The interaction algorithm and practical Fourier analysis, J. Roy. Stat. Soc. B 20, 361-372 and B 22, 372-375 / *Sloane*

Goodman, D.J. / Henry, P.J. / Prabhu, V.K. (1980), Frequency-hopped Multilevel FSK for Mobile Radio, B.S.T.J. 59, 1257-1275 / *Györfi*

Grenander, U. (1963), Probability on Algebraic Structures, Wiley, N.Y. /*Sloane*

Guivarc'h, Y. / Keane, M. / Roynette, B. (1977), Marches aleatoires sur les groupes de Lie, Lecture Notes in Math., 624, Springer-Verlag, N.Y. / *Sloane*

Guy, R.K. (1975), How to factor a number, Proc. Fifth Manitoba Conference on Numerical Math., 49-89 / *Sattler*

Györfi, L. / Kerekes, I. (1981), A Block Code for Noisless Asynchronus Multiple Access OR Channel, IEEE Trans. on Information Theory 27, 788- 791 / *Györfi*

Hain, M., Private Communications, Universität Kaiserslautern / *Jennings*

Hala, B. (1960), Autour de problème de la syllable, Phonetica 5, 159-168 / *Timmann*

Hall, M., Jr. (1967), Combinatorial THeory, Blaisdell, Waltham, Mass. / *Sloane*

Hall, M., Jr. (1975), Semi-automorphisms of Hadamard matrices, Math. Proc. Chamb. Phil. Soc., 77, 459-473 / *Sloane*

Halmos, P.R. (1956), Lectures on Ergodic Theory, Chelsea, N.Y. / *Sloane*

Halmos, P.R. (1950), Measure Theory, Van Nostrand, Priceton, N.J. / *Sloane*

Hammersley, J.H. (1972), A few seedlings of research, in Proc. Sixth Berkeley Symp. Math. Stat. and Prob., Vol. 1, 345-394 / *Sloane*

Hannan, E.J. (1960), Time Series Analysis, Methuen, London / *Sloane*

Hardy, G.H. / Wright, E.M. (1958), Zahlentheorie, Oldenburg Vlg. / *Sattler*

Harwit, M. / Sloane, N.J.A. (1979), Hadamard Transform Optics, Academic Press, N.Y. / *Sloane*

Heiberger, R.M. (1978), Generation of random orthogonal matrices, Appl. Statistics, 27, 199-206 / *Sloane*

Hellman, M.E. et al. (1976), Results of an Initial Attempt to Cryptanlyze the NBS Data Encryption Standard, Stanford University / *Schaumüller-Bichl*

Hellman, M.E. (1977), An extension of the Shannon theory approach to cryptography, IEEE Trans. Inf. Theory IT-23, 194-289 / *Beth*

Hellman, M.E. (1979), Die Mathematik neuer Verschlüsselungssysteme, Spektrum der Wissenschaft, Heft 10 / *Eier, Lagger*

Henze, E. (1979), Kryptographie, Datenschutz und Datenübertragung, Diebold Forschungsprogramm, Arbeitsgruppenbericht AB 17, 2-23 / *Beth*

Herlestam, T. (1978), Critical remarks on some public-key cryptsystems, BIT 18, 493-496 / *Beth*

Herlestam, T. (1982), On the complexity of functions of linear shift register sequences, to be presented at the 1982 IEEE International Symposium on Information Theory, Les Arcs, France / *Jennings, Herlestam*

Hess, P. / Wirl, K. (1983), A voice scrambling system for testing and demonstration, in this volume / *Sloane*

Hewitt, E. / Ross, K.A. (1963-1970), Abstract Harmonic Analysis, 2 vols., Springer Verlag, N.Y. / *Sloane*

Hewitt / Zuckerman (1960), The multiplicative semigroup of integers (mod m), Pacific J. Math. 10, 1291-1308 / *Ecker*

Heyer, H. (1977), Probability Measures on Locally Compact Groups, Springer Verlag, N.Y. / *Sloane*

Heyer, H. ed. (1982), Probability Measures on Groups, Lecures Notes in Math. 928, Springer Verlag, N.Y. / *Sloane*

Hicks, J.S. / Wheeling, R.F. (1959), An efficient method for generating uniformly distributed points on the surface of an n-dimensional sphere, Commun. ACM, 2 (No. 4), 17-19 / *Bauer, Beth*

Hitt, P. (1916), Manual for the Solution of Military Ciphers, Army Service School, Ft. Leavenworth / *Bauer*

Hopf, E. (1937), Ergodentheorie, J. Springer, Berlin, reprinted by Chelsea, N.Y. 1948 / *Sloane*

Humphreys, J.E. (1972), Introduction to Lie Algebras and Representation Theory, Springer Verlag, N.Y., second printing / *Sloane*

Ingemarsson, I. (1980), Knapsacks which are not partly solvable after multiplication modulo q, IBM Research Report RC 8515 / *Eier, Lagger*

Ito, N. / Leon, J.S. / Longqear, J.Q. (1981), Classification of 3-(24,12,5) designs and 24-dimensional Hadamard matrics, J. Comb. Theory, A 31, 66-93 / *Sloane*

Iversen, (1981), DES Chips Find a New Niche, Electronics, Nov. 17 / *Schuchmann*

Jansson, B. (1966), Random Number Generators, Stockholm / *Sloane*

Jayant, N.S. (1982), Analog scramblers for speech privacy, preprint / *Sloane*

Jennings, S.M. (1980), A Special Class of Binary Sequences, Ph. D. Thesis, London University / *Beth, Jennings*

Johnson, B. (1978), The secret war, BBC, London / *Bauer*

Kahn, (1967), The Codebreakers, Macmillan / *Bauer, Beth, Hess, Wirl*

Kahn, (1982), Why Germany lost the code war, Cryptologia 6, (No. 1), 26-31 / *Schuchmann*

Kantor, W.M. (1969), Automorphism groups of Hadamard matrices, J. Comb. Theory, 6, 279-281 / *Sloane*

Kantor, W.M. (1982), Polynomial-time perfect shuffling, preprint / *Sloane*

Karpovsky, M.G. (1977), Fast Fourier Transforms on FInite Non-Abelian Groups, IEEE Trans. on Computers, C-26, (No. 10), 1028-1030 / *Pichler*

Kasiski, F.W. (1863), Die Geheimschriften und die Dechiffrierkunst, Wittler & Sohn, Berlin / *Bauer*

Kendall, M. (1970), Rank Correlation Methods, Griffin, London, 4th edition / *Sloane*

Kennedy, W.J., Jr. / Gentle, J.E. (1980), Statistical Computing, Dekker, N.Y. /*Sloane*

Kerkhoffs, A. (1883), La cryptographie militaire, Journal des sciences militaires, Jan., Feb. 1883, Baudoin, Paris / *Bauer*

Knop, R.E. (1970), Random vectors uniform in solid angle, Comm. ACM, 13, 326 / *Sloane*

Knuth, D.E. (1976), Analysis of a simple Factorization Algorithm, TCS 3, 321-348 / *Sattler*

Knuth, D.E. (1981), The Art of Computer Programming, Vol. 2, Seminumerical Algorithms, Addison-Wesley, Reading, Mass., 2nd. edition /

Beth, Davies, Herlestam, Sattler, Sloane

Konheim, A.G. (1981), Cryptography: A primer, Wiley, Chichester, N.Y. / *Bauer, Beth*

Kowol / Mitsch, (1976), Polynomial functions over commutative semigroups, Semigroup Forum 12, 109-118 / *Ecker*

Kuipers / Niederreiter, (1974), Uniform distribution of sequences, Wiley, N.Y. / *Ecker*

Kunz, H. (1977), Approximation optimaler linearer Transformationen durch eine Klasse schneller, verallgemeinerter Fouriertransformation, Dissertation ETH 5832, Zurich, Juris Verlag, Zurich / *Pichler*

Lange, A. / Soudart, E.-A. (1925), Traité de Cryptographie, F. Alcan, Paris, preprint 1935 / *Bauer*

Lehmer, D.H. / Powers, R.E. (1931), On factoring large numbers, Amer. Math. Soc. 37 / *Sattler*

Lempel, A. (1978), Cryptology in transition: A survey, Rep. SCRC-RP-78-43, Sperry Rand, Res Lett / *Beth*

Lenstra, (1981), Integer Programming with a fixed Number of Variables, Math. Inst., Amsterdam / *Beth*

Lewis, T.G. (1975), Distribution Sampling for Computer Simulation, Lexington Books, Lexington, Mass. / *Sloane*

Li, T.Y. / Yorke, J.A. (1978), Ergodic maps on [0,1] and nonlinear pseudo random number generators, Nonlinear Analysis, Theory, Methods and Applications, 2, 473-481 / *Sloane*

van Lint, J.H. (1971), Error-correcting codes, Springer Lect. Notes Math. 201, Berlin, Heidelberg, N.Y. / *Beth*

Livingston, (1978), The congruence $a^{r+s} \equiv a^{r}$ (mod m), Amer. Math. Monthly 85, 97-100 / *Ecker*

Lloyd, S.P. (1977), Random rotation secrecy systems, unpublished memorandum, Bell Laboratories, Murray Hill, N.J. / *Sloane*

Lloyd, S.P. (1978), Choosing a rotation at random, unpublished memorandum, Bell Laboratories, Murray Hill, N.J. / *Sloane*

Logan, B.f. / Shepp, L.A. (1977), A variational problem for random Young tableaux, Advances in Math, 26, 206-222 / *Sloane*

Lüneburg, H. (1979), Galoisfelder, Kreisteilungskörper und Schieberegisterfolgen, BI, Mannheim / *Beth*

Lyapin, (1974), Semigroups, Translation of Math. Monographs, Vol. 3, Amer. Math. Soc. Prividence, R.I. / *Ecker*

MacKinnon, N.R.F. (1980), The development of speech encipherment, Radio and Elektronic Engineer, 50, (No. 4), 147-155 / *Beker, Sloane*

MacLaren, M.D. / Marsaglia (1965), Uniform random number generators, J. Assoc. Comput. Mach., 12, 83-89 / *Sloane*

MacWilliams, F.J. / Sloane, N.J.A. (1981), The Theory of Error-Correcting Codes, North-Holland, Amsterdam / *Beth, Sloane*

Marsaglia, G. (1972), Choosing a point from the surface of a shere, Annals. Math. Stat., 43, 645-646 / *Sloane*

Marsaglia, G. / Ananthanarayanan, K. / Paul, N. (1973), Random number generator package - "Super Duper", School of Computer Science, McGill University, Montreal, Quebec / *Sloane*

Marsaglia, G. / Ananthanarayanan, K. / Paul, N. (1976), Improvements on fast methods for generating normal random variables, Information Processing Letters, 5, (No. 2), 27-30 / *Sloane*

Marsaglia, G. / Bray, T.A. (1964), A convenient method for generating normal variables, SIAM Review, 6, 260-264 / *Sloane*

Martens, C. / Martens, P. (1965), Phonetik der deutschen Sprache, München / *Timmann*

McEliece, R.J. (1978), A public-key cryptosystem based on algebraic coding theory, DSN Progr. Rep. 42-44, JPL / *Beth*

McGonegal, C.A. / Berkley, D.A. / Jayant, N.S. (1981), Private communications, Bell Syst. Tech. J. 60, 1563-1572 / *Sloane*

Massay, J.L. (1969), Shift-register synthesis and BCH decoding, IEEE Trans. Inform. Theory, IT-15, 122-127 / *Beth, Sloane*

Meister, A. (1902), Die Anfänge der modernen Diplomatischen Geheimschrift, Schöningh, Paderborn / *Bauer*

Meister, A. (1906), Die Geheimschrift im Dienste der Päpstlichen Kurie von ihren Anfängen bis zum Ende des XVI Jahrhunderts, Schöningh, Paderborn / *Bauer*

Merkle, R.C. / Hellman, M.E. (1978), Hiding Information and Signatures in Trap Door Knapsacks, IEEE Trans. on Information Theory, IT-24, (No. 5), 525-530 / *Beth, Eier, Ingemarsson, Lagger, Schöbi*

Meyer, C.H. (1978), Ciphertext/Plaintext and Ciphertext/Key Dependence vs Number of Rounds for the Data Encryption Standard, Proc. of the AFIPS-NCC 1978, June 5-8, Anaheim, Cal., Vol. 47 (ed.: Gosh, Lin), 1119-1126, AFIPS Press, Montvale, N.J. / *Schaumüller-Bichl*

Meyer, C.H. / Tuchmann, W.L. (1972), Pseudorandom codes can be cracked, Electronic Design, 20 (Nov. 9), 74-76 / *Sloane*

Mihram, G.A. (1972), Simulation: Statistical Foundations and Methodology, Academic Press, N.Y. / *Sloane*

Monier, L. (1980), Algorithmes de Factorisation d'Entiers, Thèse, Paris / *Sattler*

Moore, C.C., ed. (1973), Harmonic Analysis on Homogeneous Spaces, Proc. Sympos. Pure Math. 26, Amer. Math. Soc., Providence, R.I. / *Sloane*

Morgado, (1974), A property of the Euler φ-function concerning the integers which are regular (mod m), Portugal. Math. 33, 185-191 / *Ecker*

Morris, R. (1978), The Data Encryption Standard - retrospective and prospects, IEEE Communications Society Magazine, 16 (Nov.), 11-14 / *Sloane*

Morris, R. / Sloane, N.J.A. / Wyner, A.D. (1977), Assessment of the National Bureau of Standards proposed Federal Data Encryption Standard, Cryptologia, 1, 281-306 / *Beth, Sloane*

Morrison, M.A. / Brillhart, J. (1975), A method of factoring an the factorization of F_7, Math. Comp. 29, 182-205 / *Sattler*

Muller, G.L. (1975), Riemann's hypothesis and test for primality, Proc. 7th ACM Symp. Comp., 234-239 / *Beth*

Muller, M.E. (1959), A note on a method for generating points uniformly on n-dimensional spheres, Commun. ACM 2, (No. 4), 19-20 /*Sloane*

National Bureau of Standards (1977) : Data Encryption Standard, Federal Information Processing Standards Publication (FIPS Pub) 46, National Technical Information Service, Springfield, VA / *Schaumüller-Bichl*

von Neumann, J. (1951), Various techniques used in connection with random digits, in Monte Carlo Methods, National Bureau of Standards Applied Math. Series 12, U.S. Dept. Commerce, Washington, D.C., 36-38 / *Sloane*

Nicholson, P. (1971), Algebraic Theory of Finite Fourier Transforms, Journal of Comp. and System Sc. 5 (1971), 524-547 / *Pichler*

Niederreiter, H. (1978), Quasi-Monte Carlo methods and pseudo-random numbers, Bull. Amer. Math. Soc., 84, 957-1041 / *Sloane*

Nijenhuis, A. / Wilf, H.S. (1978), Combinatorial Algorithms, Academic Press, N.Y., 2nd edition / *Sloane*

Nussbaumer, H.J. (1980), Fast fourier transform and concolution algorithms, Springer, Berlin, Heidelberg, N.Y. / *Beth*

Page, E.S. (1967), A note on generating random permutations, Applied Statist., 16, 273-274 / *Sloane*

Patterson, N. (1975), The algebraic decoding of Goppa-codes, IEEE Trans. Inf. Theory, IT-21, 203-207 / *Beth*

Pichler, F. (1980), Fast Linear Methods for Image Filtering, in: Applications of Information and Control Systems (D.G. Lainiotis and N.S. Tzannes, eds.) Reidel Publishing Corp., Denhaag, 3-11 / *Pichler*

Plackett, R.L. (1968), Random permutations, J. Royal Stat. Soc., 30, 517-534 / *Sloane*

Poe, E.A. (1966), Das gesamte Werk, Walter Verlag, Olten / *Betg*

Pohlig, S. / Hellman, M.E. (1978), An improved algorithm for computing logarithms in GF(p) and its cryptographic significance, IEEE Trans. Inf. Theory, IT-24, 106-110 / *Beth*

Pollard, J.M. (1974), Theorems on factorization and primality testing, Proc. Camb. Phil. Soc., 521-528 / *Beth*

Pomerance, C. (1981), Analysis and comparison of some integer factoring algorithms, Preprint, University of Georgia / *Sattler*

Pratt, W.K. (1969), An algorithm for a fast Hadamard matrix transform of order twelve, IEEE Trans. Computers, C-18, 1131-1132 / *Sloane*

Pratt, W.K. / Kane, J. / Andrews, H.C. (1969), Hadamard transform image coding, Proc. IEEE, 57, 58-68 / *Sloane*

Rabin, M.O. (1979), Probabilistic algorithms over finite fields, MIT Cambridge, Mass. / *Beth*

Rabin, M.O. (1979), Digitalized signatures and public key functions as intractable as factorisation, MIT Cambridge, Mass. / *Beth*

Randell, (1980), The COLOSSUS, in: N. Metropolis et al. (eds.), A History of Computing in the Twenties Century, Academic Press / *Schuchmann*

Reeds, J. (1977),'Cracking' a random number generator, Cryptologia, 1, (No. 1), 20-26 / *Sloane*

Reeds, J. (1979), Cracking a multiplicative congruential encryption algorithm, in Information Linkage Between Applied Math. and Industry (Proc. First Annual Workshop, Naval Postgraduate School, Monterey, Calif. 1978), Academic Press, N.Y., 467-472 / *Sloane*

Rejewski, (1981), How Polish Mathematicians Deciphered the ENIGMA, Annuals of the History of Computing 3, (No. 3), 213-234 / *Schuchmann*

Riordan, J. (1958), An Introduction to Combinatorial Analysis, Wiley, N.Y. / *Sloane*

Rivest, R.L. / Shamir, A. /Adleman, L. (1978), A method for obtaining digital signatures and public-key cryptosystems, Communications of the ACM, 21, (No. 2), 120-126 / *Beth, Davio, Goethals, Sattler*

Robbins, D.P. / Bolker, E.D. (1981), The bias of three pseudo-random shuffles, Aqquationes Math., 22, 268-292 / *Sloane*

Rohrbach, H. (1948), Mathematische und Maschinelle Methoden beim Chiffrieren und Dechiffrieren, MAT Review of German Science: Appl. Math., Vol. I, Wiesbaden,1939-1941 / *Bauer*

Rohwer, J. / Jäckel, E. (1979), Die Funkaufklärung und ihre Rolle im Zweiten Weltkrieg, Motorbuch Verlag, Stuttgart / *Bauer*

Ronse, C. (1980), Non-linear shift registers: A survey, MBLE Research Report R430 / *Piper*

Rose, D.J. (1980) Matrix identities of the fast Fourier transform, Linear Alg. Applic., 29, 423-443 / *Sloane*

Rosenblatt, J.R. / Filliben, J.J. (1971), Randomization and the draft lottery, Science, 167 (22 January), 306-308 / *Sloane*

Rudin, W. (1962), Fourier Analysis on Groups Intersecience, N.Y. / *Pichler*

Ryska, N. / Herda, S. (1980), Kryptographische Verfahren in der Datenverarbeitung, Informatik-Fachberichte 24, Springer Verlag, N.Y. / *Beth*

Sacco, L. (1947), Manuale di crittografia, Istituto Poligrafico dello Stato, Roma, 3rd edition / *Bauer*

Sacco, L. (1951), Manuel de cryptographie, Payot, Paris / *Bauer*

Sakasegawa, H. (1978), On generation of normal pseudo-random numbers, Ann. Inst. Statist. Math., A 30, 271-279 / *Sloane*

Schaumüller-Bichl, I. (1981), Zur Analyse des Data Encryption Standard und Synthese verwandter Chiffriersystems, Ph. D. dissertation, Universität Linz, Austria / *Schaumüller-Bichl*

Schmeiser, B.W. (1980), Random variate generation: a survey, in Simulation with Discrete Models: A State-of-the-Art Survey, edited by T.I. Oren, C.M. Shub and P.F. Roth, IEEE Press, N.Y. / *Sloane*

Schnorr, C.P. (1981), Refined analysis and improvement on some factoring algorithms, Preprint / *Sattler*

Scholz, H.-J. (1972), Untersuchungen zur Lautstruktur Deutscher Wörter / *Timmann*

Schrack, G.F. (1972), Remark on Algorithm 381, Commun. ACM, 15, 468 / *Sloane*

Schwarz, (1981), The role of semigroups in the elementary theory of numbers, Math. Slovaca 31, 369-395 / *Ecker*

Schüssler, H.W. (1973), Digitale Systeme zur Signalverarbeitung, Springer, Berlin, Heidelberg, N.Y. / *Beth*

Schwerdtfeger, H. (1950), Introduction to Linear Algebra and the Theory of Matrices, Noordhoff, Groningen / *Sloane*

Selmer, E.S. (1966), Linear Recurrence Relations over Finite Fields, University of Bergen, Norway / *Beth, Jennings, Piper*

Shamir, A. (1978), A Fast Signature Scheme, MIT Laboratory for Computer Science Report RM-107, Cambridge, Mass. / *Schöbi*

Shamir, A. (1979), How to share a secret, Com. A.C.M., Nov. 1979, 22, (No. 11), 612-613 / *Mignotte*

Shamir, A. (1979), Cryptocomplexity of Knapsack Systems, Symposium on the Theory of Complexity, Atlanta, Georgia / *Schöbi*

Shamir, A. (1980), On the power of commutativity in cryptography, in Automata, languages and programming, ICALP80, Lecture Notes in Computer Science, 85, Springer Verlag, Berlin, 582-595 / *Davio, Goethals*

Shamir, A. (1981), The generation of cryptographically strong pseudorandom sequences, presented at "Crypto 81", Univ. of Calif, St. Barbara / *Sloane*

Shamir, A. (1982), New Results on Public Key Systems, this volume / *Schöbi*

Shamir, A. (1982), A Polynomial Time Algorithm for Merkle-Hellman Cryptosystems, abstract, The Weizmann Institut / *Beth*

Shamir, A., The Cryptographic Security of Compact Knapsacks, MIT, preliminary report / *Eier, Lagger*

Shamir, A. / Zippel, R.E. (1980), On the Security of the Merkle-Hellman Scheme, IEEE Transactions of Information Theory, IT-26, (No. 3), 339-340 / *Schöbi*

Shannon, C.E. (1948), A Mathematical theory of Secrecy Systems, Bell System Technical Journal / *Gordon*

Shannon, C.E. (1949), Communication theory of secrecy systems, Bell. Syst. Tech. J., 28, 656-715 / *Beth, Sloane*

Shepp, L.A. / Lloyd, S.P. (1966), Ordered cycle lengths in a random permutation, Trans. Amer. Math. Soc., 121, 340-357 / *Sloane*

Shulman, D. (1976), An annotated bibliography of cryptography, Garland, N.Y. / *Bauer*

Sibuya, M. (1964), A method for generating uniformly distributed points on n-dimensional spheres, Ann. Inst. Stat. Math., 14, 81-85 / *Sloane*

Simmons, G.J. (1979), Cryptology: The mathematics of secure communication, Math. Intel. 1: 233-246 / *Beth*

Simmons, G.J. (1981) A system for point-of-sale or access, user authentication and identification, IEEE Workshop on Communications Security, Santa Barbara, CA., August 24-26, 1982 / *Davio, Goethals*

Sinkov, M. (1966), Elementary Cryptanalysis in Mathematical Association of America, Washington / *Bauer*

lepian, D. (1978), Prolate spheriodal wave functions, Fourier analysis and uncertainty, Part V: the discrete case, Bell Syst. Tech. J., 57, 1371-1430 / *Sloane*

loane, N.J.A. (1979), Error-correcting codes and cryptography, Academy of Sciences, N.Y. / *Sloane*

loane, N.J.A. (1981), Error-correcting codes and cryptography, in The Mathematical Gardner, edited by D.A. Klarner, Prindle, Weber & Schmid, Boston, 346-382. Reprinted in Cryptologia, 6, 128-153, 258-278 / *Sloane*

Small, (1977), Powers mod m , Math. Mag. 50, 84-86 / *Ecker*

Smith, J.L. (1971), The design of Lucifer, a cryptographic device for data communications, Report RC-3326, IBM Thomas Watson Center, Yorktown Heights, N.Y. / *Sloane*

Smith, L.D. (1956), Cryptography, Dover, N.Y. / *Bauer*

Smith / Palmer, (1979), Universal fixed messages and the Rivest-Shamir-Adleman Cryptosystem, Matematika 26, 33-52 / *Ecker*

Solovay, R. / Strassen, V. (1977), A fast Monte Carlo test for primality, SIAM J. Comput. 6, 84-85 / *Beth*

Stewart, G.W. (1980), The efficient generation of random orthogonal matrices with an application to condition estimators, SIAM J. Numer. Anal., 17, 403-409 / *Sloane*

Tashiro, Y. (1977), On methods for generating uniform random points on the surface of a sphere, Ann. Inst. Stat. Math., A 29, 295-300 / *Sloane*

Telsy Systems, Secure Voice: Reality or myth, (1979) / *Beker*

Timor, U. (1980), Improved Decoding Scheme for Frequency-Hopped Multi-level FSK System. B.S.T.J. 59, 1839-1855 / *Györfi*

Türkel, S. (1927), Chiffrieren mit Geräten und Maschinen, Graz / *Bauer*

Turyn, R.J. (1974), Hadamard matrices, Baumert-Hall units, four-symbol sequences, pulse compression, and surface wave encodings, J. Comb. Theory, 16 A, 313-333 / *Sloane*

Valerio, P. (1893), De la cryptographie, Baudoin, Paris / *Bauer*

Vandiver / Weaver, (1958), Introduction to arithmetical factorization and congruences from the standpoint of abstract algebra, Amer. Math. Monthly, 65, part 2, 53 / *Ecker*

Vernam, G.S. (1926), Cipher printing telegraph systems for secret wire and radio telegraphic communications, J. Am. Inst. Electr. Eng. XLV, 109-115 / *Beth*

Versik, A.M. / Kerov, S.V. (1977), Asymptotics of the Plancherel measure of the symmetric group and the limiting form of Young tableaux (Russian), Dokl. Akad. Nauk SSSR, 233, (No. 6), English translation in Soviet Math. Dokl., 18, 527-531 / *Sloane*

de Viaris, Marquis (1893), L-art de chiffrer et dêchiffrer les depeches secretes, Gauthier-Villars, Paris / *Bauer*

Viterbi, A.J. (1978), A processing Stellite Transponder for Multiple Access by Low-Rate Mobile Users, Digital Satellite Communications Conference, Montreal, October 23-25, 1978 / *Győrfi*

van der Waerden, B.L. (1967), Algebra, Springer Verlag, Berlin, Heidelberg, N.Y. / *Beth*

Wallis, W.D. / Street, A.P. / Wallis, J.S. (1972), Combinatorics: Room Squares, Sum-Free Sets, Hadamard Matrices, Lecture Notes in Math., 292, Springer Verlag, N.Y. / *Sloane*

Walter, P. (1981), An Introduction to Ergodic Theory, Springer Verlag, Berlin, N.Y. / *Sloane*

Warner, G. (1972), Harmonic Analysis on Semi-Simple Lie Groups, 2 vol., Springer Verlag, N.Y. / *Sloane*

Weaver, (1952), Cosets in a semi-group, Math. Mag. 25, 125-136 / *Ecker*

Wedekind, H. (1978), Zur Durchführung des §6, 1 BDSG Datenschutz und Datensicherung, 4, 181, 185 / *Horbach*

Williams, H.C. (1978), Primality testing on a computer, Ars Combinatorica, 5, 127-185 / *Herlestam*

Wunderlich, M.L. (1979), A running time analysis of Brillhart's continued fraction factoring method, Number Theory, Carbondale , Lecture Notes 751, 328-342 / *Sattler*

Wyner, A.D. (1979), An Analog Scrambling Scheme which does not Expand Bandwith, IEEE Trans. on Information Theory, 25, Part I (May 1979), Part II (July 1979) / *Pichler, Sloane*

Yao, A.C. (1982), private communications / *Sloane*

Zane, (1964), Uniform distribution (mod m) of monomials, Amer. Math. Monthly 71, 162-164 / *Ecker*

Zariski, O. / Samuel, P. (1958), Commutative Algebra, vol. 1, Van Nostrand / *Jennings*

Zierler, N. (1959), Linear Recurring Sequences, J. Soc. Indust. Appl. Math, 7, 31-48 / *Jennings*

List of Participants

Abel, Horst; Geschäftsstelle des Landesbeauftragten für den Datenschutz, Königinstraße 11, 8000 München 22

Ammann, Eckhard; Institut für Informationsverarbeitung, Universität Tübingen, Köstlinstraße 6, 7400 Tübingen

Bauer, F.L.; Institut für Informatik der Technischen Universität, Arcisstraße 21, 8000 München

Dorothea Begemann; Am Festplatz 15b, 6301 Linden

Beker, Henry; Racal-Comsec Ltd., Milford Industrial Estate, Tollgate Road, Salisbury/Wiltshire, England

Beth, Thomas; Institut für Mathematische Maschinen und Datenverarbeitung I, Universität Erlangen, Martensstraße 3, 8520 Erlangen

Beutelspacher, Albrecht; Fachbereich Mathematik der Universität Mainz, Saarstraße 21, 6500 Mainz

Bitzer, Wolfgang; AEG-Telefunken, K16 E23, Gerberstraße 33, 7150 Backnang

Blake, I.F.; Dept. of Electrical Engineering, Faculty of Engineering, University of Waterloo, Waterloo, Ontario N2L 3G1, Canada

Böhm-Beck, Engelbert; GMD Birlinghoven, Postfach 1240, 5205 St. Augustin

Bourne, Christine; Westfield College, University of London, Mathematics Department, Kidderpore Ave., London NW3, England

Camion, Paul; 3, Rue F. Couperin, 78370 Plaisir, France ; I.N.R.I.A., 78 Le Chesnay, France

Cot, Norbert; Institut de Programmation, Université de Paris VI, Place Jussieu, Paris-5, France

Davies, Donald, W.; National P. Laboratory, Teddington, Middlex, TW II OLW, United Kingdom

Davio, Marc; Philips Research Laboratory, Ave. van Becelaere, 2, Box 8, 1170 Brussels, Belgium

Dichtl, Markus; Abteilung Mathematik, Universität Ulm, Oberer Eselsberg, 7900 Ulm

Dierstein, Rüdiger; DFLR-Rechenzentrum Oberpfaffenhofen, 8031 Wessling, Obb.

Diffie, Whitfield; Bell Northern Research, East Middlefield Road, Mountain View, CA 94043, U.S.A.

Ecker, Arnim; Hahn-Meitner-Institut für Kernforschung Berlin GmbH, Glienicker Str. 100, 1000 Berlin 39

Egloff, Roland; BAUEM, Sektion Kryptologie, 3003 Bern, Schweiz

Eier, Richard; Institut für Datenverarbeitung, Technische Universität, Gußhausenstraße 27-29, 1040 Wien, Österreich

Endres, W.; TEKADE-Fernmeldeanlagen, Abt. VSP, Thurn-und-Taxis-Str.10, 8500 Nürnberg

Fedderwitz, Walter; Institut für Allgemeine Nachrichtentechnik, Callinstraße 32, 3000 Hannover 1

Fumy, Walter; Institut für Mathematische Maschinen und Datenverarbeitung I, Universität Erlangen, Martensstraße 3, 8520 Erlangen

Goethals, J.-M.; Philips Research Labs., Ave. v. Becelaere, 2, 1170 Brussels, Belgium

Gordon, John; Hatfield Polytechnic, P.O. Box 109, Hatfield Herts, ALIO 9AB, England

Grollmann, Jochen; Lehrstuhl für Informatik I, Universität Dortmund, Postfach 50 05 00, 6400 Dortmund 50

Grundhöfer, Theo; Mathematisches Institut der Universität Tübingen, Auf der Morgenstelle 10, 7400 Tübingen

Györfy, Làszlò; Budapesti Müszaki Egyetem, Hiradàstechnikai Elektronika Intêzet, Stoczek u. 2, 1521 Budapest XI, Ungarn

Hain Manfred; Fachbereich Mathematik, Universität Kaiserslautern, Erwin-Schrödinger-Straße, 6750 Kaiserslautern

Henze, E.; Institut für Angewandte Mathematik, Pockelstraße 14, 3300 Braunschweig

Herda, Siegfried; Gesellschaft f. Mathematik und Datenverarbeitung (GMD), Schloß Birlinghoven, PF 1246, 5205 St. Augustin 1

Herlestam, Tore; Bankogardsgatan 74, 25260 Helsingborg, Schweden

Heß, Peter; Institut für Mathematische Maschinen und Datenverarbeitung V, Universität Erlangen, Martensstraße 3, 8520 Erlangen

Horak, Otto; Bundesministerium für Landesverteidigung; Franz-Josefs-Kai 7-9, 1011 Wien, Österreich

Horbach, L.; Institut für Medizinische Statistik und Dokumentation, Waldstraße 6, 8520 Erlangen

Ingemarsson, Ingemar; Dept. of Electrical Engineering, Linköping Institut of Technology, Linköping 58183, Schweden

Jennings, Sylvia; Racal Research Ltd., 11 Bennet Road, Reading Berks RG2 OP 7, Reading, England

Kappas, Achim; TH Darmstadt, Institut für Datentechnik, 6100 Darmstadt

Kerekes, I.; Budapesti Müszaki Egeytem, Hiradàstechnikai Elektronika Intézet, Stoczek u.2, 1521 Budapest XI, Ungarn

König, Roman; Institut für Mathematische Maschinen und Datenverarbeitung I, Universität Erlangen, Martensstraße 3, 8520 Erlangen

Konheim, Alan G.; IBM Research Center, P.O. Box 218, Yorktown Heights, N.Y. 10598, U.S.A.

Koukkula, Hannu; Rinkutie 4 A 27, 00390 Helsinki, Finnland

Krause, Lothar; Gesellschaft für Mathematik und Datenverarbeitung (GMD), Schloß Birlinghoven, 5205 St. Augustin 1

Lagger, Helmut; Siemens AG, ZT ZTI INF 111, Otto-Hahn-Ring 6, 8000 München 83

Longo, Giuseppe; C.I.S.M. Palazzo del Torso, Piazza Garibaldi, I-33100 Udine, Italia

Lüneburg, Heinz; FB Mathematik der Universität, Pfaffenbergstr. 95, 6750 Kaiserslautern

Madlener, Klaus; Fachbereich Informatik, Universität Kaiserslautern, Erwin-Schrödinger-Straße, 6750 Kaiserslautern

Mignotte, Maurice; Centre de Calcul, Université Louis Pasteur, 67084 Strasbourg, France

Müller, Winfried, B.; Institut für Mathematik, Universität Klagenfurt, Universitätsstraße 65, 9010 Klagenfurt, Österreich

Mullin, Ronald, C.; Faculty of Engineering, University of Waterloo, Waterloo, Ontario, N2L 3G1, Canada

Nemetz, Tibor; Mathematisches Forschungsinstitut der Ungarischen Akademie der Wissenschaften, Rea'ltanoda u. 13-15, 1053 Budapest, Ungarn

Oberman, Maarten; Dept. of Switching Techniques Dr. Neher Laboratories of the Netherlands, Postal and Telecommunication services, P.O. Box 421, 2260 AK Leidschendam, Netherlands

Pichler, Franz; Lehrstuhl für Systemtheorie, Johannes-Kepler-Universität, 4040 Linz, Österreich

Piper, F.C.; Dept. of Mathematics, Westfield College, Kidderpore Ave., London NW 3 7ST, United Kingdom

Posch, Stefan; Institut für Mathematische Maschinen und Datenverarbeitung I, Universität Erlangen, Martensstraße 3, 8520 Erlangen

Rieß, H.P.; Institut für Mathematische Maschinen und Datenverarbeitung I, Universität Erlangen, Martensstraße 3, 8520 Erlangen

Rihaczek, Karl; Fabriciusring 15, 6380 Bad Homburg 1

Rösel, Gerd; Institut für Mathematische Maschinen und Datenverarbeitung, Universität Erlangen, Martensstraße 3, 8520 Erlangen

Roßbach, C.; Springer Verlag, Postfach 105280, 6900 Heidelberg 1

Sattler, Jürgen; Fachbereich Mathematik, Universität Frankfurt, Robert-Mayer-Str. 6-10, 6000 Frankfurt

Schaumüller-Bichl, Ingrid; VÖEST-Alpine Linz, FAB 31 (BG41), 4020 Linz

Schnorr, C.P.; Angewandte Mathematik, Universität Frankfurt, Robert-Mayer-Str. 10, 6000 Frankfurt

Schöbi, Paul; Institut für Kommunikationstechnik, ETH, Sternwartstraße 7, 8092 Zürich, Schweiz

Schuchmann, H.-R.; Siemens AG, ZTI INF 2, Otto-Hahn-Ring 6, 8000 München

Shamir, Adi; Applied Mathematics, The Weizmann Institute, Rehovot, Israel

Sloane, N.J.A.; Bell Laboratories, Room 2C-376, Murray Hill, N.J. 07974, U.S.A.

Sperber, Helmut; Institut für Mathematische Maschinen und Datenverarbeitung I, Universität Erlangen, Martensstraße 3, 8520 Erlangen

Sprague, Alan; Dept. of Mathematics, Ohio State University, Columbus, Ohio 43210, U.S.A.

Strehl, Volker; Institut für Mathematische Maschinen und Datenverarbeitung I, Universität Erlangen, Martensstraße 3, 8520 Erlangen

Strobel, Christina; Dovestraße 6, 8520 Erlangen

van Tilborg, Henk; Department of Mathematics and Computer Science, Eindhoven University of Technology, Eindhoven, The Netherlands

Timman, Klaus-P.; TST, H.-Knotestraße 3, 8134 Pöcking

Vary, P.; TEKADE-Fernmeldeanlagen, Thurn-und-Taxis-Str. 10, 8500 Nürnberg

Widmann, Kjell-Ove; Crypto AG, 6301 Zug, Schweiz

Wirl, Klaus; Institut für Mathematische Maschinen und Datenverarbeitung III, Universität Erlangen, Martensstraße 3, 8520 Erlangen

ecture Notes in Computer Science

49: Interactive Systems. Proceedings 1976. Edited by A. Blaser C. Hackl. VI, 380 pages. 1976.

50: A. C. Hartmann, A Concurrent Pascal Compiler for Miniputers. VI, 119 pages. 1977.

51: B. S. Garbow, Matrix Eigensystem Routines – Eispack e Extension. VIII, 343 pages. 1977.

52: Automata, Languages and Programming. Fourth Colloquium, ersity of Turku, July 1977. Edited by A. Salomaa and M. Steinby. 59 pages. 1977.

53: Mathematical Foundations of Computer Science. Proceed- 1977. Edited by J. Gruska. XII, 608 pages. 1977.

54: Design and Implementation of Programming Languages. eedings 1976. Edited by J. H. Williams and D. A. Fisher. X, pages. 1977.

55: A. Gerbier, Mes premières constructions de programmes. 56 pages. 1977.

56: Fundamentals of Computation Theory. Proceedings 1977. d by M. Karpiński. XII, 542 pages. 1977.

57: Portability of Numerical Software. Proceedings 1976. Edited V. Cowell. VIII, 539 pages. 1977.

58: M. J. O'Donnell, Computing in Systems Described by Equa- . XIV, 111 pages. 1977.

59: E. Hill, Jr., A Comparative Study of Very Large Data Bases. 0 pages. 1978.

60: Operating Systems, An Advanced Course. Edited by R. Bayer, . Graham, and G. Seegmüller. X, 593 pages. 1978.

61: The Vienna Development Method: The Meta-Language. d by D. Bjørner and C. B. Jones. XVIII, 382 pages. 1978.

62: Automata, Languages and Programming. Proceedings 1978. d by G. Ausiello and C. Böhm. VIII, 508 pages. 1978.

63: Natural Language Communication with Computers. Edited eonard Bolc. VI, 292 pages. 1978.

64: Mathematical Foundations of Computer Science. Proceed- 1978. Edited by J. Winkowski. X, 551 pages. 1978.

65: Information Systems Methodology, Proceedings, 1978. d by G. Bracchi and P. C. Lockemann. XII, 696 pages. 1978.

66: N. D. Jones and S. S. Muchnick, TEMPO: A Unified Treat- of Binding Time and Parameter Passing Concepts in Pro- mming Languages. IX, 118 pages. 1978.

67: Theoretical Computer Science, 4th GI Conference, Aachen, h 1979. Edited by K. Weihrauch. VII, 324 pages. 1979.

68: D. Harel, First-Order Dynamic Logic. X, 133 pages. 1979.

69: Program Construction. International Summer School. Edited L. Bauer and M. Broy. VII, 651 pages. 1979.

70: Semantics of Concurrent Computation. Proceedings 1979. d by G. Kahn. VI, 368 pages. 1979.

1: Automata, Languages and Programming. Proceedings 1979. d by H. A. Maurer. IX, 684 pages. 1979.

72: Symbolic and Algebraic Computation. Proceedings 1979. d by E. W. Ng. XV, 557 pages. 1979.

73: Graph-Grammars and Their Application to Computer nce and Biology. Proceedings 1978. Edited by V. Claus, H. Ehrig G. Rozenberg. VII, 477 pages. 1979.

74: Mathematical Foundations of Computer Science. Proceed- 1979. Edited by J. Bečvář. IX, 580 pages. 1979.

75: Mathematical Studies of Information Processing. Pro- ings 1978. Edited by E. K. Blum, M. Paul and S. Takasu. VIII, pages. 1979.

76: Codes for Boundary-Value Problems in Ordinary Differential tions. Proceedings 1978. Edited by B. Childs et al. VIII, 388 s. 1979.

Vol. 77: G. V. Bochmann, Architecture of Distributed Computer Systems. VIII, 238 pages. 1979.

Vol. 78: M. Gordon, R. Milner and C. Wadsworth, Edinburgh LCF. VIII, 159 pages. 1979.

Vol. 79: Language Design and Programming Methodology. Proceedings, 1979. Edited by J. Tobias. IX, 255 pages. 1980.

Vol. 80: Pictorial Information Systems. Edited by S. K. Chang and K. S. Fu. IX, 445 pages. 1980.

Vol. 81: Data Base Techniques for Pictorial Applications. Proceedings, 1979. Edited by A. Blaser. XI, 599 pages. 1980.

Vol. 82: J. G. Sanderson, A Relational Theory of Computing. VI, 147 pages. 1980.

Vol. 83: International Symposium Programming. Proceedings, 1980. Edited by B. Robinet. VII, 341 pages. 1980.

Vol. 84: Net Theory and Applications. Proceedings, 1979. Edited by W. Brauer. XIII, 537 Seiten. 1980.

Vol. 85: Automata, Languages and Programming. Proceedings, 1980. Edited by J. de Bakker and J. van Leeuwen. VIII, 671 pages. 1980.

Vol. 86: Abstract Software Specifications. Proceedings, 1979. Edited by D. Bjørner. XIII, 567 pages. 1980

Vol. 87: 5th Conference on Automated Deduction. Proceedings, 1980. Edited by W. Bibel and R. Kowalski. VII, 385 pages. 1980.

Vol. 88: Mathematical Foundations of Computer Science 1980. Proceedings, 1980. Edited by P. Dembiński. VIII, 723 pages. 1980.

Vol. 89: Computer Aided Design - Modelling, Systems Engineering, CAD-Systems. Proceedings, 1980. Edited by J. Encarnacao. XIV, 461 pages. 1980.

Vol. 90: D. M. Sandford, Using Sophisticated Models in Resolution Theorem Proving.
XI, 239 pages. 1980

Vol. 91: D. Wood, Grammar and L Forms: An Introduction. IX, 314 pages. 1980.

Vol. 92: R. Milner, A Calculus of Communication Systems. VI, 171 pages. 1980.

Vol. 93: A. Nijholt, Context-Free Grammars: Covers, Normal Forms, and Parsing. VII, 253 pages. 1980.

Vol. 94: Semantics-Directed Compiler Generation. Proceedings, 1980. Edited by N. D. Jones. V, 489 pages. 1980.

Vol. 95: Ch. D. Marlin, Coroutines. XII, 246 pages. 1980.

Vol. 96: J. L. Peterson, Computer Programs for Spelling Correction: VI, 213 pages. 1980.

Vol. 97: S. Osaki and T. Nishio, Reliability Evaluation of Some Fault-Tolerant Computer Architectures. VI, 129 pages. 1980.

Vol. 98: Towards a Formal Description of Ada. Edited by D. Bjørner and O. N. Oest. XIV, 630 pages. 1980.

Vol. 99: I. Guessarian, Algebraic Semantics. XI, 158 pages. 1981.

Vol. 100: Graphtheoretic Concepts in Computer Science. Edited by H. Noltemeier. X, 403 pages. 1981.

Vol. 101: A. Thayse, Boolean Calculus of Differences. VII, 144 pages. 1981.

Vol. 102: J. H. Davenport, On the Integration of Algebraic Functions. 1–197 pages. 1981.

Vol. 103: H. Ledgard, A. Singer, J. Whiteside, Directions in Human Factors of Interactive Systems. VI, 190 pages. 1981.

Vol. 104: Theoretical Computer Science. Ed. by P. Deussen. VII, 261 pages. 1981.

Vol. 105: B. W. Lampson, M. Paul, H. J. Siegert, Distributed Systems – Architecture and Implementation. XIII, 510 pages. 1981.

Vol. 106: The Programming Language Ada. Reference Manual. X, 243 pages. 1981.

Vol. 107: International Colloquium on Formalization of Programming Concepts. Proceedings. Edited by J. Diaz and I. Ramos. VII, 478 pages. 1981.

Vol. 108: Graph Theory and Algorithms. Edited by N. Saito and T. Nishizeki. VI, 216 pages. 1981.

Vol. 109: Digital Image Processing Systems. Edited by L. Bolc and Zenon Kulpa. V, 353 pages. 1981.

Vol. 110: W. Dehning, H. Essig, S. Maass, The Adaptation of Virtual Man-Computer Interfaces to User Requirements in Dialogs. X, 142 pages. 1981.

Vol. 111: CONPAR 81. Edited by W. Händler. XI, 508 pages. 1981.

Vol. 112: CAAP '81. Proceedings. Edited by G. Astesiano and C. Böhm. VI, 364 pages. 1981.

Vol. 113: E.-E. Doberkat, Stochastic Automata: Stability, Nondeterminism, and Prediction. IX, 135 pages. 1981.

Vol. 114: B. Liskov, CLU, Reference Manual. VIII, 190 pages. 1981.

Vol. 115: Automata, Languages and Programming. Edited by S. Even and O. Kariv. VIII, 552 pages. 1981.

Vol. 116: M. A. Casanova, The Concurrency Control Problem for Database Systems. VII, 175 pages. 1981.

Vol. 117: Fundamentals of Computation Theory. Proceedings, 1981. Edited by F. Gécseg. XI, 471 pages. 1981.

Vol. 118: Mathematical Foundations of Computer Science 1981. Proceedings, 1981. Edited by J. Gruska and M. Chytil. XI, 589 pages. 1981.

Vol. 119: G. Hirst, Anaphora in Natural Language Understanding: A Survey. XIII, 128 pages. 1981.

Vol. 120: L. B. Rall, Automatic Differentiation: Techniques and Applications. VIII, 165 pages. 1981.

Vol. 121: Z. Zlatev, J. Wasniewski, and K. Schaumburg, Y12M Solution of Large and Sparse Systems of Linear Algebraic Equations. IX, 128 pages. 1981.

Vol. 122: Algorithms in Modern Mathematics and Computer Science. Proceedings, 1979. Edited by A. P. Ershov and D. E. Knuth. XI, 487 pages. 1981.

Vol. 123: Trends in Information Processing Systems. Proceedings, 1981. Edited by A. J. W. Duijvestijn and P. C. Lockemann. XI, 349 pages. 1981.

Vol. 124: W. Polak, Compiler Specification and Verification. XIII, 269 pages. 1981.

Vol. 125: Logic of Programs. Proceedings, 1979. Edited by E. Engeler. V, 245 pages. 1981.

Vol. 126: Microcomputer System Design. Proceedings, 1981. Edited by M. J. Flynn, N. R. Harris, and D. P. McCarthy. VII, 397 pages. 1982.

Voll. 127: Y. Wallach, Alternating Sequential/Parallel Processing. X, 329 pages. 1982.

Vol. 128: P. Branquart, G. Louis, P. Wodon, An Analytical Description of CHILL, the CCITT High Level Language. VI, 277 pages. 1982.

Vol. 129: B. T. Hailpern, Verifying Concurrent Processes Using Temporal Logic. VIII, 208 pages. 1982.

Vol. 130: R. Goldblatt, Axiomatising the Logic of Computer Programming. XI, 304 pages. 1982.

Vol. 131: Logics of Programs. Proceedings, 1981. Edited by D. Kozen. VI, 429 pages. 1982.

Vol. 132: Data Base Design Techniques I: Requirements and Logical Structures. Proceedings, 1978. Edited by S.B. Yao, S.B. Navathe, J.L. Weldon, and T.L. Kunii. V, 227 pages. 1982.

Vol. 133: Data Base Design Techniques II: Proceedings, 1979. Edited by S.B. Yao and T.L. Kunii. V, 229–399 pages. 1982.

Vol. 134: Program Specification. Proceedings, 1981. Edited b Staunstrup. IV, 426 pages. 1982.

Vol. 135: R.L. Constable, S.D. Johnson, and C.D. Eichenlaub, Introduction to the PL/CV2 Programming Logic. X, 292 pages. 19

Vol. 136: Ch. M. Hoffmann, Group-Theoretic Algorithms and Gr Isomorphism. VIII, 311 pages. 1982.

Vol. 137: International Symposium on Programming. Proceedir 1982. Edited by M. Dezani-Ciancaglini and M. Montanari. VI, 4 pages. 1982.

Vol. 138: 6th Conference on Automated Deduction. Proceedin 1982. Edited by D.W. Loveland. VII, 389 pages. 1982.

Vol. 139: J. Uhl, S. Drossopoulou, G. Persch, G. Goos, M. Dausma G. Winterstein, W. Kirchgässner, An Attribute Grammar for Semantic Analysis of Ada. IX, 511 pages. 1982.

Vol. 140: Automata, Languages and programming. Edited by M. N sen and E.M. Schmidt. VII, 614 pages. 1982.

Vol. 141: U. Kastens, B. Hutt, E. Zimmermann, GAG: A Pract Compiler Generator. IV, 156 pages. 1982.

Vol. 142: Problems and Methodologies in Mathematical Softw Production. Proceedings, 1980. Edited by P.C. Messina and A. M VII, 271 pages. 1982.

Vol. 143: Operating Systems Engineering. Proceedings, 1980. Edi by M. Maekawa and L.A. Belady. VII, 465 pages. 1982.

Vol. 144: Computer Algebra. Proceedings, 1982. Edited by J. Calr XIV, 301 pages. 1982.

Vol. 145: Theoretical Computer Science. Proceedings, 1983. Edi by A.B. Cremers and H.P. Kriegel. X, 367 pages. 1982.

Vol. 146: Research and Development in Information Retrie Proceedings, 1982. Edited by G. Salton and H.-J. Schneider. 311 pages. 1983.

Vol. 147: RIMS Symposia on Software Science and Engineer Proceedings, 1982. Edited by E. Goto, I. Nakata, K. Furuka R. Nakajima, and A. Yonezawa. V. 232 pages. 1983.

Vol. 148: Logics of Programs and Their Applications. Proceedi 1980. Edited by A. Salwicki. VI, 324 pages. 1983.

Vol. 149: Cryptography. Proceedings, 1982. Edited by T. Beth. 402 pages. 1983.